Charles Gildon's
*The Life of Mr Thomas Betterton,
the Late Eminent Tragedian*

Charles Gildon's *The Life of Mr Thomas Betterton, the Late Eminent Tragedian*

An Annotated Edition, including Betterton's
The Amorous Widow

Edited by David Roberts

D. S. BREWER

Editorial matter © David Roberts 2025

All Rights Reserved. Except as permitted under current legislation
no part of this work may be photocopied, stored in a retrieval system,
published, performed in public, adapted, broadcast,
transmitted, recorded or reproduced in any form or by any means,
without the prior permission of the copyright owner

First published 2025
D. S. Brewer, Cambridge

ISBN 978 1 84384 743 4

D. S. Brewer is an imprint of Boydell & Brewer Ltd
PO Box 9, Woodbridge, Suffolk IP12 3DF, UK
and of Boydell & Brewer Inc.
668 Mt Hope Avenue, Rochester, NY 14620–2731, USA
website: www.boydellandbrewer.co.uk

Our Authorised Representative for product safety in the EU is Easy Access System
Europe – Mustamäe tee 50, 10621 Tallinn, Estonia, gpsr.requests@easproject.com

A CIP catalogue record for this book is available
from the British Library

The publisher has no responsibility for the continued existence or accuracy of URLs
for external or third-party internet websites referred to in this book, and does not
guarantee that any content on such websites is, or will remain, accurate or appropriate

CONTENTS

Acknowledgements	vi
List of Abbreviations for Frequently Cited Sources	vii
Introduction: Gildon Rehabilitated?	1
Thomas Betterton and *The Amorous Widow*	29
Note on the Text	33
The Life of Mr Thomas Betterton	39
The Amorous Widow	177
Appendix: Preface to the 1706 Edition of *The Amorous Widow*	247
Bibliography	249
Index	254

ACKNOWLEDGEMENTS

My thanks to Elizabeth McDonald at Boydell and Brewer for her faith in this project, and to Stephen Watkins for his expert comments on the manuscript. Dr Joshua Hey's equally expert copy-editing was much appreciated, as was Nick Bingham's guidance through the production process. Dr Izabela Hopkins has provided invaluable support. Over the years I have, like so many other scholars, benefitted hugely from the work and advice of the late Rob Hume. During the completion of this book my ever-loving family expanded with the arrival of a first grandson, Otto, to whom this volume is dedicated.

ABBREVIATIONS FOR
FREQUENTLY CITED SOURCES

Baines and Rogers Paul Baines and Pat Rogers, *Edmund Curll, Bookseller* (Oxford: Clarendon Press, 2007)

Cibber *An Apology for the Life of Mr Colley Cibber, Comedian and late Patentee of the Theatre Royal*, ed. David Roberts (Cambridge: Cambridge University Press, 2022)

Downes John Downes, *Roscius Anglicanus; or An Historical View of the Stage*, ed. Judith Milhous and Robert D. Hume (London: Society for Theatre Research, 1987)

Document Register Judith Milhous and Robert D. Hume, eds., *A Register of English Theatrical Documents, 1660–1737*, 2 vols (Carbondale and Edwardsville: Southern Illinois University Press, 1991)

Kewes Paulina Kewes, *Authorship and Appropriation. Writing for the Stage in England, 1660–1710* (Oxford: Clarendon Press, 1997)

LC Lord Chamberlain's Papers, National Archives, Kew

Le Faucheur Michel Le Faucheur, *An Essay upon the Action of an Orator*, trans. Anon (London: Nicholas Cox, ?1700)

Lowe Colley Cibber, *An Apology for the Life of Mr Colley Cibber*, ed. Robert W. Lowe, 2 vols (London: John Nimmo, 1889)

LS1 *The London Stage 1660–1800 Part One*, ed. William van Lennep (Carbondale and Edwardsville: Southern Illinois University Press, 1965)

LS2 *The London Stage 1660–1800. A New Version of Part Two (1700–1711)*, ed. Judith Milhous and Robert D. Hume (London: Adam Matthew, 2021)

LS3 *The London Stage 1660–1800 Part Three*, vol.1: 1729–1736, ed. Arthur H. Scouten (Carbondale and Edwardsville: Southern Illinois University Press, 1961)

vii

Abbreviations for Frequently Cited Sources

Lucian Lucian, of Samosata, *Part of Lucian made English from the originall, in the yeare 1638 ...*, trans. Jasper Mayne and Francis Hicks (Oxford: H. Hall for R. Davis, 1663)

Milhous Judith Milhous, *Thomas Betterton and the Management of Lincoln's Inn Fields, 1695–1708* (Carbondale and Edwardsville: Southern Illinois University Press, 1987)

OED *OED Online* (Oxford University Press) (www.oed.com)

PB *Pinacotheca Bettertonaeana. The Library of a Seventeenth-Century Actor*, ed. David Roberts (London: Society for Theatre Research, 2013)

Pepys *The Diary of Samuel Pepys*, ed. Robert Latham and William Matthews, 11 vols (London: Bell & Hyman, 1971–83)

Quintilian *Institutes of Oratory*, trans. J.S. Watson, ed. Curtis Dozier and Lee Honeycutt (London: Amazon, 2015); for ease of use with other editions, references to this work are given as book, chapter and paragraph numbers only

Roach Joseph R. Roach, *The Player's Passion. Studies in the Science of Acting* (Newark: University of Delaware Press, 1985)

Roberts David Roberts, *Thomas Betterton: The Greatest Actor of the Restoration Stage* (Cambridge: Cambridge University Press, 2010)

Stern Tiffany Stern, *Rehearsal from Shakespeare to Sheridan* (Oxford: Clarendon Press, 2000)

Tilley Morris Palmer Tilley, *A Dictionary of the Proverbs in England in the Sixteenth and Seventeenth Centuries* (Ann Arbor: The University of Michigan Press, 1950)

Wanko Cheryl Wanko, *Roles of Authority. Thespian Biography and Celebrity in Eighteenth-Century Britain* (Lubbock: Texas Tech University Press, 2003)

Wilson F.P. Wilson, *The Oxford Dictionary of English Proverbs* (Oxford: Oxford University Press, 1970)

Information about classical persons and topics is taken from N.G.L. Hammond and H.H. Scullard, eds., *The Oxford Classical Dictionary*, 2nd ed. (Oxford: Clarendon Press, 1970). For ease of use with other editions, references to Cicero's *De Oratore* are given in the form of book and chapter numbers only.

INTRODUCTION: GILDON REHABILITATED?

For such a notable first – that is, the first full-scale theatrical biography in English to focus on the art rather than the misdeeds of its subject – it seems surprising that for 249 years no one paid much attention to Charles Gildon's *The Life of Mr Thomas Betterton*. Betterton (1635–1710) was, after all, the foremost English actor for half a century, and is often described as part of the tradition that links Richard Burbage to David Garrick and beyond.

Published in 1710 by Robert Gosling, in association with the infamous Edmund Curll, only months after the actor's death, Gildon's book was reprinted ten years later by Robert Jeeb, who described himself as 'Bookseller, on the Pavement in YORK'. Extracts from it re-surfaced in *The History of the English Stage*, published by Curll in 1741 as Betterton's work, but which in reality was assembled by William Oldys. That book was reprinted in 1814. In 1749 the bookseller John Robinson published *An Account of the Life of that Celebrated Tragedian, Mr. Thomas Betterton* which incorporated passages from Gildon's book and inserted a passage about the actor's financial affairs missing from it. Further recycling of extracts and unedited paper and electronic editions apart, that is where the publishing history of *The Life of Mr Thomas Betterton* ended, until now.[1]

The reason lies in an article published in 1959, trashing Gildon's claim to authenticity. In the *Quarterly Journal of Speech*, W.S. Howell set out twelve exact and lengthy correspondences between Gildon's book and *An Essay upon the Action of an Orator*, a translation by an unknown hand of an oratorical treatise by the French Protestant minister, Michel Le Faucheur. Howell's conclusion was abrupt: *The Life of Mr Thomas Betterton* was the worthless work of a plagiarist. Others agreed. According to Joseph R. Roach, who on the basis of syntactic similarities alleges further theft from Thomas Wright's 1604 *The Passions of the Minde*, Gildon was guilty of 'bold-faced plagiarism'.[2] In her Oxford Dictionary of National Biography entry on Betterton, Judith

---

[1] A 1970 text published by Routledge, currently available via Google Books, has neither notes nor a scholarly introduction.

[2] Roach, p.31.

Milhous dismisses Gildon for the same reason.[3] Meanwhile, an authoritative study of Edmund Curll by Paul Baines and Pat Rogers classes the book as merely 'an essay on stage gesture, with a perfunctory biographical note at the beginning in order to attach the essay to Betterton's theatrical fame' – in other words an early instance of the celebrity coffin-chasing that would form a key plank in Curll's business model.[4]

Gildon had worked with Gosling and Curll before, and could be trusted to cobble something together when the right opportunity arose. Further examination of their business relationship reveals yet more borrowings. In his life of Betterton, Gildon took the opportunity to recycle some of his own contributions to *The Works of* Mr. *William Shakespear Volume the Seventh*, a collaboration with Curll that rode on the back of Nicholas Rowe's more scrupulous six-volume edition of Shakespeare published the year before.[5] The passage on dance that appears towards the end of the *Life* lifts passages from a translation of Girolamo Mercuriale's *De Arte Gymnastica*. Gildon's project therefore would seem to fit Baines and Rogers' description of Curll as 'a kind of resurrection-man, looking to republish texts already in the public domain'.[6]

The combination of direct and circumstantial evidence has been devastating – so much so that the comedy attached to the *Life*, Betterton's *The Amorous Widow*, has arguably received more attention than the work for which it was intended as a mere appendix.[7] To that apparently open-and-shut case might be added the fact that Gildon's dependence on Le Faucheur is greater than even W.S. Howell suspected. Verbatim, unacknowledged copying goes far beyond his twelve passages, accounting for about twenty-five per cent of the entire *Life*.

Almost alone among scholars, Cheryl Wanko has made a strong case for the importance of *The Life of Mr Thomas Betterton*.[8] In stark contrast to his immediate predecessors in theatrical biography (that is, the anonymous author of a brief life of Matthew Coppinger, and Tobyas Thomas' more

---

[3] Judith Milhous, 'Thomas Betterton', in *The Oxford Dictionary of National Biography*, ed. Lawrence Goldmann, 60 vols (Oxford: Oxford University Press, 2004), V.558.

[4] Baines and Rogers, p.49. Gildon is also credited with writing for Curll the *Memoirs of the Life of William Wycherley* (1718) and – for James Roberts, a Curll associate – a biography of Defoe, *The Life and Strange Surprizing Adventures of Mr D --- de F --- of London* (1719).

[5] See below, p.43 n.10.

[6] Baines and Rogers, p.34.

[7] For example in surveys of Restoration Drama by Robert D. Hume, *The Development of English Drama, 1660–1700* (Oxford: Clarendon Press, 1976), and Derek Hughes, *English Drama 1660–1700* (Oxford: Clarendon Press, 1996).

[8] Wanko, pp.22–50.

substantial, rogue-type biography of Joseph Haines), Gildon compares the business of acting with religious preaching and legal advocacy, both in method and respectability.[9] Like Godfrey Kneller's portrait of Betterton, the book places its subject in the same class as established members of polite society. As Wanko points out, it does so via the neoclassical passion for rules that characterizes much of Gildon's subsequent critical work, including *A Grammar of the English Tongue* (1711), *The Complete Art of Poetry* (1718), *A New Project for the Regulation of the Stage* (1720), and *The Laws of Poetry* (1720). The *Life* is partly a sequel to one of Gildon's previous productions, the 'Essay on the Art, Rise and Progress of the Stage' in Curll's Shakespeare edition. There, Gildon had applied Aristotelian principles to the work of dramatists from Aeschylus to Thomas Otway. Here, he extends the analysis to performance, and with a similar range of literary devices: staged dialogue, quotations from Shakespeare and others designed to illustrate points about correct delivery, and a tone of lament for the practices of theatre *circa* 1710. Lisa Zunshine describes the 'two discourses' that dominate writing about theatre in the eighteenth century: the ones that focus on 'the personalities, social lives and specific performances of famous entertainers', and those that present 'acting theory as a science' by laying out 'the oratorical skills of actors and actresses as compared with those of other professional speakers, such as lawyers, clergymen and politicians'.[10] Propagating both discourses, Gildon's *Life* fuses them in a single work.

As well as serving as a mouthpiece for neoclassical principles, Gildon's Betterton is a model gentleman, both modest and hospitable. He does not want his plays to be published (a wish promptly disregarded by the inclusion of *The Amorous Widow* at the end of the *Life*). The treatise on acting he allegedly produces for Gildon's hearing is, so Gildon claims, Betterton's own, though Betterton modestly hints that a friend had written it. While the actor knows his classical authorities, he is modest enough to admit that he can read them only in translation. He defers to theatrical authority, remembering with fondness the tight discipline exercised in the early years of the Duke's Company by Sir William Davenant. He insists that actors should 'keep a handsome Appearance with the World; to be really virtuous' and not abandon themselves to 'Follies and Vices, which render them contemptible to all'.[11] In Cheryl Wanko's account there is a danger in emphasizing 'hand-

---

[9]   Anon, *An Account of the Life, Conversation, Birth, Education, Pranks, Projects, and Exploits, and Merry Conceits, of the Famously Notorious Mat. Coppinger* (London, 1695), and Tobyas Thomas, *The Life of the Late Famous Comedian, Jo. Hayns* (London, 1701); for discussion, Wanko, pp.22–38.

[10] Lisa Zunshine, ed., *Acting Theory and the English Stage, 1700–1830*, vol.1 (London and New York: Routledge, 2016), p.xiv.

[11] See below, p.61.

some Appearance' when such an emphasis suggests gentility is merely a surface performance. Ultimately, Betterton's authenticity is guaranteed via professional kinship with the great Roman orators, who did after all take lessons from actors.[12]

Yet a more immediate question of resemblance disturbs Wanko's interpretation as it does the dismissive appraisals of other scholars. While Wanko invokes Michel Foucault to argue that Gildon's Betterton is a fabrication produced in order to recommend rules of good conduct in the public gaze, she also concedes that the actor was 'the perfect dramatic persona' for such a role because his 'decency' was well known.[13] One motivation for this new edition of the *Life* is the conviction that this landmark book, through its thicket of borrowings both acknowledged and otherwise, betrays genuine and specific knowledge of its subject. Author and actor had, after all, worked together, and closely.

Gildon and Betterton

In February 1700 Betterton had played Angelo in Gildon's adaptation of *Measure for Measure*, subtitled *Beauty the Best Advocate* and supplemented with '*Additions* of several *Entertainments* of *MUSICK*'.[14] The play was dedicated to Nicholas Battersby of the Inner Temple, where Betterton's *The Amorous Widow* was also performed in February 1700; the hint of a circle of obligation between actor, author and lawyer is hard to ignore.[15] John Oldmixon's Epilogue to Gildon's *Measure to Measure* was spoken by the production's Claudio, John Verbruggen, in the person of Shakespeare's ghost. Among other reflections on the modern stage, the ghost hoped that Betterton would not retire in the near future ('So, late may *Betterton* forsake the *Stage*').[16] According to *A Comparison Between the Two Stages*, the commissioning of a new version of *Measure for Measure* was a ploy to out-do Christopher Rich's rival productions of plays by Ben Jonson, which suggests that Betterton trusted Gildon to come up with a successful theatrical formula.[17]

Their working relationship extended to Gildon's next effort. In the Preface to his 1701 play, *Love's Victim*, Gildon acknowledged his 'obligation

---

[12] Wanko, p.47.
[13] Wanko, p.44.
[14] LS1 523.
[15] LS1 524.
[16] John Oldmixon, 'The Epilogue. *Shakespeares* GHOST, Spoken by Mr. *Verbruggen*', in Charles Gildon, *Measure for Measure; or, Beauty the Best Advocate* (London: Robert Parker, 1700), n.p.
[17] Anon., *A Comparison Between the Two Stages* (London, 1702), pp.26–7.

to Mr. *Betterton* in several hints he gave me in the Fable'; he further thanked Betterton's protégée Anne Bracegirdle for her performance as Guinoenda.[18] Betterton had played the male lead, Rhesus – a token of confidence he was increasingly wary of extending to other writers of new plays. In all likelihood Gildon observed his subject at close quarters, whether discussing details of plotting, attending rehearsals or, naturally, the performances themselves. There is no reason to suppose that the apparent failure of *Love's Victim* to last for more than a single performance at the Lincoln's Inn Fields Theatre dented Gildon's faith in Betterton, even though his next play, *The Patriot*, was accepted by the rival Drury Lane playhouse.[19]

There are further grounds for arguing that the *Life* is testimony not just to a man, but to a working relationship. Gildon prints a document giving details of the 1682 union of the King's and Duke's Companies, a key piece of evidence available nowhere else.[20] Since Betterton had been instrumental in securing the union, it is hardly out of the question that Gildon obtained the document directly from him. When it comes to reflections on acting, nothing in Colley Cibber's eye-witness evocation of Betterton's Hamlet (discussed in detail below) is at odds with the principles set out in Gildon's book. This was indeed, according to Cibber, an actor who preserved a classical 'medium between mouthing and meaning too little', and who studied the contours of Shakespeare's text with careful attention to complexities of feeling.[21] It is likely that Betterton himself wrote about the value of achieving the tonal perfection recommended by Gildon. In the Preface to *The Fairy Queen* (1692), Betterton's adaptation of *A Midsummer Night's Dream*, it is argued that 'he must be a very ignorant player who knows not there is a musical cadence in speaking; and that a man may as well speak out of tune as sing out of tune'.[22]

It is a classical trope that provides the framework for the meeting between author and actor described in Gildon's book. Cicero's *De Oratore* purports to record a conversation about oratory under a plane tree on the estate of a man named Crassus, specifically in imitation of a Socratean symposium.[23] Gildon offers a similar vision of intellectual hospitality, describing a visit to Betterton's 'Country House in *Reading*' during which the party 'retir'd to his Garden, and after a little Walk there, we fell into the Discourse of

---

[18]   Gildon, Preface to *Love's Victim: or, the Queen of Wales* (London: Richard Parker, 1701), n.p.

[19]   LS2 10 (*Love's Victim*) and 29 (*The Patriot*).

[20]   See *Document Register* no.1134.

[21]   Cibber, p.77.

[22]   Betterton, Preface to *The Fairy Queen* (London: Jacob Tonson, 1692).

[23]   Cicero, *De Oratore,* I.vii.

Acting.[24] There is an inconsistent attempt thereafter to sustain the illusion of a dialogue, but the location is plausible. Betterton was largely retired from 1706 onwards, and his only surviving letter shows that he did own a house near Reading.[25] There is also a marked correspondence, traced in the footnotes to this edition, between the many books and pictures referred to in the *Life* and those featured in the sale catalogue of Betterton's library.[26] The core of the *Life* is devoted to a discussion of oratorical principles in acting, and it appears Betterton did collect books on the subject, including John Bulwer's *Chirologica, or, The natural language of the hand composed of the speaking motions* (1644) and Geraud de Cordemoy's *A philosophical discourse concerning speech* (1668).[27] The *Life* further refers to painters whose work featured in Betterton's collection, and includes a fully cited contribution by Charles de St Evremond, whose work is also listed in the Betterton catalogue.[28] Gildon would doubtless have been flattered to find many of his own works among Betterton's books.[29] At the same time, the list of Betterton's roles that Gildon appended to the *Life* exceeds by dozens the ones he could have gleaned from former prompter John Downes's 1708 *Roscius Anglicanus*, although that book may in theory have furnished information about Betterton's early years. While the style of much of the *Life* is similar to that of Gildon's 'Essay on the Art, Rise and Progress of the Stage', Betterton's alleged comments on plays reveal different aesthetic priorities. In standard neoclassical fashion, Gildon's 'Essay' dismisses Shakespearean comedy and mocks the supposed absurdity of Shakespeare's time-bending choruses in *Henry V* and *The Winter's Tale*. Nothing comparable issues from the mouth of Gildon's Betterton, except praise for *The Merry Wives of Windsor*.

---

[24] See below, p.53.

[25] See Roberts, Frontispiece, and pp.173–83.

[26] *Pinacotheca Bettertonaeana* also provides evidence that Betterton may have been familiar with Gildon's non-dramatic work. It includes his *Miscellaneous letters and essays* (London: Benjamin Bragg, 1694), PB 134; *The post-Boy robb'd of his mail* (London: John Sprint, 1706), PB 105; *The new metamorphosis* (London: Samuel Briscoe, 1708), PB 105; and *The Golden Spy* (London: John Woodward, 1709), PB 133.

[27] PB 136 & 94. However, PB does not list *An Essay Upon the Action of an Orator* or works by Cicero or Quintilian.

[28] PB 75 lists a copy of St Evremond's *Recueil de diverses pièces* (La Haye: J. and D. Steucker, 1669).

[29] That is, *Miscellaneous letters and essays* (London: Benjamin Bragg, 1694), PB 134; *The post-Boy robb'd of his mail* (London: John Sprint, 1706), PB 105; *The new metamorphosis* (London: Samuel Briscoe, 1708), PB 105; *The Golden Spy* (London: John Woodward, 1709), PB 133; Gildon is not named in any of the lists of play texts at PB 161 but may feature in the miscellaneous bundles of plays.

A broader social network connected author and actor. In claiming to have represented the real Betterton, Gildon must have been aware that others would denounce him if they suspected outright fraud. Yet the *Life* is dedicated to Sir Richard Steele, whose poignant *Tatler* essay on the cloisters of Westminster Abbey served as Betterton's obituary.[30] In other words, while Gildon's *Life* is in large part an exercise in fakery, the Betterton it offers to the public is not a fake. The book is better understood as a tribute after the manner of Xenophon's *Symposium*, a work Gildon refers to, in which the author imagines a conversation enriched by the presence of Socrates himself. '*Plato* and *Xenophon* introduce *Socrates* in their Discourses, to give the greater Authority to what they say,' writes Gildon.[31] In the case of the *Life*, the conversation bears authentic traces of the man Gildon had known. That being so, however we choose to define plagiarism (not a simple matter in 1710, as will be seen below), a book by a theatre person and associate of Betterton's must be of considerable interest.

Contested Terms

When Baines and Rogers describe the *Life* as 'an essay on stage gesture, with a perfunctory biographical note', they suggest the title of Gildon's book must be misleading.[32] But in 1710 there was no secure definition of biography. When Cibber published an *Apology* for his *Life* in 1740, it was his career he had in view, not his private life. Its strictly autobiographical elements largely cease at the age of eighteen, when he becomes an actor. *Lives* were still significantly centred on the deeds and words of their subjects rather than on linear or personal chronology. The multiplicity of generic names tells its own story. What we call biography might be called 'memoir', 'memorials', 'secret history', 'life', or 'apology', each with its own species of deviation from twenty-first century practice.[33]

Gildon's *Life* is perhaps best understood as a multi-part memorial. It re-creates Betterton's presence through a combination of partly imagined words, a brief chronology, a play, and some poetry. The following inventory suggests a twelve-part tribute portfolio (or perhaps scrapbook):

(i) The Dedication to Sir Richard Steele.
(ii) The Preface.

---

[30] Richard Steele, *The Tatler*, 2–4 May 1710.
[31] See below, p.47.
[32] See above, n.4.
[33] For discussion of these different terms, see Robert D. Hume, 'The Aims and Genre of Colley Cibber's *Apology* (1740)', *Studies in Philology* 14.3 (Summer 2017), pp.662–95.

> (iii) Nicholas Rowe's epilogue to Betterton's benefit performance of *Love for Love* in 1709.
>
> (iv) The Introduction, where Gildon compares Betterton to the actors of the ancient world and concedes that even he did not embody all the qualities he says go to form an ideal actor.
>
> (v) A birth-to-death narrative of Betterton's life, including an otherwise unknown copy of the United Company agreement of 1681/2, duly quoted, with Betterton's questionable role in striking the deal examined.
>
> (vi) An account of Gildon's visit with an unnamed friend to Betterton's Reading house, and their conversation about the state of the modern stage.
>
> (vii) Betterton is reported to read from a manuscript prepared by 'a friend', to which he has added notes on contemporary performers. This is the most substantial section of the book and the one that draws heavily on the translation from Le Faucheur.
>
> (viii) Thoughts on dancing drawn from Jasper Mayne's translation of Lucian's *Dialogues* and Athenaeus' *The Deipnosophists*, adapted to reflect Betterton's own experience of hiring French dancers.
>
> (ix) A properly cited version of Charles de St Evremond's 'Of Operas, Written to his Grace The Duke of Buckingham'.[34]
>
> (x) Miscellaneous reflections on English music, Shakespeare, and the decline of English theatre.
>
> (xi) A list of plays in which Betterton acted. Judith Milhous suggests that the list was in fact drawn from Downes's *Roscius Anglicanus*, but the correspondences are hardly exact. In the current edition those have been checked against his known repertoire, with dates given where possible.
>
> (xii) Betterton's comedy, *The Amorous Widow*, thought to have been first performed *circa* 1670 but not printed until 1706.

Of those twelve components, it is clear that only two – the seventh and eighth – are subject to the charge of plagiarism. Even in those instances, however, it is worth examining what in 1710 was still a contested term.

In Paulina Kewes's words, the demand for 'explicit acknowledgement of sources intensified' during the last years of the seventeenth century, which in turn entailed 'a growing concern with the integrity of an author's *oeuvre*'.[35] That entailed separating out plagiarism from the category into which it had formerly been folded: the classical trope of *imitatio* (conscious imitation of models) which in the Renaissance 'embraced not only literature

---

[34] See below, pp.161–4.
[35] Kewes, p.96.

but pedagogy, grammar, rhetoric, aesthetics, the visual arts, music, historiography, politics, and philosophy'; as such, the practice of *imitatio* was 'central and pervasive'.[36] Julie C. Hayes points to the eighteenth century as 'the pivotal period in which classical traditions of imitation gave way to a new valorization of originality and sincere self-expression'.[37] One engine of that process was the Williamite discourse of inviolable property manifested in John Locke's *Two Treatises of Government* (1689).[38] If the pivotal moment is broadly agreed, it has not stopped some scholars, Hayes adds, from persisting in 'anachronistic habits of thought' as though 'theft is theft' whatever the cultural circumstances. No such error is committed by Margreta de Grazia or Trevor Ross, both of whom have tendered the extreme argument that plagiarism can only be treated as 'theft' where legal rights of ownership are invested in authors.[39] That issue was moot even with the passing of the 1710 Act for the Encouragement of Learning, better known as the first Copyright Act, which referred to the rights of authors but had the effect of investing those rights in booksellers, primarily with a view to breaking the monopoly of the Stationers' Company.[40]

Although the 1710 Act provides an appealingly prominent landmark in the history of plagiarism, its prominence is misleading. Paulina Kewes offers a more nuanced narrative with a close study of the often-maligned Gerard Langbaine, author of two works whose dual novelty was to catalogue plays according to author and to pursue their borrowings with relentless determination. His *Momus Triumphans* (1688) had originally been called *A New Catalogue of English Plays* until someone (hypothetically Dryden) had done a deal with the bookseller to characterize Langbaine as Momus, a carping critic. In 1691, *An Account of the English Dramatick Poets* picked its way through the nuances of source material, company rights and adaptation to provide, in Kewes's words, examples of 'external, quasi-legal, arbitration on

---

[36] Thomas M. Greene, *The Light in Troy. Imitation and Discovery in Renaissance Poetry* (New Haven: Yale University Press, 1982), p.1.

[37] Julie C. Hayes, 'Plagiarism and Legitimation in Eighteenth-Century France', *The Eighteenth Century* 54.2 (1995), p.115.

[38] Mark Rose, *Authors and Owners: The Invention of Copyright* (Cambridge, MA: Harvard University Press, 1993).

[39] Margreta de Grazia, *Shakespeare Verbatim: The Reproduction of Authenticity and the 1790 Apparatus* (Oxford: Clarendon Press, 1991); Trevor Ross, 'Copyright and the Invention of Tradition', *Eighteenth-Century Studies* 26 (1992), pp.1–27.

[40] See John Feather, 'The Book Trade in Politics: The Making of the Copyright Act of 1710', *Publishing History* 8 (1980), pp.19–44; Lyman Ray Patterson, *Copyright in Historical Perspective* (Nashville: Vanderbilt University Press, 1968); and David Saunders, *Authorship and Copyright* (London: Routledge, 1992).

matters of aesthetic value'.[41] Langbaine approaches the issue of plagiarism head on, and with important exceptions.

He begins *Momus Triumphans* by observing that plagiarism 'has reign'd in all Ages, and is as ancient almost as Learning it self', the corollary of which is that even the best-known writers are 'liable to the charge and imputation of *Plagiary*'.[42] But he is also careful to distinguish between imitation and theft. The writer who imitates a well-known classical predecessor builds on solid foundations and all but guarantees that the new work will attain a certain standard. Contemporary playwrights, however, build on sand: that is, in Langbaine's view, on French sources of dubious worth, or lesser known native drama. To borrow in plain sight from Shakespeare, Jonson or Fletcher is respectable, but ransacking Marston or Massinger is not, because (a) their work is much less familiar and the sleight-of-hand therefore less likely to be discovered, and (b) readers or audiences are made to 'pay for that which was our own before'.[43] The corollary is that borrowing from foreign authors is not only a lesser sin, but actually excusable. In Langbaine's words,

> Altho I condemn *Plagiaries,* yet I would not be thought to reckon as such either *Translators,* or those who *own* what they borrow from other Authors: for as 'tis commendable in any man to advantage the *Publick*; so it is manifest, that those Authors have done so, who have contributed to the Knowledge of the *Unlearned,* by their excellent *Versions.*[44]

Citing that passage, Kewes argues that Langbaine had in mind the interests of English consumers in a free-trading economy; he favoured 'cultural enrichment' over penalizing piracy, at least when it came to foreign texts.[45] The contradictions in Langbaine's approach are obvious, but as Kewes points out, they do not necessarily suggest a critic out of his depth. Rather, Langbaine was aware that judgments about literary plagiarism drew on a range of aesthetic, commercial and ethical constraints that may vary with each individual case. Such flexibility was evident in his treatment of different kinds of writer. He saved his worst criticism for high-profile professional writers, especially Dryden.[46] Novices, aristocrats and women he was more inclined to excuse.

---

[41]   Kewes, p.107.
[42]   Gerard Langbaine, *Momus Triumphans, or, The Plagiaries of the English Stage expos'd in a catalogue of all the comedies, tragi-comedies, masques, tragedies, opera's, pastorals, interludes, etc* (London: Samuel Holford, 1688), a1^r.
[43]   Ibid., a1^v–a3^r.
[44]   Ibid., a3^r.
[45]   Kewes, p.113.
[46]   On Langbaine and Dryden, see Kewes, pp.121–8.

Introduction: Gildon Rehabilitated?

Among the many reasons for treating Langbaine seriously, none is more compelling in the current context than the appeal his work exerted on the mind of Charles Gildon. Langbaine did not simply facilitate a shift in the diagnosis of plagiarism, but created a template for what we now classify as plagiarism to be legitimately represented as fair dealing. In 1699 Gildon published *The Lives and Characters of the English Dramatick Poets*, his completion of an undertaking left unfinished on Langbaine's death eight years before. He presumably did so by negotiation with the bookseller Nicholas Cox, who had published Langbaine's *A New Catalogue of English Plays* in 1687 and *Momus Triumphans* the following year. It seems Langbaine had promised *The Lives and Characters* to Cox, who then looked about for someone to finish the work after Langbaine's death.

That Gildon's name does not appear on the title page of *The Lives and Characters* may be a tribute to the respect in which he held his predecessor or, paradoxically, a route to self-promotion. He identified himself only as the 'Careful Hand' that 'improv'd and continued' Langbaine's work, but without overlooking the opportunity to include his own then very modest theatrical pedigree among the roster of lives and characters.[47] To 'improve' was of course to signal some critical distance from Langbaine's work. His express aim was 'to avoid his Faults, and preserve his Beauties'.[48] Chief among the faults was Langbaine's tendency to interpret as plagiarism what Gildon believed was imitation, and to bring to the claims an unwarranted ferocity. Langbaine's 'Beauties', on the other hand, lay in the extraordinarily wide reading that gave him a nose for literary resemblance between Ancients and Moderns, French and English, prose narrative and drama. As Kewes observes, experiencing Langbaine's method first hand even led Gildon presciently to conclude that Shakespeare was not the 'poet of nature' widely proclaimed since the 1623 First Folio, but a writer who worked in the shadow of classical literature.[49]

What does Gildon's autobiographical entry in *The Lives and Characters* tell us about his understanding of Langbaine's principles? It certainly demonstrates that he was a cunning but somewhat reckless manipulator of print culture. He presents his life story in the style of Langbaine while referring to events that took place after Langbaine's death. However inclined we might feel to treat his autobiographical essay with caution, some details are confirmed by other records. The entry tells us that he was born into a Catholic family in 1664 at the village of Gillingham, near Shaftesbury in

---

[47] Charles Gildon, *The Lives and Characters of the English Dramatick Poets* (London: William Turner, 1699), A5ᵛ.

[48] Ibid., A6ʳ.

[49] Kewes, p.124.

Dorset. Royalists and recusants, the family had seen its estate plundered during the Civil War, after which Gildon's grandfather was compelled to pay the remaining 'two thirds' to the government.[50] Gildon's father was admitted to Gray's Inn on 1 December 1654. The admissions register describes him as the 'son and heir of Richard G., of Motcombe, co. Dorset, gent'.[51] Motcombe is a few miles south-east of Gillingham; the former Gildon estate is now occupied by a preparatory school.

A devout Catholic, Richard Junior died when Charles was only nine, in 1673. By then the boy may already have been studying at the Catholic college at Douai. There, 'he found his inclinations point another way'. He had never shared his father's 'Zeal' for the 'Tenets of the Church of *Rome*', and the relationship soured further when Richard 'sold the best part of the Estate that our Author was born to'.[52] The will of one Richard Gildon of Motcombe drawn up in 1679 was presumably that of Charles's grandfather. It suggests that the rift may have reached the wider family, for Charles is not named in it.[53] Still, *The Lives and Characters* indicates that Gildon salvaged something. When he returned to England aged nineteen, in 1683, he rapidly spent 'the Remainder of his Paternal Estate' and married three or four years later.[54] For a time it appears his life was spent exorcising his Catholic education. He became absorbed in 'reading the Controversies' of King James's reign' and drew a line under his own upbringing:

> an Example how difficult a thing it is, to overcome the Prejudice of Education; for I am assur'd that it cost him above Seven Years Study and Contest, before he could entirely shake off all those Opinions that had grown up with him from a Child.[55]

He was helped by John Tillotson's *A Discourse against Transubstantiation* (1684), but that book was the occasion of another hard-luck story. It was 'lent him by a Lawyer, that at the same time cheated him of about Four Hundred Pounds'.[56]

---

50 Gildon, *Lives and Characters*, p.174.
51 Gray's Inn Admission Register: 1521–1887, folio 1,093.
52 Gildon, *Lives and Characters*, p.174.
53 Will of Richard Gildon in the Probate Records of the Royal Peculiar of Gillingham, P27/1/52. Richard bequeathed money or goods to his surviving sons William, John and Joseph, and his daughters Catherine and two others given only their marital names of Watts and Barnes. No money was to be paid until after the death of his widow, Frances.
54 Gildon, *Lives and Characters*, p.174.
55 Ibid.
56 Ibid., p.175.

With that, the entry moves to reflections on Gildon's use of sources, under the mask of a supposed friendship ('he being my Friend, I shall forbear all things that may argue me guilty of Partiality'). He admits that 'Necessity was the first Motive of his venturing to be an Author', an apology that colours all his work, as though financial pressure excused every subsequent instance of authorial licence. Such pressure is evidenced by his being a late starter. His first original play, *The Roman Bride's Revenge*, was written when he was 'past Thirty Two Years of Age'.[57] Before that, he had adapted Aphra Behn's *The Younger Brother*, 'which he introduc'd by the Importunity of a Friend of her and his, on the Stage' ('friends' feature prominently in Gildon's self-narratives, doubtless as a deflecting device). He presents himself as a humble interloper between aesthetic and political worlds – an improver respectful both to Behn's skill as a dramatist and to the post-1688 regime in which her Yorkist sympathies were unwelcome:

> Out of the Respect to her Memory, and a Deference, which was too nice, to her Judgment, he durst not make any Alterations in it, but what were absolutely necessary, and those only in the first and second Act, which reflected on the *Whigs*.[58]

Such respect, he claims, cost him. Had he tackled the 'jejune Stile' of the last three acts, 'in all Probability it would have been more to the Advantage of his Purse'.[59]

In his Dedication of *The Younger Brother* Gildon refers to his excision of politically controversial material and describes Behn as 'a Woman so Accomplish'd, and of so Establish'd a Fame among the Men of Sense'.[60] In the Life of Behn that follows he writes that

> Her Muse was never subject to the Curse of bringing forth with Pain; for she always Writ with the greatest ease in the world, and that in the midst of Company, and Discourse of other matters I saw her my self write *Oroonoko*, and keep her turn in Discoursing with several then present in the Room.[61]

Here it is Behn, not Shakespeare, who is the natural writer unbeholden to classical precedent. Notably absent is any suggestion that Behn was, as some of her critics alleged, a plagiarist.

---

[57] Ibid., p.175.
[58] Ibid.
[59] Ibid.
[60] Gildon, 'To Colonel Codrington', *The Younger Brother* (London: Richard Baldwin, 1696), n.p.
[61] Ibid.

When it came to his own *Phaeton*, Gildon was keen to demonstrate his belief in *imitatio* as a necessary vehicle not just for artistic excellence but for reform of the stage. It was written 'in Imitation of the Ancients' and was 'a very bold Undertaking of a Young Author, to attempt to bring so very different a way of Writing on so corrupt a Stage as ours'. The plot, as well as

> a great many of the Beauties of the Play, the Author fairly owns that he has taken from the *Medea* of *Euripides*, and in his Preface you may find his Reasons for altering the Names and Characters from what they were in the Original that he has here copied.[62]

The statement reads like a studiously learned application of Langbaine's principles: ground your work in the classics and it will be the better for it, and choose as your model a well-known play. The phrase 'fairly owns' stages an awareness that plagiarism may be alleged, but unfairly. That strategy is pursued in the play's preface:

> That I owe a great many of its Beauties to the *Immortal EURIPIDES*, I look on as my *Glory*, not *Crime*, and I have so little to fear on that Account even from my *Enemies*, that I find their chief Objection is, that I have not follow'd him yet more close.

What follows is a description of imitative process that moves from the kind of disreputable source Langbaine had condemned to one of unimpeachable authority. He had begun with 'hints' from a '*French* Opera of *Phaeton*' but once he had drafted the first two acts, 'the *Medea* of *EURIPIDES*, accidentally fell into my Hands'. Leaving aside for a moment Gildon's giveaway deployment of the accident excuse, he continues: since his own plot 'came so very near' that of *Medea*, he decided to 'make use of those Advantages the Imitation of so excellent an Author might afford'. The first of two prologues insists that the author's hand has been fully declared: '*Euripides* to Night adorns our Stage'. The second prologue again owns up to borrowing, but this time in the interests of keeping up with fashion. By scripting music and dance as part of the entertainment, Gildon has 'wisely borrow[ed] Ornaments from *France*'.[63] It sounds like the logic of someone already practised in using Langbaine's distinctions for venial ends. He admits having entertained the idea of an obvious source – another work called *Phaeton* – while his discovery of the superior *Medea* is supposedly 'accidental'. If it is not necessarily straightforward to divine his intentions, it is clear that Langbaine's work gave a needy author a plausible line of self-defence.

---

[62] Gildon, *Lives and Characters*, pp.175–6.

[63] First Prologue to *Phaeton*, spoken by George Powell; second prologue, spoken by Mrs Cross; in Gildon, *Phaeton, or The Fatal Divorce* (London: Abel Roper, 1698).

What he attempted, he claims, was more than imitation. He argues that his *Phaeton* enhances Medea's justification for her terrible deeds by making her 'the Instrument of the Gods to bring a wonderful Punishment of Perjury about, on those, whom *Power* had secured from all other means'. Gildon further stresses his distance from Euripides by explaining that he has moderated the language and motivations of Medea and Jason. He also explains that because he has created an imitation rather than a translation, he is entitled to change the names of characters. If we are entitled to interpret his emphasis on Jason's 'Perjury' as an oblique way for Gildon to deal with his nagging consciousness of plagiarism, we are similarly entitled to suspect that he was taking refuge in the concept of *imitatio* precisely because he knew his work would be interpreted as theft. The culturally ingrained comparison of Ancients and Moderns gave him further protection. Ancient Greek drama, he explains, offered genuine '*Terror* and *Compassion*' rather than noisy bluster, and the probable over the fantastic. Since there were, by definition, limits to the probable when it came to human behaviour, any act of authentic imitation was bound to give the appearance of simply recycling existing material.

He had, perhaps, also learned from his experience of *The Roman Bride's Revenge*, performed in November 1696, a little more than a year before *Phaeton*. In this, his first play, he had committed precisely the kind of indefensible recycling decried by Langbaine. No Euripides here, and noisy bluster has been let in through the front door in the shape of the recently deceased Nathaniel Lee: 'The Stile is too near an Imitation of Mr. *Lees* (the worst Qualification of that Poet, who has Beauties enough to make amends for it)'. At least the plot was original:

> The Plot I take to be of the Author's own Invention, allowing for a Hint taken from the *Camma* of *Galatea*, which is thus far improv'd, that the Husband here is alive after the Wife has drank the Poison.[64]

The 'Moral', moreover, was taken from the textbook of Roman virtues, and 'one of the most noble of any of our Modern Plays' (i.e. Lee's *Lucius Junius Brutus*) – namely that 'no Consideration in the World, ought to make us delay the Service of our Country'.[65] Unusually, the first edition of *The Roman Bride's Revenge* is fronted by a dedication written by the publisher, John Sturton, who states that Gildon had asked him 'to choose a Patron for his *Play*', a sure sign of the dramatist's disconnection from circles of influence and his neediness as a writer. Sturton's choice of William Gregory, grandson

---

[64] Gildon, *Lives and Characters*, p.176.
[65] Ibid.

of Commons Speaker Gregory, who had defied James II, also reinforced Gildon's new-regime credentials.

Among Gildon's other plays, the question of plagiarism does not arise in the prefatory material to his adaptation of *Measure for Measure*; its dependence on Shakespeare was perhaps too obvious to be stated. With *The Patriot*, his revision of Lee's previously banned *Lucius Junius Brutus*, he went to such lengths to explain his approach that he felt the need to draw back. After three densely printed pages in which he explains the changes he has made to Lee's play, he concedes that 'To run through e'ry [*sic*] particular of my Alterations would be too tedious, and perhaps invidious'.[66] If he had, by now, thoroughly mastered the art of self-defence against charges of plagiarism, he had also achieved greater prestige in the matter of patronage. *The Patriot* is dedicated to none other than Queen Anne.

So, in the light of Langbaine and the lessons Gildon had learned from him, what are we to make of his claim, boldly set out at the start of the Preface to *The Life of Mr Thomas Betterton*, that he would not have 'troubled the Reader with a Preface to this Little Treatise' but for the fact that he foresaw 'an Objection, which may be made, and that is, that I have been a Plagiary'? Was he lying in plain sight or offering a plausible defence? In terms of literary property, the question of theft is complex and requires investigation into the bookseller who had commissioned Gildon to complete *The Lives and Characters of the English Dramatick Poets*.

Nicholas Cox

Nicholas Cox had a long career in the business, working at the sign of the Golden Bible from 1673 to 1721. Two items in his catalogue set something of a pattern for his career: *An Exact Catalogue of all the Comedies, Tragedies, Tragi-Comedies, Operas, Masks, Pastorals and Interludes that were ever yet printed* (1680), a forerunner of his work with Langbaine; and *An Essay Upon the Action of an Orator*, the translation from Le Faucheur. The date of the latter book is sometimes given as 1680 but that cannot be correct; its dedicatee, the antiquarian Christopher Rawlinson, was only three in 1680 and was not known for the achievements recognized in the dedication until after the publication of his edition of the Anglo-Saxon Boethius in 1698.[67] *An Essay Upon the Action of an Orator* was not Cox's first foray into classical oratory. In 1674 he had published the portmanteau collection, *Poems, and essays with*

---

[66] Gildon, Preface to *The Patriot, or the Italian Conspiracy* (London: William Davis, 1703), n.p.

[67] *An. Manl. Sever. Boethi Consolationis philosophiae libri V Anglo-Saxonice redditi ab Alfredo ... edidit Christophorus Rawlinson* (Oxford: Sheldonian Theatre, 1698).

a paraphrase on Cicero's Lælius, or, of friendship, believed to be the work of the minor dramatist Edward Howard, whose play *The Change of Crowns* had caused a major stir in 1667.[68] It is possible that when Cox needed someone to translate Le Faucheur, he turned to Howard. Cox was himself an author. His best-selling title was his own tribute to genteel masculinity: *The Gentleman's recreation: in four parts. Viz. Hunting, hawking, fowling, fishing*, which first appeared in 1673 and was re-printed in 1674, 1677, 1686, 1697 and 1721. Cox even managed to draw Langbaine into rural territory with *The Hunter, A Discourse of Horsemanship*, which Cox published in 1685. Tellingly, one of Cox's last publications was a revised edition of Le Faucheur. *The Art of Speaking in Publick* (1721) was given the subtitle *An Essay on the Action of an Orator* and announced as 'The Second Edition Corrected' of that work. Cox seized the opportunity to refer to a contemporary clergyman whose 'extraordinary Performances and Attempts, to revive the antient Manner of Speaking in Public' had in some quarters been greeted with derision.[69] Three decades after Cox's death, the translation from Le Faucheur re-appeared as *An Essay upon Pronunciation and Gesture*, published by Charles Hitch in 1750. Hitch reproduced Cox's 'Introduction and Apology' and re-presented the translation with minor corrections.

So, if anyone could be said to have legally owned the text of *An Essay Upon the Action of an Orator*, it was not Le Faucheur or his translator, but Nicholas Cox the bookseller. There was no author to filch from. However, the fact that Gildon had worked with Cox deepens suspicions about the *Life*. He was familiar with the Le Faucheur translation and, when Betterton died and Gosling and/or Curll came calling, saw an opportunity to make use of it. He may even have relied on imagined good will on Cox's part (as he had, perhaps, on Betterton's). But the fact that Cox went on to issue a new edition of Le Faucheur suggests the bookseller saw continuing commercial value in it and would not have welcomed seeing chunks hewn into a book published by a rival, not least someone of Curll's reputation. Cox made a single foray into play publishing with the tragedy, *Courtnay Earl of Devonshire* (1705), but did not work with Gildon after *The Lives and Characters*.

Still, when all is said, Gildon and Gosling/Curll did not simply produce a pirate edition of Le Faucheur, but a selection of highlights crafted into a bigger narrative. Just as there was no offence against an author or translator, any theft from the bookseller sat on the borders of acceptability. In Langbaine's terms, what Gildon did was to make more widely available a

---

[68]   The play prompted a violent quarrel between Howard and the actor John Lacy, whom he accused of improvising lines that were offensive to the King. See Pepys, 20 April 1667 (VIII.172–3).

[69]   'The Editor's Introduction and Apology for this Edition', *The Art of Speaking in Publick* (London: Nicholas Cox, 1721), pp.xiv–xv.

foreign import that enriched the nation's cultural economy. Translators, as already observed, were for Langbaine exempt from the charge of plagiarism because they 'contributed to the Knowledge of the *Unlearned*, by their excellent *Versions*'.[70] Modifying Le Faucheur for a new audience with different concerns, Gildon might argue that he was merely doing the work of a translator. In the Preface to the *Life*, he admits to borrowing but points out that Le Faucheur himself stood on the shoulders of giants:

> I first allow, that I have borrow'd many of them from the French, but then the French drew most of them from Quintilian and other Authors.

That is indisputably true, although the scale of Gildon's borrowing exceeds Le Faucheur's. Nevertheless, much of Le Faucheur is drawn directly from Quintilian and Cicero, a dependence indicated in the notes to this edition; the sections on voice and gesture are particularly in debt to Book 11 of Quintilian's *Institutes of Oratory*. What exempts Le Faucheur from the charge of plagiarism is that he 'suppl[ied] what was lost by the Alteration of Custom, with Observations more peculiar to the Present Age'. What Gildon might argue he was doing, Le Faucheur had done before him: the characteristically Restoration business of 'improv[ing] the Ancients'.[71]

That task presumed a model of authorship different from the one pursued so relentlessly by Langbaine. 'ARTS were never brought to Perfection by one Hand', Gildon wrote, admitting that the 'Advancements' he had contributed were partial and provisional: 'a diligent Study, and judicious Observation, may produce new and more easy Rules'. But why was he 'oblig'd to have a Regard to the Action and Utterance of the Pulpit and Bar, as well as the Stage', an obligation that compelled him 'to bring my Examples from Oratory more than from the Drama'? Because Curll wanted a book with wider appeal? Or simply because *An Essay Upon the Action of an Orator* was sitting on his bookshelves waiting to be plundered? If the final paragraph of the Preface, promising a further 'Treatise for the Stage alone', is a diversionary tactic suggesting that the field is entirely within Gildon's compass, it also suggests that the *Life* did not meet with 'the Approbation of the Learned', for no such sequel appeared.

Gildon pursued his defence in the composition of the *Life*. A little way into the Reading visit, Gildon's Betterton asks to be excused in order to fetch 'a Manuscript … written by a Friend of mine, to which I confess I contributed all, that I was able'. The 'loose papers' that emerged were in 'his own Hand'; Betterton, we recall, was modest about his own writing. After a glass of wine, he began reading, taking in much of *An Essay Upon the Action of*

---

[70]   Langbaine, *Momus Triumphans*, a3[r].
[71]   Gildon, Preface to *The Life of Mr Thomas Betterton*, p.4.

an Orator, interspersed with reflections on Shakespeare and the Restoration Stage, a further manuscript allegedly loaned by a 'learned Friend' of Betterton's, and concluding with St Evremond's letter on opera to the Duke of Buckingham, duly acknowledged and placed in quotation marks. 'After this Discourse', concludes Gildon, 'we took our Leaves of Mr. BETTERTON'. The pretence that this 'Manuscript' was Betterton's is inconsistently sustained, with some glaring slips. Recalling Elizabeth Barry in Otway's *The Orphan* (1680), Betterton allegedly reads that 'I have heard her say, that she never said *Ah! Poor* Castalio … without weeping'. Betterton *was* her Castalio and on stage when she said the line, so it is not clear why he should 'have heard her say' such a thing rather than drawing on first-hand observation.[72] Then there is a passage about Charles Mordaunt, Earl of Peterborough, which illustrates the rhetoric of praise. It is lifted straight from Gildon's dedication to Mordaunt of the seventh volume of Curll's *The Works of* Mr. *William Shakespear Volume the Seventh*.[73] Leaving aside the remote possibility that Betterton had actually written such a manuscript, and that his recollections were a little dimmed by old age in 1709, it seems clear that the writing process Gildon attributes to him was exactly what Gildon himself did in producing the book: take an existing work and 'contribute all that [he] was able' to it.

One further area of Gildon's doubtful practice needs to be examined. In the Preface he refers to the 'Frenchman' whose work lies behind the *Life*. In the fictionalized encounter with Betterton, the actor refers to a further manuscript 'which he assur'd me was taken from a learned Jesuit who wrote on this Subject'. The same 'Jesuit's Observations' on the 'Natural Signification' of gestures are referred to several pages on.[74] An obvious explanation is that Gildon knew that some readers might be onto the fraud he had committed and found additional ways of putting them off the scent. If that is the case, it is odd that the Preface implies that the 'manuscript' first came to Gildon's attention directly rather than via Betterton – another instance of Gildon not quite getting his complex defence in order.

'The Frenchman'

The 'Frenchman' referred to as a Jesuit was in fact one of the most famous Protestant clergymen in seventeenth-century France. Born in Geneva in 1585, Michel Le Faucheur ministered to congregations in Montpellier,

---

[72]   See Otway, *The Orphan*, V.i.298, in *The Works of Thomas Otway*, ed. J.C. Ghosh, 2 vols (Oxford: Clarendon Press, 1932), II.78.

[73]   See below, p.132.

[74]   *Life*, pp. 79–87.

Charenton and Paris.[75] He published numerous religious tracts and was renowned for his skill at the pulpit, but he owed his fame to systematizing the principles of oratory in his *Traitté de l'action de l'orateur; ou, de la Prononciation et de geste*. It was his friend and fellow Protestant minister, Valentin Conrart, who saw the work into print soon after Le Faucheur's death on 1 April 1657. In some later editions the work is even attributed to Conrart. The book was enormously popular. At least seven French editions appeared between 1657 and 1700 (four in Paris and one each in Lyon, Leiden and Amsterdam). Melchior Schmidt's Latin translation was published under Conrart's name in 1690. The fact that Le Faucheur's name does not appear anywhere in the translation published by Cox, combined with the later confusion as to the work's original authorship, suggests that Gildon may not have known who had written it beyond the statement in the dedication to Christopher Rawlinson that it was 'Originally French'. Ignorance, together with the book's immersion in principles and examples adumbrated by Quintilian and Cicero, perhaps gave him licence to proceed.

The popularity of Le Faucheur's text rested partly on its promise of a more intuitive, even democratic, approach to rhetoric, in line with his Protestant rejection of Romish ritual. Rejecting the idea that an orator must memorize gestures, he stresses the importance of speaking in the moment to a specific audience and with a specific message. Good delivery, he urges, can make up for indifferent drafting of the written canons of invention, arrangement and style.[76]

Something in Le Faucheur's approach presumably appealed to the Protestant convert Gildon, who took seven years to 'shake off all those Opinions that had grown up with him from a Child'.[77] For different reasons it may also have appealed to Betterton, whose church connections and experience of coaching might plausibly have made the book a natural reference point and perhaps resource.

The Cox translation and Le Faucheur's text sometimes differ in emphasis. Howell points out that the English translator occasionally used 'elocution' to refer to any vocal utterance, so bequeathing a category term to an entire system of speech education.[78] Crucially, the English translation opened

---

[75] Details of Le Faucheur's career are drawn from Lynée Lewis Gaillet, 'Michel Le Faucheur', in *Eighteenth-Century British and American Rhetorics and Rhetoricians. Critical Sources and Studies*, ed. Michael G. Moran (Westport and London: Greenwood, 1994), pp.70–74.

[76] For a guide, see Richard A. Lanham, *A Handlist of Rhetorical Terms* (Berkeley: University of California Press, 1968), pp.106–16.

[77] See above, p.12.

[78] W.S. Howell, *Eighteenth-Century British Logic and Rhetoric* (Princeton: Princeton University Press, 1971), p.180.

the door to the needs of actors as well as the ministers and barristers who formed Le Faucheur's intended readership. Where Le Faucheur's aim was to educate young men in arguing virtuous causes, the English version presents good delivery as an end in itself, 'the very Life and Soul of Rhetorick'.[79] That implies the blurring of the performances of life and theatre which the translator appears at first to celebrate:

> there is nothing so taking or so much admir'd now-a-days as that which is Acted to the Life; strikes the Senses and captivates the Mind. So that Gesture, in fine, is not improperly called the Eloquence of the Body and the last Accomplishment of Speech.[80]

Apparently sensing danger, however, the translator drew back for a final reflection on the usefulness of Le Faucheur's book:

> But I will be so bold at last as to assert, that if this little Tract were rightly made use of, with a just Application, by Students either of Divinity or the Law they would have no occasion to run so often to the Play-Houses, nor fall in Love so much with comical Fopperies and extravagant Postures.[81]

Yet it was Le Faucheur himself who had invited theatrical applications of classical oratory. In the 1657 edition he explained that the great rhetorical theorists of Ancient Greece and Rome had too little to say about the mechanics of delivery.[82] Only Book 11 of Quintilian's twelve *Institutes of Oratory* provided any guidance and that, by seventeenth-century standards, was out of date. Even so, the final sentence of Book 11 must have given Gildon a cue for writing about a great actor who was also renowned for respectability: 'the orator, while he aims at the elegance of the player, may not lose the character of a good and judicious man'.[83]

The Bookseller

Gildon's previous publications had been with a variety of booksellers. Before 1710 he had worked with at least fourteen different houses – usually the sign of a hand-to-mouth existence.[84] Robert Gosling (1684–1741) was near the start of his publishing career when Gildon's book appeared. He is

---

[79] Anon, 'The Translator's Preface to the Reader', Le Faucheur, p.5.
[80] Ibid.
[81] Ibid.
[82] Gaillet, 'Michel Le Faucheur', p.71.
[83] Quintilian, p.635.
[84] That is, Benjamin Bragg, Thomas Jones, James Dowley, Daniel Brown, Henry Hills, John Lawrence, James Wilde, John Sturton, John Dunton, Abel Roper, William Davis, John Woodward, Richard Parker, and Andrew Roper.

associated with two premises: the Mitre against St. Dunstan's Church in Fleet Street, and (from 1707) at the Middle Temple Gate. His early publications largely suggest a sober trade profile, with works such as William Brown's educational manual, *Tutor clericalis instructus* (1707), and the anonymous *A Common Law Treatise of Usury* (1710). Legal publishing continued to feature in his list, including Sir Geoffrey Gilbert's *A Treatise of Tenures* (1738) and *The Laws concerning the Poor* (1718). He rose to some eminence, publishing the antiquary and MP Browne Willis' *Notitia Parliamentaria, or an History of the Counties, Cities and Boroughs in England and Wales* (1715) and a variety of theological works such as Robert D'Oyly's *Four Dissertations* (1733).[85] The fragile respectability of his business was bolstered by the career of his son, Francis, who went on to become a knighted Alderman, banker, and candidate for the Lord Mayor's office.

Gosling does not appear to have produced many books relating to the arts: an edition of Samuel Daniel's poetry (1718), Nicholas Brady's translation of the *Aeneid* (1717), and Perrault's *A Treatise of the Five Orders of Architecture* (1722) – the latter in partnership with four other booksellers – stand out among a list dominated by legal, religious and theological works. The *Life*, therefore, was a good marriage of subject and publisher: a work devoted to rules, industry and sober improvement would suit Gosling. There was also a more speculative side to his early list. One of his first titles was David Russen's *Iter Lunare: or, a Voyage to the Moon* (1707). Doubts about his credentials begin to harden when he is found working with the duplicitous Curll on six titles culminating in *A Collection of Preambles to the Patents* (1713). He is often cited by Baines and Rogers as a front for some of Edmund Curll's dealings; Curll's own master, Richard Smith, had acquired a name for 'packaging every kind of textual scrap into what he hoped would be desirable commodities' – a harsh but hardly inaccurate description of Gildon's *Life*.[86] All in all, the combination of advertised respectability, rules, translation and murky association made Gosling an ideal publisher for Gildon's *Life*. There are signs of haste, to put it kindly, in the setting of the book. Some words are scrambled ('Dufucous' instead of 'fuscous', etc), and the occasional name is mangled ('Vicians' instead of 'Vinicius'). Between pages 10 and 11 of the first edition there is clearly a passage missing; it was restored in Curll's 1741 *History of the English Stage* and is included here.[87] Given the high level of verbatim correspondence between parts of Gildon's

---

[85]   For an account of Gosling's business and that of his son, see Frank Melton, 'Robert and Francis Gosling: Eighteenth Century Bankers and Stationers', in *Economics of the British Booktrade 1605–1939*, ed. Robin Myers and Michael Harris (Cambridge: Cambridge University Press, 1985), pp.60–77.

[86]   Baines and Rogers, p.24.

[87]   See below, p.52.

text and passages in Le Faucheur, it seems likely that Gildon hand-copied some sections of the book and simply marked up others for Gosling's type-setter. However slapdash, the experience did not end their relationship. Gildon assisted with the translation from Heliodorus of *The Adventures of Theagenes and Chariclia, A Romance* (1717) for Gosling and Curll.

On Acting and Oratory

Gildon was undoubtedly devious and worked with a publisher who connived in the deceit. He sought multiple ways to deflect the allegation he knew might come his way. Yet his scrapbook tribute to Betterton displays a rounded appreciation of a man he had worked with and, like many other literary men, admired. In Wanko's words, 'Gildon's borrowing should not diminish his accomplishment and innovation'.[88] Just so, but if the book has value beyond its contribution to the history of unauthorized literary borrowing, shady publishing practice and the sociology of actors and acting, we need to be sure that it tells us something about the business of late seventeenth- and early eighteenth-century performance.

The validity of his framework is proved by several sources, not least by those who objected to acting by oratorical principles. In an edition of *The Prompter* published in 1735, Aaron Hill criticized actors who, 'instead of examining nature … look into Quintilian, not reflecting that the lessons he teaches his orator were directed to the bar, not the stage'. As an example, he singled out the absurdity of suggesting to an actor that he follow Quintilian in 'never rais[ing] his hands about the height of his eyes', a recommendation that reappears in the *Life*. Use of a mirror or paintings to cultivate stage gesture – another of Gildon's recommendations – he likewise condemns in favour of the 'imaginary graces' that come of emotional engagement. Actors who follow the oratorical school are likely to learn only 'the art of making mouths and distorting their faces into a technical and scholastic confusion between the ridiculous and the horrible'.[89]

Such criticism was usually aimed at Betterton's successors, actors such as James Quin or Barton Booth, the latter found wanting by Cibber for the solemn monotony of his acting. As Cibber describes him, Betterton himself was admirable for upholding the principle of truth to nature precisely because of his studious control of voice and gesture. When Cibber joined the United Company in 1690, Betterton was at the peak of his powers, and

---

[88] Wanko, p.40.

[89] Aaron Hill, *The Prompter*, nos.64, 66 and 118 (20 June 1735, 27 June 1735, 27 December 1735), reproduced in David Thomas and Arnold Hare, eds., *Restoration and Georgian England, 1660–1788* (Cambridge: Cambridge University Press, 1989), pp.170–3.

the young actor observed him at close quarters. It is useful to quote in full Cibber's recollection of the moment when Betterton's Hamlet saw the Ghost for the first time:

> You have seen a Hamlet, perhaps, who on the first appearance of his father's spirit has thrown himself into all the straining vociferation requisite to express rage and fury, and the house has thundered with applause, though the misguided actor was all the while (as Shakespeare terms it) tearing a passion into rags. I am the more bold to offer you this particular instance because the late Mr Addison, while I sat by him to see this scene acted, made the same observation, asking me with some surprise if I thought Hamlet should be in so violent a passion with the Ghost, which though it might have astonished, it had not provoked him. For you may observe that in this beautiful speech the passion never rises beyond an almost breathless astonishment, or an impatience limited by filial reverence, to enquire into the suspected wrongs that may have raised him from his peaceful tomb! And a desire to know what a spirit so seemingly distressed might wish or enjoin a sorrowful son to execute towards his future quiet in the grave! This was the light into which Betterton threw this scene, which he opened with a pause of mute amazement! Then, rising slowly to a solemn, trembling voice, he made the Ghost equally terrible to the spectator as to himself! And in the descriptive part of the natural emotions which the ghastly vision gave him, the boldness of his expostulation was still governed by decency: manly but not braving, his voice never rising into that seeming outrage or wild defiance of what he naturally revered. But alas! To preserve this medium between mouthing and meaning too little, to keep the attention more pleasingly awake by a tempered spirit than by mere vehemence of voice, is of all the masterstrokes of an actor the most difficult to reach. In this, none yet have equalled Betterton.[90]

There are obvious correspondences between what Cibber observed, the language he used, and the terminology Gildon borrowed from Le Faucheur. The fact that those correspondences are formed from established conventions does not make them less relevant to Betterton's practice. Key to success was the actor's grasp of the 'passion' that informed the scene: not a 'violent' one, but in Gildon's words 'produc'd naturally by the Sentiments of the Part'.[91] As Cibber would do when discussing Betterton's Brutus as well as his Hamlet, Gildon quotes Shakespeare for textual clues to the actor's method. The purpose was to 'affect both the Sense and Understanding of

---

[90] Cibber, p.77.

[91] See below, p.71. On the centrality of 'passion' in pre-Romantic theatre performance, see Blair Hoxby, *What Was Tragedy? Theory and the Early Modern Canon* (Oxford: Oxford University Press, 2015).

the Spectators with the same *Tenderness*', just as Betterton 'made the Ghost equally terrible to the spectator as to himself'.[92] Betterton's vocal crescendo similarly recalls Gildon adapting Le Faucheur: 'all his Looks, and every Sound of his Voice, like Strings on an Instrument, receive their Sounds from the various Impulse of the Passions'.[93] According to Anthony Aston, Betterton's voice was not naturally musical but achieved its effect through art: 'His Voice was low and grumbling; yet he could Tune it by an artful *Climax,* which enforc'd universal Attention, even from the *Fops* and *Orange-Girls*'.[94] Gildon makes no specific reference to such a quality but does observe that 'it seldom happens, that the same Voice is both sweet and solid'.[95] As noted above, Betterton himself is credited with emphasizing the importance of musicality in an actor's speaking.[96]

Cibber does not refer to gesture, but François Boitard's engraving of the closet scene that appears in Nicholas Rowe's 1709 edition of Shakespeare, often thought to represent Betterton, shows a left hand raised in astonishment, with the right thrust forward as though in greeting. The studied pose chimes with the *Life*; Gildon quotes Le Faucheur quoting Quintilian on the idea that gesture was both a system and a 'universal Language common to all'.[97] The *Life* often returns to the usefulness of the mirror in cultivating posture and gesture, and there is no shortage of evidence that Restoration actors rehearsed alone or by strict imitation of their predecessors.[98] When Betterton was 'Instructed' in the part of Hamlet by Sir William Davenant, he was judged to have performed 'every Particle' perfectly.[99]

It would be a mistake, however, to think that Gildon was recommending a merely superficial study of gesture. Just as he had arrived at the relatively modern conclusion that Shakespeare was a learned dramatist, he described practice surprisingly congruent with the school of actor training now called the 'Method'. When it came to passions, the actor's best route was defined by personal experience. The best tragedians of Ancient Rome 'kept their own private Afflictions in their Mind, and bent it perpetually on real Objects, and not on the Fable, or fictitious Passion of the *Play,* which they acted'.[100] He goes on to quote, directly from Le Faucheur, the examples of Polus, an

---

[92] See below, p.93.

[93] See below, p.75.

[94] Anthony Aston, *A Brief Supplement to Colley Cibber, Esq; His Lives of the late Famous Actors and Actresses*, in Lowe, II.300.

[95] See below, p.107.

[96] See above, n.22.

[97] See below, p.77.

[98] Stern, pp.154–5.

[99] Downes, pp.51–2.

[100] See below, p.91.

actor who drew on the death of his son, and Æsopus, whose performance in one play was powered by memories of his banished friend Cicero. These examples disturb conventional wisdom about late seventeenth- and early eighteenth-century acting, and find a parallel in Cibber's assertion that the best actors did not merely imitate their predecessors, but developed their own 'conception' of a role.[101]

That said, the material Gildon gleaned from Le Faucheur notably lacks a quality celebrated in later eighteenth-century performers. Seeing the Ghost, Betterton may appear to the modern reader to have acted a process of dawning recognition, traversing a broad territory of contradictory feelings. But the variety Cibber perceived was in the actor's musical line: for all their complexity, the emotions form a single, cohesive entity. James Harriman-Smith has recently demonstrated the importance of the 'transition' in appreciations of eighteenth-century acting: the ability of the actor to give physical expression to gradual or sudden changes of mood and perception.[102] The effect was to create 'points' in performance where a dynamic moment acquired iconic force. The scope of Harriman-Smith's book is determined partly by the emergence of performance criticism in the 1720s, and by the career of its presiding genius, David Garrick, whose physical style offered a startling alternative to the conventions of the oratorical school. Nevertheless, Betterton's Othello makes a brief appearance in the final chapter, where on the basis of an appreciation by Sir Richard Steele it is suggested that Betterton was also the master of the transition.[103] There is something of that quality in Cibber's tribute to Betterton. But it is also hard not to feel that the style of acting he embodied for Cibber was closer to the iconic – to the complexity and musicality of the speaking picture – than to the dynamic. In other words, if Harriman-Smith's reading of Steele's tribute is right, Gildon may have been guilty of a worse error than plagiarism. Did he misrepresent the essence of what made Betterton, in the eyes of Samuel Pepys and his wife at least, 'the best actor in the world'?[104] Yoking Betterton to time-honoured classical principles, did he overlook what was so impressive to Steele – the actor's ability to show passion not as a pose but as a rapid sequence of motions and emotions? Age does not come into it. Betterton was already well into his fifties when he first played Othello. His skill in

---

[101] On imitation, see Stern, pp.153–60. For Cibber, p.201, on Richard Estcourt imitating Anthony Leigh in Dryden's *The Spanish Fryar*: 'It was too plain that the conception was not his own but imprinted in his memory by another, of whom he only presented a dead likeness'.

[102] James Harriman-Smith, *Criticism, Performance, and the Passions in the Eighteenth Century: The Art of Transition* (Cambridge: Cambridge University Press, 2021).

[103] Ibid., pp.184–5.

[104] Pepys, 4 November 1661 (II.207).

that role, according to Steele, was to trace the 'wonderful agony which he appeared in, when he examined the circumstances of the handkerchief [...] the mixture of love that intruded upon his mind upon the innocent answers *Desdemona* makes'.[105]

An Undeserving Work?

If further evidence were needed of Gildon's duplicity in compiling *The Life Mr Thomas Betterton*, it is this. The actor's widow Mary, herself a distinguished performer as well as an acting coach, was left destitute by his death. Although Betterton was buried in the cloisters of Westminster Abbey, there was not enough money for a memorial stone. According to *The Tatler*, Mary's mental distraction was her best defence against age and poverty.[106] Friends rallied round; the company offered a pension and a benefit performance. By August 1710 she remained sufficiently needy to auction off her late husband's library and picture collection. It is comforting to imagine that Gildon's book, with its dedication to Richard Steele, the editor of *The Tatler*, may have been part of a scheme to raise funds for Mary's benefit. If that were true, Mary's name and situation would surely have featured in the prefatory material. It does not. Indeed, in the warm evocation of her marriage that features in the biographical section of the book, Gildon suggests that her 'old Age' was characterized only by her 'maintaining the Character of a good Woman'.[107] It is therefore reasonable to conclude that *The Life of Mr Thomas Betterton* was written with its author's and publisher's interests foremost in mind.

There are reasons for arguing that a work such as Gildon's *Life* does not merit a new edition. Gildon was testing the limits of Langbaine's definitions of plagiarism in a way that was calculated to deceive. But for historians of authorship that should be precisely why the book is of interest; it is a test case of how a book that appears to modern eyes unambiguously plagiarized could be presented as though it were not. For historians of the theatre the appeal is still clearer. A man of the theatre himself, Gildon knew Betterton and – even granted the possibility that he did not fully understand what made the actor so special – saw him in action. No other work of the period gives quite such a comprehensive view of how the practice of the modern stage might be rooted not just in ancient ideas but in those newly interpreted by a distinguished French rhetorician. Tiffany Stern's pragmatic conclusion is pertinent: 'given the extent to which English theatre of the time

---

[105] Richard Steele, *The Tatler* no.167, 2–4 May 1710.
[106] Ibid.
[107] See below, p.50.

was indebted to the French, the plagiarism need not discount the English relevance of the observations'.[108] *The Life of Mr Thomas Betterton* therefore merits recognition for what it is: for all its flaws, deceits and possible misrepresentations, a unique contribution to English theatre history.

[108] Stern, p.158.

THOMAS BETTERTON
AND *THE AMOROUS WIDOW*

The play Gildon and Gosling attached to *The Life of Mr Thomas Betterton* was a box office banker well into the eighteenth century. Between 1706 and 1790 it appeared in sixteen editions from booksellers in London and Dublin, one of them in a reprint of Gildon's book and five in adapted form.[1] Other plays by Betterton might have been candidates: his Webster adaptation, *The Roman Virgin*, or the lost *The Woman Made a Justice*. But the success enjoyed by *The Amorous Widow* on the Restoration stage made it an obvious candidate for inclusion in a tribute volume. Precisely when it was written and first performed is not certain. John Downes includes it in a group of plays that premiered sometime between the autumn of 1669 and late 1670, all of which reflect the growing influence of French comedy.[2] It is possible that the first edition of 1706 is itself an adaptation. Acts 3, 4 and 5 feature dance set pieces that showcased the talents of French performers brought in by Betterton from 1698 (Betterton's long-serving prompter, John Downes, took a dim view of his master's investment, describing 'Monsieur L'Abbé' and his colleagues as 'Exorbitantly Expensive').[3] For the nine seventeenth-century performances of the play recorded in *The London Stage*, there is no mention of dancing, while the scripting that surrounds the three dance episodes has a distinctly hurried quality.

The Amorous Widow has a double plot. In the Jonsonian tradition, names describe characters. The titular heroine, Lady Laycock, aged fifty and undeterred by three previous marriages, longs for a younger husband. Her niece Philadelphia is fancied by Cuningham, whose friend Lovemore pretends to woo Lady Laycock so that Cuningham can see Philadelphia. Lady Laycock is attracted to both men. When Lovemore tires of his diversionary role,

---

[1] The play was published on its own – in London unless otherwise stated – in 1706, 1710, 1714, 1725 (Dublin), 1729, 1737, 1751 (Dublin), 1755 (Dublin), 1762 (Dublin, as *The Wanton Wife*), 1768 (London, as *The Wanton Wife*), 1782 (as *Barnaby Brittle*), 1788 (as *Barnaby Brittle*), and 1790 (Dublin, as *Barnaby Brittle*).

[2] Downes, pp.64–5. The other plays were John Caryll's *Sir Salomon Single*, based on *L'École des Femmes*, and Betterton's *The Woman Made a Justice*, which appears to be an adaptation of Montfleury's *La Femme Juge et Partie*.

[3] Downes, pp.96–7; see also n.29 to the play.

Cuningham employs his falconer, Merryman, to impersonate a Viscount who is supposedly eager for Lady Laycock's hand. In the second plot, Lovemore own's amorous interests come to the fore. He pursues the wife of a glass-shop owner, Barnaby Brittle. Mrs Brittle is the 'Wanton Wife' of the play's subtitle. She is desperate to get out and amuse herself, and little wonder; she was forced to marry lower down the social ladder to repair the fortunes of her parents, Sir Peter and Lady Pride, who parade their social superiority every time they encounter their son-in-law. Lovemore employs as a messenger the hapless Clodpole, who unknowingly tells Barnaby what is going on behind his back. The second plot would take precedence later in the eighteenth century. Reduced to two acts from 1762, the play was repackaged simply as *The Wanton Wife, a Comedy*, and then again in 1782 as *Barnaby Brittle; or, a Wife at her Wit's End*, which was described – fittingly, in view of its broad physical comedy – as 'a farce'.[4]

If both plot lines seem familiar, it is because Betterton's play looks both forward and backward. The scenes where Clodpole reveals all to Barnaby may take their inspiration from Molière's *L'École des Femmes* (1662), where young Horace tells the jealous Arnolphe of his wooing of Agnès, while the Brittle plot derives from the same author's *George Dandin* (1669). The Lady Laycock plot, itself very similar to Thomas Corneille's *Le Baron d'Albikrac* (1667), seems to underlie one of the most enduring of Restoration comedies. In William Congreve's *The Way of the World* (1700), Lady Wishfort's niece Millamant is loved by Mirabell, who has pretended to woo Lady Wishfort as a way of gaining access to her. Mirabell then devises a plot to disguise his servant Waitwell as a rich uncle, with a view to trapping Lady Wishfort in a fake marriage so that she will consent to Mirabell's union with her niece. The parallels were reinforced by casting. Elinor Leigh created Lady Wishfort in 1700 and was probably already playing Lady Laycock in a production that also featured John Verbruggen, Congreve's first Mirabell, as Cuningham, and Cave Underhill, Congreve's bumptious Salopian Sir Wilful, as the countryfied Merryman. Betterton and Congreve were longstanding collaborators. The actor took a leading role in all Congreve's plays; in 1695, when Betterton and a group of senior actors broke away from Christopher Rich's United Company, Congreve's *Love for Love* followed them, even though it had been promised to Rich. Congreve admitted that *The Way of the World* had been a 'toil' to write.[5] Without memories of *The Amorous Widow*, and

---

[4]   The roles were accordingly reduced to the Brittles, Lovemore, Cunningham [*sic*], Sir Peter and Lady Pride, Damaris, Clodpole, Jeffrey and Jeremy.

[5]   Congreve, Prologue to *The Way of the World*, line 22, in the New Mermaids edition, ed. David Roberts (London: Methuen, 2020), p.11.

conceivably access to the prompt copy held by Betterton's company, his toil would have been greater.[6]

Downes outlined the first cast. Betterton's wife Mary, though only in her mid-thirties, played Lady Laycock, and Jane Long was Mrs Brittle, a part later taken by Anne Bracegirdle, Congreve's Millamant in *The Way of the World*. Betterton and William Smith played Lovemore and Cuningham, while the burden of comedy was carried, as so often, by James Nokes as Barnaby Brittle. Nokes's gift for facial acting is captured in Cibber's description of him as Dryden's Sir Martin Mar-All, and it is easy to imagine how his 'silent eloquence' and the 'piteous plight of his features' informed his performance as the bewildered shop owner Brittle.[7] By the end of the century the part had been taken by Thomas Doggett, Nokes's natural successor as the company clown and an expert in what Cibber described as 'characters of lower life'.[8] *The Amorous Widow* became popular because of the farcical energy comic actors were able to extract from the subplot. Just as reduced versions appeared in the second half of the eighteenth century, so a later critic would argue that the Brittle plot overwhelms the rest of the play.[9] Betterton's gift as a playwright certainly lay less in command of plot lines and scenes (both of which rather fizzle out, with hasty conclusions and rapid exits) than in the ability to create quirky characters that exploited the talents of a company he knew inside out. Even minor roles such as the priggish manservant Jeffrey have distinct comic traits.

The Amorous Widow has been categorized as the first in a series of 'sex comedies' that became popular during the 1670s.[10] There is obvious sexual innuendo in some characters' names, and the dialogue between Clodpole and Damaris in Act 4 touches playfully on the former's wedding night plans. But the play is hardly revolutionary. Its two plots, apparently spread out over two days, converge on a point of marked ideological safety; in particular, the 'wanton', wandering Mrs Brittle succumbs meekly to her jealous husband with a promise to obey, her actions dictated by the author's wish to tie up a narrative thread in the least controversial way possible. Greater promise, perhaps, lies in its depiction of the way class tensions cluster around the treatment of women. Sir Peter and Lady Pride, with

---

[6] The path from French sources to Congreve via Betterton is traced by John Harrington Smith, 'Thomas Corneille to Betterton to Congreve', *Journal of English and Germanic Philology* 45 (1946), 209–13.

[7] Cibber, p.104.

[8] Ibid., p.312.

[9] For example, Hume, *The Development of English Drama*, pp.264–5, and Judith Milhous, 'Thomas Betterton's Playwriting', *Bulletin of the New York Public Library* 77 (1974), 375–92.

[10] Hume, *The Development of English Drama*, p.90.

their pompous insistence that Brittle address them and their daughter in prescribed ways, are as contemptible representatives of their class as Brittle is of his. At least Sir Peter does not, like Brittle, spit on his fists as a prelude to wife beating. The play as a whole depicts a vacuum of authority in which various contenders compete for dominance discursively and physically. Its comedy, bittersweet to modern eyes, might now be described as that of a fractured patriarchy where women attempt to exploit its gaps, only to fail.

NOTE ON THE TEXT

The copy text for this edition is the 1710 *Life of Mr Thomas Betterton* contained in the database, *Eighteenth Century Collections Online*. Sections 1–11 of the work (i.e., everything up to *The Amorous Widow*) are given with original spelling and punctuation except in the case of obvious errors. A passage missing from the 1710 text that appeared in later editions is given as a footnote.

The Amorous Widow presents a more complex editorial challenge. Although the play premiered sometime before the end of 1670, it was not published until 1706, in a 1*s* 6*d* quarto (hereafter referred to as Q1). Betterton's name does not appear on Q1's title page, which announces that the play was 'Never Printed Before'. The anonymous Preface refers to the author's 'exemplary Modesty, which often requested the Gentleman, to whom he bequeathed this rich Treasure, never to divulge its Parent'. It goes on to add that if the author were known, 'his very Name would challenge a just Veneration from all the most sensible Part of Mankind, as well as strike Terror in the severest Criticks' (since the play was performed throughout the 1705–6 season, the gesture was surely futile). The notion of any playwright simply 'bequeathing' a text seems fanciful. The 1705–6 season saw a marked downturn in Betterton's theatrical commitments, an entry into semi-retirement that must have tempted him to make the most of every asset at his disposal.[1] If he did indeed sell it to the bookseller credited with the first edition, William Turner, the sale would have generated somewhere in the region of £5; what was sold would have been the manuscript rather than the prompt book, a deduction borne out by the intermittently messy, confused appearance of Q1.

Gildon and Gosling evidently thought nothing of revealing the play's authorship by including it in *The Life of Mr Thomas Betterton*; perhaps also conscious of indelicacy, they did not include the anonymous Preface. Their own title page to the play names Betterton as the author and excludes the

---

[1] On playwrights and ownership of their texts, see Judith Milhous and Robert D. Hume, *The Publication of Plays in London, 1660–1800* (London: British Library, 2015), pp.43–8.

quotation from Horace's *Ars Poetica* that introduces Q1.[2] There is a further twist. In 1710, just as *The Amorous Widow* was again being put before the public as an appendix to *The Life of Mr Thomas Betterton*, Gosling and Gildon's associate Edmund Curll reissued the 1706 edition. If that was an economic alternative for readers who wanted only a copy of the play, Curll's edition implied – presumably by chance – that Gildon and Gosling were acting indiscreetly by associating the play with Betterton.

For the purposes of comparison with Q1, the text of *The Amorous Widow* in Gildon's *Life* is referred to here as Q2. In Gildon's book it is described as 'Now first Printed from the Original Copy'. That description was intended to discredit Q1, but Q2's claim to originality is, like much else in *The Life of Mr Thomas Betterton*, dubious. However, Gildon and Gosling can at least be given credit for trying to improve on the earlier text. Q2 might be described in general terms as an imperfect attempt to apply eighteenth-century standards to the coarser lineaments of a seventeenth-century quarto. Spellings are frequently updated: to give a few instances, 'Extreamly' becomes 'extremely'; 'Extasie' turns to 'Ecstasy'; 'Fantastickly' is 'fantastically'; 'Ruine', 'Ruin'; and 'Crockadile', 'Crocodile'. Q1 abounds in colons where Q2 tends to use full stops; Q1 often gives an initial capital letter for verbs, adjectives and adverbs as well as nouns, where Q2 largely restricts itself to the latter. Some names are corrected or simply changed: in Q1, *Sans-Tarre* may be a phonetic shot at *Sans-Terre*, but is more likely an error corrected in Q2; one of Betterton's rakish heroes is *Cuningham* in Q2, where Q1 swings between that and *Cuningam*, with a majority preference for the latter. The *Geffrey* of Q1 becomes *Jeffrey* (but sometimes *Jeffry*) in Q2, while the Q1 Dramatis Personæ has Lady Laycock's niece Philadelphia played by 'Mr. Porter' rather than the 'Mrs. Porter' identified by Q2.

There are other clear-cut corrections. When Lady Laycock says she has 'not much Beauty to boast of; but Virtue, Sir, makes some amends for the Defects of the other', in Q1 Lovemore replies 'Defect?' where Q2 has the obviously preferable 'Defects?' Q2 accurately reflects the plot by having the same lady declare, 'I should think my self very happy, if I were certain of Mr. *Cuningham* or Mr. *Lovemore*'; Q1 imagines a saucier scenario by printing 'and' instead of 'or'. Instances of obviously erratic or erroneous punctuation in Q1 (for example, 'There are few but know: a little their own Value') are removed.

---

[2] 'Aut prodesse volunt aut delectare Poetæ, / Au simul & jucunda & idonea dicere Vitæ': in the translation by D.A. Russell and M. Winterbottom, 'The man who combines pleasure with usefulness wins every suffrage, delighting the reader and also giving him advice'; in their version of *Ars Poetica* contained in *Classical Literary Criticism* (Oxford: Oxford University Press, 1989), p.107.

Nevertheless, Q2 is insufficiently thorough in its revisions. In both texts, speech attributions are generally abbreviated (Lovemore to 'Love', Cuningham to 'Cun', etc). The typesetter for Q1 appears to have been confused three times by a marking of Philadelphia's name as 'Phil', interpreting it as the character beginning a speech. In each case, however, the relevant passage of dialogue makes sense only if Philadelphia is being addressed by another character. Q2 repeats the error in each case (that does not mean that *Phil* should in those instances appear in the dialogue; in this edition, it has been opened out to *Philadelphia*, which is how the character is referred to elsewhere). In both texts, Lady Laycock's designation as *Lady* turns into *Widow* from Act 3 onwards, presumably to distinguish her from Lady Pride, who had appeared earlier in the same act. Q2 also recycles errors from Q1 in the placing of stage directions. In Act 4, after Mrs Brittle beats her husband while pretending to beat Lovemore, it is clearly Brittle who '*Feels his arm and head*' rather than Sir Peter, as the lineation of both texts implies. Modernization of spelling in Q2 is erratic. Q1's 'Nooze' is corrected in Q2 to 'Noose' at the first mention, but not the second. Q2 also introduces new errors. Where Q1 has 'do not become your Forehead so well as a *Bando* did', Q2 omits the indefinite article, so implying that '*Bando*' is some personified item from the past.

In 1711 Gildon turned his attention to publishing a grammar of English, and there are some indications that when it came to punctuating *The Amorous Widow*, grammatical principles were applied that to modern ears sound alien to the rhetorical rhythms of speech.[3] Q2 frequently adds a comma where Q1 has none ('censure all for those Faults, which some few commit'; 'you'd have me go abroad like one, that sells Butter and Eggs'; 'To covet one, that is both Young and Rich', among many examples). Such instances do not resemble the random punctuation that characterizes some other eighteenth-century books – the result of printers making up their own rules as they went along, in the absence of clear guidance from authors – but rather an attempt to parse Betterton's dialogue in order to create a reading version. Like much else about *The Life of Mr Thomas Betterton*, it was an attempt compromised by the wish to put out a tribute volume as quickly as possible in the wake of the great man's death. Whatever Gildon's intentions, Q2 remains very much in the shadow of Q1. Both texts set out to offer readers the chance to experience *The Amorous Widow* on something like the same terms as audiences: rich in stage directions, with the cut and thrust of Betterton's dialogue represented in a variety of interjections,

---

[3] On the emergence of the 'grammatical' as opposed to the 'rhetorical' tradition of punctuation, see David Crystal, *Making a Point: The Pernickety Story of English Punctuation* (London: Profile Books, 2015).

changes of pace, and idioms. The promise that Q2 was 'First Printed from an Original Copy' is therefore best described as a mere advertising ploy. Q1 has the feel of a text based on a partly coherent manuscript where the printer has struggled to decode what was sometimes ambiguously written there. Like much of *The Life of Mr Thomas Betterton*, Q2 has the feel of a text that leans heavily on its predecessor.

Both texts are, compared with other comedies of the period, light in conveying a sense of place. The play begins with a disconcertingly vague signpost: 'a Room'. Only at the start of Act 3 is a specific locale – Brittle's glass shop – given; for the rest, we infer from dialogue that the setting is a street by day or night, or an interior, and that Lady Laycock is a neighbour (or even a lodger) of Barnaby Brittle's. References to St James's Park, the Mulberry Garden, Eaton's haberdashery and the Devil Tavern give a local flavour; other place names are either too generic to point to a particular location or appear plucked from the air. More vivid is the sense of *stage* place: the references to scenes opening and to characters appearing 'above' suggest an actor-author thinking first of the mechanics of theatre and the way individual performers could exploit them. It is a quality shared with – and perhaps inspired by – French comedy. If that makes the task of providing notes relatively straightforward, it may also partly explain how *The Amorous Widow* retained its popularity for so long, comparatively unanchored by a specific sense of time and place, and focusing instead on the farcical interaction of characters at the edge of their wits and tempers.

For a play published as part of the larger volume that is Gildon's *Life*, any decision about how to present the play's text is open to challenge. Should there be consistency of practice with the rest of *The Life of Mr Thomas Betterton* – in other words, a reproduction of Q2 more or less as it appears there? Or, since there is no modern edition of a play that still feels eminently performable, does the occasion warrant far greater editorial intervention? Along that spectrum, I have inclined towards the former approach. Old spelling is retained and Q2 adjusted only where there are obvious errors, where its orthography is inconsistent, or where Q1 is demonstrably superior either in substance or in avoiding the more egregious instances of pedantic parsing that characterize Q2. In both Q1 and Q2 the direction 'Aside' is given after the relevant utterance rather than before, and I have followed suit. In some instances, the directions 'Aside', 'Exit', or indications of addressees are clearly missing and have been added in this edition. 'Exeunt' is used inconsistently in Q2 and its use is regularized here, as is the pervasively erratic lineation of both texts. Prefatory material not contained in *The Life of Mr Thomas Betterton* is given as an appendix. In common with both Q1 and Q2, speech attributions are abbreviated. They have, however, been amended in two respects, again with clarity and consistency in mind.

Note on the Text

The *Lady/Widow* problem noted above has been addressed by designating Lady Laycock as *Lady L.* and Lady Pride as *Lady P.* Since we do not see the Viscount Sans-Terre but only Merryman's impersonation of him, speeches allocated to *Visc* in Q1 and Q2 are here attributed to *Merr,* as per that character's first appearance. That is consistent with the practice of Congreve's printers in attributing speeches to Waitwell rather than the fictitious Sir Rowland he pretends to be. The result is a version of Q2 that has been tidied with what are deduced to be Gildon's aims in mind, but with the consciousness that Q1 is occasionally superior. It is hoped that the result will emerge for today's readers as the bright, boisterous, and eminently playable comedy that held the London stage for a hundred years.

THE
L I F E
OF
Mr. *Thomas Betterton,*
The late Eminent
TRAGEDIAN.
WHEREIN
The ACTION and UTTERANCE of the *Stage, Bar*, and *Pulpit*, are distinctly consider'd.

WITH
The JUDGMENT of the late Ingenious *Monsieur de St. EVREMOND*, upon the *Italian* and *French* MUSIC and OPERA's; in a Letter to the Duke of *Buckingham.*

To which is added,
The AMOROUS WIDOW, or the *Wanton Wife.* A Comedy. Written by Mr. BETTERTON Now first printed from the Original Copy.

Quis Nostrum tam animo agresti, & duro fuit, ut Roscii *Morte nuper non commoveretur? Qui cum esset Senex mortuus ; tamen propter* excellentem Artem *ac Venustatem videbatur omnino mori non debuisse.*[1]

Cic. in Orat. pro ARCHIA Poeta.[2]

LONDON:

Printed for ROBERT GOSLING,[3] at the *Mitre*, near the *Inner-Temple Gate* in *Fleetstreet*, 1710. Price 3*s.* 6*d.*

---

[1] 'Which of us was so rude and uncouth as to be unmoved by the death of Roscius, whose great age was so far from preparing us for his passing that we hoped one so graceful and excellent in his art should be exempt from the common lot of mortal men?' Gildon's own translation appears below, p.xx.

[2] *Pro Archia Poeta* (c.62 BC) by Marcus Tullius Cicero (106–43 BC), a classic defence of the arts first printed in Paris in 1531, was delivered in support of A. Licinius Archias, a Greek poet deemed ineligible for Roman citizenship.

[3] For Gosling and his relationship with Edmund Curll, see Introduction, pp.1–3.

TO

Richard Steele, Esq;[4]

SIR,

THE following Piece was scarce yet an *Embryo*, when I design'd its full Growth for your Protection. For tho we Authors generally seem fond of adorning the Frontispiece of our Books with *pompous Titles*, as if we deriv'd from those not only Security but Fame to our Works; yet I can't but remember that among the *Ancients*, the Name of a *learned Friend* was of greater Consideration with the Writer, than the Dignity of a Man of Power; and that the Greatness of any Man in the *Political State*, according to them, did not raise his Authority in the Common-Wealth of Letters, above his real Merits in the *Arts* and *Sciences*, unless he ennobled it, by giving such Encouragement to them, as they very rarely in our Days meet with from the GREAT ONES.

Being, therefore, to write on an Art, which has not been much cultivated in our Nation, either in the *Practice* or *Theory*; what I had most to wish for, on the Publication of this Essay, was the Approbation of One, to whom the *Witty* and the *Learned* allow some Place in the POLITER STUDIES and FINE ARTS. An Address of this Nature is not without the agreeable Vanity of recommending a Man to the World, as a Person skilful in the Matter, of which he treats; and the Merit of Mr. STEELE, in the Kingdom of the *Muses*, is too well known to the *Beaux Esprits*, not to secure me from the Fear of the Railery of *Ascyltos* on *Encolpius*, in Petronius Arbiter – *Ut foris Caenares Poetam laudasti;*[5] or of *Manley* on my Lord *Plausible* – *That rather than not flatter, he would flatter the Poets of the Age, whom no Body else would flatter.*[6]

But I have chosen to address this Discourse to you, because the *Art*, of which it treats, is of your familiar Acquaintance, and the Graces of ACTION[7] and UTTERANCE come naturally under the Consideration of a *Dramatic Writer*. I flatter my self, that, as I am (as far as I know) the first, who in *English* has attempted this Subject, in the Extent of the Discourse before you, so I am apt to believe, that I have pretty well exhausted the

---

[4]   On Gildon's relationship with Steele, and Steele's with Betterton, see Introduction, p.7. *The Tatler* is quoted below, n.9.

[5]   'Flattering a poet in order to get asked to dinner'; from Petronius Arbiter, *Satyricon*, ed. Gareth Schmeling (Cambridge, MA: Harvard University Press, 2020), p.16.

[6]   In William Wycherley's *The Plain Dealer* (London: James Magnes and Richard Bentley, 1676) it is Olivia, not Manly, who says of Lord Plausible that 'rather than not flatter, [he] will flatter the poets of the age, whom none will flatter'; II.i.128–30 in the edition by James L. Smith (London: Ernest Benn, 1979), p.44. Betterton played the part of Manly from 1683/4.

[7]   The phrase 'the Graces of Action' occurs on p.5 of Le Faucheur, but it was proverbial.

Matter; and laid down such *General* and *Particular Rules*; as may raise the Stage from the present Neglect it lies under, to that Esteem, which it drew from the most polite Nation, that ever was in the World, and that, which it will always deserve from Men of Sense, when under a just Regulation, and adorn'd, as it ought to be, with GOOD ACTORS and GOOD PLAYS.

The *former* may be rais'd, I hope, from what I have deliver'd in the following Treatise, as the *later* from your Example, which may inspire our Authors with the Knowledge of Nature, and the Art of keeping her always in their View, adorn'd with that *Harmony*, *Decorum*, and *Order* which ought perpetually to shine in such PUBLIC REPRESENTATIONS.

I am, *SIR,*

Your Sincere Friend,
and Humble Servant

THE

PREFACE.[8]

I should not have troubled the Reader with a Preface to this Little Treatise, but to prevent an Objection, which may be made, and that is, that I have been a Plagiary, and deliver'd Rules for my own, which are taken out of other Authors. I first allow, that I have borrow'd many of them from the French, *but then the* French *drew most of them from* Quintilian *and other Authors. Yet the* Frenchman *has improv'd the Ancients in this Particular, by supplying what was lost by the Alteration of Custom, with Observations more peculiar to the Present Age.*

Arts were never brought to Perfection by one Hand, and tho I have made several Advancements my self upon those, who have gone before me, yet I know not but a diligent Study, and judicious Observation, may produce new and more easy Rules. If I have lead the Way with any tolerable Success, the Satisfaction will be too great to be lessen'd by being Succeeded with a more masterly Endeavour.

Being oblig'd to have a Regard to the Action *and* Utterance *of the* Pulpit *and* Bar, *as well as the Stage, I was compelled to bring my Examples from* Oratory *more than from the* Drama. *But if this meets with the Approbation of the Learned, I may perhaps publish a Treatise for the Stage alone. However, a Player, that is Master of those Qualities, which he ought to possess, by studying with Application this Discourse, may arrive at a Perfection which this Age has not seen.*

---

[8] On the defence mounted here, see Introduction, pp.17–19.

The Life of Mr Thomas Betterton

EPILOGUE

Spoken by Mrs. BARRY

At the Theatre Royal in Drury-Lane, April the 7th, 1709.

At Her Playing in *Love for Love*;

With Mrs Bracegirdle.

For the Benefit of Mr. Betterton.[9]

Written by N. Rowe, Esq;[10]

AS some brave Knight, who once with Spear and Shield,
Had sought Renown in many a well fought Field,
But now no more with Sacred Fame inspir'd,

---

[9] In *The Tatler* no.1 (12 April 1709), Steele recalled the support given to Betterton: 'There has not been known so great a Concourse of Persons of Distinction as at that Time; the Stage it self was covered with Gentlemen and Ladies ... This unusual Encouragement, which was given to a Play for the Advantage of so great an Actor, gives an undeniable Instance, That the true Relish for manly Entertainments and Rational Pleasures is not wholly lost'. Steele goes on to suggest that Betterton's circumstances were strained: 'we intend to repeat this Favour to him on a proper Occasion, lest he who can instruct us so well in personating Feigned Sorrows, should be lost to us by suffering under Real Ones'. It was alleged, perhaps maliciously, that Betterton made £526 4s 5d (c.£130,000 in current values) from the event thanks to patrons paying him personally and Betterton himself over-selling tickets, which was presumably the cause of the over-crowding mentioned by Steele. The official figure was £76 4s 5d (c.£19,000 in current values). See Zachary Baggs, *An Advertisement Concerning the Poor Actors, who, under Pretence of Hard Usage from the Patentee, are about to Desert their Service* (London, 1709). Baggs was in the pay of Betterton's old adversary, Christopher Rich. Betterton received a further benefit as Melantius in Beaumont and Fletcher's *The Maids Tragedy* on 13 April 1710 (LS2 218), but died a fortnight later. Elizabeth **Barry** (1658–1713), long-time stage partner of Betterton, had retired temporarily in 1707 but returned for the benefit performance before re-joining the Queen's Haymarket company for the 1709–10 season. For the *Love for Love* benefit she was joined by Thomas Doggett and Anne **Bracegirdle** (c.1671–1748), who is thought to have been Betterton's adopted daughter. All three had joined Betterton in breaking from Rich's company in 1695.

[10] Betterton had played leading roles in five plays by Nicholas Rowe (1674–1718): the title role in *Tamerlane* (1701), Memnon in *The Ambitious Step-Mother* (1700), Sir Timothy in *The Biter* (1704), Horatio in *The Fair Penitent* (1703), and the title role in *Ulysses* (1705). In the Preface to Rowe's six-volume edition of Shakespeare (1709) he is credited with researching facts about Stratford-upon-Avon and Shakespeare's family.

Was to a Peaceful Hermitage retir'd:
There, if by Chance disast'rous Tales he hears,
Of Matrons Wrongs and captive Virgins Tears,
He feels soft Pity urge his Gen'rous Breast,
And vows once more to succour the Distress'd.
Buckled in Mail he sallies on the Plain,
And turns him to the Feats of Arms again.

So we, to former Leagues of Friendship true,
Have bid once more our peaceful Homes adieu,
To aid Old THOMAS, and to pleasure you.
Like Errant Damsels boldly we engage,
Arm'd, as you see, for the defenceless Stage.
Time was, when this good Man no Help did lack,
And scorn'd that any She should hold his Back.
But now, so Age and Frailty have ordain'd,
By two at once He's forc'd to be sustain'd.
You see, what Failing Nature brings Man to,
And yet let none Insult, for ought we know,
She may not wear so well with some of you:
Tho Old, you find his Strength is not clean past,
But true as Steel, he's Mettle to the last.
If better he perform'd in Days of Yore,
Yet now he gives you all that's in his Power;
What can the youngest of you all do more?

What he has been, tho present Praise be dumb,
Shall haply be a *Theme* in Times to come,
As now we talk of ROSCIUS, and of *Rome*.
Had you with-held your Favours on this Night,
Old SHAKESPEAR's Ghost had ris'n to do him Right.
With Indignation had you seen him frown
Upon a worthless, witless, tasteless Town;
Griev'd and Repining you had heard him say,
Why are the *Muses* Labours cast away?
Why did I only Write what only he could Play?[11]
But since, like Friends to Wit, thus throng'd you meet,
Go on and make the Gen'rous Work complete;
Be true to Merit, and still own his Cause,

[11] A sentiment picked up by Cibber, p.76: 'Betterton was an actor as Shakespeare was
     an author: both without competitors, formed for the mutual assistance and illustra-
     tion of each other's genius!'

Find something for him more than bare Applause.
In just Remembrance of your Pleasures past,
Be kind, and give him a Discharge at last.
In Peace and Ease Life's Remnant let him wear,
And hang his consecrated Buskin here.[12]

---

[12] Whatever gains he made from the *Love for Love* benefit, Betterton continued to act
in tragic and other roles. At the very least, he played Thersites in *Troilus and Cressida*
on 2 June 1709 (LS2 194), Othello on 15 September 1709 (LS2 199), Hamlet on 20
September 1709 (LS2 199), and Macbeth on 17 December 1709 (LS2 205).

THE

LIFE

OF

Mr. *Thomas Betterton*, &c.

INTRODUCTION.

AS it was said of *Brutus* and *Cassius*, that they were the last of the *Romans*;[13] so it may be said of Mr. BETTERTON, that he was the last of our *Tragedians*. There being, therefore, so much due to his Memory from all Lovers of the Stage; I could not lay aside my Design of conveying his Name with this Discourse at least to a little longer Date, than Nature has given his Body. Nor can I imagine, that it can be look'd on, as injurious to our Reputation, either as Men of Candour, Figure or Sense, to express a Concern for the Loss of a Man so excellent in an Art which is now expiring, and for which Antiquity had so peculiar a Value; since it is plain from the Motto of this Book, that *Cicero* pleading the Cause of the Poet *Archias*, tells the Judge, a Man of the first Quality, that every Body was concern'd for the Death of *Roscius* the *Comedian*; or which is more emphatic, says he, *Who of us was of so brutish and sour a Temper as not to be mov'd at the late Death of* ROSCIUS? *Who, though he dy'd old, yet for the Excellence of his Art, and Beauty in Performance, seem'd as if he ought to have been exempted entirely from Death.*[14]

Whether Mr. *Betterton* or *Roscius* make a just Parallel or not in their Merits as Actors, is difficult to know; but thus far it is certain, that let the Excellence of the *Roman* be never so great, that of the *Briton* was the greatest we had: and tho we shall find, that in *Cicero*'s Time the Decorums of the Stage were more exactly observ'd, than in ours, yet we may suppose Mr. *Betterton*, in his own particular Performance, on a Foot with *Roscius*, especially when we consider that our Player excelled in both *Comedy* and *Tragedy*, the *Roman* only in the former, as far as we can discover.

---

[13] In Plutarch's *Lives*, Brutus grieves over the dead body of Cassius after the Battle of Philippi, 'calling him the last of all the Romans'; from *Shakespeare's Plutarch*, ed. Walter W. Skeat (London: Macmillan, 1875), p.144.

[14] For the source, see title page. Roscius Gallus Quintus (d.62 BC) was celebrated as an actor by Pliny and Cicero, and close associate of Catullus. His name was a by-word for excellence in acting, as evident in John Downes's celebration of Betterton's career, *Roscius Anglicanus* (London, 1708).

To give our *English* Actor yet the Preheminence, I shall here by writing his Life make him convey to others such Instructions, that if are perfectly understood, and justly practis'd, will add such Beauties to their Performances, as may render his Loss of less Consequence to the Stage. *Plato* and *Xenophon* introduce *Socrates* in their Discourses, to give the greater Authority to what they say, on those important Points which they would the more forcibly recommend to their Readers.[15] I shall, therefore, make the same Use of Mr. *Betterton*, on a Subject in which he may reasonably be thought a very competent Judge.

I know it may be objected, that the Qualifications I make him require, and the Precepts he gives, may seem to render this Art impossible for any other to attain to, as *Cicero* is said in his *Orator*, to do with the Oratorian Art.[16]

I confess that I do make him require Qualifications, of which he was not perhaps Master himself; but I presume that can be no Objection to them provided they are necessary, or at least conducive to the forming a complete Player; for we may daily hear many Painters, or even *Lovers* of the Art, who will tell you what Qualities are necessary to a great Master in History Painting, who yet do not themselves pretend to be possess'd of them. And the same will hold of many other Arts.

But if, indeed, there were any Precepts deliver'd, or any Qualifications requir'd, which would render a Mastery in this Art so difficult, that it could not be attain'd, the Objection would be far more solid, and worthy of our Notice; but I dare affirm, that as the Stages are now in the Hands and Management of the Players, there is not one Qualification set down, which is not absolutely necessary to do Justice to *Art*, in *Judgment* and *Performance*.

Nor can I find that *Cicero*, in his Book *de Oratore*, has requir'd any Impossibility in his Candidate for Eloquence; and it is evident, that has not so far discourag'd others from attempting that noble Science, but that every Age has produc'd some eminent in it, tho few or none have arriv'd to an Equality with him in the Performance for want of those very Qualities requir'd by him to the forming a *complete* Orator. Thus tho, to be a perfect Master, all the Qualities delivered be necessary, yet there is Room for Praise as well as Industry for others, who are not capable of attaining the whole. Such therefore, whose Genius is not so extensive as to comprehend the whole,

---

[15] Among other works, the *Symposium* of Xenophon (c.428–354 BC) imagines a party in which Socrates is one of the guests – perhaps an unfortunate reference for Gildon since it attracts the suspicion that his visit to Betterton's house was also imaginary. No work by Xenophon appears in PB.

[16] In Book 1, Chapter 6 of *De Oratore* (55 BC), Cicero stresses that he does not suggest that orators should know everything.

ought entirely to apply themselves to, and be content with, the *Performance*, leaving the Office of *Judging* to those, whose greater Skill and Knowledge better qualify them for Judges.

Having premis'd these things by way of Introduction, I shall now proceed to the Life of Mr. *Betterton*.

The Life of Mr. Tho. **Betterton**

MR. *Thomas Betterton* was born in *Tuttle-street, Westminster*; his Father being Under-Cook to King *Charles the First*: And when he was now come to Years sufficient, his Father bound him Apprentice to one Mr. *Rhodes* Bookseller, at the Bible at *Charing-Cross*, and he had for his Under-Prentice Mr. *Kynaston*.[17] But that which prepar'd Mr. *Betterton* and his Fellow-Prentice for the Stage, was that his Master *Rhodes* having formerly been *Wardrobe* Keeper to the King's Company of *Comedians* in the *Black-Fryars*, on General *Monck's* March to London, in 1659, with his Army, got a Licence from the Powers then in being, to set up a Company of Players in the *Cockpit* in *Drury-lane*, and soon made his Company compleat, his Apprentices, Mr. *Betterton* for Mens Parts, and Mr. *Kynaston* for Womens Parts, being at the Head of them.[18]

Mr. Betterton was now about 22 Years of Age, when he got a great Applause by acting in the *Loyal Subject*, the *Wildgoose Chase*, the *Spanish Curate*, and many more.[19] But while our young Actor is thus rising under his Master *Rhodes*, *Sir William D'Avenant* getting a Patent of King *Charles* the Second, for erecting a Company under the Name of the Duke of *York's* Servants, took Mr. *Betterton* and all that acted under Mr. *Rhodes* into his

---

[17] 'Tuttle' is a variant of Tothill, the street of Betterton's birth which still exists today. It is likely that Betterton was first employed by the bookseller John Holden, and then by Rhodes following Holden's death. There is no evidence that he was formally apprenticed to either man. The actor Edward Kynaston (c.1640–1706) was apprenticed to Rhodes as a draper in 1654. For discussion, see Roberts, *Thomas Betterton*, pp.43–50, and Christine Ferdinand, 'Thomas Betterton's Book-Trade Apprenticeship', *The Library* 23.4 (2022), pp.435–57.

[18] In December 1624 Rhodes was listed among the 'Hired Men and Assistants' of the King's Company. In the same year he became a freeman of the Drapers' Company following a thirteen-year apprenticeship. See Paula R. Backscheider, 'Behind City Walls: Restoration Actors in the Drapers' Company', *Theatre Survey* 45.1 (May 2004), p.77. On 18 August 1660 Samuel Pepys recorded seeing Rhodes's production of Fletcher's *The Loyal Subject*, in which 'one Kinaston, a boy, acted the Dukes sister but made the loveliest lady that ever I saw in my life'; Pepys I.224.

[19] Plays by Fletcher as listed below in 'Note: Gildon on Betterton's Roles'. At the time, Betterton was 24 or 25, not 22.

Company.[20] And in the Year 1662 open'd his House in *Lincolns-Inn Fields*, with the first and second part of the *Siege of Rhodes*, having new Scenes, and Decorations of the Stage, which were then first introduc'd into *England*.[21]

Tho this be affirm'd by some, others have laid it to the Charge of Mr. *Betterton* as the first Innovator on our rude Stage, as a Crime; nay, as the Destruction of good Playing; but I think with very little Show of Reason, and very little Knowledge of the Stages of *Athens* and *Rome*, where, I am apt to believe, was in their flourishing times as great Actors as ever play'd here before Curtains. For how that which helps the Representation, by assisting the pleasing Delusion of the Mind in regard of the Place, should spoil the Acting, I cannot imagine.[22]

The *Athenian* Stage was so much adorn'd, that the very Ornaments or Decorations cost the State more Money, than their Wars against the *Persians*: and the *Romans*, tho their Dramatic Poets were much inferiour to the *Greeks*, (if we may guess at those, who are perished by those who remain) were yet not behind them in the Magnificence of the Theatre to heighten the Pleasure of the Representation. If this was Mr. *Betterton*'s Thought, it was very just; since the Audience must be often puzled to find the Place and Situation of the Scene, which gives great Light to the Play, and helps to deceive us agreeably, while they saw nothing before them but some *Linsy Woolsy* Curtains, or at best some piece of old Tapistry fill'd with awkerd Figures, that would almost fright the Audience.[23]

This, therefore, I must urge as his Praise, that he endeavour'd to complete that Representation, which before was but imperfect.

Mr. *Betterton* making now the foremost Figure in Sir *William*'s Company among the Men, cast his Eyes on Mrs. *Saunderson*, who was no

---

[20] Davenant's patent was granted on 21 August 1660; on 8 October 1660 Rhodes was questioned by the Master of the Revels about his authority to act. In an agreement of 5 November 1660, Davenant made ten principal actors (including Betterton) sharers in the Duke's Company; nine were drawn from Rhodes's company. *Document Register* nos.19, 32 and 44.

[21] Lincoln's Inn Fields Theatre opened in June 1661; see LS1 29.

[22] John Dennis' riposte to Collier's *Short View* reflects on the generous support given the theatre by the Athenian state: 'The Athenians were highly sensible of the advantage which the state received from the theatre, which they maintained at a public prodigious expense, and a revenue appropriated to that peculiar use; and established a law which made the least attempt to alienate the fund capital'; Dennis, *The Usefulness of the Stage to the happiness of mankind, to government, and to religion* (London: Richard Parker, 1698), p.60.

[23] *Linsy Woolsy* (current spelling 'linsey-woolsey') is a coarse fabric made from linen and wool. In Francis Kirkman's *The Wits, or Sport Upon Sport* (1662), an image of the Red Bull Playhouse shows Falstaff and other characters on a stage backed by such a curtain.

less excellent among the Female Players, and who being bred in the House of the Patentee, improv'd her self daily in her Art; and having by Nature those Gifts which were requir'd to make a perfect Actress, added to them the Beauty of a virtuous Life, maintaining the Character of a good Woman to her old Age. This Lady therefore Mr. *Betterton* made choice of to receive as his Wife; and this proceeding from a Value he had for the Merits of her Mind, as well as Person, produc'd a Happiness in the married State nothing else could ever have given.[24]

But notwithstanding all the Industry of the Patentee and Managers, it seems the *King's House* then carry'd the vogue of the Town; and the *Lincolns-Inn Fields* House being not so commodious, the Players and other Adventurers built a much more magnificent Theatre in *Dorset Gardens*; and fitted it for all the Machines and Decorations the Skill of those times could afford. This likewise proving less effectual than they hop'd, other Arts were employ'd, and the Political Maxim of *Divide and Govern* being put in Practice, the Feuds and Animosities of the King's Company were so well improv'd, as to produce an Union betwixt the two Patents.[25] To bring this Design about, the following Agreement was sign'd by the Parties hereafter mention'd.

Memorandum, Octob. 14. 1681.[26]

"IT was then agreed upon between Dr. Charles Davenant, *Thomas Betterton*, Gent. and *William Smith*, Gen., of the one Part, and *Charles Hart*, Gent. and *Edward Kynaston*, Gent, on the other Part, — That the said *Charles Davenant*, *Thomas Betterton*, and *William Smith*, do pay, or cause to be paid, out of the Profits of Acting, unto *Charles Hart* and *Edward Kynaston*, five Shillings apiece for every Day there shall be any Tragedies, or Comedies, or other Representations acted at the *Duke's* Theatre in *Salisbury*

---

[24] Mary Saunderson (1637–1712) married Betterton some time in the winter of 1662–3. She had played stage lover to him at least since the April 1662 revival of Massinger's *The Bondman*, when she replaced Hester Davenport in the role of Cleora. For discussion of the marriage, see Roberts, *Thomas Betterton*, pp.90–2.

[25] The 'feuds and animosities' of the King's Company included Thomas Killigrew's reclaiming of his actors' shares in 1663; a quarrel between the leading actors, Charles Hart and Michael Mohun, in 1667; a dispute over ownership between Thomas Killigrew and his son Charles; and a rebellion by senior actors against their management in 1676.

[26] *Document Register* no.1134 states that the manuscript of the agreement is lost, but the details given here conform to later accounts by Charles Killigrew (see Milhous, pp.38–9). It is not clear why the document specifies Salisbury Court as the Duke's Company's home when they had moved to Dorset Garden in 1671, but it is credible that Gildon had sight of the manuscript directly from Betterton.

Court, or where-ever the Company shall act during the respective Lives of the said *Charles Hart*, and *Edward Kynaston*, excepting the Days the young Men or young Women play for their own Profit only, but this Agreement to cease, if the said *Charles Hart* or *Edward Kynaston* shall at any time play among, or effectually assist the King's Company of Actors; and for as long as this is pay'd, they both covenant and promise not to play at the King's Theatre.

"If Mr. *Kynaston* shall hereafter be free to act at the Duke's Theatre, this Agreement with him, as to his Pension, shall also cease.

"In Consideration of this Pension, Mr. *Hart* and Mr. *Kynaston* do promise to make over, within a Month after the Sealing of this, unto *Charles Davenant, Thomas Betterton*, and *William Smith*, all the Right, Title, and Claim which they or either of them may have to any Plays, Books, Cloaths, and Scenes in the King's Play-house.

"Mr. *Hart* and Mr. *Kynaston* do both also promise, within a Month after the Sealing hereof, to make over to the said *Charles Davenant, Thomas Betterton*, and *William Smith*, all the Title which they each of them have to Six and Three Pence a-piece for every Day there shall be any Playing at the King's Theatre.

"Mr. *Hart* and Mr. *Kynaston* do both also promise to promote with all their Power and Interest an Agreement between both Playhouses; and Mr. *Kynaston* for himself promises to endeavour as much as he can to get free, that he may act at the *Duke*'s Play-house, but he is not obliged to play unless he have ten Shillings *per* day allow'd for his Acting, and his Pension then to cease.

"Mr. *Hart* and Mr. *Kynaston* promise to go to Law with Mr. *Killigrew* to have these Articles perform'd, and are to be at the Expence of the Suit.

"In Witness of this Agreement, all the Parties have hereunto set their Hands, this 14th of October, 1681."[27]

I am sensible, that this private Agreement has been reflected on as Tricking and unfair, but then it is by those, who have not sufficiently consider'd the Matter; for *an dolus, an Virtus quis in Hoste requirit?*[28] All

---

[27] Charles Hart (1625–83) was one of two leading actors in the King's Company. He was the first Horner in Wycherley's *The Country Wife* (1675), created numerous roles in plays by Dryden, and retired after the Union agreement. Edward Kynaston (c.1640–1706) knew Betterton from their days working for John Rhodes before the Restoration. He continued acting in the United Company.

[28] From Virgil's *Aeneid*, 2.390. Corœbus, a Trojan, disguises himself with the armour of dead Greeks: 'Craft or courage – who cares, when an enemy has to be beaten?' In the translation by C. Day Lewis (Oxford: Oxford University Press, 1986), p.46. Hart's fellow actor, Michael Mohun, was among those who protested about the agreement, petitioning the King for the same pension rights as Hart and Kynaston

The Life of Mr Thomas Betterton

Stratagems are allow'd betwixt Enemies; the two Houses were at War, and Conduct and Action were to decide the Victory; and whatever the Duke's Company might fall short of in Action, it is plain they won the Field by their Conduct. For Mr. *Hart* and Mr. *Kynaston* performed their Promises so well, that the Union was effected in 1682, and so continu'd till the Year 1695, when the Actors under the united Patents, thinking themselves aggrieved with Mr. *Betterton* at the head of them, got a new Licence to set up a Play-house once more in *Lincolns-Inn Fields.*[29] But when the Success of that Company began to give way to the Industry of the other, and Mr. *Vanbrugh* had built a new Theatre in the *Hay-Market,* Mr. *Betterton,* weary of the Fatigues and Toil of Government, deliver'd his Company over to the new Licence.[30] But they again giving way to the new Mode of *Opera's,* the Companies were once more united in *Drury-Lane,* and the *Opera's* consin'd to the Hay-Market.[31] But Revolutions being so frequent in this *Mimic State,* Mr. *Swinny* got the chief Players over to him and the *Opera* House, among whom was Mr. *Betterton;*[32] who now being very old, and much afflicted with the Gout, acted but seldom; and the Year before he dy'd, the Town paid a particular Deference to him by making his Day worth 500*l.*[33]

Mr. Betterton was so sensible of Friendship, that tho he lost near 8000*l.* by the Father, yet he took Care of the Daughter himself, till she marry'd according to her own Inclinations.[34] Three Plays were written or translated

---

    (LC 5/191, fol.102v, in *Document Register* no.1169). Betterton appears to have owned three copies of Virgil's works: the 1654 Ogilby edition (PB 19), Dryden's 1697 *Works,* for which he was a subscriber (PB 20), and the 1709 three-volume octavo reprint of the same (PB 108).

29   In 1695 Betterton led a rebel company to Lincoln's Inn Fields to escape the management of Christopher Rich. In 1700 an order by Lord Chamberlain Jersey asserted Betterton's sole control over his increasingly fractious company (LC 5/153, p.23; *Document Register* no.1655).

30   Congreve and Vanbrugh acquired a licence for the new Queen's Theatre, Haymarket, in December 1704; according to Downes, p.99, the theatre opened on 9 April 1705. Its acoustics proved more suited to opera than plays, and in July 1705 Betterton and his fellow actors returned to Lincoln's Inn Fields (*Document Register* no.1813).

31   The Order of Union by Lord Chamberlain Kent dated 31 December 1707 (LC 5/154, pp.299–300) stipulated that operas were to be performed at the Queen's Theatre Haymarket and spoken-word drama at Drury Lane (*Document Register* no.1927).

32   Owen Swiney (1676–1754) was born in rural Ireland, graduated from Trinity College Dublin, and joined Christopher Rich's company as a general factotum in 1702.

33   For the gains from Betterton's *Love for Love* benefit performance, see above, n.9.

34   There is clearly a missing passage at this point in Gildon's text, the substance of which is supplied by the 1749 *Account*: 'He might have passed through Life with as much Ease, Satisfaction, and Peace of Mind, as any Man of his Time, as having actually saved out of his small Allowance, if not an ample, at least a competent Estate; had he not been persuaded to attempt becoming rich, which unluckily engaged him

by him, and brought on the Stage with Success; *The Woman made a Justice;* *The Amorous Widow, or the Wanton Wife*; and *The Unjust Judge, or Appius and Virginia*. But he never would Suffer any of them to be printed, tho the *Amorous Widow* from a surreptitious Copy visited the World after it had been acted almost 20 Years; but a true Copy will be added to this Book.[35]

Being now Seventy five Years of Age, and long troubled with the Stone and Gout, the latter at last, by repellatory Medicines, was driven into his Stomach, which prov'd so fatal as in a few Days to put an End to his Life.[36] He was bury'd with great Decency at Westminster-Abby.[37]

The Year before his Death being at his Country House in *Reading*, my Friend and I travelling that way, according to my Promise, I call'd to see him; and being Hospitably receiv'd, one Day after Dinner we retir'd to his Garden, and after a little Walk there, we fell into the Discourse of *Acting*. Much was said by my Friend against the present Players, and in Praise of those of his younger Days, for he was an old Man. But being pretty well tired with the Dispute as well as Walk, we sate down in an agreeable Shade, and I address'd my self to Mr. *Betterton* in this manner.

---

in a Design, which swept away all his Capital and left him in real Distress. This fell out in 1692, and though nothing could fall harder upon such a Man, and at such a Time of Life, yet he bore it with manly Patience, not only without Murmur or Complaint, but even without Mention; and was so far from suffering this severe Stroke of ill Fortune, fallen upon him, by following the Advice of one he thought his Friend, to prejudice that Friend, who ventured and lost more than himself, that, on the contrary, he continued his Friendship to his Daughter, after his Decease, and did for her all he could have done for his own' (pp.16–17). The venture was an investment in cargo from the East Indies which was seized by the French. Dr John Radcliffe also lost money. The unnamed 'Gentleman in the City' left a daughter who, according to the *Account*, subsequently married the actor John Bowman, having been raised by Betterton 'with all the Care and Tenderness of a Parent' (p.18).

[35] For *The Amorous Widow*, see Introduction, pp.29–37. LS1 168 records a performance of *The Woman Made a Justice* at Lincoln's Inn Fields in February 1670; according to Downes it ran for fourteen days (p.65). The play is an adaptation of the younger Montfleury's *La Femme Juge et Partie* (1669) and was never printed; Montfleury's play is listed in PB 93. *The Unjust Judge, or Appius and Virginia* refers to Betterton's presumed adaptation from Webster, *The Roman Virgin*, which Downes reports played for eight days in May 1669 (p.66). It was first printed in 1679 and attributed to Webster.

[36] According to Cibber, Betterton's 'distemper … flew into his head and killed him in three days' (p.88). His treatment for gout probably differed little from that practised by Dr John Hall, who in addition to a poultice prescribed a strong laxative. See Joan Lane, *John Hall and his Patients* (Stratford-upon-Avon: The Shakespeare Birthplace Trust, 1996), p.159.

[37] Betterton was probably buried in the East Cloister of Westminster Abbey; the exact location of his grave is not known.

I am sensible, that my Friend's Taste of these Pleasures was stronger in his Youth, than at this time, when the *Moroseness* of Age rebates the Edge of our Appetites in more Pleasures, than one: He would else allow that no Woman of his Time excelled Mrs. *Barry*, nor any Man your self. I mean not to flatter you, (said I, finding him a little uneasy with my Complement) for it is really my Opinion; but I must confess, I see but little Prospect, that we have of the Stage's long surviving you two, at least, in its most valuable part, *Tragedy*; for this excellent Poem loses Ground every Day in the Esteem of the Town; nor can I, by any means, attribute this entirely to the Want of Genius in our present Poets, since notwithstanding that we must allow, that they are still far from Perfection in *Tragedy*, yet we have seen much better Performances in that kind of late Years, than in the so much cried up Days of *Charles the Second*, when the Gayety of the Age made strange indigested Things, under that Title, go down, in which there was neither *Nature*, nor her Handmaid ART.[38] But I attribute this Disregard to *Tragedy* chiefly to a Defect in the *Action*, to which we may add the Sowerness of our Tempers under the Pressures of so long and heavy a War,[39] and lastly to an Abundance of odd Spectators, whom the Chance of War have enabled to crowd the Pit and Stage-Boxes, and sway too much by their Thoughtless and Arbitrary Censure, either to the Advantage or Prejudice of the *Author* and *Player*.[40]

For as War carries abundance of peccant Humours from a State, generated by the Corruptions of a long and luxurious Peace; so does it introduce a sort of Libertinism in our Diversions, contrary to Decorum and Regularity; without which no Pleasure can be truly noble. Another ill Effect of Warlike Times, is a Neglect of the politer Sciences of Peace, and a sort of Barbarism in our Gusto of all the fine Arts. To these add, the multiplying the Avenues to Wealth, whose Number increasing, increase likewise the Number of those, who are drawn into the Pursuit of Riches; which as it spreads a mean and private Spirit, of necessary Consequence makes the Love of the Public more weak and languishing.

---

[38] For example, of the 211 performances recorded in *The London Stage* for the 1708–9 season (i.e. the most recent one before Gildon's supposed visit to Betterton), only twenty-two were of tragedies. Of those, only Betterton's adaptation of Webster's *Appius and Virginia* was a premiere. *Hamlet, Macbeth, Othello* and Tate's adaptation of *King Lear* remained favourites.

[39] I.e. the War of the Spanish Succession (1701–14), fought by England and European powers against France, Bavaria, and the Spanish factions who favoured Philip of Anjou's claims to the Spanish throne.

[40] Cibber likewise complained of the 'extreme severity with which [audiences] damn a bad play', such as to discourage 'those whose untried genius might hereafter give them a good one' (p.123).

Nor is there any greater Proof of the Virtue or Corruption of the People, than their Pleasures. Thus in the Time of the Vigour of the *Roman* Virtue, Tragedy was very much esteem'd, its Dignity kept up, and the Decorum of the Stage so very nicely observ'd, that a Player standing out of his Order, or speaking a false Quantity, was sufficient for him to be hiss'd off the Stage, as *Cicero* assures us in his 3d *Paradox*.[41]

And when they gave us the most noble Examples of Virtue in their real Life, they were most pleas'd with the Representation of noble Examples on the Stage; for People are delighted with what bears the greatest Likeness to the Turn and Temperament of their own Minds. Thus when the *Roman* Virtue decay'd, or indeed was lost with their Liberty, and they subsisted and spread their Dominions more by the Merits of their Ancestors, and the *Roman* Name, made terrible by them, than by their own Bravery, then Effeminacy and Folly spread through the People, which immediately appear'd in their Sports or Spectacles; *Tragedy* was slighted; Farce on the one hand, with its *Mimes* and *Pantomimes*; and *Opera* on the other, with its emasculating Sounds, invade and vanquish the Stage, and drew the Ears and Eyes of the People who now care only to laugh, or to see things extravagant and monstrous.[42]

I wish this may not be too much our own Case. But being unwilling to guess at a hidden Cause, when there is an apparent one, I choose rather to attribute this Decay of *Tragedy* to our want of *Tragedians*, and indeed *Tragic Poets*, than to the Corruption of the People;[43] which, tho great enough, yet I hope not so desperate, as what I have mention'd in the *Roman* State.

Tho I am of Opinion, (reply'd Mr. *Betterton*) that the Decay of the Stage is in great measure owing to the long Continuance of the War; yet, I confess, I am afraid, that too much is deriv'd from the Defects of the Stage it self. When I was a young Player under Sir *William Davenant*, we were under a

---

41 The quotation is included in the 1710 text of the *Life* as a footnote: *Histrio si paulo movit extra Numerum, aut si Versus pronunciatus est Syllaba una brevior aut longior exsibilatur & exploditur* ('If a player dances ever so little out of time, if a verse is pronounced by him longer or shorter by a single syllable than it ought to be, he is hooted and hissed off the stage'). From Cicero, *Stoic Paradoxes* no.3; in the translation by Harris Rackham (Cambridge, MA: Harvard University Press, 1942).

42 This passage is similar to one from Hédelin, *The Whole Art of the Stage* (London: William Cademan, 1684), pp.146–7.

43 For tragedies and tragedians, see above, n.38. In the 1708–9 season, John Thurmond began to play Hamlet, Othello, and Antony (LS2 177–8, 191), making so little impression on Cibber that he is not even mentioned in the *Apology*. George Powell, whom Cibber characterized as lazy and debauched, played Oedipus (LS2 179), while Robert Wilks, generally more successful in comedy, played Hamlet (LS2 183). Their inferiority was emphasized by Betterton's occasional performances as Macbeth and Othello (LS2 179, 188).

much better Discipline, we were obliged to make our Study our Business, which our young Men do not think it their duty now to do;[44] for they now scarce ever mind a Word of their Parts but only at *Rehearsals*, and come thither too often scarce recovered from their last Night's Debauch;[45] when the Mind is not very capable of considering so calmly and judiciously on what they have to study, as to enter throughly into the Nature of the Part, or to consider the Variation of the Voice, Looks, and Gestures, which should give them their true Beauty, many of them thinking the making a Noise renders them agreeable to the Audience, because a few of the Upper-Gallery clap the loud Efforts of their Lungs, in which their Understanding has no share.[46] They think it a superfluous Trouble to study real Excellence, which might rob them of what they fancy more, Midnight, or indeed whole Nights Debauches, and a lazy Remissness in their Business.

Another Obstacle to the Improvement of our young Players, is, that when they have not been admitted above a Month or two into the Company, tho their Education and former Business were never so foreign to *Acting*, they vainly imagine themelves Masters of that *Art*, which perfectly to attain, requires a studious Application of a Man's whole Life.[47] They take it therefore amiss to have the Author give them any Instruction; and tho they know nothing of the Art of Poetry, will give their Censure, and neglect or mind a Part as they think the Author and his Part deserves.[48] Tho in this they are

---

[44] Pepys was told that Betterton was 'a very sober, serious man, and studious and humble, following of his study' (Pepys, 22 October 1662).

[45] Stern, p.167, cites references to morning rehearsals 'which actors notoriously came to bad tempered, and badly dressed'. Cibber, p.162, accused George Powell of 'idly deferr[ing] the studying of his parts (as schoolboys do their exercise) to the last day', in other words the final (or possibly only) run-through before the performance. The phrase 'last Night's Debauch' was proverbial: see Congreve, *The Way of the World*, ed. David Roberts (London: Methuen, 2020), p.85 (III.455).

[46] According to Cibber, 'Betterton had so just a sense of what was true or false applause that I have heard him say he never thought any kind of it equal to an attentive silence' (p.82).

[47] The economics of theatre made this an impossible ambition for all actors including Betterton, who in addition to acting and managing made money from coaching and, at least in his early years, running a bookselling business (Roberts, pp.52–3, 164–5). The most diverse portfolio career was pursued by his sometime fellow manager Henry Harris, who ran an import/export business as well as court appointments and a role at the Royal Mint (see Richard Palmer and David Roberts, 'Harris vs Harris: A Restoration Actor at the Court of Arches', *Huntington Library Quarterly* (forthcoming).

[48] Authors generally read out new plays to their casts, with mixed results. Cibber, p.85, recalled that Dryden was a tediously dry reader, while Lee was so enthusiastic that he discouraged the actors. After that reading and discussions about casting, some authors became involved in rehearsing individual actors. Cibber hints at a tendency

led by Fancy as blind as Ignorance can make it; and so wandring without any certain Rule of Judgment, generally favour the bad, and slight the good. Whereas it has always been mine and Mrs. *Barry's* Practice to consult een the most indifferent Poet in any Part we have thought fit to accept of; and I may say it of her, she has often so exerted her self in an indifferent Part, that her Acting has given Success to such Plays, as to read would turn a Man's Stomach;[49] and tho I could never pretend to do so much Service that way as she has done, yet I have never been wanting in my Endeavours. But while the young Gentlemen will think themselves Masters before they understand any one Point of their Art, and not give themselves Leisure and Time to study the *Graces* of ACTION *and* UTTERANCE, it is impossible that the Stage should flourish, and advance in Perfection.

I am very sensible (said I, finding that he had done) of the Justness of what you have said, Sir, but am apt to believe much of those Errors, which you remark proceed from want of Judgment in the Managers, in admitting People unqualified by Nature, and not providing such Men to direct them, who understand the Art they should be improv'd in.[50] All other Arts People are taught by Masters skilful in them, but here Ignorance teaches it self, or rather confirms it self into the Confidence of Knowledge, by going on without any Rebuke.[51] I have often wish'd, therefore, that some Men of good Sense, and acquainted with the *Graces* of *Action* and *Speaking*, would lay down some Rules, by which the young Beginners might direct themselves to that Perfection, which every body is sensible is extremely (and perhaps always has been) wanted on our Stage. And tho you have not had the Benefit of such an Education in the learned Languages, as some Men may have had, yet since you have read much in French,[52] and your own

---

    to learn from actors rather than authors, and admits to neglecting some roles which he thought poorly written (p.163).

[49] There are too many contenders to be certain of the reference, but Tamira in Cibber's short-lived *Xerxes* (1699) seems a likely candidate.

[50] Betterton's testimony against Christopher Rich before the 1695 breakaway included a complaint that his roles were being assigned to 'ignorant and insufficient fellows' (from 'The Petition of the Players', reprinted in Milhous, p.227).

[51] Downes's account of how Betterton first learned the part of Hamlet confirms the actor's belief in the importance of 'Masters', even though the facts are open to dispute: '*Hamlet* being Perform'd by Mr. *Betterton*, Sir *William* (having seen Mr. *Taylor* of the *Black-Fryars* Company Act it, who being Instructed by the Author Mr. *Shakespear*) taught Mr. *Betterton* in every Particle of it; which by his exact Performance of it, gain'd him Esteem and Reputation, Superlative to all other Plays' (Downes, pp.51–2).

[52] PB lists twenty-six French titles in Betterton's collection, plus approximately sixty plays in French by Poisson, Molière, Scarron, Racine, Thomas Corneille, Pierre Corneille, Quinault, Bois-Robert and Barquebois. Among his books were Guy Miège's 1677 *A new dictionary French and English* (PB 49) and Claude Mauger's 1689

Mother Tongue, by the Assistance of which Languages all Knowledge may now be obtain'd, and have besides a confess'd Genius, and a long practice in the Art, I wish I could prevail with you to deliver your Sentiments on this Head, so that from them we might form a System of *Acting*, which might be a Rule to future Players, and teach them to excel not only themselves, but those who have gone before them.

Were I, Sir, (reply'd he with a graceful Modesty) as capable as you would persuade me that you think me, I should easily be prevail'd with to communicate my Notions on this Head; but being sensible of my Incapacity, for the very Reasons you have mention'd, of my Ignorance of the learned Tongues, I must be excus'd; yet not to disappoint you entirely, I shall fetch you a Manuscript on this Head, written by a Friend of mine, to which I confess I contributed all, that I was able; which if well perus'd, and throughly weigh'd, I persuade my self our Stage would rise and not fall in Reputation.

On this he went into his House, and after a little Stay return'd to us with some loose Papers, which I knew to be his own Hand;[53] and being seated, after a Glass of Wine about, he thus began.

Being to treat of the Art of Playing, and the Duty and Qualifications of Actors, I think it will be no improper Method first to consider what Regard an Actor ought to have to his Conduct off the Stage, before we treat of what he is to do upon it.[54]

I have not found in all the Clamours against the Stage, any one that denies the Usefulness of the Drama, if justly manag'd; nay, Mr. *Collier*, the most formidable Enemy of this Diversion, (tho his *Proto-Martyr*, Archbishop *Laud*, contended so violently for the Book of Sports, and Plays were acted at Court, in the Time of the Royal Martyr, even on *Sundays*) does allow, that the Wit of Man cannot invent any more efficacious means of encouraging Virtue, and depressing of Vice.[55]

    French grammar (PB 122). PB also lists a further forty-nine works translated from the French. Betterton is believed to have visited France while planning the design of the Dorset Garden Theatre, which opened in 1671.

[53] See the Longleat letter in Roberts, frontispiece to *Thomas Betterton*. There is an obvious and suspicious discrepancy between Betterton's statement that he merely 'contributed' to a manuscript prepared by his friend and Gildon's recognition of Betterton's handwriting.

[54] Cibber observed that 'the private character of an actor will always more or less affect his public performance' (p.168) and that 'the briskest loose liver ... can never arrive at the necessary excellencies of a good and useful actor' (p.175).

[55] Jeremy Collier's *Short View* expresses admiration for Ancient Greek drama and points out that some playwrights of the earlier Seventeenth Century wrote without committing obscenity or blasphemy. Archbishop William Laud (1573–1645) was praised for his management of the Church of England in the Preface to Collier's *Miscellanies in Five Essays* (London: Samuel Keeble, 1694), n.p.; he was responsible

Hence I believe it is evident, that they suppose the Moral Lessons, which the Stage presents, may make the greatest Impressions on the Minds of the Audience; because the Instruction is convey'd with Pleasure, and by the Ministration of the Passions, which always have a stronger Remembrance, than the calmer Precepts of Reason.[56]

But then I think there is no manner of doubt but that the Lives and Characters of those Persons, who are the Vehicles, as I may call them, of these Instructions, must contribute very much to the Impression the Fable and Moral will make. For to hear Virtue, Religion, Honour recommended by a Prostitute, an Atheist, or a Rake, makes them a Jest to many People, who would hear the same done with Awe by Persons of known Reputation in those Particulars. Look but into Religion it self, and see how little the Words and Sermons of a known Drunkard, or Debauchee affect his Parishioners; and what an Influence a Divine of a pious and regular Life has on his Congregation, his Virtues preparing them to hear him with Respect, and to believe him as a Man whose Actions call not his Faith into doubt.[57] Tho the Pulpit must be allow'd to be the more sacred Place, as dispensing the most holy Mysteries of the Christian Religion; yet since the Gospel consists of the *Agenda* as well as *Credenda*, of Practice as well as Belief, and since the Practice is so forcibly recommended from the Stage by a purifying our Passions,[58] and the Conveyance of Delight, the Stage may properly be esteem'd the Handmaid of the Pulpit.

For this Reason, I first recommend to our Players, both Male and Female, the greatest and most nice Care of their Reputation imaginable; for on that their Authority with the People depends and on their Authority in great measure their Influence. They should consider, that the Infamy, that the Profession lies under is not deriv'd from the Business, which is truly valuable and noble; that the Players in Athens were honourable, and so highly esteem'd, that they were sometimes Ambassadors, and the Masters to two

---

for jailing William Prynne for his *Histrio Mastix: The Players Scourge* (1633), which criticized court theatricals. The passage lights upon a delicate subject for Betterton, who was charged with profanity in 1700 (*Document Register* no.1653).

[56] A standard argument for those who opposed Collier, such as Vanbrugh in *A Short Vindication of* The Relapse *and* The Provok'd Wife (London: Nicholas Walwyn, 1698), a copy of which is in PB 94.

[57] Cicero's *De Oratore*, 2.43, argues that those who plead causes should be morally unimpeachable. According to George Whitefield, Archbishop John Tillotson was keen to find out from Betterton why acting was often more persuasive than preaching; *The Works of the Reverend George Whitefield*, 7 vols (London: Edward and Charles Dilly, 1771–2), IV.339.

[58] Apparently a reference to Aristotelian catharsis, as described in the *Poetics*. See the translation by D.A. Russell and M. Winterbottom, *Classical Literary Criticism* (Oxford: Oxford University Press, 1989), pp.63–4.

of the most noble and glorious Orators that ever *Greece* or *Rome* produc'd; I mean, *Demosthenes* and *Cicero*, as we shall immediately see;[59] that in *Rome* it self, where the Stage had a more disadvantageous Rise, than in Athens, *Cicero* looks on it as such a piece of ill-breeding and Barbarism not to grieve for the Death of old *Roscius*, that he could suppose no Noble-man of Rome or Commoner could be guilty of.[60] He likewise calls it *an excellent Art*. All which is a sufficient Proof, that the Business it self was never infamous in either of those two Cities; nor could be here, if the Professors of it by their own loose Lives, by an open Contempt of Religion, and making Blasphemy and Profaneness the Marks of their Wit and good Breeding; by an undisguis'd Debauchery and Drunkenness, coming on the very Stage, in Contempt of the Audience, when they are scarce able to speak a Word; by having little Regard to the Ties of Honour and Common Honesty: to say nothing of the Irregularities of the Ladies, which rob them of that Deference and Respect, that their Accomplishments of Person would else command from their Beholders, especially when set off to such an Advantage as the Stage supplies in the Improvement of the Mind and Person.

This is an Evil, which, tho in the Mouths of half the Town, yet to tell those, who know themselves guilty of it, is an Affront never to be forgiven; so much more fond are they of defending their Follies, than of removing them, tho to their own Advantage; and so much in Love seem they with Infamy more, than a general Respect and Reputation. Mr. *Harrington* in his *Oceana*, proposing something about a regulated Theatre, would have all Women, who have suffer'd any Blemish in their Reputation, excluded the Sight of the Play, by that means to deter Women from Lewdness, while by that they lost the Benefit of Public Diversions.[61] If this were push'd farther, and all Ladies of the House immediately discarded on the Discovery of their Follies of that Nature, I dare believe, that they would sooner get Husbands, and the Theatre lose Abundance of that Scandal it now lies under.

Nor is this so hard a Task but even our Times, as corrupt as they are, have given us Examples of Virtue in our Stage Ladies. I shall not name them, because I would draw no Censure on those, who are not nam'd.

From what I have said I believe it is plain, that I wish such a Reformation of the People of the Stage, as would render it more reputable than it is at this Time. I would have no Man of it a common *Drunkard*, public *Debauchee*; nor so fond of his own Opinion, as to imagine that a dull Ridicule on things sacred will pass for Wit with any Man of Sense or Probity; nor would

---

[59] I.e. below, p.64.

[60] See title page: a reference to Gildon's epigraph.

[61] A free interpretation of James Harrington's *The Common-wealth of Oceana* (London: Livewell Chapman, 1656), p.182. Cibber, p.99, mocked the pretensions to purity of one actress thought to be Jane Rogers.

I have him thunder out a Volley of Oaths and Execrations to supply the Emptiness of his Discourse, with a Noise that is offensive to all Mens Ears, who are not daily conversant with the Refuse of Mankind, but acquainted with good Manners and good Breeding; nor to be vain of owing a great Deal, because by Tricks and expensive Evasions they can keep a Man from his lawful Debts, tho they might pay them with half the Money.[62] In short, I would have them keep a handsome Appearance with the World; to be really virtuous if they can, if not, at least, not to be publickly abandon'd to Follies and Vices, which render them contemptible to all; that they would live within the Compass of what their Business affords them, and then they would have more Leisure to study their Parts, raise their Reputation, and Salaries the sooner, and meet with Respect from all Men of Honesty and Sense.

The Ladies likewise should set a peculiar Guard on their Actions, and remember, that tho it may happen, that their parting with their Honour, and setting up for Creatures of Prey on all that address to them, may bring them in mercenary Advantages, yet that by keeping their Reputation entire, they heighten their Beauties, and would infallibly arrive at more Happiness (if not Wealth) in Marriages, which they can never find in making themselves subject to the Insults of Rakes, and Infirmities of Debauchees, and other Slaveries and Evils not proper to mention, which the Virtuous are free from, admir'd and ador'd by all.[63]

Thus much I thought was proper for me to say on the Conduct of our Players, Male and Female, off the Stage; which is a Lesson as well worth their learning as any I shall deliver.

Tho these are Duties which seem absolutely necessary to make our *Players* shine, and draw that Respect from the People, which now they want, yet are not these sufficient to make a good *Actor*; but there are other Lessons to be learn'd for his Qualifications on the Stage.

From his very Name we may derive his Duty, he is call'd an *Actor*, and his Excellence consists in *Action* and Speaking: The *Mimes* and *Pantomimes*

---

[62]   In other words, actors who give their audiences half measure as they do their creditors – a familiar topic for Betterton, whose former co-manager, Henry Harris, was the subject of up to fourteen legal cases for debt between 1667 and 1679. See *Document Register* nos.379, 400, 404, 414, 423, 437, 438, 457, 468, 553, 732, 956, 1009, and 1092.

[63]   The actress to whom this most readily applies was Betterton's own wife, Mary (see above, n.24). It is tempting to infer a reference to Anne Bracegirdle, who had recently appeared for Betterton's benefit (see above, n.9), but she never married or avoided 'the insults of Rakes', not least when there was an attempt by Lord Mohun to kidnap her. See Albert S. Borgman, *The Life and Death of William Mountfort* (Cambridge, MA: Harvard University Press, 1935).

did all by Gesture, and the Action of Hands, Legs, and Feet, without making use of the Tongue in uttering any Sentiments or Sounds;[64] so that they were something like our *dumb Shows*, with this difference, one *Pantomime* expressed several Persons, and that to the Tunes of Musical Instruments;[65] the dumb Shows made use of several Persons to express the Design of the Play as a silent Action; and the Nature of this is best express'd in *Hamlet*, before the Entrance of his Players in the third Act.

Enter a King and a Queen very lovingly, the Queen embracing him; she kneels, and makes shew of Protestation unto him; he takes her up, and declines his Head on her Neck. Lays him down on a Bed of Flowers; she seeing him asleep, leaves him. Anon comes in a Fellow, takes off his Crown, kisses it, and pours Poison into the King's Ear, and exit. The Queen returns, finds the King dead, and makes passionate Action. The Poisoner with two or three Mutes comes in again, seeming to lament with her; the dead Body is carry'd away. The Poisoner woes the Queen with Gifts; she seems loath and unwilling awhile, but in the end accepts his Love.[66]

I only repeat this to shew the manner of the old Time, and what they meant by dumb Shows, which *Shakespear* himself condemns in this very Play, when *Hamlet* says to the Players,—"O! it offends me to the Soul to see a robustuous Perriwig-pated Fellow tear a Passion to tatters, to very Raggs, to split the Ears of the *Groundlings*, who (for the most part) are capable of nothing but *inexplicable dumb Shows* and Noise—"[67]

But the *Pantomimes* or *Roman* Dancers expressed all this in one Person, as we have it in Mr. *Mayne's Lucian*; where *Demetrius* the *Cynic* Philosopher railing against Dancing, is invited by one of them in the Time of *Nero*, to see him perform without either Pipe or Flute, and did so; "for having impos'd Silence on the Instruments, he by himself danc'd the Adultery of *Mars* and *Venus*, the *Sun* betraying them, and *Vulcan* plotting, and catching them in a Wire Net; then every God, who was severally Spectator; then *Venus* blushing, and *Mars* beseeching; in a Word, he acted the whole Fable so well, that *Demetrius* much pleas'd with the Spectacle, as the greatest Praise, that

---

[64] Probably drawn from the translation of Lucian's *Dialogues* by Jasper Mayne and Francis Hicks (Oxford: R. Davis, 1663), p.37. PB 10 lists a copy.

[65] From Lucian, p.372.

[66] The version of *Hamlet* III.ii.126ff appears to derive from a hybrid (possibly a performance) text of the play, or perhaps the memory of either Gildon or Betterton. The phrases 'very lovingly', 'she kneels, and makes shew of Protestation to him', and the 'and' before 'exit', do not feature in any of the Shakespearean quartos. Equally, 'and he her' is not found in the folios, which have 'Lays him' rather than the quartos' 'He lays him'.

[67] Cited verbatim from *Hamlet*, III.ii.8–12, except that 'robustious' has become 'robustuous'. OED records the latter as a variant in use since the sixteenth century.

could be bestow'd upon him, cry'd out in a loud Voice, I *hear* my Friend, what you *act*; nor do I only see them, but methinks you speak with your Hands."[68]

This Instance not only shews the Difference of these *Pantomimes* from our old dumb Shews, but the Power of *Action*, which a *Player* ought to study with his utmost Application. The Orator at the Bar, and in the Pulpit, ought to understand the Art of Speaking perfectly well; but *Action* never be in its Perfection but on the Stage, and in our Time the Pulpit and the Bar have left off even that graceful Action, which was necessary to the Business of those Places, and gave a just Weight and Grace to the Words they uttered. And I wonder that our Ministers do not a little more consider this Point, and reflect, that they speak to the People as much as the Orators of *Greece* and *Rome*; and what Influence Action had on them, will be evident from some Instances we shall give in their proper Places.

ACTION indeed has a natural Excellence in it, superiour to all other Qualities; *Action* is *Motion*, and Motion is the Support of Nature, which without it would again sink into the sluggish Mass of Chaos. Motion in the various and regular Dances of the Planets surprizes and delights: Life is Motion, and when that ceases, the Humane Body so beautiful, nay, so divine when enlivened by Motion, becomes a dead and putrid Coarse, from which all turn their Eyes. The Eye is caught by any thing in Motion, but passes over the sluggish and motionless things as not the pleasing Objects of its View.[69]

This Natural Power of *Motion* or *Action* is the Reason, that the Attention of the Audience is fixt by any irregular or even fantastic Action on the Stage of the most indifferent Player; and supine and drowsy, when the best Actor speaks without the Addition of *Action*.

'Twas the Skill the ancient Players of *Athens* and *Rome* had in this, which made them not only so much admir'd by the Great Men of those Times and Places, but rais'd them to the Reputation of being Masters of two of the greatest Orators that *Athens* or *Rome* ever saw; and who had it not been for the Instructions of the Actors *Satyrus*, *Roscius*, and *Æsopus*, had never been able to convey their admirable Parts to the World.[70]

---

[68]   Cited accurately from the Mayne/Hicks translation of Lucian's *Dialogues*, pp.370–1 (see above, n.64).

[69]   A summary of ideas found in Lucretius, *De Rerum Natura*. Betterton appears to have owned two copies of Lucretius' works: the 1675 Cambridge edition published by William Morden (PB 137), and *Titus Lucretius Carus his six books of Epicurean Philosophy*, trans. Thomas Creech (Oxford: Anthony Stephens, 1683), PB 78.

[70]   Satyrus was an actor in the fourth century BC; as the following passage describes, Plutarch's *Life of Demosthenes* credits him with instructing the orator; see Plutarch, *Plutarch's Lives of Illustrious Men*, trans. John Dryden, 3 vols (New York: American

Demosthenes being, after many unsuccessful Attempts, one Time exploded the Assembly, went home with his Head muffled up in his Cloak, very much affected with the Disgrace; in this Condition *Satyrus* the Actor follow'd him, being his intimate Acquaintance, and fell into Discourse with him. *Demosthenes* having bemoan'd himself to him, and his Misfortune, that having been the most industrious of the Pleaders, and having spent almost the whole Strength and Vigour of his Body in that Employment, yet could he not render himself acceptable to the People; That Drunkards, Tarpaulins,[71] Sots, and illiterate Fellows found so favourable a Hearing, as to possess the Pulpit, while he himself was despis'd. What you say (replied *Satyrus*) is very true, but I will soon remove the Cause of all this, if you will repeat some Verses to me out of *Sophocles*, or *Euripides*. When *Demosthenes* had pronounc'd after his way, *Satyrus* presently repeating the same Verses with their proper Tone, Mien, and Gesture, gave such a Turn to them, that *Demosthenes* himself perceiv'd they had quite another Appearance. By which being convinc'd how much Grace and Ornament accrues to Speech by a proper and due Action, he began to think it of little Consequence for a Man to exercise himself in declaiming, if he neglected the just Pronunciation or Decency of Speaking. Upon this he built himself a Place under ground (which remain'd in the Time of *Plutarch*) whither he retir'd every Day to form his Action, and exercise his Voice. To shew what Pains this great Man took as an Example to our young Actors, who think not themselves oblig'd to take any at all, I shall proceed with *Plutarch*. In his House he had a great Looking-Glass, before which he would stand and repeat his Orations, by that means observing how far his Action and Gesture were graceful or unbecoming.[72]

The same *Demosthenes*, when a Client came to him on an Assault and Battery; he at large gave him an Account of what Blows he had receiv'd from his Adversary, but in so calm and unconcern'd a manner, that *Demosthenes* said, Surely my good Friend thou hast not suffer'd any one thing of what thou makest thy Complaint: Upon which his Client warm'd, cry'd aloud — How Demosthenes? *Have I suffer'd nothing?* Ay marry, replies he, now I hear the Voice of a Man that has been injur'd and beaten. Of so great

---

Book Exchange, 1880), III.146. Claudius Aesopus was a Roman tragedian in the first century BC who, as described below, gave Cicero elocution lessons. For Roscius, see above, p. 46 n.14.

[71] 'Tarpaulin': a nickname for an ordinary sailor (OED 2a).

[72] This well-known anecdote appears in Le Faucheur, p.30, who derived it from Plutarch's *Life of Demosthenes*. Betterton owned two copies of Plutarch's *Lives*: the Folio in Thomas North's translation (London: Thomas Vautroullier, 1579) and the five-volume Octavo edition by 'several hands' (London: Jacob Tonson, 1683); PB21 and 96.

Consequence did he think the Tone and Action of the Speaker towards the gaining Belief.

This was the Case of *Demosthenes*, as *Plutarch* assures us, (if I may credit the Translation, as without doubt I may;)[73] and that of *Cicero* was not much different — At first (says *Plutarch*) he was, as well as *Demosthenes*, very defective in Action, and therefore he diligently apply'd himself to *Roscius* the Comedian sometimes, and sometimes to *Æsopus* the Tragedian. And such afterwards was the Action of *Cicero*, that it did not a little contribute to make his Eloquence persuasive; deriding the Rhetoricians of his Time, for delivering their Orations with so much Noise and Bawling, saying, that it was their want of Ability to speak, which made them have Recourse to bellowing, as lame People who cannot walk, get on Horse-back and ride.

The same might be said to many of our bawling Actors, of which number *Æsopus* was not, yet so possessed with his Part, that he took his acting to be so real, and not a Representation, that whilst he was on the Stage representing *Atreus* deliberating on the Revenge of *Thyestes*, he was so transported beyond himself, that he smote one of the Servants hastily crossing the Stage, and laid him dead on the Place.[74]

But my Lord *Bacon*, in his *Advancement of Learning*, gives us a History from the *Annals* of *Tacitus*, of one *Vibulenus*, formerly an Actor on the Stage, but at that time a common Soldier in the *Pannonian* Garrisons; which is a wonderful Instance of the Power of Action, and what Force it adds to the Words.[75] The Account is this.

This Fellow, on the Death of *Augustus Cæsar*, had rais'd a Mutiny, so that *Blæsus* the Lieutenant committed some of the Mutineers to Prison; but the Soldiers violently broke open the Prison-Gates, and set their Comrades at Liberty, and this *Vibulenus*, in a Tribunitial Speech to the Soldiers, begins in this manner— "You have given Life and Light to these poor innocent Wretches — but who restores my Brother to me, or Life to my Brother? Who was sent hither with a Message from the Legions of *Germany* to treat of the common Cause; and this very last Night has he murder'd him by

---

[73] Unless this is another sleight of hand by Gildon, who did know Greek, this passage may represent the genuine reflections of Betterton, who knew Plutarch only in translation (above, n.70).

[74] An anecdote drawn from Plutarch's *Life of Cicero*. The reference is probably to a Latin translation of Euripides' play on the subject rather than Seneca's, which post-dates the life of Aesopus and may not have been designed for performance.

[75] The anecdote is drawn from Francis Bacon's *The two books of Sr. Francis Bacon. Of the proficience and advancement of learning, divine and human*, 2 vols (London: William Washington, 1605), p.70. Bacon mentions another actor, Percennius, as well as Vibulenus. Betterton owned a 1629 edition of *The Advancement of Learning*, published by William Washington, as well as five other works by Bacon (PB 51).

some of his Gladiators, some of his Bravo's, whom he keeps about him to be the Murderers of the Soldiers. Answer, *Blæsus*, where hast thou thrown his Body; the most mortal Enemies deny not Burial to the dead Enemy: When to his Corps I have perform'd my last Duties in Kisses, and flowing with Tears, command me to be slain at his Side, so that these our Fellow-Soldiers may have leave to bury us." — He put the Army into such a Ferment and Fury by this Speech, that if it had not immediately been made appear, that there was no such Matter, that he never had any Brother, the Soldiers would hardly have spar'd the Lieutenant's Life; for he acted it as if it had been some Interlude on the Stage.

There is not so great a Pathos in the Words uttered by the Soldier, as to stir the Army into so very great a Ferment, they must therefore receive almost their whole Force from a most moving and pathetic Action, in which his Eyes, Hands, and Voice join'd in a most lively Expression of his Misery and of his Loss. 'Tis true that, when an Army is tumultuous in itself, it is no difficult matter to run them into Madness; but then it must be done by some, who either by their former Interest there, had purchas'd an Opinion among them, or some one who by the Artfulness of his Address should touch their Souls, and so engage them to what he pleases. The later I take to be our Case in *Vibulenus*, who by the Advantage of his Skill in Action recommended himself and his suppositious Cause so effectually to them, as to make the General run a great hazard of his Life for an imaginary Murder.

This has made some of the old Orators give the sole Power and sovereign Command in Speech to Action, as I have read in some of those learned Men who have treated of this Subject in *English* and *French*.[76] And I am persuaded, that our Parsons would move their Hearers far more, if they added but graceful Action to loud Speaking. This often sets off indifferent Matter, and makes a Man of little Skill in any other Part of Oratory, pass for the most eloquent; this, I have read, was the Case of *Trachallus*, who tho none of the best Orators of his Time for the Competition and Writing part, yet excell'd all the Pleaders of that Age, his Appearance and Delivery was so plausible and pleasing. The Stateliness of his Person and Port, the Sparkling of his Eyes, the Majesty of his Looks, and the Beauty of his Mien; and his *Voice* added to these Qualities, which not only for Gravity and Composedness came up to that of a *Tragedian*, but even excell'd any Actors, that ever yet trod the Stage, as my Author assures us from *Quintilian. Philistus*, on the other hand, for want of these Advantages of Utterance, lost all the Beauty

---

[76] Probably a sly way to introduce the subsequent passage, which is drawn from the English translation of Le Faucheur.

and Force of his Pleadings, tho for Language and the Art of Composition excell'd all the *Greeks* of his Time.[77]

The same Advantage of *Pericles* and *Hortensius*, with this difference, *Hortensius* ascrib'd all the Success of his Pleadings to the Merit of the Writing, and convinc'd the World of his Error by publishing his Orations; *Pericles*, tho 'tis said he had the Goddess Persuasion on his Lips, and that he thundred and lightned in an Assembly, and made all *Greece* tremble when he spoke, yet would never publish any of his Orations, because their Excellency lay in the ACTION.[78]

What I have said here of *Action* in general, and the particular Examples I have given of it, is I believe sufficient to satisfy any one, that is studious of Excellence on the Stage, that it ought to be his chief Aim and Application. But next to this is the Art of Speaking, in which also a Player ought to be perfectly skill'd; for as a learned Country-man of ours observes[79] — "The Operation of Speech is strong, not only for the Reason or Wit therein contained, but by its Sound. For in all good Speech there is a sort of Music, with Respect to its Measure, Time and Tune. Every well-measur'd Sentence is proportional three ways, in all its Parts to the Sentences, and to what it is intended to express, and all Words that have Time allow'd to their Syllables, as is suitable to the Letters whereof they consist, and to the Order, in which they stand in a Sentence. Nor are Words without their Tune or Notes even in common Talk, which together compose that Tune, which is proper to every Sentence, and may be prick'd down as well as any musical Tune: only in the Tunes of Speech the Notes have much less Variety, and have all a short Time. With Respect also to Time and Measure, the Poetic is less various and therefore less powerful, than that of Oratory; the former being like that of a short Country Song repeated to the End of the Poem, but that of *Oratory* is vary'd all along, like the Divisions, which a skilful Musician runs upon a Lute."

He proceeds to our former Consideration, saying — "The Behaviour and Gesture is also of Force; as in Oratory so in Converse, consisting of almost

---

[77] Cp. Le Faucheur, p.11: 'Quintilian, on the other hand, reports it: that Trachallus was none of the best Orators of his Time, and yet out-did all the Men of that Profession in his Pleading: He made so plausible an appearance, what with the stateliness of his Person and Port, the sparkling of his Eyes, the Majesty of his Looks, and the Beauty of his Mien; besides a Voyce, that did not only come-up to a Tragedian's for Gravity and Compos'dness, but went far beyond any Actor's too that ever yet spake upon the Stage'. Le Faucheur recalled a passage from Quintilian, 12.5.5. Philistus, Sicilian orator and historian (c.432–356 BC).

[78] Le Faucheur, p.12, also refers to this anecdote. Pericles, Athenian politician (c.495–429 BC), and Quintus Hortensius, lawyer and orator (114–50 BC).

[79] Although this passage is placed in quotation marks, it appears to be a collage of phrases and ideas drawn from Aristotle's *Poetics* and Hédelin's *The Whole Art of the Stage*. The inference is that Gildon aimed to give the appearance of proper citation.

as many Motions, as there are moveable Parts of the Body, all made with a certain agreeable Measure between one another, and at the same time answerable to that of Speech, which when easy and unaffected is becoming."

A Mastery in these two Parts is what compleats an Actor: And I hope the Rules I shall give for both will be of Use to such as have truly a Genius for this *Art*; the Rules of which, like those of Poetry, are only for those, who have a Genius, and are not perfectly to be understood by those, who have not.

To begin therefore with *Action*, the Player is to consider, that it is not every rude and undesigning *Action*, that is his Business, for that is what the Ignorant as well as skilful may have, nor can indeed want: But the Action of a Player is that, which is agreeable to Personation, or the Subject he represents. Now what he represents is Man in his various Characters, Manners, and Passions, and to these Heads he must adjust every Action; he must perfectly express the Quality and Manners of the Man, whose Person he assumes, that is, he must know how his Manners are compounded, and from thence know the several Features, as I may call 'em, of his Passions. A Patriot, a Prince, a Beggar, a Clown, *&c.* must each have their Propriety, and Distinction in Action as well as Words and Language. An *Actor* therefore must vary with his Argument, that is, carry the Person in all his Manners and Qualities with him in every Action and Passion; he must transform himself into every Person he represents, since he is to act all sorts of Actions and Passions. Sometimes he is to be a Lover, and know not only all the soft and tender Addresses of one, but what are proper to the Character, that is in Love, whether he be a Prince or a Peasant, a hot and fiery Man or of more moderate and flegmatick Constitution, and even the Degrees of the Passion he is possessed with. Sometimes he is to represent a choleric, hot and jealous Man, and then he must be throughly acquainted with all the Motions and Sentiments productive of those Motions of the Feet, Hands, and Looks of such a Person in such Circumstances. Sometimes he is a Person all dejected and bending under the Extremities of Grief and Sorrow; which changes the whole form and Appearance of him in the Representation, as it does really in Nature. Sometimes he is distracted, and here Nature will teach him, that his Action has always something wild and irregular, tho even that regularly; that his Eyes, his Looks or Countenance, Motions of Body, Hands and Feet, be all of a Piece, and that he never falls into the indifferent State of Calmness and Unconcern. As he now represents *Achilles*, then *Æneas*, another Time *Hamlet*, then *Alexander* the Great and *Oedipus*, he ought to know perfectly well the Characters of all these Heroes, the very same Passions differing in the different Heroes as their Characters differ:[80] The Courage of *Æneas*, for

---

[80] Betterton played Achilles in John Banks's *The Destruction of Troy* (1678), Hamlet from 1661, Alexander in Lee's *The Rival Queens* from c.1693, and the title role in

Example, of itself was sedate and temperate, and always attended with good Nature; that of *Turnus* join'd with Fury, yet accompany'd with Generosity and Greatness of Mind. The Valour of *Mezentius* was savage and cruel; he has no Fury but Fierceness, which is not a Passion but Habit, and nothing but the Effect of Fury cool'd into a very keen Hatred, and an inveterate Malice.[81] *Turnus* seems to fight to appease his Anger, *Mezentius* to satisfy his Revenge, his Malice and barbarous Thirst of Blood. *Turnus* goes to the Field with Grief, which always attended Anger, whereas *Mezentius* destroys with a barbarous Joy; he's so far from Fury, that he is hard to be provoked to common Anger; who calmly killing *Orodes*, grows but half angry at his Threats;

> *At whom* Mezentius *smiling with a mingl'd Ire.*[82]

Thus, 'tis plain, he has not the Fury of *Turnus*, but a Barbarity peculiar to himself, and a savage Fierceness, according to his Character in the tenth Book of *Virgil*.

To know these different Characters of established Heroes, the Actor need only be acquainted with the Poets, who write of them; if the Poet who introduces them in his Play have not sufficiently distinguish'd them. But to know the different Compositions of the Manners, and the Passions springing from those Manners, he ought to have an Insight into Moral Philosophy, for they produce various Appearances in the Looks and Actions, according to their various Mixtures.[83] For that the very same Passion has various Appearances, is plain from the History Painters, who have followed Nature. Thus *Jordan* of *Antwerp*, in a Piece of our Saviour's being taken from the Cross, which is now in his Grace the Duke of Marlborough's Hands, the Passion of Grief is express'd with a wonderful Variety;[84] the Grief of the Virgin Mother is in all the Extremity of Agony, that is consistent with Life,

---

Dryden and Lee's *Oedipus* (1678). No record exists of him playing Aeneas, a role which does not feature in Banks's *The Destruction of Troy*.

[81] For Betterton and Virgil, see above, n.28.

[82] From the *Aeneid*, Book 10.1082–3, in Gildon's own translation; Mezentius (d.1176 BC) was an Etruscan king and ally of Turnus against Aeneas, who killed him in battle.

[83] Works fitting this description in PB include Thomas Stanley's *The History of Philosophy*, 3rd ed. (1687), Robert Burton's *The Anatomy of Melancholy*, 2nd ed. (1624), John Locke's *An Essay Concerning Human Understanding* (1690), Thomas Hobbes's *Elements of Philosophy* (1656) and *Hobbs's Tripos in Three Discourses* (1684), and a translation of Spinoza's *A Treatise partly theological* (1689).

[84] A reference to Hans Jordaens the Elder (1555–1630), who was born in Antwerp but later lived in Delft, where three further artists of the same name originated. PB 145 lists 'Eight large prints of *Ruben* and *Jordaens*'. The Longleat letter (Roberts, Frontispiece) shows that Betterton had dealings in works of art with at least one aristocratic household.

nay indeed that leaves scarce any Signs of remaining Life in her; that of St. *Mary Magdalen* is an extreme Grief, but mingled with Love and Tenderness, which she always expressed after her Conversion for our blessed Lord; then the Grief of St. *John* the Evangelist is strong but manly, and mixt with the Tenderness of perfect Friendship, and that of *Joseph* of *Arimathea* suitable to his Years and Love for *Christ*, more solemn, more contracted in himself, and yet forcing an Appearance in his Looks. *Coypel's* Sacrifice of Jeptha's Daughter has not unluckily express'd a great Variety of this same Passion.[85] The History Painters indeed have observ'd a Decorum in their Pieces, which wants to be introduc'd on our Stage for there is never any Person on the Cloth, who has not a Concern in the Action. All the very Slaves in *Le Brun's* Tent of *Darius* participate of the grand Concern of *Sisigambis Statira*, &c.[86] This would render the Representation extremely solemn and beautiful; but on the Stage, not only the Supernumeraries, as they call them, or Attendants, mind nothing of the great Concern of the Scene, but even the Actors themselves, who are on the Stage, and not in the very principal Parts, shall be whispering to one another, or bowing to their Friends in the Pit, or gazing about. But if they made Playing their Study, (or had indeed a Genius to their Art) as it is their Business, they would not only not be guilty of these Absurdities, but would, like Le Brun, observe Nature where-ever they found it offer any thing that could contribute to their Perfection. For he was often seen to mind a Quarrel in the Street betwixt various People, and there not only observe the several Degrees of the Passion of Anger rising in the Quarrel, and their different Recess, but the distinct Expressions of it in every Face that was concern'd.

Our Stage at the best indeed is but a very cold Representation, supported by loud prompting, to the eternal Disgust of the Audience, and spoiling the Decorum of the Representation; for an imperfect Actor affronts the Audience, and betrays his own Demerits. I must say this in the Praise of Mr. *Wilks*, he always takes Care to give the Prompter little Trouble, and never wrongs the Poet by putting in any thing of his own;[87] a Fault, which some applaud themselves for, tho they deserve a severe Punishment for their

---

[85] Large prints of two works by Antoine Coypel (1661–1772) feature in PB 142–3, but not of Jephtha's daughter.

[86] PB 145 lists one work by Charles Le Brun (1619–90), but not this one. Le Brun's paintings are referred to in Gildon's 'An Essay on the Art, Rise and Progress of the Stage' which forms the introduction to Curll's *The Works of* Mr. *William Shakespear Volume the Seventh* (1710). Sisigambis, mother of Darius and possibly Statira.

[87] Cibber, pp.163–4, also praised the 'diligence' and extraordinary memory of Robert Wilks (?1665–1732). Wilks and Betterton were in the same Queen's company from 1706. Wilks played Hal to Betterton's Falstaff in the adaptation, *Henry IV: with the Humours of Sir John Falstaff* (LS2 130), and took over some of Betterton's roles

equal Folly and Impudence. They forget *Hamlet*'s Advice to the Players —
And let those who play your Clowns speak no more, than is set down for them;
for there be of them that will of themselves laugh to set on some Quantity of
barren Spectators to laugh too; tho in the mean time some necessary Question
of the Play be then to be consider'd. That's Villanous, *and shews a most*
Pitiful *Ambition in the* Fool *that uses it.*[88] This is too frequently done
by some of our popular but half Comedians.[89] But it is, I think, a greater
Fault in a *Tragedian*, who through his Imperfectness in his Part shall speak
on any Stuff, that comes in his Head, which must infallibly prejudice the
true Expression of the Business of the Play, let it be Passion, Description,
or Narration. But notwithstanding this Supinity in general of too many of
our modern Players, we have sometimes some of them who are in earnest:
for I remember I once saw Mr. *Benjamin Johnson* (our present *Roscius*) act
Numphs with such an Engagement in the Part, that I could not persuade my
self, that it was acting but the Reality;[90] tho this often depends on the Poet
in his furnishing his Characters with Matter enough to engage the Player
to enter entirely into it, but a good Player will help out an indifferent Poet.

But this Address in the Performance can never be obtain'd without the
last Degree of Perfectness, for without that the Player can never be free from
the Apprehension of being out. Among those Players, who seem always to
be in earnest, I must not omit the Principal, the incomparable Mrs. *Barry*;
her Action is always just, and produc'd naturally by the Sentiments of the
Part, which she acts, and she every where observes those Rules prescrib'd to
the Poets by *Horace*, and which equally reach the Actors.[91]

---

    including Dorimant in *The Man of Mode* (LS2 131), Hamlet (LS2 137), and Jaffeir in
    Venice Preserv'd (LS2 141).

[88] From *Hamlet*, III.ii.36–42. In Gildon's text, Shakespeare's 'those that' is amended to
    'those who', and 'themselves' to 'of themselves' (Restoration editions of the play have
    Shakespeare's words).

[89] A notorious offender in this respect was William Penkethman (?1660–1725),
    reported to have interrupted a scene in Farquhar's *The Recruiting Officer* by insisting
    on using his own name (cited in Stern, p.184).

[90] Benjamin Johnson (c.1665–1742) is listed in Rich's Company from the 1694–5 season
    (LS1 440), but his earliest recorded role was Sir Simon Barter in Thomas Scott's *The*
    Mock-Marriage (September 1695; LS1 452); originally a scene painter, he graduated
    to acting in the provinces before joining Drury Lane. The only known dramatic
    character referred to as 'Numphs' is the son of the gentleman in Vanbrugh's *Aesop*
    (1697), who does not appear on stage. It is possible Gildon/Betterton used the term
    to describe Johnson's performance as the clownish Clodpate in Shadwell's *Epsom*
    Wells, which played at Drury Lane in December 1708 (LS2 180).

[91] For Barry, see above, n.9. The use of the present tense accurately reflects the fact she
    re-joined the Queen's company for the 1709–10 season, when Gildon's conversation
    with Betterton is alleged to have taken place.

We weep and laugh as we see others do,
He only makes me sad, who shews the way,
And first is sad himself; Then Telephus
I feel the Weight of your Calamities,
And fancy all your Miseries my own;
But if you Act *them ill I sleep or laugh.*
Your Look must needs alter as your Subject does,
From kind to fierce, from wanton to serene.
For Nature forms and softens us within,
And writes our Fortune's Charges in our Face.
Pleasure enchants, impetuous Rare transports,
And Grief dejects, and wrings the tortur'd Soul;
And these are all interpreted by Speech.
But he, whose Words and Fortunes disagree,
Absurd, unpity'd grows a public Jest.

Lord Roscommon's Translation.[92]

She indeed always enters into her Part, and is the Person she represents. Thus I have heard her say, that she never said, *Ah! poor* Castalio! in the *Orphan*, without weeping.[93] And I have frequently observ'd her change her Countenance several Times as the Discourse of others on the Stage have affected her in the Part she acted. This is being throughly concern'd, this is to know her Part, this is to express the Passions in the Countenance and Gesture.

The Stage ought to be the Seat of Passion in its various kinds, and therefore the Actor ought to be throughly acquainted with the whole Nature of the Affections, and Habits of the Mind, or else he will never be able to express them justly in his Looks and Gestures, as well as in the Tone of his Voice, and manner of Utterance.[94] They must know them in their various Mixtures, and as they are differently blended together in the different Characters they represent; and then that Rule of the present Duke of *Buckingham* will be of use to the Player as well as Poet.

---

[92] I.e. of Horace, *Ars Poetica*. The commonplace 'si vis me flere' (if you wish to move me) was widely quoted. Betterton owned a copy of Thomas Creech's 1684 translation of Horace (PB 77); Roscommon's translation, published by Henry Herringman in 1680, does not appear in PB.

[93] Thomas Otway (1652–85) wrote a series of roles for Elizabeth Barry, including Monimia in *The Orphan* (1680). It might be asked why Betterton should have 'heard [Barry] say' she always wept at this line when Betterton was her Castalio and on stage with her (albeit about to exit) when the line was spoken; see *The Orphan* in *The Works of Thomas Otway*, ed. J.C. Ghosh, 2 vols (Oxford: Clarendon Press, 1933), II.78 (V.v.298).

[94] Another commonplace set out by Le Faucheur, p.93, drawing on Quintilian, 11.1.8–11.

— For they must look within to find
Those secret Turns of Nature in the Mind;
Without this Part in vain wou'd be the whole,
And but a Body all without a Soul.[95]

Then that Conduct of the other Hopes of the *English* Stage, Mrs. *Bradshaw*, (of whom we might say in Acting, as one said of *Tasso* in Poetry, that if he was not the best Poet, he had hindered *Virgil* from being the only Poet; so that if she be not the best Actress the Stage has known, she has hindered Mrs. *Barry* from being the only Actress) would certainly be very just, for a Friend of mine discoursing with her of the Action of the Stage, she told him, that *she endeavour'd first to make her self Mistress of her Part, and left the Figure and Action to Nature.*[96]

Tho a great Genius may do this, yet Art must be consulted in the Study of the larger Share of the Professors of this Art; and we find so great a Man as *Demosthenes* perfected himself by consulting the Gracefulness of the Figure in his Glass:[97] And to express Nature justly, one must be Matter of Nature in all its Appearances, which can only be drawn from Observation, which will tell us, that the Passions and Habits of the Mind discover themselves in our Looks, Actions and Gestures.

Thus we find a rolling Eye that is quick and inconstant in its Motion, argues a quick but light Wit; a hot and choleric Complexion, with an inconstant and impatient Mind; and in a Woman it gives a strong Proof of Wantonness and Immodesty. Heavy dull Eyes a dull Mind, and a Difficulty of Conception. For this Reason we observe, that all or most People in Years,

---

[95] I.e. John Sheffield, 3rd Earl of Mulgrave and Duke of Buckingham and Marquis of Normanby (1648–1721). The extract is from his *Essay on Poetry* (London: Francis Saunders, 1697), pp.14–15. No copy is listed in PB.

[96] Lucretia Bradshaw (d.1755) is first listed among the Lincoln's Inn Fields company for the 1695–6 season (LS1 450). The 1741 *History of the English Stage*, falsely attributed to Betterton, describes her as 'one of the greatest, and most promising Genii of her Time' (p.62). The exact source of the reference to Tasso and Virgil has not been traced. Numerous works known to Gildon and Betterton compare the merits of the two poets, including Dryden's Dedication of his translation of the *Aeneid* (London: Jacob Tonson, 1697), Rapin's *Observations on the Poems of Homer and Virgil*, trans. John Davies of Kidwelly (London: Dorman Newman, 1672), and his *Reflections on Aristotle's Treatise of Poesie* (London: Henry Herringman, 1674). PB 78 lists a copy of the latter work, wrongly attributing it to Thomas Rymer.

[97] The anecdote about Demosthenes appears, differently worded, in Le Faucheur p.175; also below, p.82.

sick Men, and Persons of a flegmatic Constitution are slow in the turning of their Eyes.[98]

That extreme Propension to Winking in some Eyes, proceed from a Soul very subject to Fear, arguing a Weakness of Spirit, and a feeble Disposition of the Eye-lids.

A bold staring Eye, that fixes on a Man, proceeds either from a blockish Stupidity, as in Rusticks; Impudence, as in Malicious Persons; Prudence, as in those in Authority, or Incontinence as in lewd Women.[99]

Eyes enflam'd and fiery are the genuine Effect of Choler and Anger; Eyes quiet, and calm with a secret kind of Grace and Pleasantness are the Offspring of Love and Friendship.

Thus the Voice, when loud, discovers Wrath and Indignation of Mind, and a small trembling Voice proceeds from Fear.

In like manner, to use no Actions or Gestures in Discourse, is a Sign of a heavy and slow Disposition, as too much Gesticulation proceeds from Lightness; and a Mean betwixt both is the Effect of Wisdom and Gravity;[100] and if it be not too quick, it denotes Magnanimity. Some are perpetually fiddling about their Cloaths, so that they scarce are dress'd till they go to Bed, which is an Argument of a childish and empty Mind.

Some cast their Heads from one side to the other wantonly and lightly, the true Effect of Folly and Inconstancy. Others think it essential to Prayer, to writh and wrest their Necks about, which is a Proof of Hypocrisy, Superstition, or Foolishness.[101] Some are wholly taken up in viewing themselves, the Proportion of their Limbs, Features of their Faces, and Gracefulness of Mien; which proceeds from Pride, and a vain Complaisance in themselves; of this number are Coquets.

In this manner I might run through all the Natural Actions, that are to be found in Men of different Tempers. Yet not to dismiss the Point without a fuller Reflection, I shall subjoin here the Signification of the various Natural Gestures from a Manuscript of a Friend of mine, which he assur'd me was taken from a learned Jesuit who wrote on this Subject.[102]

---

[98]   Roach, p.31, finds a parallel between this passage and Thomas Wright's *The Passions of the Minde in Generall* (London: Anne Helme, 1620), p.27.

[99]   Le Faucheur, pp.184–5, considers the action of eyes in very similar terms.

[100] Le Faucheur often praises gravity in an orator (pp.4, 70, 167, 183, 202).

[101] Cp. Le Faucheur, pp.44–5: 'Witness Young Alcibiades that follow'd his Father's steps to a Fault. He imitated him in speaking fast and thick, one word crippling another. He toss'd up his Head, and turn'd his Neck a-skew like him too'.

[102] A curious reference when Le Faucheur was a noted Protestant minister. The word 'subjoin' may suggest the subsequent passage is offered as quoted rather than original; this is the sequence of the book which is most dependent on Le Faucheur.

Every Passion or Emotion of the Mind has from Nature its proper and peculiar Countenance, Sound and Gesture; and the whole Body of Man, all his Looks, and every Sound of his Voice, like Strings on an Instrument, receive their Sounds from the various Impulse of the Passions.[103]

The Demission or hanging down of the Head is the Consequence of Grief and Sorrow. And this therefore is a Posture and Manner observ'd in the Deprecations of the Divine Anger, and on such occasions ought to be observ'd in the Imitations of those things.

A lifting or tossing up of the Head is the Gesture of Pride and Arrogance. Carrying the Head aloft is the sign of joy, Victory and Triumph.

A hard and bold Front, or Fore-head is look'd on as a Mark of Obstinacy, Contumacy, Perfidiousness and Impudence.

The Soul is most visible in the Eyes, as being, according to one, the perfect Images of the Mind; and, as *Pliny* says, they burn, yet dissolve in Floods;[104] they dart their Beams on Objects, and seem not to see them; and when we kiss the Eyes, we seem to touch the very Soul.

Eyes lifted on high shew Arrogance and Pride, but cast down express Humbleness of Mind:[105] Yet we lift up our Eyes when we address our selves in Prayer to God, and ask any thing of him.

> *Lifting in vain his burning Eyes to Heav'n.*
> Virgil.[106]

Denial, Aversion, Nauseating, Dissimulation, and Neglect, are express'd by a turning away of the Eyes.

A frequent Winking, or tremulous Motion of the Eyes, argues malicious Manners, and perverse and noxious Thought and Inclinations.

Eyes drown'd in Tears discover the most vehement and cruel Grief, which is not capable of Ease ev'n from Tears themselves.

---

[103] Cp. Le Faucheur, pp.98–9: 'For the String sounds as it is touch'd: if it be softly touch'd, it entertains the Ear with a soft sound; if strongly, it gives you a strong and a smart one'.

[104] I.e. Pliny the Elder (23–79 AD), *Historia naturalis*; apparently a loose translation from 1.31. PB 26 lists volume 1 of the folio edition of Philemon Holland's translation, *The historie of the world Commonly called the natural historie of C. Plinius Secundus* (London: Adam Islip, 1601).

[105] Cp. Le Faucheur, pp.190–1: 'As to the lifting-up or casting-down of your Eyes, 'tis plain you must do't according to the Nature of the things you speake of: For if you speak of Heaven and Cœlestial Powers, you ought without doubt to lift up your Eyes towards Heaven; but if you speak of the Earth and Terrestrial things, you must cast 'em down upon the Ground'.

[106] From the *Aeneid* Book V; Dryden translated the line as 'In vain, with lifted Hands, and gazing Eyes'.

To raise our Eyes to any thing or Person, is an Argument of our Attention to them with Desire.

The Hand put on the Mouth is a Token of Silence by Conviction, and is a Ceremony of the Heathen Adoration.[107]

The Contraction of the Lips and the scant Look of the Eyes expresses the Gesture of a deriding and malicious Person. Shewing the Teeth, and streightening the Lips on them, shews Indignation and Anger.

To turn the whole Face to any thing is the Gesture of one, who attends and has a peculiar Regard to that one thing. To bend the Countenance downward argues Consciousness and Guilt; and, on the contrary, to lift up the Face is a Sign of a good Confidence or Innocence, Hope and Confidence.

The Countenance, indeed, is chang'd into many Forms, and is commonly the most certain Index of the Passions of the Mind. When it is pale it betrays Grief, Sorrow, and Fear, and Envy, when it is very strong. A louring and dark Visage is the Index of Misery, Labour and vehement Agitations of the Soul.

In short, as *Quintilian* observes, the Countenance is of very great Power and Force in all that we do. In this we discover when we are suppliant, when minacious,[108] when kind, when sorrowful, when merry; in this we are lifted up and cast down; on this Men depend; this they behold, and this they first take a View of before we speak; by this we love some, and hate others; and by this we understand a Multitude of things.[109]

The Arm extended and lifted up signifies the Power of doing and accomplishing something; and is the Gesture of Authority, Vigour, and Victory. On the contrary, the holding your Arms close is a Sign of Bashfulness, Modesty, and Diffidence.

As the Hands are the most habil[110] Members of the Body, and the most easily turn'd to all sides, so are they the Indexes of many Habits.

But we have two Hands, the Right and the Left, we sometimes make use of one, sometimes of the other, and sometimes of both, to express the Passion and Habit. The chief Forms of which I shall mention:

The lifting of one Hand upright, or extending it, expresses Force, Vigour and Power. The Right Hand is also extended upwards as a Token of Swearing, or taking a solemn Oath; and this Extension of the Hand sometimes signifies Pacification, and Desire of Silence.

---

[107] Cp. Le Faucheur, pp.200–1: 'they whom you speak to upon an Address, may see your Mouth, your Eyes and your Hands concurring all together, every one in its own way, to signifie the same thing'.

[108] I.e. threatening.

[109] Le Faucheur, p.182, borrowed from Quintilian, 11.3.72: 'Even before we begin to speak, by the face we express love and hate; from the face we understand a number of things, and its expression is often equivalent to all the words we could use'.

[110] OED 1: 'having the means, capacity, or qualifications to do something'.

The putting of the Hand to the Mouth is the Habit of one, that is silent and acting Modesty; of Admiration and Consideration. The giving the Hand is the Gesture of striking a Bargain, confirming an Alliance, or of delivering ones self into the Power of another. To take hold of the Hand of another expresses Admonition, Exhortation, and Encouragement. The reaching out an Hand to another implies Help and Assistance. The lifting up both Hands on high is the Habit of one who implores, and expresses his Misery. And the lifting up of both Hands sometimes signifies Congratulation to Heaven for a Deliverance, as in *Virgil*;

> *His Hands now free from Bands he lifts on high,*
> *In grateful Action to th' indulgent Gods.*[111]

The holding the Hands in the Bosom is the Habit of the Idle and Negligent. Clapping the Hands, among the *Hebrews* signify'd deriding, insulting, and exploding;[112] but among the *Greeks* and the *Romans*, it was, on the contrary, the Expression of Applause. The Imposition of Hands signifies the imparting a Power, in consecrating of Victims.

In short, *Quintilian* says of the Hands —

"It is a difficult matter to say what a number of Motions the Hands have, without which all Action wou'd be maim'd and lame, since these Motions are almost as various as the Words we speak. For the other Parts may be said to help a Man when he speaks, but the Hands (as I may say) speak themselves. Do we not by the Hands desire a thing? Do we not by these promise? Call? Dismiss? Threaten? Act the Suppliant? Express our Abomination or Abhorrence? Our Fear? By these do we not ask Questions? Deny? Shew our Joy, Grief, Doubt, Confession, Penitence, Moderation, Plenty, Number, and Time? Do not the same Hands provoke, forbid, make Supplication, approve, admire, and express Shame? Do they not in shewing of Places and Persons, supply the Place of the Adverbs and Pronouns? Insomuch that in so great a Variety or Diversity of the Tongues of all Nations, this seems to remain the universal Language common to all."[113]

---

[111]   From the *Aeneid*, Book 1. In Dryden's translation, 'the *Trojan* Chief, / With lifted Hands and Eyes, invokes Relief'.

[112]   A partially accurate reference to Thomas Goodwin, *Moses and Aaron. Civil and Ecclesiastical Rites, used by the Ancient Hebrews* (London: John Haviland, 1625), p.25.

[113]   Translated from Quintilian, 11.3.85–6. Cp. Le Faucheur's much looser version, p.194: 'As to the Hands now, they are the chief Instruments of Action, and they can vary it as many ways too as there are Things, which they are capable of signifying. For we make use of them in Accusing, Acquitting, Promising, Threatening, Intreating, Admiring or Swearing; and in representing almost all the things we speak of in the World; which require so many different Actions of the Hands: So that Quintilian

It were to be wish'd that this Art were a little reviv'd in our Age, when such useful Members, which of old contributed so much to the Expression of Words, should now puzzle our Players what to do with them, when they seldom or never add any Grace to the Action of the Body, and never almost any thing to the Explanation or fuller Expression of the Words and Passions. But to go on with my Text a very little farther. —

The stamping of the Feet among the *Hebrews* signify'd Derision and Scoffing.[114] Among the *Greeks*, &c, Imperiousness. A constant and direct Foot is the Index of a steady, certain, constant, and right Study and Aim of our Designs.

On the contrary, Feet full of Motion are the Habit of the inconstant and fluctuating in their Counsels and Resolves. And the *Greeks* thought this in Women a sign of a flagitious[115] Temper.

Thus I have gone through my Jesuit's Observations of the several Gestures and Positions of the several Parts and Members of the Body.[116] And tho some of them may to a hasty View seem trifling, and others of no great Importance, yet I am persuaded, that a Man of true Judgment may find some secret Excellencies in them, which may afford him great Helps in the rendering his Gestures beautiful and expressive.

There is no greater Proof of this, than the Example I have already urg'd of the *Pantomime* and *Demetrius* the *Cynic* Philosopher, who cry'd out to him, *I hear my Friend what you act; nor do I only see them, but methinks you speak with your* HANDS.[117] But this Speaking with the Hands, (as 'tis here call'd) I find contain a great deal of the Representation of the dancing dumb Shows of the *Mimes* and *Pantomimes*. It may be perhaps objected, that these Motions of the Hands were so well known to the Frequenters of the Theatres, that, like our talking on our Fingers with those, who understand it, there would be no Difficulty in the Representation; but that if any Stranger or Foreigner should have been there, it would have been nothing but an unintelligible Gesticulation, and what *Shakespear* calls it *unexplicable dumb Shews*;[118] whereas if these Actions and Gestures were drawn from their Natural Significancy, according to those Marks I have already given, or others referr'd to by my Quotation of *Quintilian*, they must be intelligible to

---

says very well, the other Parts of the Body help him mightily that speaks; but the Hands, as it were, speak themselves'.

[114] See above, n.112.

[115] OED 1b: infamous. Alternatively, 2: Extremely wicked or criminal.

[116] This may be a deliberate (and incompetent) strategy to mislead, or an indication that Betterton merely broke off from his manuscript before recommencing.

[117] See above, pp.61–2.

[118] *Hamlet*, III.ii.11: 'inexplicable dumb shows'.

all Nations, on first Sight to *Barbarians*, who never saw them before, as well as to *Greeks* and *Romans*, who convers'd with them every Day.

I allow the Objection, but shall remove it by a farther Account of the very same *Pantomime*, who liv'd in the Time of *Nero*: The Story is this — "A *Barbarian* Prince, who came from *Pontus* to *Rome*, about some Business with *Nero*, among other Entertainments saw this Dancer personate so lively, that tho he knew nothing of what was sung, being half a *Grecian*, yet he understood all. Being therefore to return to his Country after this Entertainment of *Nero*'s, and bid ask what he would and it should be granted, reply'd, give me the Dancer, and you will infinitely please me. *Nero* asking him of what use he would be to him? My Neighbour *Barbarians* (said he) are of different Languages, nor is it easy for me to find Interpreters for them; this Fellow, therefore, as often as I have need, shall expound to me by his Gestures."[119] So clear and intelligible were his Actions and Gestures, and so derived from the Nature of the thing represented; which is a Proof, that there are certain Natural Significations of the Motions of the Hands, and other Members of the Body, which are obvious to the Understanding of all sensible Men of all Nations. If those which I have given you from my Jesuit be not, yet I am very sure, that many of them are explain'd by him, which will be plain to a serious Considerer.

Gesture has therefore this Advantage above mere Speaking, that by this we're only understood by those of our own Language, but by Action and Gesture (I mean just and regular Action) we make our Thoughts and Passions intelligible to all Nations and Tongues.[120] 'Tis, as I have observ'd from *Quintilian*, the common Speech of all Mankind, which strikes our Understanding by our Eyes, as effectually, as Speaking does by the Ears;[121] nay, perhaps, makes the more effectual Impression, that Sense being the most vivacious and touching, according to *Horace*, as I find him in my Lord *Roscommon*'s Version;

> *But what we hear moves less, than what we see;*
> *Spectators only have their Eyes to trust, &c.*[122]

---

[119] From Lucian, *Dialogues*, p.371. As noted above, n.64, PB 10 lists a copy.

[120] Cp. Le Faucheur, p.171: 'Gesture has this advantage above Pronunciation; that, by Speech we are only understood by People of our own Country and Lingua; but by Gesture, we render out Thoughts and our Passions intelligible to all Nations, indifferently, under the Sun. 'Tis as it were the common Language of all Mankind, which strikes the Understanding in at our Eyes as much as Speaking does in at our Ears'.

[121] Quintilian, 11.3.87: 'Amid the great diversity of tongues that pervades all nations and people, the language of the hands appears to be a language shared by all men'.

[122] From Roscommon's *Horace's Art of Poetry made English* (as above, n.92), p.14.

I think I have already assign'd a tolerable Reason why *Movement* and *Action* should teach us so sensibly; nay, the very Representation of them in *Painting* often strikes our Passions, and makes Impressions on our Minds more strong and vivid, than all the Force of Words. The chief Work is certainly done by Speech in most other ways of public Discourse, either at the *Bar*, or in the *Pulpit*; where the Weight of the Reason and the Proof are first and most to be consider'd: But on the Stage, where the Passions are chiefly in View, the best *Speaking*, destitute of *Action* and *Gesture* (the Life of all Speaking) proves but a heavy, dull, and dead Discourse.

This, in some measure, will likewise reach all things deliver'd in Public, since I find *Pliny the younger* talking of People in his Days reciting of their Speeches, or Poems, by either reading them themselves, or by having them read by others, tells us, that this reading them was a very great Disadvantage to the Excellence of their Performance either way, lessening both their *Eloquence* and *Character*, since the principal Helps of *Pronunciation*, the *Eyes* and the *Hands*, could not perform their Office, being otherwise employ'd to read, and not adorn the Utterance with their proper Motions; insomuch that it was no manner of wonder, that the Attention of the Audience grew languid, on so unactive an Entertainment.[123] On the contrary, when any Discourse receives Force and Life, not only from the Propriety and Graces of Speaking agreeable to the Subject, but from a proper *Action* and *Gesture* for it, it is truly touching, penetrating, transporting; it has a Soul, it has Life, it has Vigour and Energy not to be resisted. For then the *Player*, the *Preacher*, or *Pleader*, holds his Audience by the Eyes, as well as Ears, and engrosses their Attention by a double Force. This seems to be well represented in some Words of *Cicero* to *Cæcilius*, a young Orator, on his first Cause, who would needs undertake the *Action* against *Verres*, in Opposition to *Hortensius*. After he has shown his Incapacity in many Points to accuse *Verres*, both in Ability, and in not being free from a Suspicion of a share in the Guilt, he comes at last to the Power and Art of his Adversary *Hortensius* — *Reflect*, (says he) *consider again and again what you are going to do! for there seems to me to be some Danger not only of his oppressing thee with his Words; but even of his confounding and daz[z]ling the Eyes of thy Understanding with his* GESTURE, *and the* MOTION *of his Body, and so*

---

[123] Cp. Le Faucheur, p.172: 'For this reason, Pliny Junior mentioning the Recitations which People in his Days made of their Orations and Poems to their Friends, either in reading 'em themselves or in having them read by others; says, that this Reading of them was a mighty disadvantage to their Eloquence and Character, because the main helps of Pronunciation, the Eyes and the Hands were hinder'd by't; and that it was no wonder if the Attention of their Auditors droop'd upon it'.

entirely drive thee from thy Design, and all thy Thoughts.[124] The same *Cicero,* in his Books of *Oratory,* tells us, that *Crassus* pleading against *Brutus,* deliver'd his Words with such an Accent and such a Gesture, that he perfectly confounded the la[t]ter, and put him out of Countenance, fixing his Eyes ste[a]dfastly on him, and addressing all his Action up to him, as if he would devour him with a *Look* and a *Word.*[125]

But to make these Motions of the Face and Hands easily understood, that is, useful in the moving the Passions of the Auditors, or rather Spectators, they must be properly adapted to the thing you speak of, your Thoughts and Design; and always resembling the *Passion* you would express or excite. Thus you must never speak of mournful things with a gay and brisk Look, nor *affirm* any thing with the Action of *Denial;* for that would make what you say of no manner of Authority or Credit;[126] you would gain neither Belief nor Admiration. You must also have a peculiar Care of avoiding all manner of *Affectation* in your *Action* and *Gesture,* for that's most commonly ridiculous and odious, unless where the Actor is to express some Affectation in the Character he represents, as in *Melantha* in *Marriage Ala-Mode,* and *Millamant* in the *Way of the World.* But even then that very Affectation must be unaffected, as those two Parts were admirably acted by Mrs. *Montfort* and Mrs. *Bracegirdle.*[127] But your *Action* must appear purely Natural, as

---

[124]   Cp. Le Faucheur, pp.171–2: 'Cicero discountenanced Cecilius with this Reflexion, when he would have Pleaded against Hortensius in the Accusation of Verres, and his Ambition carried him beyond his Capacity: *Consider on't* (said he to him) *and weigh the thing well; for in my Opinion you are in great Danger, not only to be baffled by his Words and his Pronunciation, but to have your Eyes dazzled too by his Gesture and the Motions of his Body; lest he should disorder all your Thoughts, amuse you and make you forget whatever you had to say'*. Le Faucheur's reference is to Cicero's *Divinatio against Quintus Cæcilius,* 11.35.

[125]   Cp. Le Faucheur, p.173: 'And when Cicero again represents the matter in his *Books of the Orator,* how Crassus baffled and fool'd Brutus once at the Barr, when he was a pleading against; he says, that he pronounced his Words after such a manner that they put him quite out of Countenance; with an Eye so stedfastly fix'd upon him; making-up all his Gesture against him, and confronting him at every turn, as if he would have swallowed him up at a Look, or in a Breath'. The reference is to the skill of Lucius Crassus as described in *De Oratore,* 2.55.

[126]   Cp. Le Faucheur, p.174: 'For if you should speak of sad things with a brisk Look and pronounce sorrow with a gay Countenance; or if you should affirm any thing with the Gesture of a Man that were denying it, 'twould take away all Authority and Credit from you Words: No Body would believe or admire you'.

[127]   Cibber, p.120, describes his 'fantastic impression' of Susanna Mountfort's performance as Melantha in Dryden's *Marriage à la Mode* (probably from 1691). On p.122 he praises Anne Bracegirdle for capturing all the 'faults, follies and affectations' of Millamant in Congreve's *The Way of the World* (1700).

the genuine Offspring of the things you express, and the *Passion*, that moves you to speak in that manner.

In fine, our *Player*, *Pleader*, or *Preacher*, must have that nice Address in the Management of his Gestures, that there may be nothing in all the various Motions and Dispositions of his Body, which may be offensive to the Eye of the Spectator; as well as nothing grating and disobliging to the Ears of his Auditors, in his Pronunciation; else will his Person be less agreeable, and his Speech les efficacious to both, by wanting all that *Grace*, Virtue, and Power, it would otherwise obtain.[128]

'Tis true, it must be confess'd, that the Art of Gesture seems more difficult to be obtain'd, than the Art of Speaking; because a Man's own Ear may be judge of the Voice, and its several Variations, but cannot see his Face at all, and the Motion of the other Parts of the Body, but very imperfectly. *Demosthenes*, as I have said, to make a true Judgment how far his Face and Limbs mov'd and kept to the Rules of good Action and Gesture, set before him a large *Looking-Glass* sufficient to represent the whole Body at one View, to direct him in distinguishing betwixt *Right* and *Wrong*, decent and indecent Actions; but yet, tho this might not be unuseful, it lies under this Disadvantage, that it represents on the Right what is on the Left, and on the contrary, on the Left what is on the Right Hand; so that when you make a Motion with your *Right-Hand*, the Reflection makes it seem as done by the *Left*, which confounds the Gesture, and gives it an aukward Appearance: And to rectify this Appearance to you from the Glass, by giving the Motions by the contrary Hands, might contract such an ill Habit, as ought with the utmost Caution to be avoided.

As to all the other Parts of Action indeed a Glass may prove very advantageous, since in it you have a faithful Representation not only of the *Face* in all its Variations of the Countenance, but of the whole Body likewise in all its Postures and Motions, and the Agreeableness and Harmony of one to the other, and the Parts with the Whole, and the Whole with the Parts. So that you may thus easily discover any *Habit* or *Gesture* that wants Grace, and Agreeableness, and any Action, which may add them to your Person, and in them that Force and Influence to [what] you utter.

For want of such a Glass there is but a more difficult thing to be apply'd to, and that is some Friend, who is a perfect Master in all the Beauties of *Gesture* and *Motion*, and can correct your Errors, as you perform before him, and

---

[128] Cp. Le Faucheur, pp.174–5: 'In fine, the Orator must manage his Gesture so nicely, that there may be nothing, if possible, in all Dispositions and Motions of his Body, which may offend the Eyes of the Spectators; as well as take care that his Pronunciation have nothing in it, which may grate and disoblige the Ears of the Hearers: Otherwise, his Presence will be less agreeable to his Audience, and his Speech it self will not have all that Grace, Virtue and Influence which it ought to have'.

point out those *Graces*, which wou'd render your Action compleatly charming.[129] 'Tis true, that some have advis'd the Learner to have some excellent Pattern always before his Eyes, and urge, that *Hortensius* was so to *Roscius* and *Æsopus*, who always made it their Business to be present at his *Pleadings* with that Attention as to improve themselves so far by what they saw, as to carry away his fine Actions and *Gesture*, and practice afterwards on the Stage, what they had seen at the *Bar*:[130] Yet can I not allow of this Imitation in Acting; for when a very young Player conceives a strong Opinion of any one of received Authority on the Stage, he at best becomes a good Copy, which must always fall short of an Original.[131] Besides, this Instance of the two *Roman* Players will not reach our Case, since they were established Players, had fixt their Characters, and manner of Playing; and only did by *Hortenius* what a Player now might do by the fine Pieces of History-Painting, carry off the beautiful Passions and Positions of the Figures, or

[129] Cp. Le Faucheur, pp.175–6: 'This made Demosthenes betake himself to speak his Harangues and his Pleadings before a great Looking-Glass, that he might observe his Gestures the better, and be able to distinguish betwixt Right and wrong, decent and indecent Actions. This method, I think, might be practic'd to purpose. There's only this disadvantage in the Glass, that it always represents on the left what is on the right, and on the right what's on the left; so that when you make a motion with the right Hand, you have the reflexion of it as if it were made with the left; which confounds the Gesture and appears a little untoward: so that if to adjust your self to the Glass, you make a motion with the left, 'tis true, it reflects the Gesture as if it were made with the right; but then you may chance to get an ill Habit by so doing, which of all things you ought to avoid. However, this inconvenience is abundantly made up to you in the advantage it gives you of seeing not only your Face in all its Countenances, but the state of your whole Body too in all its Postures and Motions: so that you may easily discover by it any thing that is unhandsome and disagreeable, either in your Habit or your Gesture; and any Action again, on the contrary, that adds grace to your Person and force to your Discourse. But for want of a Looking-Glass, you should get some of your Friends to do you this good Office; such an one, I mean, as is capable of judging whether your Gesture be good or not, upon Tryal and frequent Practice'.

[130] Cp. Le Faucheur, p.176: 'He excell'd so much in this mute Eloquence, that two of the famousest Comedians in his time, Esopus and Roscius, always made it their Business to find him out where he Pleaded, and never fail'd of attending upon his Harangues, on purpose to improve themselves; to carry away his fine Gestures with them, and to practice afterwards upon the Stage what they had learn'd of him at the Barr'.

[131] The account of Betterton's Hamlet by Downes, pp.51–2, suggests that Restoration actors learned their roles by imitating predecessors who had been 'Instructed' by the author. However, Cibber emphasizes that the best actors brought their own ideas to roles; recalling Richard Estcourt in Dryden's *The Spanish Fryar*, he writes that 'the conception was not his own but imprinted in his memory by another, of whom he only possessed a dead likeness' (p.201).

the particular Appearance of any one Passion. But after all it puz[z]les me, who am not acquainted so well with the Ancients, how to reconcile this of *Roscius* and *Æsopus* learning Gesture of *Hortensius*, and instructing *Cicero* in the same:[132] 'Tis true I have been inform'd, that *Hortensius* was Senior to *Cicero*, and therefore they might be thought to have paid that to the Bar in *Cicero*, which they had borrow'd from the Bar in *Hortensius*. But let this be as it will, the Controversy is not of that Moment as to detain us any longer.

But it may be objected, that what I have deliver'd all this Time seems rather to dwell upon *Generals*, than to come to any Particulars. I confess in this Art it is much an easier Matter to discourse in a general Manner, than to deliver particular Rules for the Direction of our Actions. Yet I believe I may venture to say, that as general as my Discourse may seem to some, those, who have any true Genius to *Playing*, will find such particular Instructions, as may be of very great use to them; and this Art, as well as most others, but especially *Poetry*, delivers such Rules, that are not easily understood without a *Genius*.

However, to gratify those, who require greater Particularities, I shall add some particular Rules of Action; which justly weigh'd, will be of use to the *Bar* and the *Pulpit*, as well as the *Stage*, provided, that the Student allow a more strong, vivid and violent Gesture to the *Plays*, than to either of the other.

I shall therefore begin with the *Government*, *Order*, and *Balance*, as I may say, of the whole Body; and thence I shall proceed to the Regiment and proper Motions of the *Head*, the *Eyes*, the *Eye-brows*, and indeed the whole *Face*; and I shall conclude with the *Actions* of the *Hands*, more *copious* and *various*, than all the other Parts of the Body.

The Place and Posture of the Body ought not to be chang'd every Moment, since so fickle an Agitation is trifling and light: Nor, on the other Hand, should it always keep the same Position, fixt like a Pillar or Marble Statue. For this, in the first place, is unnatural, and must therefore be disagreeable, since God has so form'd the Body with Members disposing it to Motion, that it must move either as the Impulse of the Mind directs, or as the necessary Occasions of the Body require.[133] This heavy Stability, or thoughtless

---

[132] Either a cunning interpolation by Gildon or a genuine representation of a conversation he had with Betterton.

[133] Cp. Le Faucheur, pp.178–9: 'As for the whole Body, it ought neither to change Place nor Posture every moment. This fickle Agitation would be as indecent as the Gesture of Curion, whom Junius compared to a Man at Sea in a Cock-boat, for tossing his Body about continually, sometimes to the right and sometimes to the left, with the greatest inconstancy imaginable: But then, on the other hand, it must neither stand like a Stock, nor be as immovable as a May-pole; for over and above that this is not Natural; God Almighty having made the Body of such a moveable Meen and of

Fixtness, by losing that *Variety*, which is so becoming of and agreeable in the Change and Diversity of Speech and Discourse, and gives Admiration to every thing it adorns, loses likewise that Genteelness, and Grace, which engages the Attention by pleasing the Eye. Being taught to dance will very much contribute in general to the graceful Motion of the whole Body, especially in Motions, that are not immediately embarrass'd with the Passions.[134]

That the Head has various *Gestures* and *Signs*, *Intimations* and *Hints*, by which it is capable of expressing *Consent*, *Refusal*, *Confirmation*, *Admiration*, and *Anger*, &c. is what every one knows, who has ever thought at all. It might therefore be thought superfluous to treat particularly of them. But this Rule I must lay down on this Head in general, first that it ought not to be lifted up too high, and stretched out extravagantly, which is the Mark of *Arrogance* and *Haughtiness*; but an Exception to this Rule will come in for the Player, who is to act a Person of that Character. Nor on the other side should it be *hung down* upon the Breast, which is both disagreeable to the Eye, in rendring the *Mien* clumsy and dull; and would prove extremely prejudicial to the *Voice*, depriving it of its *Clearness*, *Distinction*, and that *Intelligibility*, which it ought to have: Nor should the Head always lean towards the Shoulders, which is equally rustic and affected, or a great Mark of *Indifference*, *Languidness*, and a *faint Inclination*. But the Head, in all the calmer Speeches at least, ought to be kept in its just *Natural State* and *upright Position*. In the Agitation indeed of a *Passion*, the Position will naturally follow the several Accesses and Recesses of the Passion whether *Grief*, *Anger*, &c.[135]

---

such Members as dispose it for Motion, that it ought to move sometimes, either as the Soul directs or as the Body it self requires: It is also disagreeable and ungenteel for want of Variety; which becomes it so well upon every occasion or change of Discourse, and sets every thing-off to admiration'.

[134] Aston's account of Betterton's physique does not suggest an actor naturally fitted for dancing: 'Mr. *BETTERTON* (although a superlative good Actor) labour'd under ill Figure, being clumsily made, having a great Head, and short thick Neck, stoop'd in the Shoulders, and had fat short Arms, which he rarely lifted higher than his Stomach' (in Lowe, II.299).

[135] Cp. Le Faucheur, pp.179–80: 'As to the Head, 'tis needless to tell you here what Gestures and Signs, what intimations and hints it is capable of making; as of refusing, granting, confirming, admiring, of being angry, &c. because every Body knows this well enough already: So that I shall only advance two things upon the whole. The one is, that the Head ought not to be held-up too high and stretched-out extravagantly, which would be a mark of Arrogancy or Haughtiness; nor to be cast down and hang upon the Breast, which would prejudice the voyce mightily and make it less clear, distinct and intelligible; nor to lean always towards the Shoulders, which would argue an indifferency, a languor and a faint inclination: But it is always to be kept modestly upright to it's Natural State and Position, which is best. The other

The Life of Mr Thomas Betterton

We must farther observe, that the Head must not be kept always like that of a Statue without Motion; nor must it on the contrary be moving perpetually, and always throwing it self about on every different Expression. It must therefore, to steer between this *Scylla* and *Carybdis*, and shun these ridiculous Extremes, turn gently on the Neck, as often, as Occasion requires a Motion, according to the Nature of the thing, turning now to one side, and then to another, and then return to such a decent Position, as your Voice may best be heard by all or the Generality of the Audience. To this I may add, that the Head ought always to be turn'd on the same side, to which the *Actions* of the rest of the Body are directed, except when they are employ'd to express our Aversion to Things, we refuse; or on Things we detest and abhor: For these Things we reject with the *Right Hand*, at the same time turning the Head away to the *Left*.[136]

But the greatest Life and Grace of *Action* derive themselves from the *Face*. For this Reason: *Crassus* in *Cicero* remarks, that *Roscius*, tho so excellent a Player, lost his Admiration among the *Romans* on the Stage, because the Mask on his Face deny'd the Audience the sight of those *Motions, Charms*, and *Attractions*, which were to be discover'd in the Countenance.[137] I confess I am extremely surpriz'd at the Ancients Use of those Masks on the Stage, which they call'd the *Personæ*; nor could I imagine how they were made, not to destroy that Grace and Beauty of Acting, in the Management of the Lineaments of the Face, which by all that we have of that kind must be entirely hid; and yet what *Plutarch* tells us of *Demosthenes* and *Cicero*, is a Proof, that the Players of *Athens* and *Rome* were absolute Masters of Speaking and Action.[138] 'Tis true, there is much in the *Voice* to express the Passion

---

observation I make on't, is this; that it is not handsome for the Head to continue always as immoveable as that of a Statue'.

[136] Cp. Le Faucheur, pp.180–1: '[The head] must not be moving continually neither, nor throwing it self about at every turn of Expression, when the Orator advances up to the height of a Discourse; which is too common an Error. But to avoid both those awkward Extremes, it must turn softly upon the Neck, when there's occasion for't; as the Nature of the thing requires: not only to look upon those that are directly before your Eyes in the middle of an Assembly, but also to cast a Countenance now and then as well upon those that are on each Hand of you; sometimes on one side, and sometimes on the other: And after that, to hold it again in such a decent Posture as your Voyce may be most easily heard by the greatest Part of your Auditors; that is to say, looking straight forward to the middle of the Auditory. To this I must add that the Head ought always to be turn'd on the same side with the other Actions of the Body ...'.

[137] Cicero's *De Oratore* is a dialogue between characters named as Antonius, Catulus, Sulpicius, Cotta, Scævola and Crassus.

[138] Cp. Le Faucheur, pp.181–2: 'But of all the Parts of the Head, 'tis the Face that gives the greatest Life and the best grace to Action. This was the reason, why the Ancients,

artfully, yet certainly the several Figurations of the Countenance, as of the *Eyes, Brows, Mouth*, and the like, add the most touching and most moving Beauties. But this Observation before-mention'd satisfies me, that those were entirely lost by the *Personæ*; which is a Proof, that in whatever they excell'd our Actors, we have the Advantage in the making the Representation perfect, by enjoying the Benefit of exposing all the Motions of the Face.

The Character which *Lucian* gives (as I find it in Dr. *Jasper Maine*'s Translation) of those *Personæ*, makes them extremely ridiculous, and by his Description of the rest of the Tragic Equipage would make us very much doubt their Excellence in the other Parts of Acting.—

"What a deform'd and frightful Sight (says he) is it to see a Man rais'd to a prodigious Length, stalking on exalted Buskins, his Face disguis'd with a grim Vizard, widely gaping, as if he meant to devour the Spectators; I forbear to speak of his stuff'd Breasts and Fore-bellies, which make an adventitious and artificial Corpulency, lest his unnatural Length should carry a Disproportion to his Slenderness."[139]

Surely such a Figure as *Lucian* gives our *Tragedian*, must not only render him incapable of giving the Body all its just Motions and graceful Gestures, of which we are talking, and which the great Writers, as I am told, celebrate so much; but must be ridiculous to a Farce. But tho what *Lucian* represents, may be look'd upon as in the Time of the Corruption of the *Roman* Stage, yet the *Cothurni* and the *Personæ* were in use among the *Greeks*, and must have been extremely prejudicial to the Beauty of the Representation.[140] The Reason I have heard given for the first was the common Opinion, that the Heroes of former Times were larger and taller, than the Men our Cotemporaries; and I believe the first Use of the Vizard, which succeeded the besmeering the Face with Lees of Wine in the Time of *Thespis*, was chiefly to express the Looks and Countenance of the several Heroes represented, according to their Statues and Portraictures, which made the Player always new to the Audience; whereas we coming always on the Stage with the same Face, put a Force on the Imagination of the Audience to fancy us other than the same Persons.

But I think I have found out a way, which, if maturely study'd, would obtain this Variety of Countenance more artfully, and at the same time

---

as Crassus observes in Cicero, did not commend Roscius when he spake with a Mask-on; because they did not see his Face then, nor it's Motions, it's Charms and it's Attractions. So that you must take the greatest care imaginable of your Countenance, that nothing may appear disagreeable in it; for 'tis the Part most expos'd and in view, and your Auditors have their Eyes, if possible, continually fix'd upon't'.

[139] As noted above, n.64, a 1663 Folio copy of Mayne's translation of Lucian is listed in PB 10.

[140] *Cothurni* refers to buskins and *Personae* to masks.

inspire the Actor better with the Nature and Genius of his Part. I remember that some Years ago I read a *French* Book written by one *Gafferel* a Monk; who tells us, that when he was at *Rome* he went to see *Campanella* in the Inquisition, and found him making abundance of Faces; that he at first imagin'd, that those proceeded from the Torments he had undergone in that *Ecclesiastical Slaughter-House*; but he soon undeceiv'd him, by enquiring what sort of Countenance such a Cardinal had, to whom he had just before sent; for he was forming his Countenance, as much as he could, to what he knew of his, that he might know what his Answer wou'd be.[141]

If therefore a Player was acquainted with the Character of his Hero, so far as to have an Account of his Features and Looks; or of any one living of the same Character, he would not only vary his Face so much by that means, as to appear quite another Face; by raising, or falling, contracting, or extending the Brows; giving a brisk or sullen, sprightly or heavy turn to his Eyes; sharpening or swelling his Nostrils, and the various Positions of his Mouth, which by Practice would grow familiar, and wonderfully improve the Art of Acting, and raise the noble Diversion to greater Esteem. The studying History-Painting would be very useful on this Occasion, because the Knowledge of the Figure and Lineaments of the Represented (and in History-Pieces almost all, who are represented are to be found) will teach the Actor to vary and change his Figure, which would make him not always the same, as I have said, in all Parts, but his very Countenance so chang'd, that they would not only have other Thoughts themselves, but raise others in the Audience.[142] Some carry their Heads aloft and stately, others pucker their Brows, look with a piercing Eye, and the like, as I have just said; and these things throughly consider'd by the Player, would in every part make him a new Man and with more Beauty supply the *Personæ* of the Ancients, and raise our Stage to a greater Merit, than theirs could pretend to, which depriv'd the Audience of the noblest and most vivacious Part of the Representation, in the Loss of the Motions of the Face; of which we ought to take a peculiar Care, since it is on that, which the Audience or Spectators generally fix their Eyes the whole Time of the Action.[143]

Exercise and frequent Practice ought to reform the least Error in this particular, because in the Performance every one presently discovers it, tho

---

[141]   I.e. Jacques Gaffarel (1601–81), French priest, astrologer and Orientalist, whose *Curiositez inouyes sur la sculpture talismanique des Persans* (1629) was translated into English in 1650. The work is not listed in PB.

[142]   Regarding 'History-Painting', Betterton's picture collection (PB 147–50) included historical portraiture (e.g. of Henry VIII, Mary I, Charles II, James II, William III) as well as 'a small Battle' by Jan Wijck and an unidentified 'History-piece'.

[143]   While this section draws heavily on ideas from Le Faucheur and Quintilian, it is re-worked to reflect the needs of the actor.

you see it not your self. The surest way of correcting your self in this is either a Looking-Glass, or a judicious Friend, who can and will let you know what Countenance is agreeable, and what the contrary.[144] But this is a general Rule, without any Exception, that you adjust all the Lines and Motions of the Face to the Subject of your Discourse, the Passion you feel within you, or should according to your Part feel, or would raise in those, who hear and see you. You must likewise consider the Quality you represent, as well as the Quality of those to whom you speak; for even in great Degrees of the Passions the Difference and Distance of that has a greater or less Awe upon the very Appearance of the Passion. The *Countenance* must be brightened with a pleasant Gayety on things, that are agreeable, and that according to the Degrees of their being so; and likewise in *Joy*, which must still be heighten'd in the Passion of *Love*; tho indeed the *Countenance* in the Expression of this Passion is extremely various, participating sometimes of the Transports of Joy, sometimes of the Agonies of Grief; it is sometimes mingled with the Heats of Anger, and sometimes smiles with all the pleasing Tranquillity of an equal Joy. Sadness or Gravity must prevail in the *Countenance*, when the Subject is grave, melancholy or sorrowful; and Grief is to be expressed according to its various Degrees of Violence. *Hate* has its peculiar Expression composed of *Grief*, *Envy*, and *Anger*, a Mixture of all which ought to appear in the Eye.[145] When you bring or offer Comfort, Mildness and Affability ought to spread o'er your Countenance, as *Severity* should when you censure of reprehend. When you speak to Inferiors, or to little People, and your own Quality is great, Authority and Gravity ought to be in your Face; as Submission, Humility, and Respect or Veneration, when you address to those above you.

The Management of the Eyes in an *Orator* at the *Bar*, or in the *Pulpit*, seems something different from what they must be in a *Player*, tho, if we make the rest of the Actors on the Stage with him at the same time his Auditors, the Rules for one will reach the other; for so indeed they are, for all the Regard that is to be had to the Audience is that they see and hear distinctly, what we act and what we speak; that they may judge justly of our Positions, Gestures and Utterance, in regard to each other.

---

[144] See also above, p.64, 73, 82.

[145] Cp. Le Faucheur, p.183: 'But you ought still to adjust all it's Movements and Countenances, upon the Address, to the Subjects you treat of, the Passion you entertain in your own Bosom or would raise in other People's Breasts, and the Quality of the Persons to whom you speak; so as to shew a Gaiety upon things agreeable and upon Affections of Love and Joy; a sadness upon Melancholy Affairs and Passions of Hatred and Grief; a Mildness upon Consolation, and a Severity upon Censure and Reprehension …'.

The Orator therefore must always be casting his Eyes on some or other of his Auditors, and turning them gently from side to side with an Air of Regard, sometimes on one Person, and sometimes on another, and not fix them immoveably on one Part of your Auditors, which is extremely unaffecting and dull, much less moving, than when we look them decently in the Face, as in common Discourse.[146] This will hold good in Playing, if apply'd according to my former Rule; for indeed I have observ'd frequently some Players, who pass for great ones, have their Eyes lifted up to the Galleries, or Top of the House, when they are engag'd in a Discouse of some Heat, as if indeed they were conning a Lesson, not acting a Part; and *Theophrastus* himself (as I find him quoted) condemn'd *Tamariscus*, a Player of his Time, who when ever he spoke on the Stage, turn'd his Eyes from those, who were to hear him, and kept them fixt all the while on one single and insensible Object.[147] But Nature acts directly in a contrary manner, and yet she ought to be the Player's as well as Poet's Mistress. No Man is engag'd in Dispute, or any Argument of Moment, but his Eyes and all his Regard are fixt on the Person, he talks with; not but that there are times according to the Turn or Crisis of a Passion, where the Eyes may with great Beauty be turn'd from the Object we address to several Ways, as in Appeals to Heaven, imploring Assistance, to join in your Addresses to any one, and the like.

When you are free from Passion, and in any Discourse, which requires no great Motion, as our modern Tragedies too frequently suffer their chief Parts to be, your Aspect should be pleasant, your Looks direct, neither severe nor aside, unless you fall into a Passion, which requires the contrary. For then Nature, if you obey its Summons, will alter your Looks and Gestures. Thus when a Man speaks in *Anger* his Imagination is inflam'd, and kindles a sort of Fire in his Eyes, which sparkles from them in such a manner, that a Stranger, who understood not a Word of the Language, or a deaf Man, that could not hear the loudest Tone of his Voice, would not fail of perceiving his Fury and Indignation. And this Fire of their Eyes will easily strike those of their Audience, which are continually fixt on yours;

---

[146] Cp. Le Faucheur, pp.183–4: 'As for your Eyes, you must always be casting them upon some or other of your Auditors and rolling them gently about from this side to that, with an Air of Regard sometimes upon one Person and sometimes upon another; and not fix 'em like Darts that are once shot, still upon one Place of your Auditory, as many People do to their great Disadvantage: For it is so very disagreeable and dull, it affects the Persons before whom we speak, much less then when we look them decently in the Face, as we use to do in familiar and common Conversation ...'.

[147] Cp. Le Faucheur, p.184: 'Theophrastus had good Reason upon this account, for blaming an Actor call'd Tamarisque, that used to turn his Eyes away from his Auditors, whenever he spake in the Scene, and kept them fixt all the while upon one single and insensible Object'. Theophrastus of Eresos (c.371–278 BC), in his *Characters*.

and by a strange sympathetic Infection, it will set them on Fire too with the very same Passion.[148]

I would not be misunderstood, when I say you must wholly place your Eyes on the Person or Persons you are engag'd with on the Stage; I mean, that at the same time both Parties keep such a Position in Regard of the Audience, that even these Beauties escape not their Observation, tho never so justly directed. As in a Piece of History-Painting, tho the Figures direct their Eyes never so directly to each other, yet the Beholder, by the Advantage of their Position, has a full View of the Expression of the Soul in the Eyes of the Figures. Thus in the *Psyche* and *Cupid* of *Coypel*;[149] Her Eyes are directed to him as he descends on the Wing, and his to her glowing with Love and Desire, and yet all this is seen in him by those, who view the Picture. *Titian* has drawn the same Story, I mean the Loves of *Cupid* and *Psyche*;[150] but as She lies on the Bed naked, we see nothing but her Back-parts, tho *Cupid* advances his Knee to the Bed, with his Eyes fixt on her Face, which are turn'd from the Spectator. I know not what the *Italian's* Fancy was, to imagine that the Back-parts of the Mistress of Love should be more agreeable, than her Face. But this *en passant* — To return to the Subject.

The Looks, and just Expression of all the other Passions, has the same Effect, as this I have mention'd of Anger. For if the *Grief* of another touches you with a real Compassion, Tears will flow from your Eyes, whether you will or not. And this Art of Weeping, as I have read, was study'd with great Application by the ancient Players; and they made so extraordinary a Progress in it, and work'd the Counterfeit so near a Reality, that their Faces used to be all over blurr'd with Tears when they came off the Stage.

They us'd several means of bringing this passionate Tenderness to a Perfection; yet this they found the most effectual. They kept their own private Afflictions in their Mind, and bent it perpetually on real Objects, and not on the Fable, or fictitious Passion of the *Play*, which they acted.

---

[148] Cp. Le Faucheur, pp.184–5: 'Nature it self teaches you as much, and produces this effect, whensoever you are sensibly smitten with such Passions: For Example, when a Man speaks in Anger his Imagination is enflam'd and kindles a certain Fire in his Eyes, that makes 'em sparkle like Stars out of his Eye-lids; so that a meer Stranger that understood nothing of his Language, or a Deaf Man that could hear nothing of his Voyce, would not fail yet of perceiving his Indignation and Fury: And this Fire of your Eyes easily strikes those of your Auditors, who have theirs constantly fixt upon yours; and it must needs set them a-blaze too upon the same Resentment and Passion'.

[149] See above, n.85.

[150] No works by Titian are referred to in PB, although a mezzotint by John Smith, after Titian, was published in 1708. I'm grateful to Stephen Watkins for this reference.

The same Author gives us two notable Examples of this: The first is of one *Polus*, a famous Actor; he had refrain'd the Stage for some time, after the Death of a beloved Son, for the Grief for that Loss had so sensibly affected him, and thrown him into such a Melancholy, that he had no Thoughts of ever returning to his Theatrical Employment; but being at last once more on the Stage, and oblig'd to act *Electra* carrying the suppos'd Urn of her Brother *Orestes*; he went to the Grave of his own beloved Child, and brings his Urn on, instead of the suppos'd Urn of *Orestes*; which so mov'd him, and melted his Heart into such Compassion and Tenderness, at the Sight of that real Object of Sorrow, that he broke out into such loud Exclamations, and such unfeigned Tears, as fill'd the whole House with Grief, Weeping, and Lamentations.[151]

The other Example is of the famous and wealthy Player *Æsopus*, who by his rare Art in this particular did a great Piece of Service to the Commonwealth of *Rome*, in applying his Art to the recalling of *Cicero* from Banishment. For he understanding, that such a thing was in Agitation with the People, acted a Play of *Accius*, in which were some admirable Verses on the

---

[151] Cp. Le Faucheur, pp.185–6: 'For if you are afflicted with a violent Grief for your own Misfortunes, or touch'd with a great Compassion or another Man's Misery, 'twill draw Tears from your Eyes. This made the Ancient Actors apply themselves with so much Care and Concern to the acquiring a faculty of moving their Imagination to a Power of Weeping and shedding Tears in abundance upon occasion: And they succeeded so admirably well in't, wrought the Counterfeit up to such a degree, that their Faces used to be all over blurr'd with Crying after they came off the Stage. They brought this point of a Passionate Tenderness to perfection several ways; but the most effectual was this. They kept their Imagination still at work upon real Subjects and private Affections of their own, which they lay very much to Heat; and not upon the Fables or Fictions of the Play they acted, which did not touch them at all in effect. We have two notable instances of this in Story. The one, of that great Comedian Polis. He had not been upon the Stage, it seems for some time; upon the Death of one of his Sons that he lov'd dearly; which troubled him so much, that what with the Melancholy of his Temper upon the Disappointment of his Affection and the Loss of his Darling, he could hardly ever reconcile himself again to Diversion or the Theatre: But he appeared there at last however, upon Acting the *Electra* of Sophocles, and his Part was the Person of Electra her self, carrying the Urn and the Bones of her poor Brother Orestes in the Play. To do this more effectually to the Life, away he goes to his own Child's Grave; takes up his Urn and his Ashes, and brings them in his Arms upon the Stage instead of Orestes's Counterfeit. Upon this, his Imagination was so mov'd and his Heart so melted into Compassion and Tenderness at the sight of a real Object of Sorrow, that he brake out into loud Exclamations and unfeigned Tears in the Tragedy, upon the Fiction and Fate of Orestes, and filled the whole Theatre with Affliction, Lamentation and Weeping'.

Exile of *Telamon*, and the horrible Calamities of *Priam* and his Family.[152] In the speaking of these Verses, the real Sufferings of his Friend so affected him, that he made the imaginary Sufferings of the Poetical Person so moving, that he drew Floods of Tears from those, who were indifferent, and made his very Enemies blush with Tears in their Eyes at his Afflicton. And this so mollify'd the People towards *Cicero*, and gave them such a Disposition towards his Recalling and Re-establishment in his former Dignities, that he was soon after brought home in Triumph; and, as my Author assures me, *Cicero* himself tells us, with the utmost Gratitude, what his cordial Friend, this great Actor, had done for him on this Occasion.[153]

The Player therefore, nay, and the Orator too, ought to form in his Mind a very strong Idea of the Subject of his Passion, and then the Passion it self will not fail to follow, rise into the Eyes, and affect both the Sense and Understanding of the Spectators with the same *Tenderness*.[154] The Performance

---

[152] The Roman dramatist, literary historian and grammarian Lucius Accius (b.170 AD) is known to have written at least forty-six plays, many of them translations from Aeschylus, Sophocles and Euripides. Much of his dramatic output survives only as quoted by Cicero.

[153] Cp. Le Faucheur, pp.187–8: 'The other Example is of that excellent Actor Esopus; who having a mighty Affection and Zeal of Cicero; and being extremely concern'd at his Banishment, the Troubles of his Family, and other Disgraces that he lay under, he did him a signal favour once and a singular piece of good Service by the power of his tender Passion. For when he saw all the Friends of that great Man at work upon the People of Rome with their utmost Intercessions to get him Recall'd, he resolv'd to engage himself in it; to give it a lift on his part, and to strike a considerable Blow in the Affair. Upon this, he acts a Tragedy of Accius, on a Publick Occasion, which contained the fine Verses upon Telamon's Exile, and the horrible Calamities of Priam and his Family, which are related in Tully's *Tusculan Questions* and in his Oration for Sextius: But in those Verses you must think, his Imagination was not half so much struck with the false Misfortunes of the Persons in the old Fable, as with the Miseries that were too true and the real suffering of his Friend. Insomuch that the Acting of them transported him to so great a Passion and Grief, that he spake them upon the Stage, not only with a very mournful Voyce, but with Eyes also bath'd in Tears, which set all indifferent Persons that were present there a-weeping bitterly, and even made his Enemies blush with Tears in their Eyes at his Affliction. And this went a great way towards the melting of the Hearts of People and the reconciling of their Affections; towards the bringing of him Home again and the reinstating of him in his former Dignity, Reputation and Character; as Cicero himself tells us with the thankfullest Acknowledgments of the good Office, which that famous Actor, his Great and his Cordial Friend, had done him upon this occasion'. The phrase 'as my Author assures me' suggests that Gildon/Betterton has dropped back into consciously quoting Le Faucheur.

[154] Cp. Le Faucheur, p.99: 'So that the Orator would do well to adjust every Tone and Accent of his Voyce to each Passion that afflicts or overjoys him, which he would raise in others to a degree of Sympathy'. Cp. Quintilian, 11.3.62–5.

of this is express'd in *Shakespear's Hamlet* admirably well, and should be often consider'd by our young Players. —

> Ham. *Is it not monstruous that the Player here,*
> *But in a Fiction, in a Dream of Passion,*
> *Could force his Soul so to his whole Conceit,*
> *That from her working all his Visage warm'd,*
> *Tears in his Eyes, Distraction in his Aspect;*
> *A broken Voice, and his whole Function suiting*
> *With Forms to his Conceit? And all for nothing!*
> *For* HECUBA!
> *What's* HECUBA *to him , or he to* HECUBA,
> *That he should weep for her ? What wou'd he do*
> *Had he the Motive, and the Cue for Passion*
> *That I have? He would drown the Stage with Tears;*
> *And cleave the general Ear with horrid Speech;*
> *Make mad the Guilty, and appal the Free;*
> *Confound the Ignorant, and amaze indeed*
> *The very Faculty of Eyes and Ears.*[155]

This shews, that our *Shakespear* had a just Notion of Acting, whatever his Performance was;[156] for in these few Lines is contain'd almost all that can be said of Action, Looks and Gesture. Here we find the *Soul* forc'd so to his whole Conceit, *&c.* The first place is the fixing this in the *Soul*, to engage that throughly in the Passion, and then from her Working will his Visage warm, his Eyes flow with Tears, and Distractions spread over all his Face; nay, then will his Voice be broken, and every Faculty of his Body be agreeable to this strong Emotion of the Soul. Tho in the first seven Lines he seems to have expressed all the Duties of a Player in a great Passion; yet in the following seven he derives a yet stronger Action when the Object of Grief is real; which justifies what the Ancients practis'd in heightning their Theatrical Sorrow, by fixing the Mind on real Objects; or by working your self up by a strong Imagination, that you are the very Person and in the very

---

[155] Shakespeare, *Hamlet* II.ii.539–54. Here, Shakespeare's 'this Player' becomes 'the Player', while 'wann'd' becomes 'warm'd'. Richard Bentley's 1695 quarto of the play retains the original, although 'wann'd' becomes 'wand' (possibly an abbreviation of 'waned'). In the passage below, the author insists on 'warm'd'.

[156] The tradition that Shakespeare was at best a middle-ranking actor stems from Rowe's 1709 edition of the plays, which states that 'the top of his Performance was the Ghost in his own *Hamlet*'; cited in S. Schoenbaum, *Shakespeare's Lives*, 2nd ed. (Oxford: Oxford University Press, 1991), p.54. As per n.10 above, Betterton had assisted Rowe with research into Shakespeare's life.

same Circumstances, which will make the Case so very much your own, that you will not want Fire in Anger, nor Tears in Grief: And then you need not fear affecting the Audience, for Passions are wonderfully convey'd from one Person's Eyes to another's; the Tears of *one* melting the Heart of the *other*, by a very visible Sympathy between their Imaginations and Aspects.

You must lift up or cast down your Eyes, according as the Nature of the Things you speak of: Thus if of Heaven, your Eyes naturally are lifted up; if of Earth, or Hell, or any thing terrestrial, they are as naturally cast down.[157] Your Eyes must also be directed according to the Passions, as to deject them on things of Disgrace, and which you are asham'd of; and raise them on things of Honour, which you can glory in with Confidence and Reputation. In Swearing, or taking a solemn Oath, or Attestation of any thing, to the Verity of what you say, you turn your Eyes, and in the same Action lift up your Hand to the thing you swear by, or attest.[158]

Your Eye-brows must neither be immoveable, nor always in Motion; nor must they both be rais'd on every thing that is spoken with Eagerness and Consent, and much less must one be rais'd, and the other cast down; but generally they must remain in the same Posture and Equality, which they have by Nature, allowing them their due Motion, when the Passions require it; that is, to contract themselves, and frown in *Sorrow*: to smooth and dilate themselves in *Joy*; to hang down in *Humility*, &c.[159]

The *Mouth* must never be writh'd, nor the *Lips* bit or lick'd, which are all ungenteel and unmannerly Actions, and yet what some are frequently guilty of;[160] yet in some Efforts or Starts of Passion, the Lips have their share

---

[157] Cp. Le Faucheur, p.191: 'For if you speak of Heaven and Cœlestial Powers, you ought without doubt to lift up your Eyes towards Heaven; but if you speak of the Earth and Terrestrial things, you must cast 'em down upon the Ground'.

[158] Cp. Le Faucheur, p.191: 'You must also govern your Eyes according to the Passions, so as to cast 'em down upon things of Disgrace, which you are asham'd of; and to raise 'em again upon things of Honour, which you can glory in with Confidence and Credit. But it is more particularly necessary in Swearing, to turn up your Eyes towards that by which you Swear, and to lift the Hand up in the same Action'. Cp. Quintilian, 11.3.75–6.

[159] Cp. Le Faucheur, p.192: 'Your Eye-brows must neither be altogether immoveable, on the one hand, nor fickle or too full of Motion, on the other: And you must not raise them both up at every turn, as many People do upon any thing they speak with eagerness and contention; nor lift-up the one and cast down the other, as Piso did, whom Cicero reprov'd for raising one of his Eye-brows up as high as his Forehead, and hanging the other down to his Chin. But for the most part they ought to remain in the same Posture and Equality that Nature has given them'. Cp. Quintilian, 11.3.78.

[160] Cp. Le Faucheur, p.192: 'As for the Mouth, you must never wry it at all; for that's very disagreeable'. Le Faucheur goes on to repeat Cicero's anecdote about Sestius Pinarius, who always appeared to talk with a walnut in his mouth (*De Oratore*, II.67).

of Action, but this more on the Stage, than in any other public Speaking, either in the Pulpit, or at the Bar; because the Stage is or ought to be an Imitation of Nature in those Actions and Discourses, which are produc'd betwixt Man and Man by any Passion, or on any Business, which can afford Action; for all other has in reality nothing to do with the *Scene*.

Tho to shrug up the Shoulders be no Gesture allow'd in Oratory, yet on the Stage the Character of the Person, and the Subject of his Discourse, may render it proper enough; tho I confess, it seems more adapted to Comedy, than Tragedy, where all should be great and solemn, and with which the gravest of the Orators Actions will agree. I have read of a pleasant Method, that *Demosthenes* took to cure himself of this Vice of Action, for he at first was mightily given to it; he us'd to exercise himself in declaiming in a narrow and straight Place, with a Dagger hung just over his Shoulders, so that as often as he shrugg'd them up, the Point, by pricking his Shoulders, put him in mind of his Error: which in time remov'd the Defect.[161]

Others thrust out the Belly, and throw back the Head, both Gestures unbecoming and indecent.[162]

We come now to the Hands, which as they are the chief Instruments of Action, varying themselves as many ways, as they are capable of expressing things, so is it a difficult matter to give such Rules as are without Exception. Those Natural Significations of particular Gestures, and what I shall here add, will, I hope, be some Light to the young Actor in this particular. First, I would have him look back to what I have said of the *Action* of the Hands, as to their Expression of *Accusation, Deprecation, Threats, Desire*, &c. and to weigh well what those Actions are, and in what manner expressed; and then considering how large a share those Actions have in all manner of Discourse, he will find that his Hands need never be idle, or employed in an insignificant or unbeautiful Gesture.[163]

---

[161] Cp. Le Faucheur, pp.193–4: 'As to the Shoulders, there are some that shrug 'em up at every Expression; as those Grecian Witnesses, Cicero derided in his Oration for Rabirius Posthumus who made all their Gestures with the Shoulders. 'Tis a very unbecoming Vice, and you ought to shun it as a Disgrace. Demosthenes was at first addicted to it: But he soon corrected it by exercicing himself to declaim in a strait Place, with a piece of a Dart or a Dagger hung up just over his Shoulders; so that as often as he shrugg'd them up (as it was difficult for him not to do't sometimes, having gotten an ill Habit on't) the Point prick'd him, and put him in mind of his Error: Upon which, at last, he master'd the Imperfection'. Cp. Quintilian, 11.3.83.

[162] Cp. Le Faucheur, p.194: 'There are others, that in speaking, thrust out the Belly, and throw back the Head; which the Antients had good reason to condemn for an indecency and an ill Gesture'. Cp. Quintilian, 11.3.122.

[163] Cp. Le Faucheur, pp.194–5: 'As to the Hands now, they are the chief Instruments of Action, and they can vary it as many ways too as there are Things, which they are capable of signifying. For we make use of them in Accusing, Acquitting, Promising,

In the Beginning of a solemn Speech, or Oration, as in that of *Anthony* on the Death of *Cæsar*, or of *Brutus*, on the same Occasion, there is no Gesture at least of any Consideration, unless it begin abruptly, as *O! Jupiter, Oh! Heav'ns! is this to be born? the very Ships then in our Eyes, which I preserv'd,* &c.[164] extending here his Hands first to Heav'n; and then to the Ships. In all regular Gestures of the Hands, they ought perfectly to correspond with one another, as in starting in a Maze, on a sudden Fright, as *Hamlet* in the Scene betwixt him and his Mother, on the Appearance of his Father's Ghost —

> *Save me, and hover o'er me with your Wings,*
> *You Heavenly Guards!* [165]

This is spoke with Arms and Hands extended, and expressing his Concern, as well as his Eyes, and whole Face. If an Action comes to be used by only one Hand, that must be by the *Right*, it being indecent to make a Gesture with the *Left* alone;[166] except you should say any such thing as,

> *Rather than be guilty of so foul a Deed,*
> *I'd cut this Right Hand off, &c.* [167]

For here the Action must be expressed by the *Left* Hand, because the *Right* is the Member to suffer. When you speak of your self, the *Right* not the *Left* Hand must be apply'd to the Bosom, declaring your own Faculties, and Passions; your Heart, your Soul, or your Conscience, but this Action generally speaking, should be only apply'd or express'd by laying the Hand gently on the Breast, and not by thumping it as some People do. The Gesture

---

Threatening, Intreating, Admiring or Swearing; and in representing almost all the things we speak of in the World; which require so many different Actions of the Hands: So that Quintilian says very well, the other Parts of the Body help him mightily that speaks; but the Hands, as it were, speak themselves' (see Quintilian, 11.3.85–7). Le Faucheur goes on to quote not from Shakespeare but from Martial and Homer.

[164] The source has not been found; it may be an invention of Gildon's.

[165] *Hamlet*, III.iv.96–7. The engraving of this moment by François Boitard that appears in Nicholas Rowe's 1709 edition of Shakespeare (in which Betterton, a friend of Rowe's, is credited with researching Shakespeare's life), shows Hamlet with arms extended: the left one raised, the right reaching forward. Reproduced *inter alia* in Roberts, *Thomas Betterton*, p.17 and on the front cover of this edition.

[166] Cp. Le Faucheur, pp.196–7: 'You must make all your Gestures with the right Hand; and if you ever use the left, let it only be to accompany the other, and never lift it up so high as the right. But to use Action with the left Hand alone, is a thing you must avoid for its indecency'. Cp. Quintilian, 11.3.114.

[167] The quotation has not been found elsewhere, so it is probably of Gildon's own devising.

must pass from the *Left* to the *Right*, and there end with Gentleness and Moderation, at least not stretch to the Extremity of Violence.[168] You must be sure as you begin your Action with what you say, so you must end it when you have done speaking; for Action either before or after Utterance is highly ridiculous. The Movement or Gestures of your Hands must always be agreeable to the Nature of the Words, that you speak; for when you say, *Come in* or *approach*, you must not stretch out your Hand with a repulsive Gesture; nor, on the contrary, when you say, *Stand back*, must your Gesture be inviting; nor must you join your Hands, when you command Separation; nor open them, when your order is *closing*; nor hang them down, when you bid *raise such a thing*, or *Person*; nor lift them up, when you say, *throw them down*. For all these Gestures would be so visibly against Nature, that you would be laugh'd at by all that saw or heard you. By these Instances of faulty Action, you may easily see the right, and gather this Rule, that as much as possible every Gesture you use should express the Nature of the Words you utter, which would sufficiently and beautifully employ your Hands.

It is impossible to have any great Emotion or Gesture of the Body, without the Action of the Hands, to answer the Figures of Discourse, which are made use of in all Poetical, as well as Rhetorical Diction; for Poetry derives its Beauty in that from Rhetoric, as it does its Order and Justness from Grammar; which surprizes me, that some of our modern taking Poets value themselves on that, which is not properly Poetry, but only made use of as an Ornament, and drawn from other Arts and Sciences.[169]

> Thus when *Medea*, says,
> *These Images of* JASON,
> *With my own Hands I'll strangle*, &c.[170]

---

[168] Cp. Le Faucheur, pp.197–8: 'And so when Jesus Christ commands the faithful Servant to cut-off his right Hand, if it offend him; I would represent that Action, if 'twere my Business, with the Gesture of the left, because there's no other to do't; for the right Hand cannot cut-off it self ... The right Hand applies it self very pertinently to the Breast, when the Orator speaks of himself, and declares his own Faculties and Passions; his Heart, his Soul, or his Conscience: I say barely, applies it self; for it must be done only by laying the Hand gently upon it, and not by beating on't, as some People do. You must every where avoid making use of the left Hand alone. But there are some Men naturally left-Handed, and 'tis impossible for them to forbear using the left Hand sometimes, because they have been accustomed to it from their Infancy'. Le Faucheur's passage bears a strong resemblance to another in Bulwer's *Chirologia*, p.89.

[169] Another passage that closely resembles Bulwer's *Chirologia*, p.117. Bulwer ends his passage with a quotation from Book 7 of Ovid's *Metamorphoses*, 132–4, in which Jason takes Medea's hand, promising to marry her.

[170] Presumably suggested by Bulwer's use of *Metamorphoses*, Book 7.

'tis certain the Action ought to be express'd by the Hands to give it all its Force.

In the lifting up the Hands to preserve the Grace, you ought not to raise them above the Eyes; to stretch them farther might disorder and distort the Body; nor must it be very little lower, because that Position gives a Beauty to the Figure: Besides, this Posture being general on some Surprize, Admiration, Abhorrence, &c. which proceeds from the Object, that affects the Eye, Nature by a sort of Mechanic Motion throws the Hands out as Guards to the Eyes on such an Occasion.

You must never let either of your Hands hang down, as if lame or dead; for that is very disagreeable to the Eye, and argues no Passion in the Imagination. In short, your Hands must always be in View of your Eyes, and so corresponding with the Motions of the Head, Eyes and Body, that the Spectator may see their Concurrence, every one in its own way to signify the same thing, which will make a more agreeable, and by Consequence a deeper Impression on their Senses, and their Understanding.[171]

Your Arms you should not stretch out sideways, above half a Foot from the Trunk of your Body, you will otherwise throw your *Gesture* quite out of your Sight, unless you turn your Head also aside to pursue it, which would be very ridiculous.

In Swearing, Attestation, or taking any solemn Vow or Oath, you must raise your Hand; an Exclamation requires the same Action: But so that the *Gesture* may not only answer the *Pronunciation*, or *Utterance*, but both the Nature of the thing, and the Meaning of the Words. In public Speeches, Orations, and Sermons, it is true your Hands ought not to be always in Motion, a Vice which was once call'd the *Babbling of the Hands*; and perhaps, it may reach some Characters, and Speeches in Plays;[172] but I am

---

[171] Cp. Le Faucheur, pp.200–1: 'If you lift-up the Hand, it ought not to be higher than the Eyes, and but very little lower: Whereas there are some that raise it extravagantly up to the Sky, as if they threatened the Stars. The same Proportion ought to be observed in holding the Hand down; and you must have a care also of doing as some People do, when they are Preaching in a Pulpit; who hang down their right Hand now and then as if it were Dead; which is extremely disagreeable to the Eye and dispassionate to the Fancy. 10thly, In fine, your Eyes must always have your Hands within view: They must always be within compass of your Head, and lash-out as little as possible, either over or under, higher or lower than the Eyes: So that they whom you speak to upon an Address, may see your Mouth, your Eyes and your Hands concurring all together, every one in its own way, to signifie the same thing; which will make a deeper and more agreeable impression both upon their Senses and their Understandings'. Cp. Quintilian, 11.3.112–13.

[172] Cp. Le Faucheur, p.201: 'You ought not to stretch-out your Arms, sideways, farther than half a Foot at most from the Trunk of your Body: Or, else you will throw your Gesture quite out of sight, unless you turn your Head aside to see it; which would

of Opinion, that the Hands in Acting ought very seldom to be wholly quiescent, and that if we had the Art of the *Pantomimes*, of expressing things so clearly with their Hands, as to make the Gestures supply Words, the joining these significant Actions to the Words and Passions justly drawn by the Poet, would be no contemptible Grace in the Player, and render the Diversion infinitely more entertaining, than it is at present. For indeed *Action* is the Business of the Stage, and an Error is more pardonable on the right, than the wrong side.

There are some *Actions* or *Gestures*, which you must never make use of in Tragedy, any more than in Pleadings, or Sermons, they being low and fitter for Comedy or Burlesque Entertainments. Thus you must not put your self into the Posture of one *bending a Bow, presenting a Musquet*, or playing on any Musical Instrument, as if you had it in your Hands.[173]

You must never imitate any lewd, obscene or indecent Postures, let your Discourse be on the Debaucheries of the Age, or any thing of that Nature, which the Description of an *Anthony* and *Verres* might require our Discourse of.[174]

When you speak in a *Prosopopœia*, a Figure by which you introduce any (thing or) Person speaking, you must be sure to use such Actions only, as are proper for the Character, that you speak for. I can't remember at present one in Tragedy, but in Comedy *Melantha*, when she speaks for a Man, and answers him in her own Person, may give you some Image of it.[175] But these seldom happen in Plays, and in Orations not very frequently.

---

be very ridiculous. 12thly, You must raise your Hand in Swearing; and God himself, when he speaks to Men with an Oath, whether in his Promises or his Menaces, says in Several Places of his Speech, that he lifts up his Hand: That is to say; he Swears, that he will either bless them in his Mercy or punish them in his Anger. The same thing is to be done upon an Exclamation; so that the Gesture may answer the Pronunciation, and both of 'em may be adjusted to the Nature of the Thing'. Cp. Quintilian, 11.3.84.

[173] Cp. Le Faucheur, p.202: 'There are some Actions which you must never attempt to represent with your Hands, nor put your self in the Posture of those that make use of 'em; as of Fencing, of bending a Bow, of presenting a Musquet, of playing upon an Instrument of Musick, as if you had the Spinette or Virginals under your Fingers, or a Harp in your Hands'.

[174] Cp. Le Faucheur, pp.202–3: 'You must take great care to avoid imitating those Actions which are Base, Filthy and Dishonest, by any Gesture of the Hands or Movement of the Body; as in the making a Description of the Debaucheries and Impurities of a Mark Antony, a Verres, or any other lewd Person'. Gaius Verres, prosecuted by Cicero, was a notoriously acquisitive politician.

[175] I.e. the *précieuse* character in Dryden's *Marriage à la Mode* (see above, n.127), and specifically to the scene where she reads a letter from Rhodophil and replies to it; III.i.254–71 in the edition by Mark S. Auburn (London: Edward Arnold, 1981). Quintilian, 9.2.30, discusses prosopopæia in similar terms.

Thus I have gone through the Art of Action or Gesture, which tho I have directed chiefly for the Stage, and there principally for Tragedy; yet the *Bar* and the *Pulpit* may learn some Lessons from what I have said, that would be of mighty use to make their Pleadings and Sermons of more Force and Grace. But, I think, the *Pulpit* chiefly has need of this Doctrine, because that converses more with the Passions, than the *Bar*; and treats of more sublime Subjects, meritorious of all the Beauty and Solemnity of Action. I am persuaded, that if our Clergy would apply themselves more to this Art, what they preach would be more efficacious, and themselves more respected; nay, have a greater Awe on their Auditors. But then it must be confess'd it is next to impossible for them to attain this Perfection, while that Custom prevails of reading of Sermons, which no Clergy in the World do but those of the Church of *England*. For while they read they are not perfect enough in what they deliver, to give it its proper Action and Emphasis, either in Pronunciation or Gesture. But the *Tatler* has handled this particular very well; and if what he has said will have no Influence upon them, it will be much in vain for me to attempt it.[176]

The *Comedians*, I fear, may take it amiss, that I have had little or no Regard to them in this Discourse. But I must confess, tho I have attempted two or three Comical Parts, which the Indulgence of the Town to an old Fellow has given me some Applause; for yet Tragedy is, and has always been, my Delight.[177] Besides, as some have observ'd, that Comedy is less difficult in the Writing; so I am apt to believe, it is much easier in the Acting; not that a good *Comedian* is to be made by every one that attempts it, but we have had, almost ever since I knew the Stage, more and better *Comedians*, than Tragedians; as we have had better *Comedies*, than *Tragedies* writ in our Language, as the Critics and knowing Judges tell us.[178] But being willing to raise Tragedies from their present Neglect, to the Esteem they had in the most polite Nation, that ever *Europe* knew, I have endeavour'd to contribute my Part towards the improving of the Representation, which has a mighty Influence on the Success and Esteem of any thing of this Nature.

---

[176] In *The Tatler* no.66, 10 September 1709: 'there are none who puzzle me so much as the Clergy of Great-Britain, who are, I believe, the most learned body of men now in the world; and yet this art of speaking, with the proper ornaments of voice and gesture, is wholly neglected among them'.

[177] In fact Betterton had played more than fifty known roles in comedy; as recently as the 1708–9 season he had played Heartwell in Congreve's *The Old Batchelor* and Falstaff in his own adaptation of *Henry the Fourth* (LS2 181), as well as Valentine in the benefit performance of Congreve's *Love for Love* described above, n.9.

[178] Possibly reflecting the views of Thomas Rymer, *The Tragedies of the last age Consider'd* (London: Richard Tonson, 1678). PB 78 lists a copy.

I might here add some Observations on the Errors in the Action of our present Players, but as that would be an invidious Talk, so they may easily be discover'd by those Rules I have laid down of a just Performance. I shall therefore now proceed to the other Duty of a Player, which is the Art of *Speaking*; which, tho much the least considerable, yet according to our modern *Tragedies*, I mean those, which have been best receiv'd, is of most Use. For those Poets have very erroneously apply'd themselves to write more what requires just *Speaking*, than just Acting. And our Players, generally speaking, fall very much short of that Excellence ev'n in this, which they ought to aim or arrive at; but too plainly prove what *Rosencraus* describes— *An Airy of Children, little Yases, they cry out on the Top of the Question, and are most tyrannically clapt for't; these are now the Fashion, and so berattle the common Stages (so they call 'em) that many wearing Rapiers are afraid of Goose-Quills, and dare scarce come thither.*[179] And tho in what I have before quoted from *Hamlet* (in his Account of the Actor's Action and Behaviour) do happily express the Soul and Art of Acting, which *Shakespear* has drawn the compleat Art of Gesture in miniature, in the quoted Speech, yet all the Directions, which he gives, relate (except one Line) wholly to *Speaking*.

Hamlet. "Speak the Speech, I pray you, as I pronounc'd it, trippingly on the Tongue. But if you mouth it, as many of our Players do, I had as lieve the Town-Cryer had spoke my Lines. Nor do not saw the Air too much with your Hand thus, but use all gently; *For in the very Torrent, Tempest, and I may say the Whirlwind of Passion, you must acquire and beget a Temperance, that may give it Smoothness.* Oh! it offends me to the Soul to see a robustous, *perriwig-pated* Fellow tear a Passion to Tatters, to very Rags, to split the Ears of the Groundlings, who for the most part are capable of nothing but inexplicable *dumb Shows* and *Noise*. I could have such a Fellow whipt for o'erdoing Termagant: It out *Herod*'s Herod. Pray you avoid it — Be not too tame neither, but let your own Discretion be your Tutor. Suit the *Action* to the *Word*, the *Word* to the *Action*, with this special Observance, that you o'ertop not the Modesty of *Nature*. For any thing so overdone is from the Purpose of Playing, whose End both at the first and now was and is to hold as 'twere the Mirror up to *Nature*; to show Virtue her own Feature; scorn her own Image, and the very Age and Body of the Time, his Form, and Pressure. Now this over-done, or come tardy of, tho it make the Unskilful laugh, cannot but make the Judicious grieve: *The Censure of which* One, *must in your Allowance o'ersway a* Whole Theatre *of others.* Oh! there be

---

[179] *Hamlet*, II.ii.335–40. The spelling 'Rosencraus' may reflect the Bentley/Herringman edition of *Hamlet* (1695), in which the *Dramatis Personae* gives 'Rosincraus' (the text itself has 'Rosencrantz'). It is unlikely that Betterton misremembered the name; the likelihood is that Gildon did and referred to the 1695 *Dramatis Personae* to refresh his memory.

Players, that I have seen play, and heard others praise, and that highly, (not to speak it prophanely) that neither having the Accent of *Christians*, nor the Gate of *Christian, Pagan, or Norman,* have so *strutted* and *bellow'd, that I have thought some of Nature's Journey-Men had made Men, and not made them well, they imitated Humanity so abominably.*

Player. "I hope we have reformed that indifferently with us, Sir.

Ham. "Oh! reform it altogether. And let those, who play the Clowns, speak no more, than is set down for 'em; for there be of them, who will themselves laugh, to set on some Quantity of barren Spectators to laugh too; tho in the mean time, some necessary Question of the Play be then to be consider'd: that's villanous, and shews a most *pitiful Ambition* in the Fool, that uses it".[180]

If we should consider and weigh these Directions well, I am persuaded they are sufficient to instruct a young Player in all the Beauties of *Utterance*, and to correct all the Errors he might, for want of the Art of Speaking, have incurr'd. By pronouncing it *trippingly on the Tongue*, he means a clear and disembarrass'd Pronunciation, such as is agreeable to Nature and the Subject on which he speaks. His telling the Actor, that he had as lieve the Town-Cryer should speak his Lines, as one that mouth'd them, is very just; for if Noise were an Excellence, I know not who would bear away the Palm, the *Cryer*, or the Player; I'm sure the Town-Cryer would be less faulty, his Business requiring Noise. *Nor do not saw the Air with your Hand thus*, but *use all* GENTLY: This is the only Precept of Action, which is extremely just; and agreeable to the Notions of all, that I have met with on my full Enquiry among my learned Friends, who have read all that has been wrote upon Action, and who reckon *rude* and *boistrous* Gestures among the faulty; Art always directing a moderate and gentle Motion, which *Shakespear* expresses by *use all gently*. Besides this *sawing of the Air*, expresses one, who is very much at a Loss how to dispose of his Hands, but knowing that they should have some Motion, gives them an aukward Violence. The next Observation is extremely masterly — *For in the very* TORRENT, TEMPEST, *and I may say the Whirlwind of Passion, you must acquire and get a Temperance, that may give it* SMOOTHNESS. I remember among many, an Instance in the Madness of *Alexander* the *Great*, in *Lee*'s Play, Mr. *Goodman* always went through it with all the Force the Part requir'd, and yet made not half the Noise, as some who succeeded him;[181] who were sure to bellow it out in such a manner, that

---

[180] *Hamlet*, III.ii.1–42.

[181] Cardell Goodman (c.1649–99) joined the King's Company in 1673. He took over from Charles Hart the role of Alexander in Lee's *The Rival Queens* and was succeeded in it by William Mountfort from around 1686. Upon Mountfort's death in 1692 Betterton took it on. When he resigned it, 'the play for many years after never was able to impose upon the public' (Cibber, p.82). Actors who subsequently played

their Voice would fail them before the End, and led them to such a languid and enervate Hoarseness, as entirely wanted that agreeable *Smoothness*, which *Shakespear* requires, and which is the Perfection of beautiful Speaking;[182] for to have a just Heat, and Loudness, and yet a *Smoothness* is all that can be desir'd. *Oh! it offends me to the Soul*, he goes on — Methinks some of our young Gentlemen, who value themselves for great Players, nay, and Judges too of the Drama, set up for Critics, and who censure and receive or reject Plays, should be asham'd of themselves, when they read this in *Shakepear*, whose Authority they seem so fond of on other Occasions; but it is with them here, as with some Enemies of Reason on other Occasions, who are against Reason, when Reason is against them, tho none so clamorous for it at other Times, that is, they are fonder of Error than Truth, when they can be more remarkable, and clapt by the Million, by continuing in their Error, than by quitting it — But that is a *pitiful Ambition* indeed, and unworthy a Master of any Art. *Tully* likens these Bellowers to Cripples, that fly to Noise to cover their Ignorance, as the other to a Horse to help their Lameness, and with this Noise they triumph with the Ignorant;[183] but *Homer* never reckon'd *Stentor* among his fine Speakers.[184] So that tho a strong and firm Voice be a very good Ingredient in a Speaker, yet he ought to have a peculiar Care not to offend a nice Ear, by putting it upon the stretch too much. For this Reason when *Carneades* (not yet of so great Authority among the Philosophers) was declaiming in the Schools, the Master lent him word to moderate his Voice a little; but on his requiring a Pitch from him, the Master reply'd, let his Voice be your Tone, with whom you talk. So that the Loudness or Lowness of the Voice is to be modell'd according to the Place of Speaking, and the Audience; that it be not too low, or too loud.[185] An equal Care ought to be taken of the Action, that it be not

---

the role less successfully were John Verbruggen and George Powell; Aston claimed that Powell 'maintained not the dignity of a king but out-Heroded Herod ... while Betterton kept his passion under and showed it most' (II.301).

[182] Cp. Le Faucheur, pp.68–9: 'In time, you must endeavour to give your Voyce such a Smoothness, that the Turns, the Tones and the Soft measures of it may please the Ear of your Auditor, though he understand nothing at all either of your Language or of the Subject of your Discourse'. Cp. Quintilian, 11.3.65.

[183] Cp. Le Faucheur, p.81: 'For to strain it up always to such an extraordinary height, would not be to Preach or to Plead, but to make a noise, like those loud-tongued Orators in the time of Tully, whom he compares to Cripples that got a Horse-back because they could not walk a foot: They made a bawling because they knew not how to Speak'.

[184] In Homer's *Iliad*, 5.785–6, Stentor is said to have a voice as loud as fifty men. PB 19 lists a copy of Ogilby's folio edition of the *Iliad* and the *Odyssey*.

[185] Carneades of Cyrene (c.214–129 BC), philosopher and founder of the Third Academy; his writings were preserved in those of his pupil, Clitomachus of Carthage (c.187–110 BC).

rude and desultory, nor beyond Measure active; *Quintus Haterius* had a Servant always behind him, when he spoke in Public, who by touching his Garment, when the Ardour of Discourse had made him fly out, recall'd him to the just Medium of Action.[186] The Ancients indeed (if my Authors mislead me not) were extremely against that insolent tossing of the Body about, when there was no Occasion.[187] *Sextus Titius* was a very sharp and loquacious Man, but was so dissolute and enervate in his Action and Gestures, that a sort of Dance arose out of his Gesticulation, which was call'd by his Name.[188] Nor was *Manlius Sura*, whom when *Domitius Afer* had seen whilst he was Acting or Speaking, running up and down, dancing, tossing his Hands about, throwing down his Gown now, and then gathering it up again, he said, this Man does not act or use Gestures, but miserably aims at something he does not understand.[189] Some of the Ancients, not content with this Agitation of the Body, that they like the Antisophist of *Virginius*, travell'd a many Miles in their Declamations; which made *Cassius Severus* require some Goal, or Bound to be set them, as in Races, beyond which their Excursions should not reach.[190] Some strike their Chins, some their Thighs, and some their Foreheads in Trifles, and others perpetually buffet the Pulpit, or Place of Action; some proceed so far, as to pull off their Hair. These Vices of Action are not fit for any one, much less for grave People, and on grave Occasions. For tho the Passions are very beautiful in their proper *Gestures*, yet they ought never to be so extravagantly immoderate, as to transport the Speaker out of himself. Tho this has a peculiar Regard to the Bar and the Pulpit, yet has it an equal Authority over the Stage, allowing only for the greater Latitude, which is proper to that Place, which would be shocking in the other. But then *Shakespear* would not have his *Player* too tame neither, for that indeed is an Error in the other Extreme; it enervates the Discourse, and makes the whole Passion languish, which ought to warm you with a just and comfortable Heat, and enlivening Fire.[191] Altho Action be of great Use and Force in *Speaking*, Sedateness being to be

---

[186]   Haterius Quintus (5 BC–26 AD), Roman orator noted for improvising his speeches.

[187]   Cp. Le Faucheur, pp.178–9: 'This fickle Agitation would be as indecent as the Gesture of Curion, whom Junius compared to a Man at Sea in a Cock-boat, for tossing his Body about continually, some-times to the right and sometimes to the left, with the greatest inconstancy imaginable'.

[188]   Probably a reference to Gaius Titius, orator and dramatist of the second century BC, cited, like the others in this passage, by Cicero in his *Letters to Brutus*, which in Gildon's day was part of *De Officiis*.

[189]   The antics of Manlius Sura are recorded in Quintilian, 11.3.124.

[190]   A rephrasing of Le Faucheur, pp.205–6.

[191]   Terms drawn from Galenic medicine, for example in *Galen's art of physick*, trans. Nicholas Culpeper (London: Peter Cole, 1652).

express'd in some things, in others *Severity*, and Vehemence, yet never Madness in any thing, which happens to those, who wanton in a sort of tragical and howling Voice upon every Trifle. Some, on the contrary, are viciously opposite to these, who act so tamely and so coldly, that when they ought to be angry, to thunder and lighten, as one may say, they are no fuller of Heat, than a wet Hen, as the Saying is;[192] and turn over a *Thyestean* Scene in the calm Tone of a mere Reader;[193] which made *Cicero* say to *Callidius*, when he sedately told of his being like to be poison'd, *If you did not feign all this Story, could you deliver it in this manner?* gathering from his Action, that he spoke not feelingly enough for a Reality.[194] Such are fitter to comfort the Sick, than to *speak* in public. In this much is left to the Nature of the Subject, and for this Reason *Shakespear* leaves it to his Discretion. Yet notwithstanding he leaves his Discretion to be his Guide, he soon directs that Guide, by bidding him *suit the Action to the* WORDS, *and the Words to the* ACTION; and not *to overtop* the Modesty of, that is, to go beyond *Nature*, which is to be the Rule of just Acting. But then the same Difficulty will arise here as in Writing, where all sides agree, that Nature is the sovereign Guide and Scope; but then they are not so agreed in what *Nature* is: The Skilful lay down those Signs, Marks, and Lineaments of *Nature*, that you may know when she is truly drawn, when not; the Unskilful, which is the greater and more noisy part, leave it so at large, that it amounts to no more, than every one's Fancy, which would make Contradictions Nature; for what pleases one, he calls Nature; what pleases another, that he calls Nature; and I heard once a Man of the Stage, in great Vogue for I know not what off the Stage, say *Nonsense* was natural, when Nature has been urg'd as the Rule of good Writing; whether he meant it a *Witticism* or not, I never thought it worth while to examine, being sensible, that NONSENSE is very natural to some, ev'n tho they set up for, and are ev'n admir'd by a Set of People for their Wit.[195]

I instance this, to show that there seems a Necessity of some Marks, or Rules to fix the Standard of what is *Natural*, and what not, else it is a loose vague Word of no manner of Use or Authority. But this is what *Shakespear* supposes our Actor to know, and therefore he proceeds to tell him what the

---

[192] Not sufficiently proverbial to feature in either Tilley or Wilson, but OED (Phrase 3a and 3b) suggests a synonym for anger.

[193] John Crowne's *Thyestes* was probably performed by the King's Company in March 1680 (LS1 285–6). The play is an orgy of violence and rhetorical excess. A translation of Seneca's play had been published in 1674, with the addition of a burlesque *Mock-Thyestes*.

[194] Anecdote drawn from Le Faucheur, p.116.

[195] Possibly a reference to Cibber, who would go on to defend his own follies (*Apology*, p.28).

End of a Player was and is, *viz. to hold as it were the Mirrour up to Nature, to shew Virtue her own Feature: scorn her own Image, and the very Age and Body of the Time, his Form and Pressure.*[196] To attain a just Praise in which, besides the Knowledge of them, the Player must neither over or under-act his Part. As I have already laid down such Observations, as may be of great Use to the *Actor* in his Acting and Gesture, so I shall now set down some, which will give an Insight into the Art of *Speaking*, or regulating and modelling the Voice in such a manner, as may render the Utterance pleasing to the Ear.

Before I come to the Directions for the Beauties of Speaking, I think it will not be amiss to insert here a Paper given me by a Friend, of the several natural Defects and Vices of a Voice, taken from the 26th Chapter of the Second Book of *Julius Pollux*'s *Onomastics*, which he makes about twenty in number.[197]

The first he calls *Black*, drawing the Metaphor from the Eyes to the Ears. For as Black strikes the Eyes more dully, so does this sort of Voice penetrate the Ears with greater Difficulty, and carries with it less of the Pleasant, but something on the contrary of the *dismal* and *horrid*.

Next the *dusky* or *brown*, differs from the Black only, by being something less obscure, but is yet very far from that Brightness of a pure Tone of Voice.

Rough or *unpleasant*, such as your very strong Voices generally are, with which the pleasing Sweetness is seldom mingled; and *Seneca* puts it down for a wonder, that *Cassius Severus* retain'd a Sweetness in his Voice, tho it was extremely strong and robust;[198] for it seldom happens, that the same Voice is both sweet and solid.

The opposite to this he calls *small* or *weak*, such is their Voice, who seem rather to pip like a young Chicken, than to speak like humane kind.

Strait or *slender*, which is slenderly melted thro' the narrow Channel of the Throat, and fills not the Ears of the Hearers.

Dusucous, that which is not heard without Difficulty, or that which is very importunately troublesome to the Ears.[199]

---

[196] *Hamlet*, III.ii.20–3.
[197] Julius Pollux, Greek scholar and rhetorician of Egyptian origin who flourished in the second century AD, and author of *Onomasticon*. No copy is recorded in PB and there does not appear to have been an English translation until 1775, so this passage cannot be attributed to Betterton, unless his 'friend' translated it.
[198] Adapted from Le Faucher, pp.85–6, but with 'Tully' replaced by 'Cassius Severus'. No copy of Seneca's works is recorded in PB.
[199] The term does not appear anywhere else. It may be a printer's error for 'fuscous', meaning cloudy or dull.

The *confus'd*, which is not distinguish'd with full articulate Sounds.

The *jarring*, untuneable, absonous, and unharmonious.

Unmelodious, neglected, without Beauty or Grace.

Rude, uncouth, untractable, unmanageable, like unbroken Colts.

Unpersuasive, that is not adapted to Persuasion, such as theirs, who have a perpetual Identity of Tone in Discourse; a *Monotony*.[201]

Rigid, that which with Difficulty admits any Variation.

Hard or *harsh*, which offends the Ears with a sort of bouncing and cracking Noise.

Desultory or *broken*, which is when the Discourse leaps or bounds, as it were with unequal Distances and Sounds, confusedly mixing short and long, flat and sharp, high and low, so that the Discourse goes lamely on with the Inequality of all these together; the same is call'd the *fickle* or *inconstant*.

The *austere*, *sour* or *dismal*, which strikes the Ears with an unpleasant Sound, something like that of creaking Wheels.

The *infirm* or *feeble*, by which the weak and broken Breath is spread and dispers'd into a hoarse Smallness.

Brazen, which like the vehement Clinking of Brass is perpetually assaulting our Ears.

The *sharp* or *acute*, which strikes and penetrates the Ears with a shriller Sound, than it ought. For the most acute Sounds are not the most fit for Speaking in Public; which is made too thin, too cutting, and of too great a Clearness.

The contrary Virtues enumerated by the same Author are these.

The *high*, which being sent from good Lungs and Chest perfectly fills the Ears.

The *lofty*, that which is not only more fully heard, but by its own Firmness becomes durable.

The *clear*, that sounds sprightly, and is not blurr'd with any Defects.

The *smooth, spreading, explicit*.

The *grave, bass*, or *full*, such as generally is the Voice of the most manly and robust Singers, which if mingled with Sweetness is the most valuable

---

[200] Actually taken from Cicero, Oration 20 in *The Orations of Marcus Tullius Cicero*, trans. Charles Duke Yonge, 4 vols (London: H.G. Bohn, 1851), I.172. Cicero refers to the city of Aspendus, home to a harpist who could 'sing everything within himself' and make others believe he was a statue. 'Subsurd' is probably a botched attempt at 'surdus', Latin for 'deaf'.

[201] A quality Cibber associated with his and Betterton's colleague Barton Booth (Cibber, pp.92 and 362).

Voice, that is; but when it wants this Sweetness, it scatters and spreads out into wild and desolate Enormity.

The *candid* and *pure*, which affects the Ears, as White does the Eyes, and is therefore contrary to the Vice of Voice call'd the *black*.

The *pure* and *simple*, and as it were refin'd from all Vices and Defects.

The *sweet*, which delights with the Flower, as I may say, of a good Grace.

The *alluring*, that abounds in delicate Modulating, and harmonious Warblings.

The *exquisite*, polish'd and rich.

The *round* and *simple*, and most adapted to Persuasion.

The *tractable* or *Voice at Command*, which easily rises from the lowest Note to the highest, and with as much Ease falls from the highest to the lowest, and every where divides it self into all the pleasing Variety of Notes.

The *flexible*, that is wholly without Roughness, Stiffness, that obeys the Modulation, as Wax does the Fingers.

The *voluble* or swift, such as that of the best Orators, in the closest and hottest of the Argument.

The *delicious*, beautiful in a kind of graceful Softness.

The *sounding* or *canorous*,[202] fit to sing with Musical Instruments.

The *full*, perspicuous, and easy to be heard.

The *splendid*, and *shining* with an agreeable Softness.

These are the several sorts, or kinds of Voices, and their Virtues, which proceed merely from Nature, which yet receive from Art their Brightness, Improvement, and Perfection.

As these are the Virtues and Vices of the Voice, so we shall now proceed to the Beauties and Defects of *Pronunciation*: The chief Excellencies of which are agreed by the Masters of the Art to be *Purity, Perspicuity, Ornament*, and *Hability* or *Aptitude*.[203]

Purity is, as we may say, a certain Healthfulness of Voice, which has in it nothing vicious; which is obstructed by the Voice we have call'd *subsurd* or deafish, rude, noisy, hard, rigid, inconstant or uncertain, thick or gross; or by one, that is small, strait, empty, infirm, soft, or effeminate. On the contrary, a Delivery, which is easy, open, pleasant, genteel; and in which nothing sounds clownish or foreign, is a great Help to *Pronunciation*, as *Quintilian* justly observes.[204] *Cicero*, with equal Justice, and for the same Reason, in his Book *de Oratore*, condemns a Voice, that is soft, womanish, untuneable, absurd, ungenteel and rustical.[205] And he directs his Speaker to

---

[202] OED defines 'canorous' as 'singing, melodious, musical; resonant, ringing'.

[203] What follows is paraphrased from Quintilian's *Institutes* and Cicero's *Orations*, and acknowledged as such.

[204] Book 1.11 of Quintilian concerns the teaching of correct pronunciation.

[205] A re-working of Cicero, *Orations*, pp.388 and 397.

a *Delivery*, that is neither harsh, nor disorderly, nor clownish, nor gaping, but close, equal, or of the same Tenor, and smooth. To these we must add the Tone and Accent, by which Men are known. This Virtue is obtain'd by Nature and Use, which is of very great Consequence in these Affairs; for which Reason Boys should inure themselves to a right Pronunciation from the Beginning; since we find, that in learning foreign Tongues, those seldom reach the Purity of them, who apply not themselves to them till in Years.

The PERSPICUITY, and Light of *Pronunciation* consists of a certain articulate Expression of all the Syllables, and their proper Points and Stops; of which these are the Precepts of *Quintilian*.[206]

The *Pronunciation* will be *perspicuous* and *clear*, first if the whole Words are entirely sounded, part of which is sometimes devoured, part neglected by most, who by indulging and dwelling too much on the Sound of the foregoing Syllables, express not sufficiently the last: But as the making Words have a plain Pronunciation is necessary, so is it very troublesome and odious to run it to a Computation and Enumeration of every Letter, and we must observe nicely in what Place the Discourse is to be sustain'd, and as it were suspended. And this, as is plain, is to be attain'd by Art.

The ORNAMENT is the cultivating and Clearness of the Voice; and to this a great Help is naturally deriv'd from a Voice, that is easy, great, happy, flexible, firm, sweet, durable, clear, pure, penetrating, high, and adorn'd indeed with all those Virtues, we have already enumerated out of *Julius Pollux*. To this we must add, the beautiful Composition of the whole Instrument or Body, as the Firmness of the Chest and Lungs, Goodness of Breath, and that not easily giving way to, or falling under Labour and Fatigue.

HABILITY or APTITUDE is a pleasing Variety of *Pronunciation*, according to the Diversity of the Subject, and in a constant Equality. For as the best Style is perpetually equal or consistent with it self, and yet is according to the Subject now grave, now florid, and now gently abated; so is a valuable Utterance always the same, and never deviating from its Excellence, yet derives all its Beauty and Glory from those agreeable Varieties, which according to the Nature of the Things it delivers, it admits. It is impossible to express how great and charming the Grace of the Art of varying the Voice, how much it enlivens the Hearers, and refreshes the Speaker himself by an agreeable Change of his Labour. On the contrary, a *Monotony*, or perpetually Speaking in the same unvary'd Tone, quite destroys the Speaker, and dispirits the Auditors, making them languish under a tiresome Oscitation.[207] As we cannot always stand, or sit, or walk, but relieve our selves by

---

[206] The following passage is paraphrased from Quintilian, 11.3.33–57.
[207] I.e. drowsiness.

an alternate Use of them, so in *Pronunciation*, we love a grateful Variation of the Voice directed by a just Equality.

The Voice therefore, according to *Quintilian*, in *Joy* should be full, simple, pleasant, and flowing;[208] in Dispute, extended with all its just Force and Nerves; in *Anger*, vehement and sharp, or acute, close, compact, mixt with frequent Respirations; but more slow in raising *Envy*, since few but Inferiours have Recourse to this.

In Insinuations, Confessions, Atonements and the like, the Voice must be gentle and temperate; when you persuade, admonish, promise, or Comfort it ought to be grave; and contracted in Fear, and Bashfulness and Modesty; strong in Exhortations, in Disputations round, fine and smooth; in Pity and Compassion, turning dolefully, and as it were on purpose more obscure. In Expositions and Discourses, direct; and in a Tone, that is a Medium betwixt an acute and grave. It is rais'd with our Passions, and falls again with them, being higher or lower according to either. Whoever can do all this has attain'd the highest Perfection of *Pronunciation*.[209]

Cicero, in his 3d Book *de Oratore*, divides Pronunciation into many kinds;[210] into *gentle* and *fierce*; contracted and diffus'd; with a continu'd Breath, and with an Intermission of the same; *broken* or *cut*; with a varying or direct Sound; slender and *great*. These, says he, are expos'd for Colours to the Actor, as to the Painter to draw his Variations.

Anger loves an acute Sound, vehement, and full of Respirations.

Commiseration or *Pity*, one that is flexible, full, interrupted, and doleful.

Fear, one low, not without Hesitation, and abject.

Force and *Power*, one vehement, earnest, imminent, but carry'd on with a certain Gravity.

Pleasure, one effusive, gentle, tender, joyful, and remiss.

Grief and *Trouble*, one grave, and oppress'd with every draining.[211]

---

[208] Quintilian, 11.3.40.

[209] Le Faucheur, pp.99–120, expands upon Quintilian's points.

[210] I.e. *De Oratore* III.58.

[211] Cp. Le Faucheur, p.99: 'If your Speech proceeds from a violent Passion, it produces a violent Pronunciation; if it comes from a Peaceable and Gentle Thought, the pronunciation again is as Peaceable, Gentle and Calm: So that the Orator would do well to adjust every Tone and Accent of his Voyce to each Passion that afflicts or overjoys him, which he would raise in others to a degree of Sympathy. He will shew his Love best by a Soft, a Gay and a Charming Voyce; and his Hatred, on the contrary, by a Sharp, Sullen and Severe one. He'll discover his Joy well with a Full, Flowing and Brisk Voyce; and his Grief, on the other side, with a dull, Languishing and Sad Moan; not without breaking-off abruptly sometimes, with a Sob; and fetching-up a Sigh or a Groan from the heart. His Fear will be best demonstrated by a Trembling and Stammering Voyce, somewhat inclining to uncertainty and apprehension. His Confidence, on the contrary, will be easily discover'd by a Loud and a Strong Voyce,

Thus far my Paper, in which, I think, is contain'd the Art of Speaking beautifully on all Occasions; for there is nothing, that an Actor can talk of on the Stage, whether in Passion, or out of Passion, a Pleader at the Bar, or the Divine in the Pulpit, but what must fall under some of these Heads. I therefore recommend to the Study of my *Speaker* a perfect Application to what is here deliver'd. Yet, as this may not appear so obvious to many, who may desire to understand this Art, and may be capable of arriving at some Perfection in it; I shall proceed to give my Learner some more plain Lights, and which may serve, as a thorough Paraphrase and Explanation of what I have here deliver'd.

The first Consideration in the Art of Speaking, is to satisfy the Ear, which conveys all Arts and Sciences to us, and is the natural judge of the Voice. The Speaker therefore ought to be heard and understood with Ease and Pleasure, to which a Voice clear, sweet and strong, is necessary to be heard all over the Audience. Such a Voice as *Quintilian* gives *Trachallus*, would be very useful, who pleading a Cause in one of the four Courts in the *Julian Forum*, was not only heard in that but in all the rest, so well to be understood, and merit Applause; but tho every Man cannot obtain a Voice like this, yet if he cannot fill the Place, where he speaks, he's not fit to speak.[212]

Some Men have such a Voice naturally, others attain it by the Improvement of Art and Exercise. As has been said of *Demosthenes*, who was as defective in Speaking as in Action and Gesture: He had naturally a weak Voice, and Impediment in his Speech, and a short Breath; and venturing withal these Disqualifications to speak in public twice, he was hiss'd both Times. But by his Industry and Application, he removed all these Obstructions. He daily in his under-ground Apartment exercis'd himself, by speaking what he had read aloud, so that his Organs gradually open'd, and his Voice sensibly clearing, grew every Day stronger, than the former. His Tongue was so gross and clumsy, that he mumbled his Words, nor could utter them clear and plain; nay, he could not pronounce an (*R*) at all; he was so short winded, that he could not speak many Words together without taking his Breath, which was but a sort of broken-winded Pronunciation; and these Difficulties produc'd a wonderful Difficulty, which was the surmounting the great Noise of a Publick Assembly.[213]

---

always keeping-up to a decent Boldness and a daring Constancy. And he cannot give his Hearers to understand his Anger better than by a sharp, impetuous and violent Voyce; by taking his Breath often, and speaking short upon the Passion'. Cp. Quintilian, 11.3.62–4.

[212] Cp. Le Faucheur, p.4, as cited above, p.66 n.77.

[213] Cp. Le Faucheur, p.39: 'For the first and second time Demosthenes pleaded at Athens in his natural way of speaking, without observing any rule of the Voyce, he was hissed for his bad Delivery, and the remarkable vices of his Pronunciation; but

First, he cur'd the Grossness of his Tongue, by putting Pebble-stones in his Mouth, whilst he spoke for some time; he cur'd himself of his short Breath, by running up Hills, and repeating upright as he went some Verses, or Sentences of Speeches, which he had by Heart; which strengthen'd his Lungs, and made him long-winded: The Noise of Public Assemblies he conquer'd by Speaking with his utmost Contention of Voice in his Orations to the Roaring of the Sea, when loudest, and so became the most compleat Speaker of his Age.[214]

'Tis true *Demosthenes* overcame these Difficulties, or at least Historians make us believe so; but this should be no Reason for admitting any one into a Play-house, who lies under such Defects, as this great Orator, by unspeakable Diligence, remov'd. For if a Man's Voice be good for nothing, by Reason of any Indisposition of the Organs, as the Tongue, Throat, Breast, or Lungs; if he have any considerable Lisping, Hesitation, or Stammering, he is not proper for the Stage, the Pulpit, or the Bar.

But I have given this Instance of *Demosthenes*, for the Sake of some, who may be on the Stage, and furnish'd with an admirable Genius, yet for Want of Breath, or by the Feebleness of their Voice, cannot exert their other beautiful Qualities. Let them always speak out in their private Study, and in *Rehearsals*; it is an exercise, which has been judg'd beneficial to the Health, provided, that you do not overstrain your Voice. Thus we find in *Plutarch*, (for I read all the Ancients I can meet with in French or English)[215] whilst he advises other bodily Exercises for the Health of others, to those, who speak in *Public*, be it on the Stage, or elsewhere, he prescribes Discoursing, or making Speeches often, or Reading with as exalted a Voice, as Nature will

---

after he had been trained up to it a while under Masters of the Art, he was heard with universal applause and Humm'd to admiration'. Le Faucheur drew on Cicero's account of Demosthenes in *De Oratore,* 1.61.

[214] Cp. Le Faucheur, p.57: 'First, he cured the grossness of his Tongue by putting Pebble-stones in his Mouth that he pick't-up out of the purling Streams; which was a very troublesome experiment to him, and hindered his Speech mightily at first; but afterwards, when he came to practice without Pebbles in his Mouth, he found the good effects of it in the Liberty of his Tongue and the Facility of Speaking. He brake himself of breathing-short, in the next place, by running up-hill and repeating over certain Verses of some Sentences of his Harangues that he had by Heart, bolt upright as he went; which strengthened his Lungs and made him long-winded. And last of all, he conquer'd the clamour of Assemblies, by going now and then to the Sea-shore, when it was most troubled, boisterous, and roaring at Full-Sea; saying off some or other of his Orations there aloud, and striving to raise his Voyce above the murmuring noise of the Waves'. Cp. Quintilian, 11.3.54.

[215] Gildon claims to be representing Betterton's voice here; the actor did own a 1579 Folio copy of Thomas North's translation of Plutarch's *Lives* (PB 21) as well as the 1683 translation 'by several hands' (PB 96).

well bear; and he says, it is his Opinion, that this Exercise is more healthy, and useful for this End, than all others; since while the other Motions set only the Limbs at work, and stir the external Members, the Voice employs a nobler part of the Body, and strengthens the Lungs, from which it receives its Breath; it augments the natural Heat, thins the Blood, cleanses the Veins, opens all the Arteries, prevents every Obstruction, and hinders the gross Humours from thickening into Distempers.[216]

Let every Syllable have its distinct and full Sound and Proportion, when you use this Exercise, and then you need not fear muffling your Words, or Stammering. But besides this Vice of Utterance, you must avoid a broad way of speaking with your Mouth wide open, and of bellowing out a great Sound, but so confus'd and inarticulate, that tho you may be heard a great way off, yet the Sound will convey no more to the Understanding, than the Roaring of a Bull, or any other Beast. This proceeds from an Affectation, and a false Opinion, that this enormous Loudness gives a Majesty and Force to what they say; whereas it robs it of its Articulation, which is the very Being of Speech, and hinders its being understood, which is the very End of Speaking.[217]

There are, in short, two things to make the Speaker heard and understood without Difficulty; first, a very distinct and articulate Voice, and next a very strong and vigorous Pronunciation. The first is the most important;

[216] Cp. Le Faucheur, p.59: 'And therefore Plutarch very well recommends several Exercices of Body to other People, that may conduce to the Health as well as divert; but he appoints no other for those Persons that speak upon publick occasions, than what their Profession obliges them to in course: That is, to be often discoursing and haranguing, or at least reading out a loud and raising up the Voyce as High as Nature will well bear. An Exercice, in his Opinion, far more wholesome and useful for this purpose than all others; for says he, while other motions only set the Limbs at work and stir the External Members of a Man, the Voyce exercises a Nobler Part of the Body and strengthens the Lungs that give it breath. It augments the natural Heat, thins the Blood, cleanses the Veins, opens all the Arteries, prevents every obstruction, and keeps the gross Humours from thickening into a mischief'.

[217] Cp. Le Faucheur, pp.62–3: 'There are some persons again that are affected with another vice, which the Greek Rhetoricians call Plateasm: That is to say; a Broad way of Speaking with the mouth wide open, and of bellowing out a great sound, but nothing so confused and inarticulate as the noise of it: Insomuch that a Man may hear them a great way off with ease, but understand no more of their Bawling than of the Bruit of Wild Beasts. Now this is not Nature's Fault, but a Vice of meer Affectation and Conceit. For these noisy People affect to speak open-mouth, and phancy that this thundering Clatt of theirs gives Power and Majesty to their Speech: But, on the contrary, 'tis this deprives it of it's greatest Virtue and Perfection, which is to be well Heard every word on't, and well understood in all it's Parts. Besides that it robs it of it's very Being a Speech too; for there's not a Word in it, but only an Inarticulate Huddle of Sound and Voyce'.

for an indifferent Voice, with a distinct Pronunciation, shall be far more easily understood, than one, that is stronger and more audible, but which does not articulate the Words so well.[218]

But it is not sufficient to be heard without Difficulty, but it ought to be the Object of your Endeavours to be heard with Pleasure and Satisfaction. To this End you must consider, whether your Voice have any of the fore-mention'd Vices or Defects, whether it be harsh, hoarse, or obsequious, and enquire into the Cause, whether it be from Nature, or an ill Habit; for 'tis your Business to render your Voice as sweet, soft, and agreeable to the Ear, as you possibly can. If the Defect proceeds from only an *ill Habit*, you ought to practice a contrary manner, if you would make your self fit for this Affair.[219] But if it proceed from Nature, in the Defect of any, or all of the Organs of the Body employed in it, tho we have the Examples of *Cicero* and *Demosthenes* of Success, yet at this time, and in this Employ, I think, it is scarce worth the while to aim, by a great deal of uncertain Labour, at the correcting Nature, when there are other Employments fitter for you.

Next to the Fineness of the Tone, the Variation of it is what will make the Auditors pleas'd and delighted with what they hear; you ought therefore to employ much Care and Time in learning the Art of varying the Voice, according to the Diversity of the Subjects, of the Passions you would express or excite, stronger or weaker, higher or lower, as will be most agreeable to what you say.[220]

---

[218] Cp. Le Faucheur, pp.64–5: 'First, there are two things requisite to qualifie a Man for this Work: That is, a very Distinct and Articulate Voyce, and a very Strong and Vigorous Pronunciation; but the former is the more important and necessary of the Two. For a Man that has only an indifferent Voyce, if his Pronunciation be but Distinct, he shall be understood with far more ease than another that has a stronger and more Audible Faculty of Speaking, but does not articulate his words so well'.

[219] Cp. Le Faucheur, p.67: 'It is not enough for the Orator to be Heard only without difficulty and pain, but he must endeavour to be Heard also, if possible, with Pleasure and Delight. And therefore you must make it your main business, in the first place, to render your Voyce as Sweet and Soft, and Agreeable to the Ear as you can: So that if you be naturally inclined to any thing either of a Harsh, Hoarse, or Obstreperous Voyce, you must enquire into the cause on't for cure. And if you find it comes only from an ill Habit you have got, or so; you ought to take up a resolution of unpractising it as soon as possible, and of running up a Counter-Custom against it, of better Service and Satisfaction to the Publick'.

[220] Cp. Le Faucheur, p.71: 'The only thing, after this, I can recommend to your care and your time, is to put your self upon varying your Voyce according to the diversity of the Subjects you are to set forth, of the Passions you would either express your self, or excite in others, and of the several parts of your Speech; according to the variety of Words, Stronger or Weaker, Higher or Lower, as will best serve your Turn and answer their quality. For as a Scraping Fiddler that should harp always upon one String, would be Ridiculous; and his Musick Intolerable: So there is nothing can

The Life of Mr Thomas Betterton

Tho I have already touch'd on this Point both in my Remarks on what I quoted from *Shakespear* about Speaking, and in the Paper inserted on the Virtues of *Pronunciation*, yet I cannot dismiss this Subject without some farther Reflections, because we have had some Actors of Figure, who have an admirable Tone of Voice, the Beauty of which they have perverted into a Deformity, by keeping always in the very same Identity of Sound, in the very same Key, nay, the individual Note;[221] for as in Music, so in Speaking, 'tis the Variety, which makes the Harmony; and as for a Fiddler or Lutinist, or any other Performer in Music, to strike always the same String and Note, would be so far from tolerable Music, that it would be ridiculously insufferable and dull, so can nothing grate the Ear so much, or give the Auditors a greater Disgust, as a Voice still in the same Tone, without Division or Variety.[222]

'Tis true, this Vice is too general among most Speakers, but not in the last Degree. Few arrive to the true Art of varying the Voice with that Beauty and Harmony, which is in Nature, because they do not study what the Words, Subject, and Passion to be express'd properly require. A good Voice, indeed, tho ill manag'd, may fill the Ear agreeably, but it would be infinitely more pleasing, if they knew how to give it the just Turns, Risings, Fallings, and all other Variations suitable to the Subjects and Passions. But those very fine Voices, which in spight of their being ill govern'd please, are very uncommon. But this Vice renders such Voices, as are ordinarily met with, to the last Degree disagreeable.

But this *stiff Uniformity of Voice* is not only displeasing to the Ear, but disappoints the Effect of the Discourse on the Hearers; first, by an equal way of Speaking, when the Pronunciation has every where, in every Word and every Syllable the same Sound, it must inevitably render all Parts of the Speech equal, and so put them on a very unjust Level. So that the Power of the Reasoning Part, the Lustre and Ornament in the Figures, the Heart, Warmth, and Vigor of the passionate part being express'd all in the same Tone, is flat and insipid, and lost in a supine, or at least immusical

---

grate the Ear of your Auditors so much, and give them so great a disgust as a Voyce still in the same Key, to the Tune of Hum-Drum, without either Division or Variety'. The ideas are largely drawn from Cicero, *De Oratore*, III.51 but see also Quintilian, 11.3.42.

[221] Quintilian, 11.3.57, deplored the 'singing tone'. There may also be a reference to Barton Booth, whose style Cibber found 'too grave' (p.362). Booth played the Ghost to Betterton's Hamlet and is said to have found the experience overwhelming; see Thomas Davies, *Dramatic Miscellanies*, 3 vols (London: Thomas Davies, 1783–4), III.32. He became a leading actor during the 1705/6 season.

[222] Cp. Le Faucheur, p.71: 'For as a Scraping Fiddler that should harp always upon one String, would be Ridiculous; and his Musick Intolerable: So there is nothing can grate the Ear of your Auditors so much, and give them so great a disgust as a Voyce still in the same Key, to the Tune of Hum-Drum, without either Division or Variety'.

Pronunciation.[223] So that, in short, that which ought to strike and stir up the Affections, because 'tis spoken all alike, without any Distinction or Variety, moves them not at all. Next there is no greater Opiate in Speaking, nothing so dull and heavy, and fit to lull us asleep, as a whole Discourse turning still on the same *Note* and *Tone*;[224] and indeed it savours of the Cant, which was formerly in some of the Dissenter's Pulpits, which they have of late very much reform'd in their young Men.

I believe a great deal of this is owing to our erroneous way of Education, where the School-Mistresses first, and afterwards the Masters, teach or suffer the Boys to cant out their Lessons in one unvary'd Tone for so many Years, which grows up with us, and is not overcome at last without Application; tho Nature and Reason, if we would consult them, would guide us into a more pleasing and excellent Road.[225]

Nature tells us, that in Mourning, in Melancholly, in Grief, we must and do express our selves in another sort of Tone and Voice, than in Mirth, in Joy, in Gladness: Otherwise in Reproof of Crimes, etc. than in Comforting the Afflicted: Otherwise when we upbraid a Man with his Faults, than when

---

[223] 'Immusical' is first recorded by OED in 1626.

[224] Cp. Le Faucheur, pp.72–3: 'I say that this stiff uniformity of the Voyce is not only unpleasant to the Ear, but prejudices the Discourse it self extremely too, and disappoints the effect it should have upon the Hearers, for two reasons. The one is, that an equal way of Speaking, when the Pronunciation is all of a piece and every where upon the same Sound, renders all the Parts of the Speech equal too upon a very unjust level; for it takes away all power from that which has the greatest strength of Argument in the reasoning part, and all Lustre from that which has the greatest splendour of ornament in the figurative part of a Discourse, throughout the whole Work: So that, in short, that which ought to strike the Passions most, moves them not at all in effect, because it is spoken all alike so, and flabbered over without any distinction or variety. The other, that there is nothing lulls us a Sleep sooner, nothing so dull and heavy as a long Discourse without ever turning the Tone or changing a Note for't: and there are many Persons, although they should fix never so stedfastly upon such a Speaker and resolve to hear him with the utmost regard and attention, would not be able yet to hold up their Eyes 'till he had half-done, upon this deficiency of his Pronunciation'.

[225] Cp. Le Faucheur, p.74: 'I could find no other cause of it at last, but bad Education. For they that teach Children to read, learn 'em ill custom of pronouncing every word a like, in the same Cant and Tone; the fault of most School-mistresses: And when these Children again advance into Grammar or Rhetorick, they fall perhaps into no better hands, of Masters that teach them their Rudiments in the same measure and method, without ever taking care to correct the ill habit of Speaking they have got; but rather giving them a bad example themselves by pronouncing every word they read or say off-book, with the same Accent, and quite another tone than what we use in our daily Discourse and Common Conversation, then instructing Youth in the variation of the Voyce for publick business'. Cp. Quintilian, 1.1.1–12.

we ask Pardon for our own; otherwise when we threaten, than when we promise, pray, or beg a Favour; otherwise when we are in a good Humour, the Passions all calm, and the Mind in perfect Tranquillity, than when we are rais'd with Anger, or provok'd by ill Nature.[226]

This Variation is so founded in Nature, that should you hear two People, in a Language you do not understand, talking together with Heat, the one in *Anger*, the other in *Fear*; one in *Joy*, the other in *Sorrow*, you might easily distinguish the Passions from each other by the different Tone, and Cadence of their Voice, as well as by their Countenance and Gesture; nay, a blind Man, who could not observe those, by the Voice would easily know the Distinction.[227]

From this it is plain, that as this Variation of the Voice is founded in Nature, so the nearer you approach to Nature, the nearer you come to Perfection; and the farther you are from her, the more vicious is your *Pronunciation*. The less affected the better, for a natural Variation is much the best; the easiest way of arriving at which, is a just Observation of common Discourse, and to mind how you speak your self in Conversation; how a Woman expresses her Passion for an Injury receiv'd, her Grief for the Loss of a Husband, or any thing dear to her, and from these Observations endeavour to form your Pronunciation in public, with this only difference, that you consider how much louder your Voice ought to be to be heard in all those Particulars, at such a Distance as the Stage, the Bar, or the Pulpit.[228] The best Actors change their Voice according to the Qualities

---

[226] Cp. Le Faucheur, p.75: 'Nature it self tells us that we ought to pronounce our selves otherwise when we speak of Melancholy and Mournful Things, then we should do a Merry-making upon Joy or Pleasantry; otherwise, when we reprove people for committing some Great Crime or other, than when we are a comforting them that are in Affliction; otherwise, when we upbraid a Man with his faults, then when we would ask Pardon for our own; otherwise again, when we threaten; otherwise, when we promise, or pray a thing and humbly beg the favour; otherwise, when we are in a good humour, the Passions calm, and the Mind serene; and otherwise, when we are upon the transports of Choler and ill Nature'.

[227] Cp. Le Faucheur, pp.75–6: 'This variation is so natural to us, that if we should hear two persons haranguing both together in a Language we did not understand at all, the one in Anger, and t'other in fear, one of them speaking with joy, and t'other, with sorrow: We might easily distinguish the Passions of the one from the other, not only by their countenance and their gesture, but by the different Tone and Cadence of the Voyce'.

[228] Cp. Le Faucheur, p.76: 'For the nearer it comes up to Nature, the more perfect it is; and the further off from it, the more vicious. The less affected, still the better; for a natural variation is best. The only way then to get this knack of varying the Voyce, is to make your own reflections upon common Chat, and to take notice of any ordinary Discourse, either in Town or in Table-Talk. You are likewise to mind how you Speak your self, when you are in Company; what a Woman says in a Passion for an

of the Persons they represent, and the Condition they are in, or the Subject of their Discourse; always speaking in the same Tone on the Stage, as they would do in a Room, allowing for the Distance.[229]

We must, therefore, vary the Voice, as often as we can; but the only Difficulty is to know how to do it artfully, and with Harmony; to the accomplishing which, I shall give the following Directions.

There are three chief Differences of *Highness* or *Lowness*, of *Vehemence* and *Softness*, and *Swiftness* and *Slowness*. The Speaker therefore is to observe a just Measure in all these Distinctions thro' all that he has to say. He must be sure to keep a true Medium of the Voice, both the Extremes being vicious and disagreeable. First, as to its *Height*, you must have a Care of either raising it always to the highest Note it can reach, or letting it down to the *lowest*. To strain it always to the Height, would be a *Bawling* or a *Monotony*, a Cant, or Identity of Sound.[230] For besides the Ungenteelness and Indecency of the Clamour and Noise to the Hearer, it wears the Throat of the Speaker into a Hoarseness, and the Ears of the Hearer into an Aversion. To sink the Voice likewise into the lowest and most base Note, and to keep it always in the same Tone, would be to mutter, not to speak, and few of the Audience would be able to hear a Word, that was said.[231]

---

injury done her, and how she pronounces upon the loss of her dear Husband or her Child'.

[229] Cp. Le Faucheur, p.77: 'Our best Actors change their Voyce thus, according to the different quality of persons and the diversity of Subjects; and they speak as naturally upon the Stage, and in the same Tone too, as they would in a familiar Club-room; saving that they are obliged to accent their words louder there, and to proportion the force and vehemence of their Voyce to the vastness of a Theatre'.

[230] Cp. Le Faucheur, pp.80–1: 'As the Body has three dimensions, for it's Length, Breadth and Thickness; so the Voyce has three principal differences, of Highness or Lowness, of Vehemence or Softness, and of Swiftness or Slowness. The Orators business is to keep up a just measure in all these distinctions, and to observe that variety, throughout the whole Speech, which we have asserted for so necessary a Virtue. But the chief thing will be to maintain a true medium of the Voyce, because both the extremes of it are vicious and disagreeable. And therefore, first, with a regard to the height of it, we must have a care of raising it always to the highest Note it can reach, on the one hand, or of debasing it always to the lowest it will go, on the other'. Cp. Quintilian, 11.3.17.

[231] Cp. Le Faucheur, p.81: 'For, over and above the indecency and ungenteelness of Clamour and Noise, it very much offends the Throat of the Speaker to a Hoarseness, and the Ears of the Hearer to an aversion. To sink the Voyce likewise, on the contrary, into the lowest base, and keep it always in the same tone, would be to mutter rather than to Speak; and it would make a very silent meeting, where a Man could not be heard at all, or be heard but by a very few people, and the rest of the Auditors might go away as they came, not one word the wiser for him'. Cp. Quintilian, 11.3.51–2.

Nor must a Man force his Voice perpetually to the last Extremity; for not being able to sustain it long in that Key, it would fail him all of a sudden; like the String of a Musical Instrument, that breaks when screw'd up too high. Without observing these Directions, he would either like *Adrian* the *Phœnician*, mention'd by *Philostratus*, lose his Voice in the midst of his Discourse, and murmur out the later part in so low a Tone as not to be heard; or like *Zosimus* the Freedman of *Pliny* the younger, over-straining himself, vomit Blood, and endanger his Life.[232] A Man of a weak Constitution, and in Years, ought to have a Care of such an intemperate way of Speaking, lest he incur the Fate of King *Attalus*. He (as I have read) made once a Speech at *Thebes*, in a public Assembly, in which being transported into an Action so violent for the Debility of his old Age, he was of a sudden struck speechless, and without the least Motion or Appearance of Life; so that he was forc'd to be carry'd home to his Lodgings, whence soon after being convey'd to his Palace at *Pergamus*, he dy'd.[233]

On the other side, you ought not to be too supine or remiss either in your *Action* or *Speaking*, because so effeminate and soft a Dissolution of the *Voice* betrays a Feebleness, and destroys the Energy of what you say, nor raises the Passions of any one, that hears above a common and dispassionate Discourse.[234]

---

[232] Cp. Le Faucheur, pp.82–3: 'For the vehemence of the Voyce in the next place, a Man must not force it upon every turn to the last Extremity. For he would not be able to hold it long-up to this violence, till it would fail him all o'the sudden; like the Strings of a Musical Instrument, that break when they are wound up a Pin too high. In this case, he would either have the same fortune with Andrian the Phœnician, that Philostratus speaks of, who suffered himself to be transported into such a Tragical Fit of Speaking, that he lost his Voyce in a moment, and was forced either to hold his Tongue, or to mourn it out so Faint and so Low, that people could hardly hear him and much less understand what he said: Or else, he would run the risqué of Zosimus the Freeman of Pliny Junior; who having overstreined himself with the violence of his Rehearsals, vomited Blood upon't'. Philostratus of Athens (c.170–240), author of *Lives of the Sophists*.

[233] Cp. Le Faucheur, pp.83–4: 'A Man of a Weak Constitution, and in Years especially, ought to beware of this Intemperance, for fear of falling into King Attalus's misfortune. He made a Speech once at Thebes, in a publick Assembly; and being transported upon it into an Action too Violent for his Crazyness and old Age, he was struck Speechless all of a sudden, without the least motion of appearance of Life in him, so that he was forced to be carried home to his Lodging: But a little while after, he was conducted from thence to his Palace at Pergamus, and there he Died'. Le Faucheur derived the story from Livy's *History of Rome* (?1–12 CE).

[234] Cp. Le Faucheur, p.84: 'On the other hand, an Orator ought not to be too Remiss neither in his Action, nor too Mild-spoken: For such a soft resolution of the Voyce argues an Infirmity, and too much mildness destroys the Energy and Force of a Speech, because a dispassionate Discourse raises no body's Affectations a pitch above common Story and ordinary Taste'.

The Life of Mr Thomas Betterton

Next, as to the Swiftness and Volubility, it ought not to be precipitate. This was the Fault of one *Serapion*, of whom *Lucillius* gives *Seneca* an Account, and says, That his Fancy slow'd so quick, that hud[d]ling Word on Word, one Tongue seem'd not sufficient for the Precipitation of his *Pronunciation*.[235] But this, on several Accounts, is a very vicious way of Speaking. This Vice is not only unseemly on all grave Subjects, but an Obstacle to the End propos'd by them, which is Persuasion. For without allowing Time to consider what you say, how can you convince? But on the Stage indeed the Case is something different, because there are Parts, and some particular Speeches, where such an extravagant Volubility is beautiful; as in several Places of the Part of *True Wit* in the *Silent Woman*, and some other Parts:[236] But that we shall see anon, when we come closer to Particulars. This running on Post without any Pause, is also prejudicial to the Speaker himself; for there is nothing hurts the Lungs more, than such a Violence and Precipitation of Speech, as allows no Intermission for the regular drawing the Breath, which has cast some into Consumptions, and cost them their Lives.[237]

But when I give Caution against this Vice, I would not have you throw your self into the contrary Extreme; for when I would not have you run so very fast with your Tongue, I would not have you suppose, that I prescribe such a Slowness of Utterance, that is like a sick Man's Walking, who can hardly draw one Leg after the other; whereas what I aim at is, that the Tongue of the Speaker should keep Pace with the Ear of the Auditors, being neither too swift for them to follow, nor too slow for their Attention. I find in an Author on this Subject, *Vicians* noted for this, that his Slowness of Delivery was so great, that he spoke scarce three Words together without a Pause, or Intermission. But there can be no manner of Pleasure to hear a Man drawl out his Words at this Rate; his Speech, to be of Value, must be more florid, but then it ought to glide like a gentle Stream, and not pour down like a rapid Torrent.[238]

---

[235] Cp. Le Faucheur, pp.84–5: 'Thirdly, As to the Swiftness and volubility of the Orator's voice, he ought to moderate it in such a manner as to avoid all precipitation … This was Serapion's weak-side also, of whom Lucilius wrote to Seneca, that he spake exceeding fast and thick, one word upon the neck of another; insomuch that one single Tongue seem'd insufficient to express the vast multitude and hurry of his Thoughts, so much did the Fruitfulness of his phancy precipitate his Pronunciation'.

[236] Betterton played Morose in Jonson's *Epicœne, or the Silent Woman* from 1684/5.

[237] Cp. Le Faucheur, p.88: 'there's nothing, over and above, so hurtful to the Lungs, as to speak with violence and precipitation, without any intermission or ever drawing breath for't: Insomuch that it has cast many Persons into deep Consumptions, and cost some of them their Lives too'.

[238] Cp. Le Faucheur, p.89: 'There's no manner of pleasure in hearing a Man drawl-out his words so, one after another, that one might very well bid him, Speak, or hold his Tongue. His Speech must be more fluent, before it be good for any thing; but then

There is a certain Latitude for the Variation of the Voice, extending to five or six Tones; so that the Speaker has room enough for varying his Voice, without striking on the two Extremes, by forming out of these five or six Notes a just and delightful Harmony.[239]

Next, the Speaker must govern his Voice, in Regard of its Violence and Softness, with such a Moderation, that tho he force it not to that last Extremity, which hurts Nature in himself, as well as jars upon the Ear of the Hearer; nor languish, on the other hand, so far, as to fall into the lowest Degree of Softness and Effeminacy, he may yet give his *Pronunciation* more or less Vehemence, or Mildness, according to the different State of his Subject, and the Quality of his Speech. But in this, as well as in the *Swiftness* and *Slowness*, he must let the Subject and Passions of his Discourse be the Guide of his Judgment. Nor must he, when he would vary his Voice, start out of one Tone into another with too remarkable a Distinction of the latter from the former; but slide from one to the other with all the Moderation, Softness and Address in the World; else to those, who see you not, it will seem the Speech of some other Person.[240]

Were I sure of such Readers, as could reduce these general Rules to particular Cases, I need not give my self the Trouble of descending to Particulars: But that there may be no Help wanting, that I am able to procure, I shall come to Rules for all the several Variations of the Voice, tho they might in some Measure be gather'd from what has been urg'd on this Head, both in what regards the Quality of the Subjects, the Nature of the

---

it ought to flow like the gliding Stream, not as a rapid Torrent'. 'Vicians' is probably a printer's error for Vinicius Publius, the Augustan orator mentioned by the elder Seneca in *Controversiae*, VII.5, and by Le Faucheur, p.89.

[239] Cp. Le Faucheur, p.89: 'the medium of the Voyce I mention does not consist in an indivisible point, but admits of a certain Latitude and certain degrees'.

[240] Cp. Le Faucheur, p.90: 'As for the violence of the softness of it, in the next place; his business will be to govern it with such a moderation; that although he neither force it to the utmost of violence that either hurts nature or offends the Ear, on the one hand; nor make it languish to the last degree of softness or effeminacy, and droop into contempt, on the other: he may yet give his pronunciation more or less vehemence and mildness, at discretion, at the different circumstances of his Subject or the qualities of his Speech shall require. And as to the swiftness or slowness of it at last, though the Orator avoid an extraordinary dullness in speaking, on this side, as well as an extravagant precipitation on that, he may never the less speak faster or slower, upon occasion, according to the best of his judgment; and be as quick, voluble and smart, more or less, as he pleases, if it do but answer the Subject and Passions of his Discourse'.

Passions, the several Parts of the Discourse, the Figures made use of, and the Varieties of Words and Phrases.[241]

I shall begin with the Subjects, of which there are several sorts; as, *Things Natural, the good or evil Actions of Men, the happy or unfortunate Events of Life,* &c. All which ought, as they are of a very different kind, to be spoken with as different an Air and Accent. In speaking of Things Natural, when you design only to make your Hearers understand you, there is no need of Heat or Motion, a clear and distinct Voice and Utterance is sufficient; because the informing the Understanding being here all the Business, the moving the Will and Passions has nothing to do. But if from this you rise to strike your Auditors with Admiration of the Wonders of Providence, in its *Beauty, Wisdom* and *Power,* you must do it in a grave Voice, and a Tone full of Admiration.[242]

If your Discourse be on the Actions of Men, either as *just,* and *honourable,* which you would by Praise recommend to the Esteem or Imitation of those, who hear you; or *unjust* or *infamous,* which you would deter them from by Invective; the Voice must be adapted to the Quality of either; expressing the Just and Honest with a full, lofty, and noble Accent, with a Tone of Satisfaction, Honour, and Esteem; but the *unjust, infamous,* or *dishonourable,* with a strong, violent and passionate Voice, and a Tone of Anger, Disdain and Detestation.[243]

---

[241] Cp. Le Faucheur, pp.92–3: 'he must have Particular Rules also for all the changes and variations of the Voyce that are necessary to set-off his Discourse with a taking Air of Elocution, according to the quality of the Subjects he treats of, the nature of the Passions he would shew in himself or raise in others, the several parts of his Discourse, the different Figures he makes use of, and the variety of his words and his Phrase'.

[242] Cp. Le Faucheur, p.93: 'To begin then with the Subjects of Discourse which the Orator may chance to fall upon; there are several sorts of them: As Things natural, the good or evil action of men; the happy or unhappy events of Life: And these things being all of a very different nature, ought to be spoken with a quite different account and air. If you've occasion to speak of natural things, with an intention only to make your hearers understand you and no more, there's no need of any great heat or motion upon the matter; but as a clean and distinct Voyce will do't; because your business here is not to move the Will and Affections, so much as to inform the Understanding. But if your design be to make them admire the Wonders of his Bounty, of his Wisdom and of his Power that created them; you must then do it with a Grave Voyce and a Tone of Admiration'.

[243] Cp. Le Faucheur, pp.93–4: 'If our Discourse fall upon the Actions of Men; either just and honest, that we would have our Auditors value as much as we esteem them our selves, by the way of Panegyrick and Commendation, or unjust and infamous, that we have a mind to make them abhor as much as we abhor them our selves, by the way of invective or Philippick: We must then adjust our Voyce to the quality of the one and the other; expressing the Just and Honest with a full, lofty and noble accent,

If your Discourse be on the Events of human Life, those are some fortunate or happy, others unfortunate and miserable; you must likewise vary your Voice according to the Difference. When you congratulate the Fortunate, your Tone and Accent is brisk and chearful; when you condole the Unfortunate, the Accent must be sad and mournful.[244]

As all the Subjects of Natural Things are not alike for their Grandeur, Beauty and Lustre, as the Heavens and Earth, the Planets and Herbs and Insects, and therefore not to be deliver'd with the same Voice, and State of Magnificence of *Pronunciation*; so are not the Actions and Events of human Life happy or unhappy, good or bad, of the same Import; a great and profligate Crime, or a barbarous and extraordinary Cruelty, are of greater Consequence, than a little and common Peccadillo. The Interest and Honour of Life is of greater Importance, than the Interest of many; the brave Actions of an illustrious Conqueror, of a MORDANT or an EUGENE, than those of a *Wat Tyler* or *Jack Straw*; the Destruction or Safety of a *whole Kingdom*, than the Loss or Gain of a *private Person*. So they require a different, and some a more vehement Accent and Pronunciation, than others; for a great Tone and Accent to trivial and common Occurrences, would be as ridiculous and absurd, as to speak in a plain, low, unconcern'd familiar Tone on the most noble and illustrious Affairs.[245]

---

with a Tone of satisfaction, honour and esteem; but pronouncing upon the unjust and infamous, with a strong violent and Passionate Voyce as well as with a Tone of Anger, Disgrace and Detestation'.

[244] Cp. Le Faucheur, pp.94–5: 'If it be upon the events of Humane Life, some are Fortunate and others Unfortunate: So that the Orator must then also vary his Voyce according to this difference; speaking of the Fortunate, as in Congratulations, with a brisk and a Cheerful Air; and of the Unfortunate, on the contrary, as in Funeral Orations, with sad and mournful Accents: For Mirth best answers the Character of Good-Fortune; and Moan, the story of Disappointment and Affliction. The one is the Subject of Gaiety and Good humour, and t'other of Melancholy and Moroseness'.

[245] Cp. Le Faucheur, pp.95–6: 'As to the Actions and Events of Humane Life, good or bad, happy or unhappy; they are not all of the same size and import: And because a Great Crime or an Extraordinary Cruelty is of worse Consequence than a common venial Pecadillo; because the interest of Honour and of Life is of greater concern than the Interest of Money; the noble exploits of a Brave Conqueror than the vulgar Actions of a Captain of the Mobb, the safety or the destruction of a whole Kingdom than the profit or the disadvantage of a Private Person: They also require a quite different Elocution according to the diversity of the Subject; some of them a far more vehement Accent and Passionate Pronunciation than others. For it would be ridiculous to speak Common and Ordinary Things, that happen every day, with a Tragical Concern or a Tone of Admiration; and as absurd on the other hand, to speak of Great Affairs and matters of extraordinary moment with a low unconcerned and familiar Voyce'. For 'Mordant', see below, n.263. Gildon also refers to Prince Eugene of Savoy (1663–1736), combatant at the Siege of Vienna and the Battle of Blenheim;

Tho these things perhaps, at first View, may seem more closely to relate to set Speeches, Orations, or Sermons, yet if the Actor will throughly consider them, they are of no less Concern to him, since whatever he speaks of on the Stage, will fall under some of these Heads, or, at least, these Subjects will often fall in his way to discourse of in Tragedy. But what follows will, beyond Contradiction, be of immediate Use to him, since it is directive of the Accents and Tones according to the Passions; and the Passions are or ought always to be in every Part of the *Tragic Scene*; and which, if more introduc'd by our Poets, would get them much more Reputation, as well as Money.

If the *Speaker* will but weigh these Subjects, I have just mention'd, well, and strongly imprint them in his Imagination, they will infallibly give such lively Ideas, as must raise in himself the Passions of *Joy* or *Sorrow*, of Fear or Boldness, of Anger or Compassion, of Esteem or Contempt; and if these are fully and emphatically represented, and utter'd with that *Variety* of Tone and Cadence, which they ought to be, they cannot fail of moving the very same Affections in his Auditors.

When you are therefore to speak, you ought first with Care to consider the Nature of the Thing of which you are to speak, and fix a very deep Impression of it in your own Mind, before you can be throughly touch'd with it your self, or able by an agreeable Sympathy to convey the same Passion to another.[246] The String of a musical Instrument sounds according to the Force and Impulse of the Master; if the Touch be gentle and soft, the Sound is so too; if strong, the Sound is vivid and strong. It is the same in Speaking as in Music, if violent Passion produce your *Speech*, that will produce a violent Pronunciation; but if it arise only from a tranquill and gentle Thought, the Force and Accent of the Delivery will be gentle and calm; so that the Speaker ought first to fix the Tone and Accent of his Voice to every Passion, that affects him, be it of Joy or Sorrow, that he may by a sympathetical Force convey it to others.[247]

---

and Wat Tyler, leader of the 1381 Peasants' Revolt, in which Jack Straw participated (see Friedrich W. Brie, 'Wat Tyler and Jack Straw', *The English Historical Review* XXI, ed. Reginald L. Poole (London: Longmans, Green and Co., 1906), pp.106–11.

[246] Cp. Le Faucheur, p.97: 'Those Objects I have just mentioned, being well weighed and imprinted in your imagination, will give you such Idea's as are able to raise in your own breast the Passions of Joy or of Sorrow; of Fear or of Boldness; of Anger or of Compassion; of Esteem or of Contempt: and if they be well represented and pronounced with that variety which they ought to be, they will move the very same Affections also in your Hearers. The Orator must therefore, first consider the thing he's to speak of, with care, and carry a deep impression of it in his mind, before he be either sensibly touch'd with it himself or able to move others upon it with a more effectual Sympathy'.

[247] Cp. Le Faucheur, p.99: 'If your Speech proceeds from a violent Passion, it produces a violent Pronunciation; if it comes from a Peaceable and Gentle Thought, the

Thus will he best express *Love* by a gay, soft and charming Voice; his *Hate*, by a sharp, sullen, and severe one; his *Joy*, by a full flowing and brisk Voice; his *Grief*, by a sad, dull and languishing Tone; not without sometimes interrupting the Continuity of the Sound with a Sigh or Groan, drawn from the very inmost of the Bosom. A tremulous and stammering Voice will best express his *Fear*, inclining to Uncertainty and Apprehension. A loud and strong Voice, on the contrary, will most naturally show his *Confidence*, always supported with a decent Boldness, and daring Constancy. Nor can his Auditors be more justly struck with a Sense of his *Anger*, than by a Voice or Tone, that is sharp, violent and impetuous, interrupted with a frequent taking of the Breath, and short Speaking.[248] Thus *Hotspur* in *Henry* IV. of *Shakespear*.

Hots. He said he would not ransom MORTIMER,
Forbad my Tongue to speak of MORTIMER,
But I will find him when he lies asleep,
And in his Ear I'll hollow MORTIMER.
Nay, I'll have a Starling shall be taught to speak
Nothing but MORTIMER, *and give it him,*
To keep his Anger still in Motion.
Why look ye, I am whipt and scourg'd with Rods,
Nettl'd and flung with Pismires, when I hear
Of his vile Politician BULLINGBROOK, *&c.*[249]

And King Lear in the same Poet.

---

pronunciation again is as Peaceable, Gentle and Calm: So that the Orator would do well to adjust every Tone and Accent of his Voyce to each Passion that afflicts or overjoys him, which he would raise in others to a degree of Sympathy'.

[248] Cp. Le Faucheur, pp.99–100: 'He will shew his Love best by a Soft, a Gay and a Charming Voyce; and his Hatred, on the contrary, by a Sharp, Sullen and Severe one. He'll discover his Joy well with a Full, Flowing and Brisk Voyce; and his Grief, on the other side, with a dull, Languishing and Sad Moan; not without breaking-off abruptly sometimes, with a Sob; and fetching-up a Sigh or a Groan from the heart. His Fear will be best demonstrated by a Trembling and Stammering Voyce, somewhat inclining to uncertainty and apprehension. His Confidence, on the contrary, will be easily discover'd by a Loud and a Strong Voyce, always keeping-up to a decent Boldness and a daring Constancy. And he cannot give his Hearers to understand his Anger better than by a sharp, impetuous and violent Voyce; by taking his Breath often, and speaking short upon the Passion'. Le Faucheur's subsequent example is taken from Terence's *Adelphi*.

[249] A running together of two speeches from *1 Henry IV*, I.3.219–41, with 'holla' changed to 'hollow'. Betterton's lightly edited version of the play, *King Henry IV with the humours of Sir John Falstaff*, opened at Lincoln's Inn Fields in January 1700 (LS1 522), with the actor as Falstaff.

LEAR. *Detested Kite, thou lyest!*
My Train are Men of choice and rarest Parts,
That all Particulars of Duty know,
And in the most exact Regard support
The Worships of their Names! O most small Fault!
How ugly didst thou in CORDELIA *show?*
Which like an Engine wrench'd my Frame of Nature
From the fixt Place; drew from my Heart all Love
And added to the Gall. O LEAR! LEAR! LEAR!
Beat at this Gate that let thy Folly in,
And thy dear Judgment out.——

And again immediately.

Hear! Nature hear! dear Goddess hear!
Suspend thy Purpose if thou dost intend
To make this Creature fruitful,
Into her Womb convey Sterility;
Dry up in her the Organs of Increase,
And from her Derogate Body never spring
A Babe to honour her. If she must teem,
Create her Child of Spleen, that it may give,
And be a thwart, denatur'd Torment, like her.
Let it stamp Wrinkles in her Brow of Youth;
With cadent Tears fret Channels in her Cheeks;
Turn all her Mother's Pains and Benefits
To Laughter and Contempt; that she may feel
How sharper, than a Serpent's Tooth it is
To have a thankless Child.[250]

Both these Speeches, with that of *Hotspur*, must be spoke with an elevated Tone and enraged Voice, and the Accents of a Man all on Fire, and in a Fury next to Madness.[251] The same may be said of *Othello* in the following Speech.

[250] From *King Lear*, 1.4.262–89. Betterton's only recorded appearances in the role of Lear were in the 1681 version by Nahum Tate, who adapted these two speeches significantly. The printer appears to have had some difficulty with the manuscript in the second speech, rendering 'Derogate' as 'Dewgate'. PB 97 lists a copy of Nicholas Rowe's six-volume 1709 edition of the works of Shakespeare; it may be significant that either Gildon or Betterton (or both) did not regard Tate's as the true version of the play.

[251] Cp. Le Faucheur, p.101: 'He must needs speak those words with an elevated Tone; an enraged Voyce ... in a Fury next to a Distraction'.

OTH. *Villain! Be sure thou prove my Love a Whore;*
Be sure of it; give me the Ocular Proof,
Or by the Worth of my eternal Soul,
Thou hadst better have been born a Dog,
Than answer my wak'd Wrath —
If thou dost slander her, or torture me,
Never pray more; abandon all Remorse
On Horrors Head, Horrors accumulate;
Do Deeds to make Heaven weep, all Earth amaz'd,
For nothing canst thou to Damnation add
Greater than that.[252]

Old *Capulet* in *Romeo* and *Juliet*.

How now!
How now! chop Logic? What's this?
Proud! and I thank you! and I thank you not!
Thank me no Thankings; nor proud me no prouds;
But fettle your fine Joints 'gainst Thursday *next,*
To go with Paris *to St.* Peter's *Church,*
Or I will drag thee in a Hurdle thither.
Out you Green-sickness Carrion; out you Baggage;
Out you Tallow-Face.

And before in the same Play.

Old CAP. *He shall be endur'd.*
What good Man Boy—I say he shall. Go to -—
Am I the Master here or you? Go to --
You'll not endure him! God shall mend my Soul,
You'll make a Mutiny among the Guests!
You'll set cock-a-hoop! You'll be the Man![253]

'Tis plain from the Expressions between short Sentences in both these Speeches, that the Actor should speak puffing and blowing, and take his Breath at every Point, as if his Passion had choak'd up his Delivery, and he

---

[252] Again, a running together of separate speeches, this time from *Othello*, III.3.362–77. Betterton is thought to have played the title role from 1690.

[253] Two speeches from *Romeo and Juliet*: 3.5.149–57 ('How now!') and 1.5.74–9 ('He shall be endur'd'). Betterton played Mercutio from 1662.

could not for Anger and Choler utter more Words together.[254] The same
may be said of the first Speech of *Hotspur's*.

I cannot but here give a Description of a valiant Anger, or the Heat of a
noble Warrior in Fight, out of *Shakespear's Harry V.* because it gives a lively
Image of all the Looks and Actions belonging to it.

HEN. *But when the Blast of War blows in our Ears,*
Then imitate the Action of the Tyger.
Stiffen the Sinews, summon up the Blood;
Disguise fair Nature with hard-favour'd Rage;
Then lend the Eye a terrible Aspect,
Let it pry through the Portage of the Head,
Like the Brass Cannon let the Brow o'erwhelm it,
As fearfully as does a galled Rock
O'erhang and jutty his confounded Base,
Swell'd with the wild and wasteful Ocean.
Now set the Teeth, and stretch the Nostrils wide,
Hold hard the Breath, and bend up ev'ry Spirit
To its full Height. —[255]

If a Player would study this Speech, he would find such Looks and Motions
would inspire him with more Life on the Representation of such a Character, than he would otherwise feel.

To move Compassion, the Speaker must express himself with a soft,
submissive and pitiful Voice,[256] as *Arthur* in *King John*, when Hubert shows
him the King's Order for burning out his Eyes with a hot Iron.

ARTH. *Have you the Heart? When your Head did but ake,*
I knit my Handkerchief about your Brows,
(The best I had, a Princess wrought it me)
And I did never ask it you again;
And with my Hand at Midnight held your Head,

---

[254] Cp. Le Faucheur, pp.101–2: 'It is plain by Sostrata's expressions inserted there between
those short Sentences, that the Actor spake puffing and blowing, and took his Breath
at every Period: As if his Passion had choak'd-up his Pronunciation, and he could
not utter more words together for vexation and Choler'.

[255] *Henry V*, 3.1.5–17. There is no evidence that Betterton played Shakespeare's Henry
V and no reference to any performances of the play in LS1. He played Owen Tudor
in the Earl of Orrery's *Henry the Fifth* in 1664. The subsequent comment indicates
awareness of the somatic nature of Shakespeare's writing.

[256] Cp. Le Faucheur, p.102: 'If the Orator be mov'd with a Compassion which he would
influence upon others, he must express himself with a very soft, submissive and
pitiful Voyce'.

The Life of Mr Thomas Betterton

And like the watchful Minutes to the Hour,
Still and anon chear'd up the heavy Time,
Saying, What lack you? and where lies your grief?
Oh! what good Love may I perform for you?
Many a poor Man's Son would have lain still,
And not have spoke a loving Word to you.
But you at your sick Service had a Prince, &c.[257]

And *Anthony* in *Julius Cæsar*, in the Beginning of his Speech on *Cæsar's* Death.

ANT. *Friends,* Romans, *Country-men, lend me your Ears,*
I come to bury CÆSAR, *not to praise him.*
The Evil, that Men do, lives after them,
The Good is oft interred with their Bones.
So let it be with CÆSAR. *The noble* BRUTUS
Has told you, CÆSAR *was ambitious.*
If it were so, it was a grievous Fault,
And grievously has CÆSAR *answer'd it.*
Here under Leave of BRUTUS *and the rest,*
(For BRUTUS *is an honourable Man,*
So they are all, all honourable Men)
Come I to speak in CÆSAR's *Funeral.*
He was my Friend, faithful and just to me;
But BRUTUS *says he was ambitious,*
And BRUTUS *is an honourable Man, &c.*[258]

'Tis plain, that *Arthur* spoke (if it were well acted) with a low Tone, and slender and humble Accents, pleading for his Life; turning his Voice on such Tones, as were fittest to incline the Affections. The same may almost be said of *Anthony's* Speech, where he pleaded to the People to move their Pity first, and then to raise a stronger Passion, nay, even their Rage; endeavouring first to melt them with a low and submissive Voice, and yet not without Passion, but that Passion is mingled with a great deal of Tenderness, that shew'd a

---

[257] *King John*, 4.1.41–52. A document dated 12 January 1669 includes *King John* among plays assigned to the King's Company, but there is no record of a performance until Garrick's revival in February 1745, when it was advertised as 'Not acted in 50 years' (LS3 1154).

[258] *Julius Caesar*, 3.2.73–87. The play was popular throughout the Restoration period. Cibber praised Betterton's restraint as Brutus (pp.78–9), as he had the same actor's Hamlet (p.77), finding in that performance the kind of complexity of response demanded in the subsequent passage.

Mind sensibly touch'd and afflicted with the Oppression and Murther of his Friend.

I have read in a French Author,[259] that Cicero, in his *Tusculan Questions*, tells us, that the whole Theatre was fill'd with Melancholly and Grief, when the Actor pronounc'd these Words, of the Ghost of an unbury'd Corps.

> *Awake, O Mother! break off your careless Slumbers,*
> *Think on your wretched Son, yet uninterr'd;*
> *Cover, oh! cover soon his poor defenceless Body,*
> *From wild devouring Beasts of Prey,*
> *That soon my scatter'd Limbs and mangled Corps*
> *May bear away, &c.*[260]

Tho this was spoke with a deplorable Voice, yet to do this well, there are several Manners of softening the Voice necessary to express the different Qualities of the Words uttered, and the Characters of the Things mention'd in the Discourse; which are much better convey'd to the Learner *vivâ voce*, than by Precept.[261]

But to proceed to other *Passions*, and the Variations and Inflections of the Voice proper to them: If you were to give the Character of a great and brave *Hero*, with a visible Esteem of him, he must do it with a lofty

---

[259] In fact, Le Faucheur, p.107, which this passage reproduces almost verbatim (see below, n.261).

[260] In Cicero's *The Tusculan Questions* this is reported to be from a play by Lucius Accius featuring the death of Hector; in the translation by George Alexander Otis (Boston: James B. Dow, 1839), pp.77–8.

[261] Cp. Le Faucheur, pp.106–7: 'To this purpose, the same Author again, Tully in his First *Tusculan Question*, says; that, when these Verses, out of one of the Antient Tragedians, which represented a young Man Dead, and Unburi'd yet; rowzing-up the Earth in the Character of her Son, and invoking his Mother.

> *Mother, awake! thy careless rest deferr;*
> *Think on thy Son, and his poor Bones interr:*
> *Before wild Birds, and Beasts, for Prey that roar,*
> *My scatter'd Limbs and mangled Corps Devour.*

When these Verses, I say are spoken with a doleful and deplorable Voyce, they fill the whole Theatre with Grief and Melancholy. But for the Speaker to do this well, there are several ways of softening the Voyce requir'd, according to the different quality of the Words he makes use of and the Character of things he treats of in his Discourse: However, 'tis far more easier to be Taught off the Lip in express Language than in Writing'.

and magnificent Tone, and a Voice noble as the Theme[262]— As if you were speaking of the Earl of *Peterborough*.[263]

His Merits are too PUBLIC *to need a Recital, his Friends with Joy, and his Enemies with Regret confess, and all* Europe *is Witness to them with Amazement; nothing can be said of his Courage or Conduct, of which there are not attested Proofs in the Hands of all Men: The Taking and Relief of* BARCELONA, *the Stony Cliffs of* ALBOCAÇAR, *the Surrender of* NULES *and* MOLVIEDRO, *the Relief of* VALENTIA, *and the Reduction of that Kingdom, and the Promise of all* SPAIN, *by the particular Force of his own Genius, and various other Wonders, testified by that Royal Hand, into which his Valour and Conduct only put a* SCEPTRE. *What should I say of his Generosity, a heavenly Quality, and which must be visible in all the Actions of a Hero truly great! What, I say, can I speak, equal to those noble Proofs, which remain on Record to all Posterity? He was always liberal of his* OWN TREASURE, *but justly frugal of* THAT *of the* PUBLIC; *when he took whole Countries almost without Men, and maintain'd Armies without Money. But what can all the Art of the best Orator say, equal to that unparalle'd Act of Beneficence to the* PUBLIC, *when his Lordship refus'd a Compensation for the Loss of his Baggage at* HUETE; *where, with a Generosity peculiar to his Lordship, he transferred the Amends due to himself to the Advantage of the Public, by obliging the Inhabitants to furnish the Confederate Army with Magazines of Corn (sufficiently then wanted by them) large enough to suffice a Body of 20000 Men for two Months. This is an Action, as unfashionable, as noble, and too likely to raise Envy, as well as Admiration, when the* Public *is the Bubble of private Interest, and Heroes have the Art of uniting their own Gain with the public Good*.[264]

Should this be spoke in a low and languishing Voice, it would be flat, cold and insipid, and altogether beneath the Honour of the Hero; but let

---

[262] Cp. Le Faucheur, p.107: 'We come now to other Passions of the Mind and other variations or Inflexions of the Voyce to shew how our Orator shall acquit himself in the Action of them to the best advantage. If he would give his Audience a Character of some Brave Hero and testifie his own Esteem of the Person, he should do't with a Lofty and a Magnificent Tone, and his Voyce must be as noble as his Strains'.

[263] I.e. Charles Mordaunt, 3rd Earl of Peterborough (1658–1735), English general at the 1705 Siege of Montjuic, Barcelona. This passage is lifted from the dedication to Mordaunt of *The Works of* Mr. *William Shakespear Volume the Seventh* (London: Edmund Curll, 1710), A3, which Gildon assisted in preparing for Curll as a supplement to Rowe's six-volume edition of 1709; the dedication is signed 'S.N.', presumably a pseudonym. Mordaunt's conduct, more controversial than this passage implies, sparked a series of publications, among them George Farquhar's unfinished epic poem, *Barcellona*. PB includes several works of Iberian history.

[264] Before the siege Mordaunt had endured a series of quarrels with his fellow generals and paid for mercenaries from his own pocket following disagreement about government funding.

them be spoke with that noble Accent, and be animated with a lofty Tone of Voice, agreeable to the Hero's Spirit and Magnificence, then they will not appear wholly unworthy of the Subject.[265]

If a Man is to speak in Contempt of any one, he ought to express that Contempt in the scornful *Tone*, but without any Eagerness, Passion, or Violence of *Voice*, for those show *Anger*;[266] and where there is Anger, justly speaking, there is not Contempt, the Object of which is suppos'd to be below our Anger, and unable to give us Pain. Any thing therefore of this Nature must be spoke calmly, and without any great Emotion; for if you speak on this Occasion with a passionate Voice, discovering a great Concern or Indignation, you plainly contradict your own Design, your Contempt being express'd in only Words, and not in Deeds;[267] you must therefore always avoid this Error, when you treat any Man with Scorn and Derision, or expose the Folly of any ridiculous Argument or Thing: for to be vehement on a Trifle, would be like using a Club against a Worm, which you might crush to pieces with your Foot.[268]

But if you have had any Inhumanity, or barbarous Injustice offer'd you, of which you would complain, you must then speak after quite another manner; you must express your Grievance and your Affliction in a Tone more elevated and strong, proportioning your Passion and Vehemence of Voice to the Greatness of the Injustice done you; for to speak without Emotion in such a Case, is to persuade the Hearer, that you do not feel the Injury, for if you did, it would produce an Utterance much more outragious.

---

[265] Cp. Le Faucheur, pp.109–10: 'Let a Man speak those fine words with a Low and Languishing Voyce, and nothing can appear more Cold, Flat, or Insipid; nothing more unworthy, either of the Eloquence of Cicero, or of the Honour of Pompey. But, on the other hand, let him pronounce them with a Noble Accent and animate them with a lofty Tone of the Voyce answerable to their own Spirit and Magnificence; and then they will appear in their proper Lustre, quicken the Hearers with Admiration, and entertain as if they came from the Mouth of Tully himself yet, Sixteen Hundred years and more after his Death'. Gildon substitutes the passage about Peterborough for Tully's oration on the Manilian Law.

[266] Cp. Le Faucheur, p.110: 'If the Orator would shew the Contempt he has of a Man, and expose him to his Auditors, he must do't with a Scornful Tone; but without any Passion, Eagerness or Violence of the voyce: As Cicero spake to Cœcilius, who pretended to be preferr'd before him for Pleading in the Accusation of Verses'.

[267] Cp. Le Faucheur, p.114: But if he had spoken with a passionate voyce, and shew'd any great concern or indignation in the matter, he had palpably contradicted his Design. For then he had declar'd his contempt of him only in Word; but in Deed, thought him worthy of his Anger and Rhetorick'.

[268] Cp. Le Faucheur, p.115: 'if he should put himself upon the last effort of his voyce and his Eloquence for a trifle, against silly people and insignificant arguments; as if he should make use of Hercules's Club to kill a Worm, which is easily trod to pieces and crushed underfoot'.

A Client coming to *Demosthenes*, on a Case of Assault and Battery, related his Story with so little Concern, that he plainly told him, he could not believe, that there was the least Reality in what he said; on which the Client replying with a loud Voice and agitated Spirit, *How! do you not believe me?* Ay now (says he) I believe you, this is the Voice of a Man, that has felt the Bastinado. And this Art of Speaking was so well known to the Ancients, that I find *Cicero* quoted on this Occasion, urging the Calmness and Indifference of *Callidius's* Pleading, where Heat and Concern were requir'd, as an Argument against the Reality of what he pleaded for his Client.[269]

I cannot pass from this Head of varying the Voice according to the Passion you are to express, without this Rule, (which indeed will be of more use to the Bar and Pulpit, by Reason of the Length of their Discourse, than to the Stage, tho it be not unuseful even to that) when you come to cool on a violent Passion, and recover your self from a Transport, you ought to lower the Tone of your Voice in such a manner, as may express that Languidness of your Faculties and Speech, which the Stretch and Extent of your Passion has produc'd. And I would advise all those, who would speak with Beauty and Harmony in these various Inflexions of the Voice, often to read with Caution and Attention aloud the best and most passionate Tragedies, and those Comedies, which may afford the greatest Variety, and such Dialogues as approach nearest to the Stile of the Dramatic Poets. For as a certain Author observes, nothing can be more serviceable to the Improvement of Action and Eloquence.[270]

---

[269] Cp. Le Faucheur, pp.115–16: 'But if the Orator have a Barbarous Injustice to complain of, that has been done him by an Enemy, as Demosthenes did of those abuses he had receiv'd at the hands of Midias upon the Feast of Saturn; he must speak in another manner, and express his Affliction and Grievance with an Elevated Tone; proportioning the vehemence and passion of his voyce to the Cruelty of the Injury: And certainly he could not do't otherwise, without doing himself wrong; for if he should speak it without any Heat or Concern, People would neither believe the Case or be True nor himself really aggrieved; and all that he could say then of the Indignity, would never avail him in Court before the Judges of his Complaint. This was the reason Demosthenes reprimanded a Man once that came to him upon an Assault and Battery, and desired him to plead his Cause for him; telling him the plain truth of the matter with a great deal of simplicity, and shewing no manner of concern or vexation by his voyce. Why, says the Councellor, *I cannot believe what you tell me.* But another Man having told him the same story over again in a Great Passion, with a Spirit of Fury and Revenge for the Affront. *Well! I believe you* (says he) now you speak with the Accent and Zeal of a Man that has been assaulted and drubb'd. And this was to shew him with what tone of the voyce he ought to speak upon Oppression and Injury, either to be believed or to make his Cause Good'.

[270] Cp. Le Faucheur, pp.117–18: 'Besides, not to omit any thing that may contribute to the advancement of so necessary a Work, as the several inflexions of the voyce are in point of speaking, I must add this; That the only way to acquire the Faculty of

The Life of Mr Thomas Betterton

I must, by the way, add a Word or two, which the Stage has not much to do with, unless in such Speeches, as imitate Orations, or solemn and public Addresses, which have not a Right to have much place in the Drama; and that is, the Art of varying the Voice according to the several parts of the Oration, Pleading, Sermon, or Discourse, which you deliver.

You must therefore begin with a low and modest Voice, both in Regard of that Deference, which you should pay to the Auditors, and for the better Management of your Voice, taking with you the calm State of the Hearers, when you begin to speak, and to raise it by degrees up to such a Height of Passion and Warmth, as may be necessary for your Purpose, and the Energy of the Subject;[271] else first you would put your self out of Breath, for want of a prudent Conduct at your first start, so that you would be unable to return to that Moderation, which allows ways to heighten the rest and more important parts of your Speech to a degree above the Beginning.

On the other hand, I do not propose, that you should begin in so very low a Voice, as not to be heard by more, than a few, who stand or sit nearest to you; but tho you must speak even at first with a Voice so clear and distinct, that every individual Person of your Audience, that attends, may hear you without Difficulty or Trouble; yet it must contain nothing of that Force and Energy, which is proper to Passion. I am therefore only for having the Beginning insinuating, soft and easy, delivered in a Tone more low, and an Address more humble, than the other Parts of the Discourse.[272]

This Rule, 'tis true, does admit of an Exception for there are some Beginnings, which do not fall under it, which are those, which we call *abrupt*,[273] as that of *Ajax* in *Ovid*.

---

varying the voyce upon all kind of Subjects as well as Passions, is to be often reading of Comedies, Tragedies, and Dialogues aloud, or some other Discourses of Authors, whose Stile comes nearest up to the Dramatick: For nothing can be more serviceable to the Emprovement of Action and Elocution'.

[271] Cp. Le Faucheur, p.119: 'The Exordium ought to be spoken with a low and a modest voyce; for to begin with modesty is not only agreeable to the Auditors, as it is a virtue which shews how great an esteem we have of them and demonstrates the respect we pay to their presence; but a necessary qualification also for the Orator, to manage his voyce discreetly and to work it up by degrees of moderation to a higher pitch of warmth and Passion'.

[272] Cp. Le Faucheur, p.120: 'However, I do not mean that he should begin so low neither, as to be heard only by a very few People, just under his nose; but, on the contrary, I would have him speak-up, at first, so clear and distinct, as to be heard without difficulty or trouble by every Man of his Auditors that would give himself the liberty of attending'.

[273] Cp. Le Faucheur, p.121: 'But this rule yet will admit of an Exception; for there are some Exordiums do not fall under it, which we may call unexpected or abrupt, from

> *Before the Ships, ye Gods, then must I Plead?*
> *And is* ULISSES *then compar'd to me?*[274]

Nor has the Speaker any Occasion of raising his Voice to any great stretch of Passion in the *Proposition* or Narration of his Discourse, this being the Place of informing his Hearers in the Matters in Question; so that the Voice here has only need of being a degree higher, than in the Beginning: But he must take Care to be very distinct and articulate, it being the Groundwork of the Whole, and the Force and Vigour of the following Reasons and Arguments taking all their Life from hence; it ought therefore to be perfectly heard and understood, or the Foundation being defective, the Fabric must fall to the Ground. The Difference of Actions and Events in the *Narration* must vary the manner of the Delivery; yet this is not the proper part of the Speech, for the Contention of Voice, which must be chiefly refin'd for the other parts: For the greatest Stress of the Discourse lies in confirming our own Arguments, and refuting those of the Adversary. When the Speaker comes to the summing up the whole, after the Confutation, he ought to make a little Pause, and begin it again with a lower Tone, and a different Accent from the last Cadence of his Voice; then raising himself, he should break out into a louder Voice, and carry it on to the End with more Gaiety, Magnificence, and Triumph of Pronunciation, which would seem born of his Assurance in the Justice of his Cause, now sufficiently made good, and the Conviction and Satisfaction of his Hearers in that and his Integrity. And then he should conclude with Joy and Satisfaction.[275]

---

a Term of Art, and the Common Ex Abrubto of the Schools; as that of Cicero's is, in his first Oration against Cataline'.

[274] Gildon translates from Ovid, *Metamorphoses*, 13.131–2, which imagines an argument between Ajax and Ulysses. The passage replaces Le Faucheur's choice of an example from Cicero. PB lists five separate editions of Ovid's works.

[275] Cp. Le Faucheur, pp.125–6: 'In the next place, the Orator need not put himself in a Passion nor raise his voyce to any great vehemence upon the Proposition of Narration of his Speech; for his business in this part is only to inform his hearers, or to instruct his Judges, and to give them a right understanding of the matter in question. So that 'tis enough here for the Pronunciation to be a degree higher than that of the Exordium; only he must take care all the while to be very Articulate and Distinct upon it, because the Narration lays the groundwork of the whole Discourse and contains the virtue of all those reasons that are to be drawn from it: And therefore it mightily imports and concerns him to have it well heard, if he would Build well or raise any great Arguments upon that Foundation. There must needs be some difference too, in the manner of speaking it, according to the different quality of Actions and Events in the relations: But this is not the proper place yet for the vehemence and contention of the voyce, which must be kept in reserve for a better occasion and the following parts of the Speech'.

But to omit none of those Helps to this Art, which I have been able to meet with in my little Reading, I must add a few Words, which will assist in this varying the Voice, a Quality so necessary for a Speaker of any kind in *Public*, and that is, by running through those Modes of Speech, or Manners of expressing the Mind, which I find call'd Figures of Speech, or *Rhetoric*; which some call the Lights of Speech, deriving to it both Grace and Variety, there being so peculiar an Air, Ornament and Novelty proper to each, that they are spoken with a different Tone from the rest of the Discourse.[276] I begin therefore with that, which is call'd an EXCLAMATION. — As it would be ridiculously flat and insipid to pronounce this with no louder a Voice and more passionate Accent, than the rest of the Discourse;[277] so the very Nature of the thing gives you the Reason of it; as, *Oh Horror! O unheard of Cruelty! Unequalled Impiety! to stand in fear neither of Man nor God! What a Feast was that of* THYESTES! *Oh! monstrous Barbarity! to feed the Father with the Flesh of his own Son! to make the Parents Bowels the Grave of his own Child! Well might the fiery Chariot of the Sun turn back, and not give Light to so hellish a Deed,* &c. To speak these Words without an Elevation of Voice, would be to make them flat and insipid, and to rob them of their Force and Energy.[278]

The same exclamatory way of Speech must be used in Swearing, or a solemn Denunciation, Oath or Vow; as, that which I find quoted of *Demosthenes*, in his Oration for *Ctesiphon*, which was, it seems, much admir'd by the Ancients. In that Point you have not fail'd, no— *I swear by our great Ancestors, who won the Battle of* MARATHON *with so much Hazard and Bravery! by those, who maintain'd the Fight at* PLATEA *with so much Generosity and Glory! by those, who contended with so much Courage in the Sea-Fight of* SALAMIS! *by those, who so bravely fell at* ARTEMISIUM! *and by all those gallant Warriors, whose Deeds merited public Monuments with all the Ensigns of Honour, Fortune and Fame!*[279]

---

[276] Quintilian, 9.3, offers a similar list of figures of speech.

[277] Cp. Le Faucheur, p.128: 'As Figures are the lights of Speech, that render it most agreeable both for variety and Good Grace, every one of 'em carrying a long with it a particular Air, Ornament and Novelty: So they are to be spoken with a different Tone from the rest of the Discourse, upon an Exclamation. The very name of that Figure shews the reason; for nothing would appear so Flat and Ridiculous, if it were not pronounced with a louder Voyce and a more Passionate Accent than any other'.

[278] Cp. Le Faucheur, p.129: 'If he had spoken those words without any Elevation of the Voyce, had he not deprived them of all their Clatt, Ornament and Force?' The passage concerning Thyestes does not correspond to Seneca's play or the versions of it written by 'F.W' (1674) and John Crowne (1681), so it is presumably Gildon's own invention.

[279] Closely based on Le Faucheur, p.130, who relied on Demosthenes; see *The Three Orations of Demosthenes Chiefe Orator among the Grecians*, trans. Thomas Wilson (London: Henry Denham, 1570), pp.127–9.

It cannot be doubted but *Demosthenes*, who had study'd Action and Utterance with so much Application, spoke this with that Elevation of Tone, and Contention of Voice, as was necessary to touch his Hearers with Warmth, and not chill them with a calm Indifference of *Pronunciation*.

There is a Figure, which comes, or may come often, into the Speeches of the Pulpit, which is the Introduction of some other Person speaking, which they call a *Prosopopœia*,[280] and this has been often us'd on the Stage, in Comedies especially, as in the former Instance I have given of *Melantha*, if that ought not rather to be referr'd to [as] a Diologism.[281] That the Person ought to change his Voice, who introduces this, is evident, and that by the Character of him he introduces, that he may shew, that it is not he but the Person introduc'd, that speaks, For Instance: If a grave, venerable old Man be thus brought in, the *Force* of the Voice, and the manner of Utterance must be grave and severe, and so answerable to the Person; and thus if a young Rake or *Debauchee* be introduc'd, it must be loose and effeminate.

When you address your Speech to any Man or thing by way of *Apostrophe*, you ought to consider your own Design, and the Circumstances of him that you address to.[282] If you direct your Discourse to anything inanimate, you must raise your Voice above the ordinary and common Tone, as to one deaf, or who want their perfect Hearing;[283] as, *Oh! sacred Thirst*

---

[280] Strictly speaking, where 'an imaginary or absent person is represented as speaking or acting'; Richard A. Lanham, *A Handlist of Rhetorical Terms* (Berkeley: University of California Press, 1968), p.83.

[281] For Melantha in Dryden's *Marriage à la Mode*, see n.127 above. OED 1 defines 'dialogism' [*sic*] as 'The rhetorical device of presenting a reasoned argument in the form of a dialogue between two or more people, with opposing or contrasting views expressed by the different participants'.

[282] Apostrophe: 'Breaking off discourse to address directly some person or thing either present or absent' (Lanham, p.15).

[283] Cp. Le Faucheur, pp.131–2: 'In a Prosopopœia, nature her self shews us; First that the Orator ought to change his Voyce, to the end it may appear as if it were not a speaking, but some other Person brought in by the by: And secondly, that he must vary it according to the Diversity, Character and Business of the Persons that he introduces, and feigns a speaking in this Disguise. For instance, in those two Prospopœia's which Cicero makes use of in his Oration for Celius; the one of the Venerable Old Man Appius, the other of the young Rake Clodius, a Debauchée; who may not see with half an eye how differently they are to be spoken; and how that ought to be Grave and Severe; but this loose and effeminate, according to the different qualities of the Persons? Read over the one and the other in the Speech it self, and you will easily judge of them for the Pronunciation. But if you would bring in a Man talking himself, upon a point of deliberation, and arguing in his own breast what he should do in the matter, you must manage it with a low voyce, and introduce him as if he were only speaking to himself and within the compass of his own Ears, with a design not to be overheard by any body else'.

of Gold, how you constrain our mortal Breasts, &c. Ye Walls! ye Beds! ye conscious Pillows tell, &c. Thus if you address your self to Heaven, you must do it in a higher Strain and loftier Tone of Voice, than if you were speaking to Men, who are here on a Level with you; *To thee, O* Jove! *I make my last Appeal. Ye Stars, ye wandring Planets of the Night, and thou bright Sun the Source and Prince of Light, I call you all to witness my true Fire,* &c.

When you bring in two Persons in a *Dialogue* talking together, by way of Question and Answer, you must certainly change your Voice by turns, as if two Men, or a Man and Woman, were talking together;[284] of which, that which I have now twice already mention'd will be a just Example.

Upon all these Conferences and Dialogisms, we must always observe to pronounce the Answer with a different Tone from the last Cadence of the foregoing Question or Objection.[285]

When the Speaker presses his Adversary close, and insists upon the same Arguments still, pressing it home upon him several ways, over and over again, 'till he seems asham'd of it, and confounded at the Repetition, his Voice must be *brisk*, pressing and insulting, where he lays the main Stress of what he aims at[286] — My Author furnishing me with so good an Example of this from *Cicero*, when he defends *Ligarius* against *Tubero*, who accus'd him to *Cæsar*, as having been in *Pompey's* Army at *Pharsalia*; and I choose it rather than any Instance from the *Drama*, because that Speech is famous for having made *Cæsar* drop his Papers, and declare himself vanquish'd by Eloquence, when he had decreed, that he would not forgive *Ligarius* before he came to hear him — *What,* Tubero, *did you in the Battle of* Pharsalia *with your Sword drawn? At whose Breast did you aim the Point? What was the Sense of your Weapon? the Design of your Arms? and the Intention of your Appearance there? Where were your Thoughts, your Desires, your Wishes, your Expectations? What meant those Eyes, that Zeal, that Passion, that*

---

284 Cp. Le Faucheur, p.135: 'Upon a Dialogism, or Conference, where two Persons are brought in as 'twere Dialoguing one another, one of 'em moving the Question and t'other making the Answer, you must change your voyce by turns, as if two Men were really a talking together'.

285 Cp. Le Faucheur, p.136: 'Upon these Conferences and Rencounters, we must always observe to pronounce the Answer with a different Tone from the last Cadence of the foregoing Question and Objection'.

286 Cp. Le Faucheur, p.137: 'In the Figure call'd Epimone by the Greeks, and which we may call Insistance, whereby the Orator presses his Adversary to a pinch and dwells upon it; insisting still the same argument, and expressing it home to him several ways over and over till he seems asham'd of it, and confounded at the Repetition: Here the Orator must make use of a brisk, pressing and insulting voyce, where he lays the main stress of his Speech and clinches it upon the hearers'.

The Life of Mr Thomas Betterton

Hand, that Weapon? But I urge this Matter too hard upon him. The Youth is asham'd, and in Confusion at the Conviction I'll say no more.[287]

When you avow your Liberty of Speaking without Fear, let the Danger be what it will, which the Rhetoricians call *Parrhasia*, the Voice must be full and loud, exalted with Confidence of Success or Boldness, not to be daunted with any Apprehension.[288] Nor can I omit an Example of this likewise from the same Orator, because it is excellent and pathetic. *Oh! Clemency most admirable! and worthy of eternal Praise, Honour, and Memory!* CICERO *has the Boldness to confess himself guilty before* CÆSAR *of a Crime, for which he cannot suffer another to be wrongfully accus'd; nor is he under any Apprehensions from the Resentment of his Judge on this Account. Behold how undaunted I am, Sir, in the Confidence of your Goodness; behold the great Lights of Generosity and Wisdom, which from your Aspect favour me in what I say, I will raise my Voice to a Loudness, if I can, sufficient to make all the People of* Rome *hear what I say! The War now being not only began, but almost ended, I went over to your Enemy's Camp freely, voluntarily, on my own Choice, before this finishing Blow put an end to it at* PHARSALIA.[289]

In a *Gradation* or *Climax*, the Voice must with the Sentence climb up by several Degrees of the Sentence to the Period;[290] as, *Luxury is born in the City, out of Luxury there is a Necessity that Avarice should arise, from Avarice*

---

[287] Cp. Le Faucheur, p.137: 'As when Tully says in his Oration for Ligarius: "What did you, Tubero, in the Battel of Pharsalia, with your Sword drawn there? Against whose breast did you direct the point of it? What was the sense of your Weapon, the design of your Arms the Intention of your appearance? Where were your thoughts, your wishes, your desires, your expectations? What meant those Eyes, that Zeal, that Passion, that hand, that Weapon? But I urge the thing too far upon him: The young Man is asham'd, and in Confusion at the Conviction; I'll say no more."'

[288] Parrhesia or Parrosia refers to outspokenness (Lanham, p.73).

[289] Cp. Le Faucheur, pp.140–1: 'Upon a Parrhesia, or the bold Figure of taking the liberty to say every thing we have a mind to say, let the danger be what it will, where there's any confidence in the Cause, or any fear of losing the Point, our voyce must be full and loud, as upon these words of Tully in his Oration for Ligarius. "Oh admirable Clemency; worthy of eternal praise, honour and memory. Cicero has the boldness now before Cæsar to confess himself guilty of a Crime, for which he cannot endure another should be falsly arraign'd, neither does he fear the private resentments of his Judge for't. See how undaunted I am now, upon the confidence of our Goodness. See the great lights of Generosity and Wisdom that countenance me from your Royal Aspect. I will raise my voice as loud as I can, that all the People of Rome may hear me. The War being begun, Sir, and almost ended, I went over to your Enemy's Camp before the finishing stroke of it, upon my own choice and without any Compulsion".

[290] Cp. Le Faucheur, p.142: 'Upon a Climax, or a Graduation; where the Discourse climbs up by several clauses of a Sentence to a Period or Full Point; 'tis manifest that the voyce must be rais'd accordingly by the same degrees of elevation to answer every step of the Figure, till it is at the utmost height of it'.

140

must spring audacious Boldness, which must beget all manner of Wickedness and Mischief.[291]

MARS *saw the Nymph, and seeing did desire,*
And having wish'd, he quench'd his amorous Fire.
The Eye the dangerous Poison soon let in,
And by the Eye the Heart began to sin,
Till the whole Body did the Crime complete, &c.[292]

The *Suppression* or *Aposiopesis*, is a suppressing of what might be farther urg'd;[293] and in this the Speaker must lower his Voice a Tone or two, and pronounce the foregoing Words, that introduce it with the highest Accent;[294] as, *Æolus* in *Virgil*.

Which I—
But first the raging Floods, 'tis fit that I compose.[295]

In a *Subjection*, where several Questions are put, and an Answer subjoin'd to ev'ry one of them:[296] He that speaks must vary his Voice, by giving the Question one Tone, and the Answer another; either by asking the Question higher, and giving the Answer lower, or the contrary, according to the Place where he would have the Force lie.[297]

In the *Opposition* or *Antithesis*, the Contraries must be distinguish'd by giving one a louder Tone, than the other; as, *Truth breeds us Enemies, Flattery Friends.* The Romans *hate* PRIVATE *Luxury, but love* PUBLIC *Magnificence.*

---

[291] A translation of Cicero's defence of the businessman P. Quintius; in the translation by Charles Yonge, 'In a city, luxury is engendered; avarice is inevitably produced by luxury ...' etc. From 'The Speech of M.T. Cicero as the Advocate of P. Quintius', in *The Orations of Marcus Tullius Cicero*, I.60.

[292] Gildon's free adaptation from Ovid's *Metamorphoses*, IV.435–45.

[293] Either stopping suddenly to leave a statement unfinished or leaving the auditor to deduce what is being referred to (Lanham, p.15).

[294] Cp. Le Faucheur, p.143: 'Upon an Aposiopesis, or holding one's peace and concealing what might be said farther in the matter, the Orator must lower his voyce a tone or two, and pronounce the foregoing words that introduce it with the highest Accent'.

[295] Gildon's own translation of the *Aeneid*, I.135–6, where Neptune orders Aeolus to calm the storm he has created.

[296] I.e. subjection, where the speaker 'suggests the answer to his own question' (Lanham, p.94).

[297] Cp. Le Faucheur, p.144: 'In a Subjection, where several questions are put and an answer made to every one of them, the Orator must vary his voyce, and give the Interogation one Tone, and the Answer, another'.

Repetition or *Anadiplosis*, which is a Repetition of the same Word, and the Speaker must give the Word in the second place a louder and stronger Sound, than in the first place.[298]

> *Y* *Harmonious Nine, to* GALLUS *tune my Song,*
> *To* GALLUS, *whose Love,* &c.
> *And yet he lives, not only lives, but comes*
> *Into the very Senate-House.*[299]

There is another Repetition, where the same Word is more, than once repeated, either in the Beginning of several Sentences, or in the several Clauses of the same Sentence, where the Word must be sounded always in the same Tone, but differently from the other Parts of the Discourse.[300] *Does not the Nightly Guards of the Palace touch you at all? Not at all the Watches of the City? Not at all the Peoples Fear? Not at all the Agreement of all honourable Men? Not at all this fortify'd Place of the Senate-Meeting,* &c. *You lament the Loss of three* Roman *Armies,* MARK ANTONY *destroyed them: You resent the Death of so many noble Citizens,* MARK ANTONY *was their Death; the Authority of the Senate is invaded,* MARK ANTONY *invades it.*

As for Sentences, some are very short, and those not spoken in a Breath, would be maim'd; there are others, which are something longer, yet withal do not exceed the Power of an easy Pronunciation, in one Breath if you can; for a Period so pronounc'd, sounds rounder and handsomer, and appears with more Beauty and Force, than it would do with several Breathings. To this End you must endeavour by Practice to attain a long Wind, as *Demosthenes* did by the Instructions of *Neoptolemus* the Actor. But when the Period is long, you ought to fetch your Breath at the several Members of the Periods, that is to say, after two Points, or a *Semi-colon*, or at least after a *Comma*, for to do it otherwise or oftner, would be extremely disagreeable. For nothing is more intolerable and clownish, than to break off in the middle of a Word or Expression. 'Tis proper to make a Pause at the End of every Period; but

---

[298] Cp. Le Faucheur, p.144: 'Upon the Figure which the Greeks call Anadiplosis; That is to say, a redoubling, or an immediate repetition of the same word…The Orator must give the same word repeated here a different sound, and pronounce it the second time over far louder and stronger than at the First'.

[299] The first two lines are a loose translation of the opening of Virgil's tenth Eclogue; for PB and Virgil, see n.28 above.

[300] Cp. Le Faucheur, p.147: 'In an Anaphora, where one and the same word is repeated over and over in the beginning either of several Sentences one after another, or of several clauses of the same Sentence'. This figure is sometimes referred to as Epanalepsis (Lanham, p.42).

it must be short on those, that are short, and longer on those, which are of greater Extent.[301]

When you have a Period, that requires a great Contention and Elevation of Voice, you must manage your Voice with the greater Moderation on those, which precede it; but by employing your whole Force upon those, you are oblig'd to speak this more important one more languidly, which requires more Vigour and Vehemence. This was a Beauty, which was always observ'd by the two famous Actors of the *Romans*, *Roscius* and *Æsopus*. For in speaking these Verses,

> *The noble Warriors generous Choice and Buckler*
> *Is Honour, not the Blunder of the Field,*[302]

he did not pronounce them with all that Vehemence of Action and Utterance, that some now would, but simply, and with Moderation, that he might exert himself in this following Exclamation, which naturally requir'd more Force and Emotion of Admiration and Astonishment.

> *What is't I see! all arm'd, all arm'd he comes!*
> *E'en to your Sacred Temples! &c.*[303]

---

[301] Cp. Le Faucheur, pp.151–4: 'For there are some Sentences very short; each part of which is but a simple expression and consists only of one single Proposition ... Those Periods may not only be pronounced with one Breath; but can hardly be pronounced otherwise, without prejudice to the expression .... There are some Sentences again, longer ... And those may be pronounced all at a Breath too, if the Voice be naturally good for any thing: and however, you ought also to do it as well as you can; for a Period so pronounced looks rounder, and appears with more Beauty and Force, than it would do upon several Breathings by fits. For this purpose, you must make it your main Business to acquire a long-winded Habit by Study and Exercise: but that must be done by degrees: For Nature is not chang'd in an instant from a short Breath to a long one. Nature indeed is absolutely necessary in the matter; but Art also can do much towards the accomplishing of this end: and we read in the Bibliotheca of Photius, that Demosthenes, who had naturally a very short Breath; finding that he had need of a very long one to speak upon Publick Occasions, gave Neoptolemus the Stage-player, and a great Actor of Comedy, a thousand Drachms to teach him this Art; which he became Master of at last to perfection by the force of Practice and by exercising himself upon all the difficulties of Respiration. You must likewise exert your Faculties, as he did, and neither spare any time, nor pains, nor cost, to make your self long-winded and an Orator'. Cp. Quintilian, 11.3.52–5.

[302] Altered from Le Faucheur, pp.161–2 ('The brave Warrior's noble choice and shield, / Is Honour, not the Booty of the Field').

[303] Also altered from Le Faucheur, pp.161–2 ('What is't I see! He comes Arm'd, / Even into our very Temples!').

Nor did *Æsopus*, with the utmost Contention of Voice, say — *Where shall I find Relief and whither fly?* but more softly and languidly, and without any immoderate Action; the Force of which he reserv'd for the following Exclamation — *O! my Father! O! my Country! O! House of* PRIAM. --- which his Voice would not have supply'd without that Care. Thus the Painters represent some parts of a Picture in Shades and Distances, to heighten the rest with greater Light.[304]

But tho I have said something of Sentences in their several Kinds, yet I must add a Hint or two of Words likewise.— In them you must regard the common Pronunciation of Custom, and the Conversation of those, who

---

[304] Cp. Le Faucheur, pp.154–5: 'There are other Periods that have a longer Train yet, and take a larger Tour than either of the former; which you cannot pronounce without taking your Breath once or twice … You must pronounce the first part of that Period without ever taking Breath for't; but you cannot pronounce the second in the same manner: So that you ought rather to make a pause upon't than force your Voice to an Absurdity and run your self quite out of Breath; which would be very ungenteel and indecent. Only you must take care by the Way to stop in proper and convenient Places: that is to say, after two Points, a Colon, or a Semi-colon, or at least after a Comma; for to do it otherwise, or oftener, would be a thing extremely disagreeable. Nothing is more untoward, and uncourtly, than to break off in the middle of a Word or an Expression'. Also Le Faucheur, pp.162–3: 'For Roscius did not rehearse these Verses.

> *The brave Warrior's noble Choice and Shield*
> *Is Honour, not the Booty of the Field.*

with all the vehemence of Action and Gesture, that he might have done; but altogether simply, with moderation and conduct, to the end that falling immediately upon this exclamatory Period;

> *What is't I see! he comes Arm'd,*
> *Even into our very Temples!*

he might act it more earnestly, represent it more strongly, and accent it with greater Admiration and Astonishment. And Esopus did not pronounce these Words,

> *Where shall I find Relief?*
> *Or whither shall I fly?*

with all the contention of Voice and Accent within the compass of his Power; but softly or languidly, and without any immoderate Action at all; having a regard all the while to what immediately follows;

> *But, O Father, O Country,*
> *O House of Priam!*

which he could not have spoken with all necessary Exclamation, if he had already spent himself and as it were exhausted his Voice beforehand upon former Emotion and Violence'. Le Faucheur's passage draws freely on Cicero, *De Oratore*, III.26.

speak well; avoiding the ill Accent, and Pronunciation of the several Dialects of the different Countries, either in the Quantities of Syllables, or the Sound of the Vowels, either longer or shorter, or broader or narrower; and you must avoid these Faults, not only in the Country People, but of those of the City and Court it self, where Affectation often destroys the genuine and just Pronunciation.[305] Next remember to pronounce emphatical Words with an Emphasis, Force and Distinction; as, *certainly, assuredly, infallibly, undoubtedly, necessarily, absolutely, expresly, manifestly*, which are Words of a very strong and positive Pronunciation. Words of Praise and Extolling; as, *admirable, incredible, incomparable, ineffable, inestimable, glorious, glittering, pompous, triumphant, illustrious, heroic, august, majestic, adorable*, which are Terms of Honour, and must be pronounc'd in a magnificent Tone. Or Words, that express our Dispraise or Detestation; as, *cruel, heinous, wicked, detestable, abominable, execrable, monstrous*, and such like, are all to be pronounc'd with a passionate and loud Voice. Words that complain and lament; as, *unfortunate, miserable, fatal, mournful, pitiful, deplorable, lamentable, sorrowful*, require a melancholy Tone and Accent.[306] There must be a more, than common Stress on Words of Quantity; as, *grand, high, sublime, profound, long, large, innumerable, eternal*; as well as on Words of Universality; as, *all the World, generally, every where, always, never.* Here the *Pronunciation* must be grave, and of an high *Accent.* As for Terms of Lessening, or Contempt and Slight; as, *pitiful, insignificant, little, low, despicable, feeble,* &c. they must be pronounc'd with a very low, lessening, abject Voice, and an Accent of the greatest Scorn and Disdain. To speak otherwise in all these Cases, than I have laid down, would be ridiculous, and to speak so will effect that Variation of Voice, which is so necessary to finish a complete Speaker. In fine, remember to pronounce all your Words with an audible Voice, especially those, which conclude a Period; which is

---

[305] Cp. Le Faucheur, p.163: First, you must observe to pronounce them according to common custom and the ordinary Conversation of those that speak well. In every Country or Province, there are certain vicious Pronunciations and Dialects, that are peculiar to particular People'.

[306] Cp. Le Faucheur, pp.166–7: 'My next Observation is this; that he must pronounce emphatical Words with an emphasis and a distinction: Whether it be to affirm strongly; as, certainly, assuredly, infallibly, expressly, manifestly, are Words of a very strong and positive Pronunciation: or, to Praise and Extol; as, admirable, incredible, incomparable, ineffable, inestimable, glorious, flittering, pompous, triumphant, illustrious, heroic, August, majestic, adorable, are terms of Honour that must be pronounced with a magnificent Tone: or to dispraise and detest; as cruel, heinous, wicked, detestable, abominable, execrable, monstrous, which are all to be pronounced with a most Passionate and loud Voyce: or, to complain and lament: as, unfortunate, miserable, fatal, mournful, pitiful, deplorable, lamentable, are all sorrowful Words and require a melancholy Accent'.

chiefly to be taken Care of, when the Period ends with Syllables of a weak and dull Sound in themselves.[307]

I have thus run through the whole Art of *Acting* and *Speaking*, or rather, as *Shakespear* calls it, of ACTION and UTTERANCE, in which I have had a just Regard to the PULPIT and the BAR, as well as to the STAGE; in Complaisance to which, I have chosen to give Examples rather oftentimes from *Oratory*, than from the *Drama*, since the *Actor* may learn his just Lessons from that former, as from the latter. I have, in short, laid down such Rules, as if throughly consider'd, and reduc'd judiciously to Practice, will form the *Gesture* with that Beauty, as to strike the Eye with Wonder and Pleasure; and teach the Tongue to utter with that Grace and Harmony, that the Ear will be equally ravish'd, and both convey so sensible a Delight to the Mind, that the Success will be much more glorious in the *Pulpit* and on the Stage, than is at present found from the Endeavours of either. I confess, I know not whether Oratory be at all useful at the *Bar*, where *Evidence*, *Proofs*, and Methods of Court, generally prevail, or where Justice and Equity ought to carry the Point. Besides, the Subjects, which are furnish'd at the Bar, are in themselves *low* and mean, and afford nothing great and awful, as both the *Pulpit* and the *Stage* always do, or ought to do.

I have given you a Collection of the natural Significations of several *Gestures*, and shown how Nature expresses her self in the several Emotions, which she feels; I have shewn you how Art improves these *Gestures*, and on what Occasions they are proper, and how to make them Graceful; I have likewise shewn you how you are to model your Voice to make your Utterance harmonious, shewn the Defects of *Voice* or *Tone*, and its Beauties and Varieties, and laid down Rules how you may avoid that intolerable Vice of

---

[307] Cp. Le Faucheur, pp.167–8: 'He must also lay more stress upon Words of Quantity; as, grand, high, sublime, profound, long, large, innumerable, eternal; as well as upon Words of Universality; as all the World, generally, every where, always, never: Here the Pronunciation must be pois'd to a certain gravity and height of Accent. As for those terms of extenuation and slight; as, pitiful, insignificant, little, low, mean, despicable, feeble, he must pronounce 'em with a very low, lessening, abject Voyce, and an Accent of the greatest scorn and disdain. For the purpose: If a Divine a Preaching, should bring in a Soul labouring under the sense of many great Infirmities, and saying: *When I search'd into the Faith of my Heart, I found it so weak, so imperfect, so languishing, &c.* To speak that Resentment with an elevated Tone or any great Contention of the Voyce, would be a ridiculous Pronunciation, and contrary to the very Nature of things, as well as the Rules of Sence, Reason and Reflection. For those Words of weak, imperfect, languishing, require a doleful Accent, an Accent of Moan, and a low as well as a slow Voyce. This Distinction of the Pronunciation, besides that it is more agreeable to the things signified by such Words, will serve over and above for the variation of the Voyce, which the Orator must always make it his Business to observe'.

Monotony, or always sounding the same Note on all Occasions, without any or with very little Variation. Thus I have run through the *Passions*, the Figures of Diction, Sentences, nay, and even Words; each of which afford infinite Variety to the Voice, if the Student will make it his Business to understand and practise them.

I shall therefore now conclude with those Qualities and Qualifications of a *complete Actor*, which however difficult to attain they may seem, are yet sufficiently, from what I have said, proved to be necessary.

He ought, therefore, to understand History, Moral Philosophy, Rhetoric, not only as far as it relates to Manners and the Passions, but every other Part of it, at least as far as it teaches the Rules of Elocution.[308] He ought not to be a Stranger to Painting and Sculpture, imitating their Graces so masterly, as not to fall short of a *Raphael Urbin*, a *Michael Angelo*, &c.[309] But that which is the most necessary Quality, that a Player ought to cultivate, which should be open, and much at Command; and the Praise *Thucidides* gave *Pericles*, he should endeavour to obtain, that is, *to know what is fit, and to express it*. He must know how to give the proper Graces to every Character he represents, those of a *Prince* to a *Prince*, those of a *Merchant* to a *Merchant*, and so of all others; for generally speaking, let the Part be what it will, the Person, Mien, Action, Look, is the same, that is, that of the Player, not of the Person represented. He should have farther a penetrating Wit and clear Understanding; he must also be a good Critic in the Art of the Stage, I mean, in the Poetical Performances, that he may choose the Good, and reject the ill.

Besides these Qualifications of Mind, his Body ought to have several, that are not very common in our Days. He should not be too tall, nor too low and dwarfish, but of a moderate Size; neither over-fleshy, which is prodigious, nor over-lean, like a Skeleton.[310] Tho this is a thing so little regarded by our Managers or Audience, yet I find, that it was of Consequence in the nicer Nations of Antiquity, as those Instances may show, which *Lucian* tells you, were of a People, who were no dull Observers. — "The Citizens of *Antioch* (says he) are most ingenious, and much addicted to the *Stage*, and so given to remark what is said and done, that no Passage escapes them; seeing, therefore, on a Time a *little short* Fellow enter, and act *Hector*, they cry'd out with one Voice, This is *Astyanax*, but where is *Hector*? Another time, a great tall long Fellow acting *Capaneus*, attempting to scale the Walls of *Thebes*, they told him, he might mount the Walls without a Ladder; at

---

[308] Cp. Le Faucheur, p.36: 'And therefore the Præcepts of Moral Philosophy are both very useful and necessary to reform them, and to teach them Better Manners'. The same argument is explored at length in Cicero's *De Oratore*, Book 1.

[309] PB 139–46 lists a number of engravings after the work of Italian masters, including one of Michaelangleo's *Last Judgment*.

[310] For Betterton's own physique see n.134 above.

The Life of Mr Thomas Betterton

another Time a big and corpulent Dancer endeavouring to rise high, we have need, cry'd they, to underprop the Stage, &c."[311]

A Player, therefore, should be of an active, pliant and compacted Body, which may be improv'd by learning to dance, fence and vault.[312] With these Qualities and Qualifications, and a thorough Knowledge of what I have written, he may justly be allow'd a complete Player. But before I put an End to this Discourse, I shall give an Instance or two of Affectation and Over-acting from *Lucian*. "I once (says he) saw a Dancer (or Actor, for in his Sense they are the same) who tho before of a good Reputation for his Art, I know not by what mischance, disgrac'd himself by Over-Action.— For being to represent *Ajax* distracted after his being vanquish'd by *Ulysses*, he acted not a Madness, but was himself distemper'd. For he rent the Garment of one of those, who stamp'd in Iron Shoes, and snatching a Cornet from one of the Fidlers, struck *Ulysses*, who stood by insulting on his Victory, such a Blow on his Head, that if his Helmet had not sav'd him, and born off the Violence of the Stroke, he had perished, and fal'n prostrate at his Feet.

Tho the whole Theatre of Spectators, as mad as *Ajax*, stampt, shouted, and shook their Cloaths; for the Rout and Ideots, who knew not Decorum, nor were able to distinguish false Action from true, took this as a great Expression of Fury; and the better bred and more understanding, tho they blush'd at what was done, yet shew'd not their Dislike, as much as by their Silence, but colour'd the Actor's Folly by their Commendations, tho they saw not the Madness of *Ajax* acted, but that of the Representer. So that not yet contented, the Gentleman play'd a Prank much more ridiculous; for descending into the Pit, he sat down betwixt two, who had been Consuls, who were much afraid of themselves, lest this frantic Actor should take one of them for a Sheep. Which Passage some extoll'd, others derided; others suspected, that his Over-Imitation had cast him into a real Madness. Others report, that after he came to himself, he was so asham'd of what he had done, that upon the true Apprehension of his Distemper, he fell sick for Grief, and plainly profess'd it. For those of his Faction desiring him to act *Ajax* over again to them, *When I come next on the Stage*, said he; *in the mean time, 'tis enough for me once to have plaid the Madman*. But his chief Discontent

---

[311] As noted above, n.64, PB 10 lists the Mayne/Hicks translation of Lucian; this quotation is cited verbatim from p.375 of that work. In Aeschylus' *Seven Against Thebes*, Capaneus is described as a 'giant warrior'; in the translation by John Stuart Blackie, *The Lyrical Dramas of Aeschylus* (London: J.M. Dent, 1906), p.272. Since his actions are described rather than shown, the reference may be to an unknown play.

[312] While Betterton's physique may not have equipped him naturally for dancing or vaulting (above, n.134), he appeared in numerous roles that required skill with the sword.

sprung from an *Antagonist* or *Anti-Actor*, who represented *Ajax* raving so gracefully and discreetly, that he gain'd a great Applause."[313]

Tho, I fear, I may have tir'd you with all these Rules and Observations, which immediately relate to the Actors; yet I cannot conclude without saying something of our Theatrical Dancing and Musick, as being by *Aristotle* himself allow'd part or an Appendix of the Stage.[314] Under the last Head of Music, I shall presume to say something of *Opera's*, which have of late been dangerous Rivals of the Drama, tho clogg'd with many adventitious or accidental Absurdities more, than the very *Opera* consider'd in it self contains, tho those are so very many and very visible, that they exclude it from the rational Diversions.[315]

I am sensible, that what I am going to say may look like a Condemnation of my own Practice, when I had the Management of the House, and that is in regard of good Dancing.[316] Yet considering, that I was oblig'd, on Account of Self-Defence, to enter into those Measures, I hope what I say here cannot be look'd on as a Deviation from my own Principle; or if it be, I may be allow'd to alter my Opinion in things of this Nature, when we find great Divines do the same every Day in Matters of far greater Importance.

I know very well, that in this I shall run against the Stream of the Town, I mean of those, who generally make up the Audience; but then I consider, that I am an old Man, and have contracted such a Value for the *Drama*, by so long a Conversation with it, that I would willingly leave for a Legacy to my Successors, a Stage freed from those intolerable Burthens, under which it groans at present by the Depravity of the Taste of the Audience, which as it has risen in Dignity has (I am afraid) fal'n in Purity and Judgment.

About an hundred Years ago, there were about five or six Play-houses at a Time in this Town, tho at that Time much less extended and populous, than at present, all frequented and full; and the Players got Estates, tho the Stage

---

[313] Cited verbatim from the Mayne/Hicks Lucian, pp.377–8.

[314] In the *Poetics*, for example, Aristotle notes that in tragedy 'some parts are in verse alone and others in song'; *Poetics*, p.57. PB does not include any translations of Aristotle but does feature René Rapin's *Reflections on Aristotle's treatise of poesie*, listed on p.78.

[315] A view of the new genre of opera that was widely shared, for example by Joseph Addison in *The Spectator* no.18 (21 March 1711). Such was the threat posed to spoken word drama that in January 1707 a production of Shakespeare's *Julius Caesar* was billed 'For the Encouragement of the Comedians Acting in the Haymarket, and to enable them to keep the Diversion of Plays under a separate Interest from the Opera' (LS2 137).

[316] Downes, pp.96–7, complained that 'In the space of Ten Years past, Mr. *Betterton* to gratify the desires and Fancies of the Nobility and Gentry; procur'd from Abroad the best Dances and Singers ... who being Exorbitantly Expensive, produc'd small Profit to him and his Company, but vast Gain to themselves'.

was yet in its Infancy, rude and uncultivated, without Art in the Poet, or in the Decorations, and supported by the *Lower Sort of People*, and yet these LOWER SORT OF PEOPLE discover'd a natural Simplicity and good Taste, when they were pleas'd and diverted with a Drama so naked, and unassisted by any foreign Advantage.[317]

But in our Times (forgive so bold a Truth) the People of Figure, who in Reason might have been expected to be the Guardians and Supporters of the noblest and most rational DIVERSION, that the Wit of Man can invent, which at once instructs and transports the Soul, were the first, nay, I may say, the only People, who conspir'd its Ruin, by prodigal Subscriptions for *Squeaking Italians*, and cap'ring Monsieurs; and the more infamously to distinguish their poor and mean Diversions from those more noble of the Public, they would have no Play at all mingled with them, lest the World should think, that they pay'd any Deference to Poetry, Wit, and Sense; or that their Satisfaction and Delight reach'd farther, than their Eyes and Ears. But what was yet worse, their Taste was so far sunk, that they were pleas'd with what shock'd a nice Ear, and what could not divert a curious Eye. For first, the best of *French Dancers* are without Variety; their Steps, their Posture, their Risings are perpetually the *same* UNMEANING *Motion*; a *French Dancer* being at best but a *graceful Mover*, full of a brisk and senseless Activity, unworthy the Eye of a Man of Sense, who can take no Pleasure worth attending, in which the Mind has not a considerable Share.

Were our modern Dancers like the *Mimes* and *Pantomimes* of the *Romans*, (tho even those grew into Esteem in the Wain and Corruption of that Empire) our Dotage on them might have been thought more excusable; since one of them, as I have shewn from *Lucian*, by the Variety of his Motions and Gesticulations, would represent a whole History, with all the different Persons concerned in it so plainly and evidently, that every body, that saw him, perfectly understood what he meant.[318]

In this indeed it might be pretended, that there was something to strike the Mind, and rationally entertain it, every Action depending on the other, and all directed to one End. But to be fond of our modern Dancing is still to be Children, and fond of a Rattle, that makes perpetually the very same Noise. All that could be said of *Ballon*, (or any other Dancer of more Reputation) is, that his Motion was easy and graceful, the Figures he threw his Body into, fine, and that he rose high with Freedom and Strength; or, in

---

[317] Probably drawn from oral history as conveyed, for example, by Sir William Davenant to Betterton (see Introduction, p.25), but possibly reinforced by James Wright's *Historia Histrionica; an historical account of the English Stage* (London: William Haws, 1699), p.29.

[318] See above, n.64.

short, that he was an active Man.[319] But is that, or would indeed the *Roman Pantomimes*, be a sufficient Ballance for the Loss of the *Drama* to any Man of common Sense?

But before the Depravity of the *Roman State*, nay, ev'n in *Greece*, Dancing was esteem'd, and always perform'd in their Plays, either Tragedies or Comedies, having those, which were proper and peculiar to each, and not to be used promiscuously in both: nay, we find, that ev'n the *Pantomime* Art was in great Perfection, in which *Telesis* the Dancer, was so great a Master, that when he danc'd the seven Captains besieging of *Thebes*, he set before the Eyes of the Spectators, by his Gesticulations and Motions all that they perform'd in that Siege.[320]

Nay, Dancing was there in so much Esteem, that *Socrates* being reflected on for frequenting too much the *Ægyptian* Performances of that kind, reply'd, that Dancing contain'd all Musical Exercises; and the ancient Poets *Thespis, Cratinus, Phrynicus*, &c. were call'd Dancers, not only because they added Dances to their Fables or Plays, but also because they taught to dance. Nay, 'tis certain, that the Art of *Dancing* was so much in Esteem in *Greece*, that *Pindar* calls *Apollo* himself the Dancer.[321] But then we must remember, that all these *Dances* contain'd not only an extraordinary Exercise for the Body, but an Instruction to the Mind, both in the Subject represented by the Figures in the Art of War, which was taught by the *Pyrrhic* and other Dances.[322]

For this Reason I suppose, the Poets assign'd Dancing to Children, (except in the more robust Performances of Warlike Dances) and the Figures of the Dances always express'd the things, that were sung by the Voice, preserving always in them something manly and great, and they were call'd *Hyporchemata*, as it were, Dances subservient to the Voice; and therefore they always condemn'd those, whose Steps and Figures did not

---

[319] Claude Balon (1671–1744) of the Paris Opera was hired by Betterton in April 1699 to perform for five weeks at a reported cost of 400 guineas (LS1 510).

[320] Telesis or Telestes often performed in Aeschylus' tragedies and was renowned as an innovative dancer. See Lillian B. Lawler, 'Phora, Schêma, Deixis in the Greek Dance', *Transactions and Proceedings of the American Philological Association* 85 (1954), pp.148–58. This section on dancing draws on the Mayne/Hicks translation of Lucian, pp.356–66.

[321] Pindar (518–438 BC) became a priest of Apollo. For his Odes and their many associations of the god with dancing, see William Mullen, *Choreia. Pindar and Dance* (Princeton: Princeton University Press, 1981). He was a poet more often imitated than reprinted in seventeenth- and eighteenth-century London. Thespis, Athenian poet, active c.530–520 BC; Cratinus, author of Old Attic comedy, active c.450–26 BC; Phrynichus, tragedian, active c.511–476 BC

[322] According to Plato's *Laws*, the Pyrrhic or Pyrrhichois dance featured quick movements that demonstrated how to evade and inflict injury on an enemy in battle.

express or correspond to the Voice.[323] 'Tis likewise plain from *Lucian*, that the *Mimes* and *Pantomimes* of his Time express'd in Figures what they sung, whether the Rape of *Proserpina*, the Loves of *Mars* and *Venus*, or any other of the Poetical Fables:[324] For in his Enumeration of the Faults of Dancers, he says — "There are many, who out of Ignorance (for 'tis impossible, that all should be knowing) commit great Solecisms in Dancing, such, I mean, whose Actions are irregular, and not to the Tune, as they say, when the Foot says one thing, and the Instrument another: Others keep Proportion to the Music, but their Presentments, as I have often seen, are dispropotion'd to the right Time. For you shall have one, who endeavouring to act the Birth of *Jupiter*, and *Saturn's* eating his Children, dances the Sufferings of *Thyestes*, by reason of the Affinity of the Fables. Another being to act *Semele* burnt with Lightning, likens *Glauce* to her born long after, not enough regarding the Song, that is sung."[325]

But I shall call into my Assistance on this Subject a Manuscript lately left with me by a Friend, better acquainted with these Matters, than I can pretend with all my modern Helps to be.[326]

These Dances, says a certain Author, were in Imitation of those things, which the Words of the Songs express'd. One of them is thus describ'd by *Xenophon*, in his *Expedition of Cyrus*, as perform'd before them at a Feast with *Seuthes* the *Thracian*.

"After we had (says he) pe[r]form'd our *Libations* to the Gods, and sung the *Pæana*, (that is, in plain *English*, after we had said Grace) first, some *Thracians* rose up, and arm'd danc'd to the Flute, rising lightly and high, waving and brandishing their Swords, till two of them to the Tune dealing Blows to each other, that when one of them fell artificially down, they all imagining that he was wounded, shriek'd out aloud. Immediately he, who seem'd to have wounded him, as he lies there spoils him of his Arms, and singing the Praises of *Sitalcas*, makes his Exit. The Rest of the *Thracians* then take up the suppos'd dead, (who indeed had felt no harm) and bear him off. After this enter'd the *Magnesians* and the *Œnianes*, and perform'd the Dance call'd *Semlutes* with their Arms, which is thus.

"A Plough-man with his Arms by his Sides drives in the Oxen and Plough, and sows his Corn, turning every Minute from one side to the other,

---

[323] The hyporchema was a representational, mixed gender dance used in the worship of Apollo.

[324] Lucian, p.371.

[325] Cited verbatim from Lucian, p.376. 'Glauce' is presumably the daughter of Creon of Corinth and wife of Jason, killed at the hands of Medea either by arson or flammable poison.

[326] Note the production of a further manuscript by Betterton's (probably) fictional friend.

as if he were afraid, or apprehensive of some Danger. Presently a Robber approaches, and the Plough-man handling his Arms, fights the Robber, (putting himself betwixt him and his Plough) adapting all the Motions of his Body to the Notes of the Flutes; but in the End the Robber vanquishing the Plough-man, binds him, and bears him off; and sometimes, on the contrary, the Plough-man the Robber."[327]

There were indeed many Kinds of Dancing among the Ancients, which some, according to *Homer*, reduce to three;[328] the first was call'd *Cubistic*, which *Xenophon* and *Suidas* say was an Art of Dancing on the Head, whilst they acted various Motions and Gesticulations with their Hands and Legs.[329] The second sort was call'd *Sphæristic*, or the *Play at Ball*, because they danc'd playing with a *Ball*, all the while they kept Time to the Music. The third kind was plainly call'd *Orchesis* or *Dancing*. *Plato*, in his Book of Laws, divides Dancing into *Military*, Peaceable or proper for Peace, and the Medium betwixt both.[330] That he call'd Military, which imitated by rising on high, or falling back, or inclining to any side, the Assaults of Enemies, their Attacks, Evasions, and Defences, and resembled by various Figures the *Darters*, or those, who fight with close Weapons; and *Plato* was so fond of this sort of Dance, that he ordains in his Republic, that some should be paid by the *Public* to teach it to both Men and Women; believing, that by this alone there would be a very great Help obtain'd towards the Perfection of military Discipline. In Confirmation of which we find, that the *Lacedemonians* receiv'd Dancing among their Exercises as useful to War.[331]

[327] This passage does not appear in known English translations of Xenophon, including the most recent one by Francis Digby and John Norris' *Kyrou paideia, or The institution and life of Cyrus the Great written by that famous philosopher and general, Xenophon of Athens* (London: Matthew Gilliflower, 1685).

[328] See *The Iliad*, VII.238–41 and XVI.617–18, and *The Odyssey*, 288–316. As Gildon writes below, there was a widespread belief that dance was an essential skill for a warrior; see Everett L. Wheeler, '*Hoplomachia* and Greek Dances in Arms', *Greek, Roman, and Byzantine Studies* 23.3 (1982), pp.223–33.

[329] '*Suidas*' refers to the Suda Lexicon, a tenth-century encyclopaedia that draws on ancient literature; it was common to assume (incorrectly) that Suidas was an author. In his biography of Cyrus, Xenophon writes of various kinds of dancing, including somersaults. See Xenophon, *The Historie of Xenophon containing the ascent of Cyrus into the higher countries*, trans. John Bingham (London: John Haviland, 1623), pp.103–4.

[330] In Book VII of the *Laws*, Plato names the Pyrrhic or war dance, and the Emmelia or peace dance; see *The Laws of Plato*, pp.199–202. Gildon also drew on a translation of Hieronymus Mercurialis, *The Art Gymnastica Libri Six* (Amsterdam, 1672), p.135.

[331] I.e. citizens of Lacedaemon, also known as Sparta, famed for its discipline in war and life.

The Life of Mr Thomas Betterton

It would swell this Discourse too much, to pick all, that the Authors yet extant could furnish on the several Heads of these two Divisions of Dancing, that is, of *Homer* and *Plato*; I shall therefore keep wholly to the last of the former, that is, the *Orchesis* or *Simple Dancing*, deferring to speak of the *Cubistic* and *Sphæristic* till some other time.

Aristotle, in the Beginning of his Poetics, having said, that all the Parts and Kinds of Poetry agree in this, that they are all Imitations; he divides Imitations into divers Kinds, or ways of Imitation, as by *Harmony*, or *Verse*, &c. or into Degrees, as *better*, or *like*, or *worse*; or into divers Modes or Forms and Manners, as Action, or Introduction, or Narration, or assuming the Person of others, or not; and proceeding, he says, this of Dancers, that they imitate by Number alone without Harmony, for they imitate the Manners, Passions and Actions by the numerous Variety of Gesticulation. Hence it appears, that Dancing was nothing else but a certain Faculty of imitating the Manners, Passions, and Actions of Men, by the Motions and Gestures of the Body, made by a certain Artifice, Number and Reason. For when he had told us in the seventh Book of his Politics, that there was nothing in Nature, which more fully express'd the Similitude of things, than *Number* and *Song*, he justly adds, that Dancers in the Imitations of Actions make use of *Number*.[332] How this Imitation could be effected by numerous Motions, *Plutarch* in his fifteenth Problem expresses this most clearly of all Men after *Aristotle*; who tells us, that Dancing had three Parts, the *Bearing*, *Figure*, and *Indication*; because all Dancing consists of Motions, Habitudes, or States of Body, and Pauses, as Harmony of Tones and Intervals, or Stops, he says, the Bearing or *Lation* was only the representative moving of any Passion or the Actions;[333] but the *Figure* the Habitude or State of Body and Disposition, in which the Motion or *Bearing* ended; for the Dancers pausing near the Figure or Image of *Apollo*, *Pan*, or *Bacchus*, their Bodies being form'd to their Likeness, continu'd elegantly a-while in that Posture. But that the Indication was not properly an Imitation, but a Declaration of some certain thing, either of the Earth, or the Heavens, or something else relating to either, express'd by numerous and regular Motions. As the Poets, when they imitate make use of fictitious sometimes, or metaphorical Words; but when they inform or instruct, employ only those, which are proper. In like manner, the Dancers, when they imitate make use of Figures, and Habitudes, or States of the Body; but when they declare or inform, they employ the things themselves with the foresaid Indications. So that Art or Faculty of Dancing, according to *Plato*, *Aristotle*, and *Plutarch*

---

[332] Gildon summarizes Books II–IV of Aristotle's *Poetics*. Book VII of the *Politics* refers to the health of citizens without reference to dancing.

[333] *Lation* is an obsolete astrological term referring to the motion of the planets.

The Life of Mr Thomas Betterton

consists in Imitation, made only by Motion; and the Dancers themselves do nothing else but imitate the Manners and Affections, by moving themselves in Number, and using Gesticulations in Order, by *Bearings* or *Lations*, or Figures, or declare by Indications or Information; or else at once declare to all the Manners, or represent to all at once the Manners, Passions and Actions of Men.[334] Hence it was that *Simonides*, with a great deal of Reason, us'd to call *Dancing a silent Poesie, and Poesie a Speaking Dancing.*

But *Plutarch*, even in his Time, complains, that True Dancing was much degenerated from Music, to which it was join'd, and fal'n from that Celestial Art, which it once was, into the *tumultuous and unlearned Theatres* held a most absolute and tyrannic Sway; and there is no Man of Knowledge but is sensible, from that Time to our Days, how much more it is corrupted.[335]

It is not sufficiently known, who first taught Men this sort of Dancing, unless you will allow what *Theophrastus* tells us in *Atbenæus*, that *Andro*, a Flutinist of *Catana*, first added to his Music apt and proper and elegant Motions; whence the Ancients call'd Dancing *Sicilising*, *Catana* being a City of *Sicily*.[336] After whom *Cleophantes* of *Thebes* and *Æschylus* invented many Figures of Dancing, which were call'd by a *Sicilian* Name *Balliomous*, as *Athenæus* insinuates from the Authority of *Epicharmus*; and from this Name *Hieronymus Mercurialis* derives the Italian Name of *Balli*, as our *Balls* seems to be deriv'd from that.[337]

Dances were perform'd to the Sound of Wind Music, or the Lute, or any other Instrumental or Vocal Music. But *Homer, Plato, Xenophon, Aristotle, Strabo, Plutarch, Gallia, Pollux*, and *Lucian*, give an Account of an infinite

---

[334] Distilled from Aristotle, *Poetics*, Books II–IV.

[335] The reference to Plutarch appears to derive from Philemon Holland's translation, *The Philosophie, commonlie called, The Morals* (London: Arnold Hatfield, 1603), pp.786 and 799–801. Simonides of Ceos (c.556–468 BC) was a noted lyric poet.

[336] A debate about the origins and different types of flute appears in *The Deipnosophists; or, Banquet of the learned of Athenæus*, IV.78–83, trans. Charles D. Yonge (London: H.G. Bohn, 1853–4), pp.278–87. Gildon's reference to 'Andro' appears to be drawn from the citation in that work of Theophrastus' 'Treatise on Enthusiasm'. 'Catana' refers to the Sicilian town of Catania.

[337] Also drawn from *The Deipnosophists*. Cleophantes was a Greek physician of the third century BCE recognized by Pliny the Elder and Galen; the fifth-century BCE comic playwright Epicharmus is cited in *The Deipnosophists*, Book XVI. Gildon's 'Balliomous' may be a misspelling of Bucoliasmus, a herding dance. Girolamo Mercuriale (1530–1606) was a celebrated physician and prolific author of *De Arte Gymnastica* (Venice, 1569) and *De Pestilentia* (Padua, 1577). The passage from here to 'Dancing was perfected' (below, p.157) is taken almost verbatim from the translation, *The Art Gymnastica Libri Six*, pp.129–33.

Number of various Kinds of Dancing.[338] Those that were in most Esteem deriv'd their Names either from the Countries where they were invented, or in great Request, or from the Inventor or Manner of Performance. Those which took their Names from Countries were, the *Laconic, Trœxenic, Empyrephyrian, Cretensian, Ionic, Mantinean,* &c. From the Inventor and Manner of Performance, as the *Pyrrich* from one *Pyrrichus* a *Lacedæmonian*, or, as others would have it, from *Pyrrhus* the Son of *Achilles*; in which Dances they danc'd arm'd either with a Song or without it, as we find by a piece of old *Basso Relievo*.[339]

But these *Pyrrich* Dances were divided into several Kinds, or had several Names; as, among the *Cretans*, the *Orsitan*, and *Epichidian*; among the *Ænianensetans*, and *Magnetes*, the *Carpeans*, which *Xenophon* mentions in the V. of his Expedition of *Cyrus*.[340] There were besides, those call'd *Apochinos* or *Mactrismos*, which were danc'd by Women, and for that Reason call'd *Martyriæ*. Others had greater Variety, and were more solemn; as, the *Dactil, Jambic, Emmelian, Molossic, Cordux, Sicinus, Persian, Phrygian, Thracian*, and *Telesias*; the last so call'd from one *Tilenius*, who first danc'd it in Arms, in which Dance *Ptolemus* kill'd *Alexander* the Brother of

---

[338] Gildon's borrowing notwithstanding, dancing features often in works represented in PB: among the sixteen references to dancing in the *Iliad*, there are examples of festival and war dances (16.213 and 654), and wedding and harvest dances (18.495 and 571); in Plutarch's *Lives*, among twenty references, Theseus performs a religious dance at Delos (p.29), nude dancing features in the Life of Lycurgus (p.163) and war dances in the Life of Nuna Pompilius (p.237); Lucian's *Dialogues* contains 124 references to dancing, including 'the Bracelet', a 'kind of dance common to young men, and virgins' (p.359). Of the other authors mentioned here, PB lists works only by Plato (PB 76). *Gallia* probably refers to the poet Caius Cornelius Gallus (?b.69 BC). Accounts by the Greek historian Strabo (64/3 BC–21 AD) informed numerous works of historical geography in the seventeenth century, as did the works of Julius Pollux of Naucratius (second century AD).

[339] John Weaver's *An Essay towards the History of Dancing* (London: Jacob Tonson, 1712), p.107, appears to draw on this passage, itself a rephrasing of Book XIV of *The Deipnosophists* (see n.336, above). The reference is to dances from Sparta (in the region of Laconia), Troezen (the setting for Euripides' *Hippolytus*), Epirus (in the north west), Crete, Ionia (part of modern day Turkey) and Mantinea, west of Argos.

[340] This passage on ancient dances is taken not from Xenophon but from *The Deipnosophists*, Book XIV: 'There were other Dances call'd *Mad Dances* or *Cernophorus, Mongas, Thermaustris*, or the popular or plebeian *Anthema*, in which the Dancers moving themselves, sung to the Tune they danc'd, *Where are my Roses? Where are my Violets? Where are my Lillies? Where are my beauteous Swarms of Bees?* Some were ridiculous; as, the *Mætrismos, Apodimas, Sobas, Morphasmus, Glaux*, and the *Lion*. There are besides, the *Scenic Dances*, as the *Tragic, Comic, Satyric*, and the *Lyric*, as the *Porrichian, Gymnopædican*, and *Hyporchœnatican*, the manner of Dancing all which is not the Business of our present Discourse'.

156

Philip. Other Dances were call'd *Turning* or *Versatile*, because the Dancers turn'd round in a Ring.

There were other Dances call'd *Mad Dances* or *Cernophorus, Mongas, Thermaustris*, or the popular or plebeian *Anthema*, in which the Dancers moving themselves, sung to the Tune they danc'd, *Where are my Roses? Where are my Violets? Where are my Lillies? Where are my beauteous Swarms of Bees?* Some were ridiculous; as, the *Mætrismos, Apodimas, Sobas, Morphasmus, Glaux*, and the *Lion*.[341] There are besides, the *Scenic Dances*, as the *Tragic, Comic, Satyric*, and the *Lyric*, as the *Porrichian, Gymnopædican*, and *Hyporchænatican*, the manner of Dancing all which is not the Business of our present Discourse; it is sufficient to know, that in this third Division of Dancing were not only all these Kinds, we have mention'd, but many more, to which *Lucian* appropriated a whole Book, and that they likewise made use of a great Diversity of Motions both of the Hands and Feet.[342] For since all Motion is compos'd of *impelling* and *drawing* according to *Aristotle*, so the Dancers either thrust on their Bodies, or drew them, either upwards or downwards, from the Right to the Left, and the contrary, backwards and forwards; from which Motions after wards were compos'd simple Walking, Winding and Turning, Procursion or Sallies, Leaping or Rising, Divarication or spreading of the Legs to a Distance, Claudication or halting, Ingeniculation or a bowing the Knee, or a Curtesying, Elation or bearing up haughtily, the shaking of the Feet, Permutation or changing or altering the Motion, *&c.* out of all which the whole Art of Dancing was perfected.

Tho this be but an imperfect Sketch of the Excellence of the Dancing of the Ancients, and gathered from such Fragments, as the Injury of Time has left us; yet it is plain, that they were all directed to express or imitate something, which was an Advantage, that few or none of our modern (especially *French*) Dances have.[343]

But since there is no Man, who shall accurately consider the several Species of Dances in use among the Ancients, but will find, that they did not want the Order of Time, Reason, Proportion, and Musical Harmony, and therefore may be apt to think them not unlike the Hobby-Horse Dancing of our Days, which both Men and Women use for the promoting of Lust;[344] but there is no body but may perceive this Difference between theirs

---

[341] See above, n.336.

[342] For Lucian, see above, n.64.

[343] For John Downes on Betterton's difficulties with French dancers, see above, n.316. For Claude Balon, n.319. Antoine L'Abbé (c.1667–1758) danced at the Paris Opera from 1688 and first appeared in London in 1698. It is thought that Marie-Thérèse de Subligny (1666–c.1735) accompanied Balon on his first visit to London; she returned to Betterton's Lincoln's Inn Fields Theatre in December 1701.

[344] I.e. associated with pagan traditions and holidays.

The *Life of Mr Thomas Betterton*

and ours, that theirs were employ'd as Exercises often, and conducive to Health, ours after Supper, Feasts, and in the Night Time. Theirs were always directed to express some Passion or Action, or Story of the Gods or Men, ours to nothing but striking about to shew a useless Activity. And yet how much greater Deference has been paid to *L'Abbe, Ballon, Subligniy,* and the rest, than to *Otway, Shakespear,* or *Johnson?* And while our own Poets were neglected, the *French* Dancers got Estates; and this by the Influence of those, who at the same Expence might have made their own Names and their Country famous for the Encouragement of the politest Arts and Sciences, now neglected to a Degree of Barbarity, greater, than most Nations on this side *Lapland.*

I must own, that the Excuse of our Leaders seems greater and more reasonable in the Indulgence they shew to Music, in their Subscriptions for *Italian* Singers;[345] tho so sensible a Man as Monsieur St. *Evremont* evidently gives the Palm of Singing to his own Nation — "*Solus gallus cantat,* says he, *none but the* Frenchman *sings.* I will not be injurious to all other Nations in maintaining what an Author has publish'd, the SPANIARD *weeps,* the ITALIAN *grieves,* the GERMAN *hollows,* the FLANDERKIN *howls,* and *only the* FRENCHMAN *sings;* I leave him to all these pretty Distinctions, and shall only back my Opinion with the Authority of *Loüigi,* who could not endure to hear an Italian sing Airs, after he had heard *Vyert, Hilaire,* and *La Petite Varenne* sing. Upon his Return to *Italy,* he made all the Musicians of that Nation his Enemies, saying openly at *Rome,* as he had at *Paris,* that to make pleasant Musick, *Italian* Airs should be in a *French* Man's Mouth — It is very certain, he was much disgusted with the *Harshness* and *Rudeness* of the *greatest* Masters of *Italy,* when he had tasted the Sweetness of the *French,* the *Neatness* and *Manner* of the *French.* — The *Italians* with their Profoundness in Music, bring their Art to our Ears without any Sweetness, &c."[346] Whether

---

[345] Two Italian *castrati* dominated the opera stage during the early 1700s. Valentino Urbani (fl.1690–1722), known as Valentini, made his London debut in February 1706, while Nicolo Grimaldi (1673–1732), known as Nicolini, made his in December 1708. Valentini was paid £537 for the 1712–13 season (*Document Register* no.2222).

[346] The subsequent passage in quotation marks is either loosely transcribed from Ferrand Spence's translation of St. Evremond's 'Of Operas, Written to his Grace The Duke of Buckingham', in St. Evremond's *Miscellanea, or, Various discourses* (London: Samuel Holford, 1686), pp.41–50, or a new translation of the original. PB 75 lists a copy of the original, *Recueil de diverses pieces* (La Haye: J.&D. Steucker, 1669). Charles de St. Denis, Sieur de St.Evremond (1614–1703), soldier and essayist, lived in England from 1661 to escape persecution in France. Charles II appointed him governor of the duck islands in St James's Park. He is commemorated in Poets' Corner. For Luigi, see below, n.358. Vyert is a misspelling: Pierre de Niert (c.1597–1682) was a celebrated singer and teacher. Among his pupils were Mlle Hilaire Dupuis, related to Lully, and a Mlle Varenne.

this Man of an acknowledg'd fine Taste be in the right or not, I leave to the Judges of the Art; but I am sure, if he has shewed himself but an indifferent Critic in Music, he has shewn himself a good *Patriot*, in preferring his own Country-men to a Company of *Stroling Foreigners*, who in my poor Opinion have little Advantage of either of us, but that of coming a great way, and requiring a great deal of Money, and the Witchery of being a *Foreigner*; when scarce any Nation has given us, for all our Money, better Singers, that Mrs. *Tofts* and Mr. *Leveridge*, who yet being of our own Growth, maintain but a second or third Character among worse Voices.[347]

But were these Foreigners as excellent, as they themselves would be thought, yet to be drawn wholly by Sound, tho the most harmonious, that Art and Nature can supply, is neither the greatest nor the justest Praise.

It must, however, be allow'd, that Music discovers a wonderful Power, a Power not to be resisted; but I am afraid, that Power acts more on the Body, than the Mind, or by the Body on the Mind; the Ear has a pleasing Sensation at melodious Sounds, and that gratifies the Mind, which cannot naturally be uneasy when the Body is delighted with agreeable Sensations: But this proves Music as transporting, as it is to be but sensual Pleasure, and deriving no part from Reason, nor directing any part to the Gratification of the rational Soul. But then this Power and Force of *Music* is heighten'd by the Addition of Poetry, which among the Ancients even in Dancing (as we have seen) was very seldom left out; for passionate Words give a double Vigour to Harmony, and make for it a surer way to the Heart, than when the Soul is unconcern'd in the bare and solitary Notes. And Vocal Music is agreed by all to be the most noble, and most touching, that Tone being esteem'd the most excellent, which comes nearest to *Vocal Sounds*.

Music therefore ought still, as originally it was, to be mingled with the *Drama*, where it is subservient to Poetry, and comes into the Relief of the Mind, when that has been long intense on some noble Scene of Passion, but ought never to be a separate Entertainment of any Length.

But tho we allow the Vocal the Preheminence of all other sorts of Music, yet we cannot without the greatest Absurdities receive even that on Subjects improper for it, or in a manner unnatural, that is, as it is offer'd to us in our *Opera's*, with which of late the Town (I mean the leading part of the Audience) has been perfectly intoxicated, and in that drunken Fit has thrown away more Thousands of Pounds for their Support, than would

---

[347] Catherine Tofts (c.1695–1756), soprano, drew the praise of Cibber: 'The beauty of her fine proportioned figure and exquisitely sweet, silver tone of her voice – with that peculiar, rapid swiftness of her throat – were perfections not to be imitated by art or labour' (p.253). Richard Leveridge (1670–1758), bass and composer, sang roles for Purcell and Handel, and later acquired a name for singing and composing comic ballads.

have furnish'd us with the best Poetry, and the best Music in the World, without declaring against common Sense.[348] *Opera's* have been said to be the Invention of modern *Italy*, e'er the Return of Learning, and in the midst of that barbarous Ignorance, with which the Inundations of *Vandals, Goths, Huns* and *Lombards* had o'er-whelm'd it; but I think it is pretty plain, that the *Romans* were, before that, sunk as far from their ancient Learning and Sense, as Virtue and Warlike Glory; and *Lucian* puts it beyond Controversy, that the Entertainment, which we now call *Opera's*, was in use in his Time, when he says, after he had been ridiculing the Tragedies of his Age —

"And also his Clamour from within, he breaks open, and unlocks himself, and most *ridiculously* SINGS his own Sufferings, and renders himself by the very Tone odious; yet as long, as he personates some *Andromache*, or *Hecuba*, his Singing is tolerable, *but for a* HERCULES *to enter dolefully* SINGING, *and to forget himself, and neither regard his Lion's Skin or Club, must needs to a judging Man appear a Solecism.*"[349]

But this, as I have said, was in the Corruption of the *Roman* State, under the Empire, when Learning was almost again engross'd by the *Greeks*, and scarce any else appear'd in Books of Note but that Nation, as those of *Plutarch, Sextus, Lucian*, &c. for it was never so in *Greece*, as is plain from the *Alcestis* of *Euripides*; where the Servants of *Admetus* are scandaliz'd at the Singing of *Hercules*, when *Alcestis* lay dead in the Palace, and the Family with its Lord were all in the extremest Grief and Sorrow; which is a plain Argument, that the rest of the Play was spoken, and not sung.[350] Mr. *Barns* indeed, who is the Author of extraordinary Conjectures, fancies, that the *Greek* Tragedies were sung like our *Opera's*; whereas what we have here instanced, and the Constitution of the Chorus in its Division into *Strophe, Antistrophe*, and *Epod*, prove the contrary. But this may pass from a Gentleman, who would fain persuade us, that *Solomon* was the Author of the *Ilias*.[351]

What insinuated into him this Notion, was the Words he gives us, which imply no more but that Harmony of Speaking, which we have been endeavouring to recommend to the Study of our present *Players*. But if this were really true, (whereas it is directly contrary to Truth) yet I cannot imagine,

---

[348] Closely based on St Evremond, 'Upon Opera's'.

[349] Cited verbatim from Lucian, p.363.

[350] The reference is to Euripides, *Alcestis*, lines 759–61 in the translation by Philip Vellacott (Harmondsworth: Penguin, 1953), p.67. The fragile argument that singing cannot be criticized in song reflects the pervasive suspicion of opera.

[351] Joshua Barnes (1654–1712), Regius Professor of Greek at Cambridge from 1695, produced editions of Euripides, Homer and Anacreon. PB 136 lists a copy of Barnes's *Aulikokatoptron* (London: Benjamin Tooke, 1679). Barnes's lectures on his theory that Solomon was the author of the *Iliad* were published as *Homērou Ilias kai Odysseia eis autas scholia* (Cambridge: Cornelius Crownfield, 1711).

that any Authority can justifie that, which is absurd in it self. But because the Authority of a Man, that is receiv'd in the World, and allow'd to be a Man of a fine Taste, and admirable Sense, may be more prevalent with most Pretenders to Wit, than Reason it self, I shall here transcribe what Monsieur St. *Evremont* has deliver'd to the Public on this Head, both in regard of his Reputation, and for the Justness of his Reasoning, which is the best Confirmation of an Authority; and tho what he says be on the *French Opera's*, it will hold stronger against the *Italian*. He writes to the late Duke of *Buckingham* in the following manner.[352]

"I have long, my Lord, had a Mind to give you my Thoughts, and deliver my Sentiments on the Difference betwixt the *Italian* and *French* way of Singing.

"The Discourse we had of it at the Dutchess of *Mazarine's* has rather added to, than satisfy'd that Desire, which I will now wholly gratify, by these few Thoughts I now send you upon it.[353] I shall therefore begin with avowing freely to you, that I am no Admirer of those musical Plays or Tragedies, which we see in our Time; I own indeed, that their Magnificence gives me some Pleasure, that their Machines have sometimes something surprizing, the Music in some Places may be charming, and the whole together seems wonderful; but then you must grant me on the other hand, that these Wonders are extremely tedious, for where the Mind has so very little to do, the Senses, after the first Pleasure, which the short-liv'd Surprize affords, must languish and die. The Eyes grow weary of being continually fixt upon the glaring Objects. In the Beginning of the Consorts, the Audience observe the Justness of the Concords, and let none of the Varieties escape them, that join in the making up the Sweetness of the Harmony; soon after the Instruments stun us, and the Music seems no more to the Ears, but a confus'd and undistinguishable Sound. But who can support the dull Tediousness of the *Recitativo*, which has neither the Charm of Song, nor the agreeable Force of good Speaking? The Soul tir'd out with a long Attention to that, in which it can find nothing affecting, retires into it self to find some secret Emotion, by which it may be touch'd; and the Mind, having in vain expected Impressions from without, has Recourse to empty Musings, or grows dissatisfy'd with it self for being so useless to its own Satisfaction. In a Word, the Fatigue is so great and so universal, that we only think how to get out; and all the Pleasure the tir'd Spectator can propose to himself, is the Hopes of a speedy End to the *Show*.

---

[352] Again, based on St Evremond's 'Of Opera's'. See n.346.
[353] Hortense Mancini, Duchesse de Mazarin (1646–99), niece of Cardinal Mazarin and a former mistress of Charles II.

"The Reason[354] why generally I soon grow weary at an *Opera*, is, *That I never yet saw any* OPERA, *which did not appear to me most despicable, both in the Disposition of the Subject, and in the Verses.*[355] *Now 'tis in vain to charm the Ear, and flatter the Eye, if the Mind remain unsatisfy'd, my Soul being in better Intelligence with my Mind, than with my Senses, struggles against the Impressions it might receive, or at least fails in giving an agreeable Consent to them, without which e'en the most delightful Objects can never afford me any great Portion of Pleasure.*

"'Tis true, a *Foolery* set off, and *hautgout* with Music, Dances, Machines, and Decorations, is a pompous and magnificent *Foolery*, but yet it is still but a FOOLERY:[356] 'Tis an ugly Ground to beautiful Ornament, through which I yet discover the Ground with a great deal of Dissatisfaction.

"There is another thing in *Opera's* so contrary to Nature, that it always shocks my Imagination, and that is, *the singing the whole from one End to the other, as if the Persons had ridiculously conspir'd to treat in Music both of the most common and most important Affairs of human Life.* Can any Man persuade his Imagination, that a Master calls his Servant, or sends him of an Errand *singing*? That one Friend communicates a Secret to another *singing*? That Politicians deliberate in Council *singing*? That Orders in Time of Battle are given *singing*? And that Men are *melodiously kill'd with Sword, Pike or Musket*? This is to lose the very Life and Soul of Representation, which no Man of Sense doubts, but is preferable to Harmony.[357] For Harmony ought to be no more, than a bare Attendant on Poetry; and the great Masters of the Stage have chose to add it, not as essential or necessary, but as pleasing, after they have regulated all that relates to the Subject and Discourse.

"In the mean time, by these means the Idea of the Master of Musick or Composer takes Place of the Heroe of the Opera, and justles him quite out of our Thoughts. *Loüigi, Cavallo* and *Cesti* are represented to our Imagination; for the Mind being unable to apprehend or conceive a *singing Hero*, comes directly on him, who made the Music;[358] nor can any one deny, but

---

[354] Here, Gildon's book adds a note: 'This Reason is worthy our Wits Consideration, who can value themelves on their Understanding, yet bear Nonsense in Music for four hours together, nay, and extol it too'.

[355] Here, Gildon's book adds a further note: 'This is spoken of the French Opera's of Quinaut, which as far excel all the Italian Opera's, in Disposition and Verse, as Dryden does Quarles'.

[356] 'Hautgout' means highly seasoned.

[357] In other words, poetry and drama should be thought of as superior to music: a brusque intervention in the time-honoured debate about the hierarchy of artistic forms.

[358] The three composers named here are: Luigi Rossi (c.1597–1653), who wrote an *Orfeo* opera at the request of Cardinal Mazarin in 1646; Pier Francesco Cavalli (1602–76), who composed over forty operas and, like, Rossi, was invited to Paris by Mazarin,

that *Baptiste* in the *Opera's* represented in the *Palace Royal* is a thousand times more thought on, than *Theseus* or *Cadmus*.[359]

"I pretend not, by what I have said, to exclude all manner of Singing from the Stage, for it must be allow'd, that there are some things there which ought to be sung, and others, which may be sung without sinning against Probability, Decency and Reason. Vows, Prayers, Praises, Sacrifices, and generally all, that relates to the Service of the Gods, are sung in all Nations, and in all Times; tender and mournful Passions express themselves naturally enough by a kind of Tone; the Expression of LOVE *in its Birth*, the Irresolution and Doubts of a Soul toss'd by the several Emotions of that Passion, are the Subject for *Stanzas*, or *Lyric* Poesy, and so is that for Music. Every Man knows, that the *Greeks* introduc'd the *Chorus* on their Stage, and I'm of Opinion, that we have the same Reason to follow their Example on ours.

"The Business of the *Drama*, in my Opinion, ought to be distributed in this manner. Whatever relates to Conversation, to the Intrigues and Affairs, to Counsel and Action, is only proper in the Mouth of the *Actor*, but highly ridiculous in that of a *Singer*. The *Greeks* made noble *Tragedies*, in which something was *sung*; the *Italians* and *French* make those, which are detestable, in which every thing is *sung*!

"Would you know what an *Opera* really is? I'll tell you,' — *It is a very* ODD MEDLEY of POETRY and MUSIC, in which the Poet and Master of Music are equally on the Rack for one another, and take a great deal of Pains to compose a very Scurvy-Piece. Not but you may sometimes find agreeable[360] Words, and very fine Airs in them, but you will find with much more Certainty, before any one of them be done, a Dislike of the Verses, where the Poet's Genius has been stinted, and a perfect Satiety of the Singing, when too long a Service has jaded the Composer.

"Did I think my self Master of Capacity enough of advising those Persons of Consideration and good Breeding, who are pleas'd with this

---

in this case to write *Ercole amante* for the 1662 wedding of Louis XIV; and Pietro Antonio Cesti (1623–69), sometime friar, latterly *maestro di cappella* to Archduke Ferdinand of Austria, and composer of *Il Pomo d'Oro* for the wedding of Leopold I and the Infanta Margherita in 1666, a production often referred to as the most elaborate opera production ever.

[359] Jean-Baptiste Lully (1632–87), a Florentine by birth, was Louis XIV's Master of Music, composing over twenty operas and discouraging potential rivals such as Cavalli (n.358 above). His *Thésée* premiered in 1675, and *Cadmus et Hermione* in 1673, the latter of which was performed in England in 1686 (see Andrew R. Walkling, *Masque and Opera in English, 1656–1688* (Aldershot: Ashgate, 2019), p.228.

[360] Gildon adds a note: 'This is only in the French Opera's, neither the Italian nor ours can pretend to them'.

Entertainment of the Theatre, I would counsel them to recover their vitiated Palate, and relish again our good Plays, our *Tragedies* and *Comedies*, where Music may be introduc'd without wounding the Representation, there they might have a musical Prologue, and in the Interludes they might have the Music animated with[361] Words, that might be the Life of what had been represented. And after the Play is ended, an *Epilogue* might be sung, or some Reflections on the finest things in the Play. This would fortify the Idea, and rivet the Impressions they had made in the very Hearts of the Audience.

"By this means you might supply enough to satisfy both the Senses and the Mind; the Charm of Singing relieving the bare *Representation*, and the Force of Action the Length of the *Music*."

Thus far Monsieur St. *Evremont*; and I forbear giving you his Discourse about the mutual Dislike the *French* and *Italians* have for the *Opera's* of each other, because that Controversy is not much to our Purpose; and our *Italians* have not long ago publish'd a Book, call'd, *The Comparison of the* French *and* Italian *Music*, in which the *French* Author gives up the Cause to the *Italians*, in return of *Loüigi's* giving it up formerly to the *French*.[362] Tho if I had any thing to do with this Controversy, I should very much doubt the Judgment of the *Frenchman* from one Instance of many, where he admires the *Italians* for Singing out of Tune, that they may give the better Relish to the fine Harmony, that succeeds; as if a Man should admire it as a Perfection in another to speak Nonsense first, to give the better Taste to Sense afterwards.

I confess, I was a little surpriz'd, to hear of and see this Book with Notes by Seignior *H—* or some Creature of his; for I thought they would never have ventur'd so far out of their Depth, as to launch from mere *Sound* into Sense, from pricking musical Notes, to Writing;[363] since that was the only

---

[361] Gildon adds a note: 'He means by this what Horace says of the Chorus, thus translated by the Lord Roscommon,

> A Chorus should supply what Action wants,
> And has a generous and manly Part;
> Bridles wild Rage, loves rigid Honesty,
> And strict Observance of impartial Laws,
> Sobriety, Security, and Peace;
> And begs the Gods to turn blind Fortune's Wheel,
> To raise the Wretched, and pull down the Proud, &c'.

[362] I.e. the translation believed to be by John Ernest Galliard from François Raguenet, *A Comparison between the French and Italian musick and opera's* (London: William Lewis, 1709).

[363] The translation from Raguenet is accompanied by 'A Critical Discourse' thought to be Galliard's work. 'Seignor H' may be a mocking reference to the opera producer

effectual way they could take to convince the World, that we were impos'd on by those, who were not content to bubble us of our Money for Airs and Recitativo's, unless they told us to our Faces, that we knew nothing of the mat[t]er, and must, therefore, receive whatever Stuff they would be graciously pleas'd to bestow upon us.

But this Author puts a great Stress on the *Taking* of his Compositions, and the Miscarriage of those of others, when he had before deny'd, that we knew any thing of the Matter. But if he allow that, as a Test of the Excellence of his *Opera*, that will be much stronger for Mr. *Henry Purcel*, whose Music supported a Company of young raw Actors, against the best and most favour'd of that Time, and transported the Town for several Years together, as they do yet all true Lovers of Music.[364] Let any Master compare *Twice ten hundred Deities*, the Music in the *Frost Scene*, Several Parts of the *Indian Queen*, and twenty more Pieces of *Henry Purcel*, with all the *Arrieto's, Dacapo's, Recitativeo's* of *Camilla, Pyrrhus, Clotilda*, &c. and then judge which excels.[365] *Purcel* penetrates the Heart, makes the Blood dance through your Veins, and thrill with the agreeable Violence offer'd by his Heavenly Harmony; the *Arietto's* are pretty light Airs, which tickle the Ear, but reach no farther; *Purcel* moves the Passions as he pleases, nay, *Paints* in Sounds, and verifies all that is said of *Timotheus*.[366] Music, as well as Verse, is subject to that Rule of *Horace*;

John James Heidegger (1666–1749), who would go on to hire at enormous cost the warring sopranos Faustina Bordoni and Francesca Cuzzoni.

[364] Henry Purcell (1659–95) wrote the incidental music for a number of key productions by and/or featuring Betterton, including *The Prophetess* (1690), *Amphitryon* (1690), *The Gordian Knot Unty'd* (1690), *King Arthur* (1691), *Cleomenes* (1692), *The Fairy Queen* (1692), *Oedipus* (1692), *The Old Batchelor* (1693), *The Richmond Heiress* (1693), *The Double Dealer* (1693), *The Comical History of Don Quixote* (1694), and *Theodosius* (1694). His music for *The Indian Queen* (1695) was performed after Betterton and colleagues had split from Rich's Company.

[365] The aria 'Ye twice ten hundred deities' is sung in Act 3 of *The Indian Queen* by the sorcerer Ismeron, a bass role first taken by Richard Leveridge (see above, n.347). The 'Frost Scene' features in Act 3 of *King Arthur* and is often held to be one of Purcell's finest achievements, its crescendo of shivering strings and chromatic harmonies setting a new standard in programmatic music. *Camilla* refers to the adaptation of Bononcini's 1696 opera by Owen Swiney and Nicholas Haym, staged at Drury Lane in March 1706 (LS2 121) and a runaway success. Haym's *Pyrrhus and Demetrius*, adapted from Alessandro Scarlatti's opera of 1694, opened at the Queen's Theatre Haymarket in December 1708 (LS2 181). Francesco Conti's *Clotilda* played at the same theatre from March 1709 (LS2 186).

[366] I.e. Timotheus of Miletus (c.450–c.360 BC), lyric poet, author of *The Persians*, and credited with revolutionizing the art of music.

He that would have Spectators share his Grief,
Must write not only well, but movingly.[367]

This was *Henry Purcel*'s Talent; and *his* Music, as known as it is, and as often repeated as it has been, has to this Day the very same Effect. But all the Airs of these *Opera's*, as they touch nothing but the Ear, so they vanish as soon, as that is tyr'd with the Repetition; that is, they live but a Year at most; so that *Purcel*'s being compos'd to penetrate the Soul, and make the Blood thrill through the Veins, live for ever; but those foreign Whims, which have cost us above twenty thousand Pounds, are lost before the Castratos have spent the Money they brought them in.[368]

But it has by this very Book been said, that our Taste is improv'd, much amended since the Time of *Henry Purcel*, and that we should not now relish any of his Things.[369] To this I answer, that I find the best Judges of Music, those who are Masters of the Composition, as well as Performance, prefer what he has done to all the *Opera's* we have had, on our Stage at least. I would therefore fain know how our Taste is mended? Do the promiscuous Audience know more of the Art of Harmony and Music? No — not one in a thousand understands one single Note. How shall these therefore give the Preference of this new *Music*, to that of *Henry Purcel*'s? The Masters must decide it, you reply perhaps — That indeed would bring it into a small Compass, to the Decision of a very few, and yet not to be determin'd; for the *English* Masters have still a Veneration for *Purcel*; and the foreign Masters have too visible an Interest to be the Deciders. The only way is by the Rules of Art; for what goes beyond them is nothing but Extravagance, and no Beauty; and if the *Italians* sing out of Tune by way of Perfection, they must enjoy the Advantage, which all Men else in the World will condemn as no Harmony, and by Consequence can be no Beauty or Excellence in Music, the very Soul of which is *Harmony*.

---

[367] Gildon adds the Latin with a literal gloss: 'Non faris est pulchra esse Poemata dulcia funto & quocunq; volenr animum Auditoris agunto. *It is not enough, that the Poem be beautiful, but it should be sweet, and turn the Mind where-ever it pleases*'. The quotation is from Horace, *The Art of Poetry*, lines 99–100.

[368] A document probably dating from April 1709 outlines the terms Owen Swiney proposed to the castrato Nicolo Grimaldi, known as Nicolini: three-year contract for 800 guineas plus £150 per opera supplied (*Document Register* no.2005). Downes points out that English operas were also very expensive. Among the Purcell/Betterton shows listed above, n.364, *The Prophetess* was 'set out with Coastly Scenes, Machines and Cloaths', while *The Fairy Queen* 'in Ornaments was superior' and 'all most profusely set off' (Downes, p.89).

[369] A reference to the gist rather than the exact wording of *A Comparison between the French and Italian musick and opera's* (above, n.362), p.65.

But to return from this Digression, in Vindication of our *English Music*, to the Absurdities of *Opera's*; I think the Degeneracy of the Age is but too apparent, in the setting up and encouraging so paltry a Diversion, that has nothing in it either manly or noble.

But, says a certain Gentleman, the Business of the Stage is to *please*, and if this Pleasure be found in *Opera's*, what signifie all the objected Absurdities? Tho this be a very ridiculous Defence, and will hold of the most scandalous and dullest things in Nature; yet I have heard it urg'd by Men of allow'd Wit, and indeed, who had more of that, than of Reason, and Judgment, which is founded on that. But if this be really a good Argument, *Clinch* of *Barnet*, *Bartholomew-Fair* Drolls, nay a *Jack-pudding* Entertainment in *Moor-Fields* are noble Entertainments, for all these please, and have as good a Title to the Stage, as *Opera's*, nay, from Reason a better, as not subject to so many Absurdities.[370] But this is consecrated by the Taste of Quality.— If the Taste of Quality sink to that of the *Canaille*, it is not the Persons can give it a Reputation, since their beloved *Cowley* has told us of a *great Vulgar*, as well as *small*.[371]

Would therefore a Man of Sense be for a Diversion, which levels his Understanding with that of the Refuse of the *Mob*? Yet the following of *Opera's* does this, and insisting in their Vindication, that whatever pleases deserves Encouragement, since it is a Scandal to be pleas'd with some things, as proving but a weak Capacity, or a very unpolish'd Taste.

There are some Pleasures, which none but Men of fine Sense, and a Gust for the Art, can distinguish, as in Painting, Graving, &c. while the Vulgar look with an equal Eye on the best and the worst. A certain Country Squire of my Acquaintance was drinking in a Country Alehouse, in which seeing several notable Cuts, as of the *Prodigal, Robin Hood* and *Little John* and some other scurvy Prints, worse than ever *Overton* sold,[372] he turn'd to the

---

[370] *Clinch* of *Barnet* refers to the impressionist known as Clench (d.1734), who appeared at Drury Lane in 1701–2 and caused a sensation with vocal imitations of organs, flutes, bells and dogs (LS2 cxliv). Comic sketches or 'drolls' were performed during the three August days of Bartholomew Fair, sometimes by actors from the regular theatres (LS2 xxxvii). A *Jack-pudding* was a clown who set up a stall in public spaces to provide crude comic entertainment.

[371] *Canaille* means rabble, riff-raff. Abraham Cowley's essay, 'Of Greatness', observes that 'The mightiest princes are glad to fly often from these majestic pleasures (which is, methinks, no small disparagement to them) as it were for refuge, to the most contemptible divertissements, and meanest recreations, of the vulgar'; in *The Essays of Abraham Cowley* (London: Sampson Low, Son, and Marston, 1868), p.79. No works by Cowley feature in PB.

[372] This prominent family business began in 1665 when John Overton took over a shop on Pye Corner. It was his son Henry, operating from premises outside Newgate, who 'catered to the lower end of the market', selling 'cheap prints wholesale to chapmen

Gentleman, who sate next him, and said, — *Well! this Painting is a noble Art* — And indeed a Graving of old *Vanhove's*,[373] or worse, if any worse can be, would please the Vulgar, as well as one of *Edlinch, Audrand,* or any of the *Italian Cuts*; and a Piece of a mere Sign-Dauber is as valuable in the Eye of a gross and common Understanding, as one of *Raphael's* or *Thornhill's*.[374] And so in *Music*, a *Taber* and *Pipe*, a *Cymbal* or *Horn-pipe*, will ravish the Mob, more than the admirable Mr. *Shoar* with his incomparable Lute; and the Ballad Tune *Lilly Bullero* more, than a fine *Sonato* of *Corelli*.[375] And thus in Poetry, the *Million* will prefer *Bunnyan* and *Quarles* to *Milton* and *Dryden*;[376] yet sure no Gentleman of fine Taste and Genius in all these things, but would be asham'd to urge such an Argument as Pleasing, since all these, which are scandalous, *please* the most in Number.

---

    who came to stock up with goods to sell on their travels'; from Sheila O'Connell, 'The Print Trade in Hogarth's London', in *The London Book Trade. Topographies of Print in the Metropolis from the Sixteenth Century*, ed. Robin Myers, Michael Harris and Giles Mandelbrote (Delaware and London: Oak Knoll Press and the British Library, 2003), p.72.

[373] By 'old', Gildon may mean Denys van Hove, artist of the Flemish School active in Antwerp in the early seventeenth century, rather than Pierre van Hove, decorative artist of the same region and active in the early eighteenth century. PB lists 155 sets of drawings and engravings, some from the Flemish School; no van Hoves are mentioned.

[374] Given the context, probably a reference to Loduwyck Edelinck, Flemish School, sixteenth century. Other members of the Edelinck family, the brothers Gérard and Jan, enjoyed greater success and worked in Paris; PB 144 lists an engraving of a portrait by Gérard. 'Audrand' could refer to any of the nine members, spread across three generations, of the Audran family of engravers between Charles (1594–1674) and his great nephew Louis (1670–1712). The least distinguished, befitting the context here, was Benöit (1661–1721). PB 139–46 lists seventeen different sets of Italian engravings ('*Italian Cuts*'). PB 140 also lists a set of engravings by Raphael of Urbino (1483–1520) but none by James Thornhill (1675–1734), who at the time of writing was painting murals at the Royal Naval Hospital in Greenwich.

[375] John Shore, friend of and collaborator with Purcell, trained as a lutenist and instrument maker but was also, like his father Mathias, an eminent trumpeter. He was a regular performer in the pit at Drury Lane. His sister Katherine, a fine singer, married Colley Cibber in 1693. The first London edition of Arcangelo Corelli's *XII Sonatas of Three Parts* was published in 1705; music for the popular march 'Lilli burlero' (c.1687) is sometimes attributed to Purcell, an attribution of which the author of the above statement seems unaware.

[376] In *The Way of the World* (1700), Congreve also had a dig at the popularity of these authors by including them in Lady Wishfort's restricted library; 3.1.54–6 in the edition by David Roberts (London: Methuen, 2020). No works by John Bunyan (1628–88) or Francis Quarles (1592–1644) feature in PB, whereas Dryden and Milton are represented seven times, including the Bentley/Tonson 1688 Folio edition of *Paradise Lost* (PB 5).

It is therefore as scandalous to be pleas'd with any thing irrational and absurd on the Stage, in Comparison of the *Drama*, as with *Jack-pudding*, or a *Bartholomew Droll* off it; or to prefer to *Edlinch, Audrand*, a *Vanhove*, &c. or a Consort of Tongs and Keys, or Cymbal and Bagpipe to Mr. *Shoar's* Lute, or the Competitions of *Corelli*.

But, says another, if All that is absurd and irrational should be excluded the Theatre, you must banish a great many of the most celebrated Pieces of the Stage; as, *Othello*, which is compos'd of Parts shocking to Reason, and full of Absurdities; the *Maid's Tragedy*, which Mr. *Rhimer* has justly condemn'd, and several others, which no Man has been able to vindicate from Faults equal to those urg'd against *Opera's*.[377] And since our Reason must be shock'd either with *Harmony*, or without it, pray let us have *Opera's*, where the Composer's pleasing Art makes Amends for the Poet's Fooleries. Nay, says another, I will undertake to prove, that there is scarce one Play, that has met tolerable Success, or is very much esteem'd, and call'd a Stock-Play, but what is as absurd, and shocking to Reason, as most *Opera's*; and what is worse, the Authority, which they have obtain'd with the *Many* is so great, that when you attempt to speak against them, both your *Wits* and *Witlings* cry out, *That you're past Shame*.

If indeed, pursues he, you could advance the *British* Stage to the Excellence of that of *Athens*, it would want neither *Reason* nor *Music*, but the happy Mixture would be admirable, and the Diversion divine; but as the Stage is, both in Players and Plays, I cannot discover so mighty a Difference in the Merit of the two Diversions, but that a Man's Sense is as justifiable in the frequenting the one, as the other.

I must confess, this last Objection has too much Weight in it, but then if the Encouragers of this Folly had bestow'd half as much in the Reformation of the Stage, it would have rais'd it to an Equality with, if not above that of Athens it self, tho that State employ'd immense Sums in the Decorations of it, and the setting out of the Plays; and if any one Man of Power and Interest would heartily engage on the Part of good Sense, Poetry, and the Honour of his Country, we should soon remove this Objection, and discard the Dregs of *Italy* with their harmonious Nonsense.[378]

But there are others, who tell us, that it is the illness of our present Plays, that excuses their Fondness of *Opera's*. But this is without the least Shadow of Reason or Truth; nor can they in any point prove our Plays to be

---

[377] On Rymer. PB 78 lists Rymer's *Tragedies of the Last Age consider'd and examin'd* (London: Richard Tonson, 1678), in which *The Maid's Tragedy* and *Othello* are referenced, but not the same author's *A Short View of Tragedy* (London: Richard Baldwin, 1693), in which those plays' allegedly implausible and sordid plots are submitted to lengthy scrutiny.

[378] For John Dennis on support given by the Athenian state, see above, n.22.

worse, than those of an hundred Years ago, since it would be too palpable an Instance of their profound Ignorance or extravagant Prejudice, which is below a Man of Sense and Judgment, as may easily be made appear in Tragedy only, of which we are scarce yet arriv'd to a just Notion. Nor was there much of Comedy known before the Learned *Ben Johnson*, for no Man can allow any of *Shakespear's* Comedies, except the *Merry Wives of* Windsor.[379] There are indeed excellent Humours scatter'd about, and interwoven in his other Plays; but *Ben Johnson* was the first, that ever gave us one entire Comedy. Since him we have had *Etheridge, Wicherly, Shadwel*, and *Crown* in some of his Plays, with the Rest of King Charles the IId's Reign.[380] And since the Revolution, Mr. *Congreve* in three Plays has merited great Praise, and very well distinguish'd his Characters and hit true Humour.[381] Mr. *Vanbrook* too has shewn Abundance of rude, unconducted and unartful Nature; his Dialogue is generally dramatic and easy.[382] Nay, after these our very Farce Writers deserve more Esteem, than the taking Plays of an hundred Years ago, as having as much Nature, more Design and Conduct, and much more Wit.[383]

---

[379] Performances of Shakespearean comedy were scarce during Betterton's lifetime; *The Merry Wives of Windsor* has more performances recorded in *The London Stage* between 1660 and 1710 than any other. Betterton played Falstaff in the play at least from April 1704 (LS2 64); the play was revived for his benefit performance the following month (LS2 66). In the 'Essay', Gildon wrote that the play 'wants but little of a perfect Regularity' (p.lix).

[380] Morose in *Epicœne* was Betterton's sole recorded role in a Jonson comedy (see above, n.236); the plays had been assigned to the King's Company in 1660 and were falling out of favour in the theatre by the time the King's and Duke's were joined in 1682. Betterton played leading roles in Etherege's *The Comical Revenge* (1664) and *The Man of Mode* (1676), and took over Manly in Wycherley's *The Plain Dealer* (originally a King's Company play) from 1683/4. He is known to have appeared in at least four plays by Thomas Shadwell – *Epsom Wells* (1672), *The Libertine* (1675), *The Virtuoso* (1676), and *Bury Fair* (1689) – and seven by John Crowne: *Juliana* (1671), *The History of Charles the Eighth of France* (1671), *The Countrey Wit* (1676), *The Misery of Civil War* (1680), *Henry the Sixth* (1681), *Regulus* (1692), and *The Married Beau* (1694).

[381] Betterton played leading roles in all of Congreve's plays. If critical and popular success are the criteria, the three plays referred to here are probably *The Old Batchelor* (1693), *Love for Love* (1695), and *The Mourning Bride* (1697). *The Way of the World* (1700), now regarded as Congreve's masterpiece, was less successful in the theatre.

[382] Betterton created the role of Sir John Brute in Vanbrugh's *The Provok'd Wife* (1697) and appeared in *The Mistake* (1706). Cibber praised the 'clear and lively simplicity' of Vanbrugh's writing (p.149).

[383] Vanbrugh himself was a leading translator of French farces. His *The Cuckold in Conceit* (now lost) was based on Molière's *Le Cocu Imaginaire* and opened in March 1707 (LS2 143). *Squire Trelooby*, a version of Molière's 1669 farce, *Monsieur de*

The Life of Mr Thomas Betterton

From hence it appears, that this Objection of the Degeneracy of the present Stage, from what it was formerly, as an Excuse for frequenting *Opera's*, is nothing but a mere groundless Pretence; and that if we met now with as much Encouragement from our dignify'd Audience, as that did from the Vulgar; or if our Judges could distinguish betwixt *good* and *bad* so far, as to encourage the former, and explode the latter, they would soon have Plays more worthy the *English* Genius, and *Opera's* would retire beyond the *Alps*.

After this Discourse, we took our Leaves of Mr. BETTERTON, and return'd to *London*: I was pleas'd with his Story of the extravagant Actor,[384] since it is a very pleasant Lesson for a great many of our modern Players, and which might it self cure them of Extravagances too much in vogue.

I subjoin here a Catalogue of the Plays, in which Mr. *Betterton* made some considerable Figure.[385]

The Loyal Subject.	*The Wild Goose Chase.*
Maid in the Mill.	*The Spanish Curate.*
The Mad Lover.	*Richard the IIId.*
Pericles Prince of Tyre.	*Henry the Vth.*
A Wife for a Month.	*Sir Solomon Single.*
Rule a Wife and have a Wife.	*The Woman Made a Justice.*
The Tamer Tam'd.	*Amorous Widow.*
The Unfortunate Lovers.	*The Unjust Judge.*
Aglaura.	*Epsom Wells.*
Changling.	*Macbeth.*
The Bo[n]dman.	*King Lear.*
The Wits.	*The Rover.*
Hamlet Prince of Denmark.	*Sir Foppling Flutter.*
Romeo and Juliet.	*Circe.*
Adventures of Five	*Hours Siege of Troy.*
Twelfth Night	*Anna Bulloin.*
The Villain	*The Libertine.*
The Rivals	*Virtuoso.*
Henry VIIIth	*Spanish Fryar.*
Love in a Tub	*Oedipus.*

Pourceaugnac, was written with Congreve and William Walsh and opened in March 1704 (LS2 62). *The Mistake* was based on Molière's *Le Dépit Amoureux* (1656) and opened in December 1705, soon after another Molière adaptation, *The Cheats of Scapin*, the 1676 translation of *Les Fourberies de Scapin* (1671) by Thomas Otway (LS2 109 and 111).

[384] I.e. above, p.56 n.45.

[385] On the relationship between Gildon's list and other evidence of Betterton's roles, see below 'Note: Gildon on Betterton's Roles'.

Cutter of Colemanstreet	*Orphan.*
The Dutchess of Malfey	*Titus and Berenice.*
Mustapha	*Theodosius.*
Cambyses	*Plain Dealer.*
The Grateful Servant	*Mock Astrologer.*
The Witty Fair One	*Valentinian.*
The School of Complements	*Amphytrion.*
The Warrior's Weathercock	*Cleomenes.*
Fatal Marriage	*Troilus and Cressida.*
Double Dealer	*Cæsar Borgia.*
Prophetess	*The Way of the World.*
Love for Love	*Ambitious Step-Mother.*
Mourning Bride	*Fair Penitent.*
Heroic Love	*All for Love.*
Harry the IVth.	*The British Enchanters.*

And many others too long to insert.

FINIS

Note: Gildon on Betterton's Roles

Gildon lists 70 plays in which Betterton appeared, but without naming the roles. His addition, 'And many others too long to insert', points to the 182 roles listed in Roberts, *Thomas Betterton*, pp.232–8, which draws on Judith Milhous' 'An Annotated Census of Thomas Betterton's Roles, 1659–1710', *Theatre Notebook* 29 (1975), pp.22–45 and 85–94. Dates relate to the first known performance featuring Betterton. A bold **D** indicates where Gildon could have gleaned his information from John Downes's *Roscius Anglicanus* (London, 1708). There are 36 such instances, just over half Gildon's total. The distribution of dates suggests that Gildon began with the intention of providing a chronological survey before leaping forward to performances by Betterton which he remembered. Later in the list there is a semblance of groupings according to playwright.

The Loyal Subject by John Fletcher (1660). Betterton played Archas.
[The] Maid in the Mill by John Fletcher and William Rowley (1660). Role not known.
The Mad Lover by John Fletcher (1660). Betterton played the title role.
Pericles Prince of Tyre by William Shakespeare and George Wilkins (1660). Betterton played the title role.
A Wife for a Month by John Fletcher (1660). Role not known.
Rule a Wife and have a Wife by John Fletcher (1660). Betterton played Michael Perez. **D**
The Tamer Tam'd. by John Fletcher (1660). Role not known.
The Unfortunate Lovers by William Davenant (1660). Role not known.
Aglaura by John Suckling (1660). Role not known.
[The] Chang[e]ling by Thomas Middleton and William Rowley (1660), Betterton played De Flores. **D**
The Bo[n]dman by Philip Massinger (1660). Betterton played Pisander. **D**
The Wits by William Davenant (1661). Betterton played the Elder Palatine. **D**
Hamlet Prince of Denmark by William Shakespeare, adapted by William Davenant (1661). Betterton played the title role. **D**
Romeo and Juliet by William Shakespeare (1662). Betterton played Mercutio. **D**
[The] Adventures of Five Hours by Samuel Tuke (1663). Betterton played Don Henrique. **D**
Twelfth Night by William Shakespeare (1661). Betterton played Sir Toby Belch. **D**
The Villain by Thomas Porter (1662). Betterton played Brisac. **D**
The Rivals by William Davenant (1664). Betterton played Philander. **D**

Henry VIIIth by William Shakespeare (1663). Betterton played the title role. **D**

Love in a Tub [i.e. *The Comical Revenge*] by George Etherege (1664). Betterton played Lord Beauford. **D**

Cutter of Colemanstreet by Abraham Cowley (1661). Betterton played Colonel Jolly. **D**

The Dutchess of Malfey by John Webster (1662). Betterton played Bosola. **D**

Mustapha by Roger Boyle, Earl of Orrery (1665). Betterton played Solyman.

Cambyses by Elkanah Settle (1671). Betterton played the title role. **D**

The Grateful Servant by James Shirley (1661/2). Role not known.

The Witty Fair One by James Shirley (1666/7). Role not known.

The School of Complements by James Shirley (1666/7). Role not known.

The Warrior's Weathercock [probably *Woman is a Weathercock*] by Nathan Field (1666). Role not known.

[The] Fatal Marriage by Thomas Southerne (1694). Betterton played Villeroy.

[The] Double Dealer by William Congreve (1693). Betterton played Maskwell.

[The] Prophetess by John Fletcher and Philip Massinger, adapted by Betterton (1690). Role not known.

Love for Love by William Congreve (1695). Betterton played Valentine. **D**

[The] Mourning Bride by William Congreve (1697). Betterton played Osmyn.

Heroic Love by George Granville (1697). Betterton played Agamemnon.

Harry the IVth by William Shakespeare, adapted by Betterton (1700). Betterton played Falstaff. **D**

The Wild Goose Chase by John Fletcher (1660). Role not known.

The Spanish Curate by John Fletcher and Philip Massinger (1660). Role not known.

Richard the IIId by William Shakespeare (1691/2). Betterton played Edward IV. Alternatively, John Caryll's *The English Princess* (1667), in which Betterton played Richard III. **D**

Henry the Vth by Roger Boyle, Earl of Orrery (1664). Betterton played Owen Tudor. **D**

Sir S[a]lomon Single by John Caryll (1670). Betterton played the title role. **D**

The Woman Made a Justice by (?) Thomas Betterton (1670). Role not known; does not appear in Roberts or Milhous.

Amorous Widow by Thomas Betterton (?1670). Betterton played Lovemore. **D**

The Unjust Judge [i.e. *The Roman Virgin*] by John Webster, adapted by Thomas Betterton (1669). Betterton played Virginius. **D**

Epsom Wells by Thomas Shadwell (1672). Betterton played Bevil. **D**

Macbeth by William Shakespeare, adapted by William Davenant (1664). Betterton played the title role. **D**

King Lear by William Shakespeare, adapted by Nahum Tate (1681). Betterton played the title role. **D**

The Rover [part 1] by Aphra Behn (1677). Betterton played Belvile.

Sir Foppling Flutter [i.e. *The Man of Mode*] by George Etherege. Betterton played Dorimant. **D**

Circe by Charles Davenant (1677). Betterton played Orestes. **D**

Siege of Troy [i.e. *The Destruction of Troy*] by John Banks (1678). Betterton played Achilles.

Anna Bulloin [i.e. *Vertue Betray'd*] by John Banks (1682). Betterton played Piercy.

The Libertine by Thomas Shadwell (1675). Betterton played Don John. **D**

[The] Virtuoso by Thomas Shadwell (1676). Betterton played Longvil.

[The] Spanish Fryar by John Dryden (1680). Betterton played Torrismond.

Oedipus by John Dryden and Nathaniel Lee (1678). Betterton played the title role. **D**

[The] Orphan by Thomas Otway (1680). Betterton played Castalio. **D**

Titus and Berenice by Thomas Otway (1676). Betterton played Titus.

Theodosius by Nathaniel Lee (1680). Betterton played Varanes. **D**

[The] Plain Dealer by William Wycherley (1683/4). Betterton played Manly. **D**

[The] Mock Astrologer [i.e. *An Evening's Love*] by John Dryden (1685/6). Role not known.

Valentinian by John Wilmot, Earl of Rochester (1684). Betterton played Aecius. **D**

Amphytrion by John Dryden (1690). Betterton played Jupiter.

Cleomenes by John Dryden (1692). Betterton played the title role.

Troilus and Cressida by William Shakespeare, adapted by John Dryden (1679). Betterton played Troilus.

Cæsar Borgia by Nathaniel Lee (1679). Betterton played the title role. **D**

The Way of the World by William Congreve (1700). Betterton played Fainall.

[The] Ambitious Step-Mother by Nicholas Rowe (1700). Betterton played Memnon. **D**

[The] Fair Penitent by Nicholas Rowe (1703). Betterton played Horatio.

All for Love by John Dryden (1685?). Betterton played Antony. **D**

The British Enchanters by George Granville (1706). Betterton played Caelius.

THE
Amorous Widow:
OR, THE
WANTON WIFE.
A
COMEDY.

As it is Perform'd by

Her MAJESTY's Servants

Written by the late Famous
Mr. *THOMAS BETTERTON.*

Now first Printed from the Original Copy.

LONDON:
Printed in the Year 1710.

Dramatis Personæ[1]

SIR *Peter Pride.* A great Boaster of his Honour, his Valour, what a noble Family he is deriv'd from, and of their mighty Courage. } Mr. *Freeman.*

Cuningham. A Gentleman in love with Philadelphia, and is much courted by the Widow. } Mr. *Verbruggen.*

Lovemore. His Friend, in love with Mr. *Brittle's* Wife, and endeavours to have an Intrigue with her; but the Widow courts him too. } Mr. *Betterton.*

Barnaby Brittle. An old Citizen that keeps a Glass-shop, marry'd to Sir *Peter Pride's* Daughter. } Mr. *Dogget.*

Jeffrey. Servant to *Cuningham*, in love with *Prudence.* Mr. *Fieldhouse.*

Clodpole. A simple Country Fellow that *Lovemore* employs in sending Letters to Mrs. *Brittle.* } Mr. *Bright.*

Merryman. A Falconer to *Cuningham,* who takes upon him to represent the Viscount *Sans-Terre,* that is to marry the Widow. } Mr. *Underhill.*

Lady Laycock. An amorous old Widow, that courts every one she can for Marriage, fancying her self so engaging, that all that see her must love her. } Mrs. *Leigh.*

Lady Pride. Wife to Sir *Peter*, a formal old Lady that boasts much of her Gentility, and of her great Name and Family. } Mrs. *Willis.*

Mrs. *Brittle.* Their Daughter, Wife to *Barnaby Brittle*; a Cunning, Intrieguing Coquet, that always over-reaches her Husband. } Mrs. *Bracegirdle.*

Philadelphia. Niece to the Widow, in love with *Cuningham.* } Mrs. *Porter.*

Prudence. Maid to the Widow. Mrs. *Hunt.*

Damaris. Maid to Mrs. *Brittle*, that assists her in her Intrigues. } Mrs. *Prince.*

---

[1] This represents the cast from the mid-1690s onwards. For the original cast, see Introduction, p.30.

THE
Amorous Widow:
OR, THE
WANTON WIFE.

ACT I. Scene a Room.

Enter Philadelphia *with a Letter, follow'd by* Jeffrey.

Phil. I should believe Mr. *Cuningham* very constant, if I had Faith enough to credit this Letter, *Jeffrey.* What Complaints are here? But 'tis the Stile that all young Lovers write.

Jeff. Pray, Madam, believe me; you know I am a Man of Integrity. I cannot dissemble. Let him write what he pleases. If he did not love you, do you think I'd tell you so?

Phil. When he has Opportunity, I must confess, he says kind things to me.

Jeff. Take my Word, Madam, my Master is not like other Men—Unless he loves a Lady, and loves her passionately too, he never troubles himself to compliment her much.

Phil. Never? Yes, *Jeffrey*; sometimes, you know, he compliments my Aunt.

Jeff. That's a convincing Proof of his Love to you; you cannot think him reduc'd to the Necessity of making Love to an antiquated Piece, with design to know her otherwise than to obtain the Happiness of seeing you? But I shall tell him, Madam—

Phil. Tell him I have receiv'd and read his Letter.

Jeff. Is that all, Madam?

Phil. All! Yes. Are you not content with that?

Jeff. Any indifferent Person, that had Hands, and could but read, would have done as much as that.

Phil. Well; tell him then, in time perhaps I may—

Jeff. My Master, Madam, can't endure to depend on a perhaps.

The Amorous Widow: Or, The Wanton Wife

Enter Prudence.

Pru. Quick, quick, up to your Chamber, Madam.

Phil. What's the Matter? Is my Aunt coming hither?

Pru. She's at your Heels. Go up the Back-Stairs quickly.

Phil. Farewell, *Jeffrey*; commend me to thy Master.   (*Exit* Phil.

Jeff. For what, I beseech you? Is not my Master bewitch'd, to court a Lady a whole Year, and she hardly tell him she loves him yet?

Pru. Alas! She's but a Novice. Let me alone with her; I'll order the Business so, that if thy Master be discreet and passionate enough in his Expressions, he wins her Heart, I'll warrant you.

Jeff. He can say nothing to her, but that damn'd Aunt of hers is harkning to't still. What Pleasure can she find in Love at fifty?

Pru. Fie, *Jeffrey*, you must say five and twenty.

Jeff. I wonder any Woman can have the Impudence to live, and trouble Mankind after that Age.

Pru. There never was a Woman so old, but she retain'd a good Opinion of her self.

Jeff. Then she dresses her self so fantastically, that all may see she strives to appear Young in defiance of Nature. She is more gawdy in that she calls Half-Mourning, than a young Bride is on her Wedding-Night. The Devil's in her if she believes any one can love her. 'Tis jeering her, but to be commonly civil to her.

Pru. A little Flattery fires her. She believes all that is said to her. And he that does not make love to her, and compliment her, shall not be twice admitted to her House.

Jeff. O reverend Beauty! On my Conscience, if I would grease her Chops with a few Compliments, she'd mump[2] and smile upon me.

Pru. No doubt on't.

Jeff. When shall my Master have an Opportunity to speak freely to *Philadelphia*?

---

2   *mump*: 'To utter indistinctly or inarticulately, as with toothless gums' (OED 1).

Pru. Mr. *Lovemore* is thy Master's Friend, and is better belov'd here than he imagines. You must persuade him to amuse the Aunt, that Mr. *Cuningham* may have Convenience to court the Niece.

Jeff. Mr. *Lovemore's* tir'd with playing that part so often; he is cloy'd with the Aunt, and swears he'll have no more of her.

Pru. I'm sure her Niece and I endure much more. Tell him, 'twill be Charity in him to relieve us.

Jeff. 'Twill be hard[3] to persuade him to it.

Pru. This old Lady of mine has languish'd for a young Husband ever since Sir *Oliver Laycock* dy'd. She cares not what Estate he has, or what Religion he's of, so he be but young and lusty. Where is the great Viscount *Sans-Terre* thy Master told her of? Methinks he's long a-coming.

Jeff. Some cross, unlucky Business hinders him.

Pru. She has lately receiv'd some Letters, that have given a full Account of him.

Jeff. So much the worse. What is it?

Pru. They say his Fortune is not very much, but he is greatly born, and very pleasant; and that he is so great a Lover of Musick, he has not a Servant but can Sing or Dance, or Play upon some Instrument. You may know when he's come by the Noise; the Fiddlers will welcome him to Town, for all from *Westminster* to *Wapping* pay him Homage.

Jeff. Wou'd he were but marry'd to her, *Prudence*.

Pru. Whether he marries her or not, is not our Business, *Jeffrey*. Let him but fool with us till thy Master has gain'd her Niece, and then our Work is done.

Jeff. Well, we have had enough of thy old Lady *Laycock*. Let us now talk of our own Affairs; speak, dost thou love me, *Prudence*?

Pru. A pleasant Question! Do you doubt it now?

Jeff. If you would have me credit you, swear it.

Pru. Sure you are jealous, *Jeffrey*?

Jeff. You're somewhat near the Matter. I know your Humour well enough; you love a bold audacious Fellow, that will say any thing, and such a one we have come to Town, one *Merryman* our Falconer; I fear you'll like him better than you do me.

---

[3] Q1 has 'very hard'.

The Amorous Widow: Or, The Wanton Wife

Pru. Oh Fool! Why should you think so?

Jeff. I have some Honour in me; but he's a Fellow that has eaten Shame, and drank after it. He is more impudent than a Court Page, and will take no Denial.

Pru. Hold your Tongue, here's my Lady.

Enter Lady Laycock.

Lady L. What Business has *Jeffrey* with you?

Pru. His Master sent him to know, whether he might have leave to wait upon your Ladyship this Morning.

Lady L. Yes; tell him, I expect him.

Jeff. He durst not come, because Mr. *Lovemore*'s with him.

Lady L. Go tell 'em, if they please to come, they shall be welcome both.

Jeff. I shall, Madam. (*Exit* Jeff.

Pru. You see what Power your Beauty has. Neither can live a Moment without seeing you.

Lady L. No, they have other Business with me, *Prudence*: they came from *Paris* lately, and brought me a Letter from my Brother; and I believe they come for my Answer now.

Pru. But does not one of 'em love you, Madam?

Lady L. I have some Reason to believe he does; Mr. *Lovemore* has spar'd no Pains to persuade me to quit my Widow-hood.

Pru. I have been told, Madam, that Widow-hood is a Gift Heaven seldom bestows but on its Favourites; you are rich, and know how troublesome Marriage is. For my part, I believe the fairest Hair, the beautiful'st Curls do not become your Fore-head so well as a *Bando* did; but every one, Madam, knows their own Necessities.

Lady L. I confess, Widow-hood has its Conveniencies; but if Marriage be a Trouble to some, 'tis a Pleasure to others, *Prudence*.

Pru. You had the Experience of it thirty Years; how did you like it, Madam? They say, Sir *Oliver Laycock* lov'd your Ladyship.

Lady L. For all that, he was jealous; and, what's worse, was old.

Pru. Very well; therefore you resolve to have a young One now, Madam?

182

The Amorous Widow: Or, The Wanton Wife

Lady L. You cannot blame me for that? Can you, *Prudence*?

Pru. Oh no, 'tis well known Youth is comfortable. But, methinks, you should take one a little nearer your own Age, Madam. A very young Man may be too treacherous for you, Madam.

Lady L. Why, is my Age so visible?

Pru. No, Madam; with a little Help of Art you have some Remains of Beauty still. You have something about your Eyes as pleasant now, as others have at twenty.

Lady L. 'Tis a very malicious World we live in, *Prudence*; they are so apt to censure and speak of any single Woman, that one ought to marry to avoid that Scandal.

Pru. Some that are young are forc'd to marry, to avoid Detraction; others wou'd rather all that's ill should be said of them, than to have no Notice taken of 'em. I knew a young Lady that pin'd to a Consumption, because she liv'd three Years about the Court, and never had the Honour to be lampoon'd. The Truth is, none that are Beautiful and Young can avoid Envy, but few are so malicious, to speak against the Old.

Lady L. There is no Age exempt from Scandal, *Prudence*. When we are young, they say we sell our selves; when old, we are forc'd to hire, to buy our Lovers.

Pru. You know what they say, Madam, of the old Marchioness, your Friend, that was so admir'd, so courted in her Youth; who, when she found she was forsook by all, was forc'd to hire a Player by the Quarter.[4] How soon the poor Fellow was tir'd too! How like a Sheep-biter[5] he look'd after the first two Months!

Lady L. This *London* is a very wicked Place; 'tis impossible to live without Scandal here.

Pru. I'm afraid they'll say as much of you, Madam, if you bargain for a Husband. To covet one that is both young and rich, is too much in Conscience, Madam.

Lady L. Thou know'st, *Prudence*, Wealth is not the thing I seek.

Pru. Then, Madam, the Business is done; the Viscount *Sans-Terre* shall be your Husband, Madam.

---

4   *by the quarter*: every three months.
5   *Sheep-biter*: probably in the sense given by OED 4, 'a dog that runs after mutton' (i.e. old lamb).

The Amorous Widow: Or, The Wanton Wife

Lady L. Ah *Prudence*! If he were but as handsome as—

Pru. Ah Madam, that's too much.

Lady L. Why may not I wish for it?

Pru. Consider his Quality, Madam, and 'bate[6] him something for that. One thing I must advise you: be not too prodigal of your Gold at first; to be liberal sometimes will be convenient, and make him kinder to you.

Lady L. For all this, I should think my self very happy, if I were certain of Mr. *Cuningham* or Mr. *Lovemore*.

Pru. A little Jealousy will inflame 'em. They'll be more pressing when the Viscount comes.

Lady L. But yet methinks, *Cuningham* and my Niece—

Pru. What, Madam?

Lady L. Are always whispering.

Pru. He only compliments her, Madam. She's too young to make Love seriously.

Lady L. With your Favour, there's no trusting to that. To my Knowledge, there are those younger than she, that understand what Love is but too well.

Pru. That's true, Madam; but *Philadelphia* is so innocent, that no Man can make Love to her, but to divert himself. Here she is, Madam.

Enter Philadelphia.

Lady L. What does she come for? I'll send her packing quickly.

Pru. Consider what you do, Madam. How can Mr. *Lovemore* entertain your Ladyship, unless his Friend may divert himself the while with rallying with your Niece?

Lady L. For all that I could wish—

Pru. Pray trouble not your self. Trust me, I'll watch her, Madam.

Phil. Will your Ladyship go to *Eaton's*?[7] The Coach is at the Door.

---

6   *bate*: abate, make allowance for.

7   *Eaton's*: the Eatons were a well-known family of mercers and haberdashers who traded from the Royal Exchange, rebuilt after the Fire in 1669. John Eaton was a prominent mercer in the 1660s who dealt in lace among other goods; he died in 1682. Records of Hearth Taxes show a John Eaton of Foster Lane, Cheapside, who was prosperous enough to have eight fireplaces. See D.J. Keene and Vanessa Harding,

The Amorous Widow: Or, The Wanton Wife

Lady L. No, I'll not go yet.

Phil. If you stay long, Madam, the best *Poynt*[8] will be sold before you come.

Lady L. No matter. Ha! What ails the Girl! How strangely she looks! Her Eyes are hardly open yet!

Phil. How, Madam?

Lady L. Then her Head's dress'd awry. How it disguises her! Lord! How frightfully it looks!

Phil. Truly, Aunt, 'tis dress'd just as the Fashion is.

Lady L. Fetch her Hood, *Prudence*; I'll have her put it on till it be mended.

Phil. I dress'd it to please no body but my self, Madam.

Lady L. I'll have you dress your self now to please me. Come, put it on.

Pru. My Lady's in the Right. Never was any thing more ridiculous. Here, put on the Hood, I am sure this is much handsomer.

Lady L. Why don't you put it on?

Phil. I can't endure it, Madam—

Lady L. Do, I say.

Pru. So. Now it is as it should be; all modest Maids should be dress'd so. But here's Mr. *Cuningham* and Mr. *Lovemore*.

Enter Cuningham, Lovemore *and* Jeffrey.

Love. Your Servant, Madam; you see how we love your Company, by giving you this Trouble in a Morning.

Cun. 'Tis a Happiness we are much envy'd for.

Lady L. You are welcome, Gentlemen. Pray command this House as freely as your own.

Love. Why does this Lady hide her Face? Pray, Madam, let us see you.

Lady L. Forbear, Sir, I beseech you. She has had the Tooth-Ache lately. If she takes off her Hood, she'll catch cold, and bring the Pain again.

Historical Gazetteer of London Before the Great Fire, available at www.british-history. ac.uk/no-series/london-gazetteer-pre-fire, and www.british-history.ac.uk/london-hearth-tax/london-mddx/1666/st-botolph-aldersgate'aldersgate-street.

[8] *Poynt*: i.e. lacework made entirely by needle.

Phil. I thank your Ladyship for your Care of me. But the Pain has been gone so long, I don't fear it now.

Love. Nay then, we must have it off.

Phil. What say you, Madam? Shall I pull it off?

Lady L. Yes, Impertinence; I see you have a Mind to shew your self.

Pru. 'Tis the Nature of all young Girls to do what they are forbidden.

Cun. I come not to trouble your Ladyship for your Letter to my Lawyer; your countenancing my Business will be of great Advantage to me.

Lady L. This, Sir, is what my Brother commands me. You shall see I take delight to serve his Friends.

Love. Madam, You promis'd me that Honourable Title.

Lady L. Do you pretend to it?

Love. Yes, Madam, more, than any one.

Lady L. I have not much Beauty to boast of; but Virtue, Sir, makes some amends for the Defects of the other.

Love. Defects? (Cuningham *courts* Philadelphia) Pray, Madam, wrong not your self so much.

Lady L. There are few but know a little their own Value. And tho' a Woman be not fam'd for a great Beauty, yet if she be agreeable, there are those will like her well enough.

Love. You have that in Perfection, Madam.

Lady L. In that, Sir, I know you do not flatter. *Philadelphia* —

Phil. Madam.

Cun. Then, Madam, you like my Choice of this Suit.

Phil. Extremely well. Was it your own Fancy, Sir?

Cun. I am not asham'd to own it, since you ask it, Madam.

> (*They counterfeit to be talking about Fashions,*
> *whilst seemingly* Lovemore *courts the Aunt.*

Pru. I'll listen to 'em— He talks to her of nothing but new Fashions.
You may, Madam, venture to discourse without disturbance.   (*To* Lady L.

Lady L. Pray, Sir, tell me freely: how old do you think I am?

The Amorous Widow: Or, The Wanton Wife

Love. Faith, Madam, if you were not a Widow, I should think you a Girl scarce twenty.

Lady L. Now, Sir, you flatter me. You might have said Thirty. I do not love to disguise my Age.

Love. How! Thirty, Madam! And look so youthful: I'll not believe it, 'tis impossible!

Lady L. You do not know what Misery I endur'd whilst my old Husband liv'd. The Griefs I had upon me would have distracted another Woman. Alas! Sir, 'tis not Age but Sorrow has broke me.

Love. It makes me sad to hear you tell it, Madam, and vexes me to think an old Man should enjoy such Happiness.

Lady L. You do not know how many Tears I have shed.

Love. 'Tis some Comfort, Madam, to remember he did not live long with you.

Lady L. Truly, Sir, Fifteen Years.

Pru. Yes, and Fifteen to that.   (*Aside.*

Lady L. Having been so unfortunate in a Husband, you may believe I have but little Encouragement to venture, Sir, again. For I am very happy now I am alone.

Love. You do wisely, Madam; for she deserves not to be pity'd, that rashly runs into the same Misfortune; and therefore you have, Madam—

Lady L. Nay, Sir, I have not forsworn Marrying yet.

Love. Pray, Madam, where do you use to walk in the Evening? Into St. James's Park?[9]

Lady L. Not very often, Sir.

Love. Or into the Mulberry Garden?[10] Is not the Wilderness very pleasant?

---

[9]   *St James's Park*: a stock setting for Restoration comedies and a fashionable meeting place; extended and regularly used by Charles II, and newly laid out according to French principles. Rochester's poem, 'A Ramble in St James's Park', portrays it as a den of promiscuity; here, as below, Lovemore makes a joke at Lady Laycock's expense.

[10] *Mulberry Garden*: next to St James's Park, since occupied by Buckingham Palace. Pepys's experience says something about Lovemore's sense of humour: 'a very silly place, worse than Spring-Garden, and but little company and those a rascally, whoring, roguing sort of people; only, a wilderness here that is somewhat pretty';

The Amorous Widow: Or, The Wanton Wife

Lady L. If I like my Company, Sir, I never mislike the Place.

Love. Have you seen the new Paradise, Madam?[11] 'Tis much superiour to the former.

Lady L. I have heard as much. But, Sir—

Love. Let me have the Honour to wait upon you thither presently.

Lady L. Not yet, Sir; after Dinner, if you please. But tell me, Sir, do you think me such an Enemy to Marriage, that were I sure a young Gentleman lov'd me, and lov'd me truly, I would be so uncivil to refuse him?

Love. When I consider what you endur'd in Sir *Oliver Laycock*'s time, I think you ought to do it, Madam; and that Man's unjust, that urges you to break your Resolution.

Lady L. Pray do not mistake me, Sir; I have made no such Resolution yet.

Love. Nay, Madam, since you are displeas'd at what I said, we'll change the Discourse. Pray, Madam, do you think the young Lord *Lucky* has that Interest at Court, that Fame reports he has?

Lady L. Lord, Sir, this is a strange wild Answer to my Question. Let me tell you, Sir, if I have any Merit, Wealth or Beauty, there's one in the World deserves 'em all.

Pru. Good! How she teazes him! (*Aside.*

Love. But has that one no Fault, Madam?

Lady L. You know him very well, Sir.

Love. I know him, Madam!

Lady L. Yes, you, Sir. 'Tis your self.

Love. 'Sdeath! What will become of me now? (*Aside.*

Enter a Servant.

Serv. Madam—

Lady L. What now?

Serv. The Marchioness is come to visit you.

Pepys, 20 May 1668 (IX.207). Pepys visited the site fresh from disliking Sir Charles Sedley's comedy of love intrigue, *The Mulberry-Garden* (1668).

[11] *Paradise*: another sly allusion to sexual pleasure, this time via the newly enclosed area of the Mulberry Garden.

Lady L. Troublesome Creature. Go one of you and entertain her quickly.

Pru. Which of us, Madam?

Lady L. Go you, *Philadelphia*, and keep her Company till I come.

Phil. I shall, Madam. (*Exit* Phil.

Cun. Pray, Madam, what is this Marchioness?

Lady L. Oh, Sir! A most eternal Talker. Her Tongue goes like the Larum of a Clock, as fast, and to the same Tune still. She's almost sixty, and yet pretends to Beauty, and loves Courtship most unreasonably. Say but a kind thing to her, and you win her Heart. The Truth is, she has not much Reputation; but the Respect I give her is to her Quality and to her Person. But she's an Original in her kind, Sir.

Love. Oh blind, blind Creature! She draws her own Picture, and laughs at it.
(*Aside.*

Cun. Sure, Madam, her Conversation must be very pleasant?

Lady L. She has been much courted in her Youth; but 'twould make one die to hear her boast of her Lovers now. How this Knight sighs, and that Lord dies for her; when all the while I know what Necessity the poor Creature is reduc'd to. I would have brought her hither, but I know we never should have been rid of her. Excuse me a Moment, I'll send her away, and return presently. Your Servant, Gentlemen. (*Exit* Lady L.

Cun. How now, Friend—What's the Matter? Why dost look so sullenly?

Love. I play the Ass here any longer! No; if I do, may I turn Pudding to a Rope-Dancer, and shew Tricks next *Bartholomew* Fair.[12]

Cun. Nay, but Friend, dear Friend—

Love. Tell not me of Friendship. What Man would endure to be so plagued as I have been. I have parry'd with my best Skill the dangerous Thrusts that ever were made at me. To tug at an Oar, or dig in a Mine in *Peru*, is Recreation to it. But the first time to offer Marriage to me! I sweat to think on it.

---

[12] The rope dancer Jacob Hall was renowned for his displays at Bartholomew Fair, held annually in the last week of August. On 29 August 1668 Pepys judged Hall's performance 'a thing worth seeing, and mightily followed'. 'Pudding' (spelled 'Pudden' in Q1) refers to the buffoonish character Jack Pudding who often featured in booth and street performances. Before seeing Jacob Hall in 1668, Pepys watched 'a ridiculous, obscene little stage-play, called 'Marry Andrey' [i.e. Merry Andrew]; a foolish thing, but seen by everybody' (IX.293).

The Amorous Widow: Or, The Wanton Wife

It made me tremble twice, for fear she should have forc'd my Neck into her muddy Noose of Matrimony.

Cun. We have no other way to blind her.

Love. 'Tis all one to me.

Cun. If thou lov'st my Life, Friend, do not forsake me now.

Love. Pray live, if you please, and give me leave to do so too. Should I again be left alone with her, the best I can hope for is Distraction.

Pru. How do you like the Niece?

Cun. She's all Perfection.

Pru. How do you thrive? Do you find her kind, Mr. *Cuningham*?

Cun. She has promis'd me a Meeting this Afternoon, if thou canst but remove the Aunt from us.

Pru. I'll try what I can do, but Mr. *Lovemore* is the only Man in her Favour.

Cun. Dear Friend, try but this one.

Love. I'll be hang'd, drawn, and quarter'd for a Traitor first, and have my Limbs hung up for the Birds to feed upon.[13] No, no, I have my Belly full, I thank you, and some to spare.

Pru. But now I think on't, where's this Viscount all this while? His Arrival wou'd be of great use in this Affair.

Love. Prudence advises well. Methinks he's long a-coming.

Cun. Why, you must know, there is one *Merryman* just come up out of the Country; he is my Falconer. Upon Occasion, the Fellow is bold, and very apt, and has not been seen much in Town. What think you of him to act awhile, till some more lucky Occasion present it self?

Love. 'Tis a lucky Thought, and may be of use. Where is he?

Jeff. In the Pantry, a-ramming down a Wedge of Roast-Beef to keep out the Town Air, and making Sport with a simple Country Fellow he has brought out of the Country with him to see the Town; one *Clodpole*, he calls him.

---

[13] This brutal punishment was a familiar sight in 1660s London, partly because of the treatment of signatories to Charles I's death warrant. The last UK instance was in 1820, for the five men involved in the Cato Street Conspiracy, and the practice was not formally abolished until the Forfeiture Act of 1870.

The Amorous Widow: Or, The Wanton Wife

Love. 'Twould not be amiss to examine him, and instruct him how to behave himself, before he is too much known.

Jeff. No body of the Family has seen him yet, but the Butler; and he, I know, will be secret. I'll step and call him to you, Sir, if you please?

Cun. Do so. (*Exit* Jeff.

In the mean time, *Prudence*, there's something to buy thee a Pair of Gloves.
(*Gives her Money.*
Pru. Oh, dear Sir! How long have I deserved this? Please to command me any thing within my Power, and conclude it done.

Enter Jeffrey *with* Merryman *dress'd like a Falconer.*[14]

Jeff. Sir, I found him just passing by the Door, and have told him part of the Business.

Love. Well, Friend, dost think thou can'st act the Part of a Viscount for a little while?

Merr. What sort of a Lord is he to be?

Cun. Oh! An Amorous Resolute sort of a Person, that's much given to love Musick. You shall have all things that's fitting for a Man of such Quality.

Merr. Well, Sir, let me be once set out with a good Equipage, and leave the rest to me.

Love. Come with us, Friend, and we'll instruct thee fully in thy Part.

Merr. Well, give me but my Cue of Entrance, and let me alone to act my Part.

Cun. Let's about it then. (*Exit* Love., Cun. *and* Merr.

Jeff. Prudence—

Pru. What's your Will?

Jeff. One Kiss.

Pru. 'Pshaw! Is that all? (*He kisses her.*

Jeff. All! I say no more, but—Ah *Prudence, Prudence*!

Pru. What damnable whining Tone hast thou got, ha?

---

[14] *dress'd like a Falconer*: i.e. presumably at least with gloves, a waistcoat, hawking bag, hat, and perhaps a lure and other accessories.

The Amorous Widow: Or, The Wanton Wife

Jeff. I am afraid of this Viscount, *Prudence.*

Pru. Away, you Fool; I have other things to trouble my Head withal—Farewell.

Jeff. Adieu. (*Exeunt severally.*

ACT II.

Enter Cuningham *and* Philadelphia.

Cun. Why, Madam, are you so unwilling to credit what my constant Passion, so long in vain, has urg'd? Do you not believe I love you? Oh! Did you but know what I endure, when you refuse to hear me, you would in Charity have some Compassion on my wounded Soul.

Phil. I dare not hear this Language from you, Sir.

Cun. What are you afraid of, Madam?

Phil. All Men say the same things, Sir, till they have won our easy Hearts to pity and believe you; then straight you slight your Conquest, and leave us to pursue our Ruin.

Cun. Be not so cruel to censure all for those Faults, which some few commit; for all, I must confess, do not stand excus'd. But, Madam, you cannot be so great a Stranger to my Love, as not to think it real; or so great an Enemy to your own Worth, to believe it has not Power to enslave a Heart, that's guarded more securely than mine—But no more—your Aunt—

Enter Lady Laycock.

Lady L. So Niece, I see your squeamish Stomach can digest all sorts of Diet, tho' ne'er so strictly charg'd to the contrary. Mr. *Cuningham,* what Business have you with her? I wonder you are not asham'd to be always following of her at this rate, and endeavouring to take Advantage of her foolish Youth; for she is but a Girl yet, and not fit for the Conversation of a Man; nay, or indeed to be trusted with her self.

Cun. Madam—

Lady L. Go, go, indeed you are much to blame. What will the World judge, think you? Or what Excuse can I make, for suffering such Doings in my House? And you, Huswife! How dare you disobey my Commands? Is this the Respect you pay to me, and to my Quality? I believe, in a little time I must make it my whole Imploy to invite home young Gallants, forsooth, to pleasure you, whilst I, as if I were your Slave, must retire, and wait till you

The Amorous Widow: Or, The Wanton Wife

are serv'd first. 'Tis come to a fine pass indeed; but I'll put an End to it all, and keep you always lock'd up in your Chamber, I will so.

Phil. I told you, Sir, what would be the Event of your Projects, but you would not be said nay. I must be an Instrument to make your Passion known, and none so fit to be trusted with such an Affair as I; but henceforward if you can't speak for your self, you may hang or drown, as you pretend, for me, for I'll no more get Anger for you.

Cun. What does she mean? (*Aside.*

Lady L. What's that you say?

Phil. Mr. *Cuningham* here, Madam, is always urging me to tell your Lady-ship the Passion he has for you.

Lady L. Saucy Slut!

Phil. As if he could not speak for himself, but must be still plaguing me, and swearing how long, how well, and how tenderly he loves you; then sighs and cries, Oh *Philadelphia*! Can I live without her? But she, cruel as she is, has vow'd to die unmarried.

Cun. Oh the Devil! What will become of me now? (*Aside.*

Phil. Then raves worse than any one in *Bedlam*,[15] crying, And must I then lose her so? Oh! Death to all my Hopes! I must not, cannot, will not! and a thousand such like things, which I'm resolv'd never to hear again. So, Sir, don't trouble me any more, but e'en speak what you have to say to her your self. (*Exit.*

Lady L. Is this true, Mr. *Cuningham*? I did not think there was a Man living, which cou'd love at that rate, and with such Constancy.

Cun. Oh! Madam! What shall I say, since all is still in vain! Your Vow, your cruel Vow, has vanquish'd all my Hopes; then where should I seek for Peace, but in my last Retreat, the Grave. Farewell; I cannot bear to stay, for every Look adds new Poisons to my Soul. (*Is going.*

Lady L. Stay, Sir—I have made no such Vow. If your Passion—

Cun. Oh Madam, forbear! I know your Goodness to be such, that rather than be the Instrument of what may happen, you would seemingly comply

---

[15] I.e. Bethleham Royal Hospital, since 1377 for detention of the 'distracted'. In 1670 it was located at Bishopsgate; in 1676 it was moved to a new building in Moorfields designed by Robert Hooke.

The Amorous Widow: Or, The Wanton Wife

with any thing I can ask. Pardon me, Madam, I have been too much deceiv'd already.

Lady L. Pray stay, Sir, do not mistake—

Enter Philadelphia *with a Piece of* Poynt.[16]

Phil. Oh, Madam, here's the finest Piece of *Poynt* I ever saw, and the cheapest; pray, Madam, look at it.

Lady L. Saucy Intrusion. How durst you come without being call'd? How often have I told you this, you Minx. Be gone, and leave it in the next Room, till I please to come and look on't.

Phil. Madam, the Woman that brought it is in haste, she bid me tell your Ladyship.

Lady L. Let her go about her Business, if she can't wait, for I'll not come yet.
(*Exit* Philadelphia.

How horribly unlucky was this to disturb me, just as I was going to tell him of my Intentions, and of my Concern for his Passion. (*Aside.*

Cun. I believe I am troublesome, Madam. Farewell. (*Is going.*

Lady L. No, pray stay, Sir, I have something to say to you, but that young Slut interrupted me.

Cun. Oh the Devil! (*Aside.*

Lady L. But as I was going to say, I did indeed resolve not to marry any more; and when you have heard me out, you'll say I had Reason. You must know, in my Husband Sir *Oliver's* Days, I had not that Liberty, perhaps, as other Ladies of Quality took; for, to say Truth, my airy Temper and my Youth at that time, made my Husband grows jealous, tho' without Cause, Heaven knows.

Cun. That I dare swear, if all were of my Mind. (*Aside.*

Lady L. Which made him lead me a very uneasy Life; so that it made me resolve on many Things at that time, and one was this: that if ever Sir *Oliver* should die, I never would marry again; but I don't remember that I swore to it. Or if I had, you have such a way with you, 'twould be very hard to deny you any thing, Mr. *Cuningham.*

Cun. Oh, Madam!—Your Charity comes now too late: I am past all Hope.

---

[16]   See above, n.8.

The Amorous Widow: Or, The Wanton Wife

Lady L. Oh, dear Sir, say not so! For since you say your Disease is grown to that Extremity, that unless your Love meet Reward—

Cun. Talk not of Impossibilities. I know how much you prize your Honour. And since you have vow'd never to marry, I have nothing left to hope for else.

Lady L. 'Tis true, Mr. *Cuningham*, I would not have my Honour suffer; but what remains beside that I can do, to save you from what may be dangerous, shall not be wanting.

Enter Prudence *and* Philadelphia.

Pru. Oh, Madam! Madam! The rarest News—The Viscount *Sans-Terre*, whom you have so long expected, is just arriv'd, and is coming hither with a huge fine Equipage, Fiddles, and other Instruments.

Lady L. Oh dear! How I'm surpriz'd! I would not have him see me thus for all the World. *Prudence*, set my Curls right, and alter my Knots. Quickly, don't stand fumbling—Look if the Paint be firm.

Pru. 'Tis pretty well, Madam; there's here and there a small Crack, but 'twill not be discern'd at distance.

Lady L. Quickly, good *Prudence*. Put me a little better in Order. You'll pardon me, Sir. You see what a Fright I'm in.

Cun. Pardon, quotha! The Devil take me, if any thing could be more freely granted.   (*Aside.*

Enter [Merryman as] *the Viscount* Sans-Terre, *with Musick, and a good Equipage; attended by* Lovemore *and several Gentlemen. The Viscount* [Merryman] *sings as he enters.*

A CATCH.
From the North I came,
Where I heard of the Fame
Of the Lady Laycock's *Beauty;*
I had pass'd for an Ass,
Had I stay'd where I was,
And not done a Viscount's Duty.

Merr. Oh! are these the Ladies? By your Favour, Sweet Lady.   (*Kisses* Phil. A delicate Morsel, by this Hand. Madam, I see that Fame has justly spoke your Praise. You are indeed the Wonder of all your Sex. How fair she is!

Lady L. What does he mean?

195

The Amorous Widow: Or, The Wanton Wife

Merr. Pray, Madam, what young Gentlewoman is that, whose matchless Beauty seems to fill the Place with more than common Brightness? Sure 'tis some Goddess, dropt from Heaven for Men to worship! Fair Angel, pardon this rude Attempt: the Honour only of your fair Hand.   (*Kisses* it. For till I touch it, I cannot think you mortal.

Lady. Oh, dear Sir! You make me blush.

Merr. Pray, Lady, is this pretty young Gentlewoman your Niece?   (*To* Phil.

Phil. This Fellow must be a Fool, or he could ne'er mistake so grossly. (*Aside.*

Pru. Now we shall have rare Sport. Sure he's blind to mistake you for your Aunt.   (*To* Phil.

Love. Pray have a little Patience, Madam, and you'll see the Event. (*To* Phil.

Merr. Lady, I bless those Stars that have directed me to so happy a Choice; therefore few Words are best. If you like me as well as I do like you, e'en send for a Parson—   (*To* Phil.

Lady L. Hold, Sir, sure you mistake!

Love. Now—Now it works.   (*Aside to* Phil.

Merr. What say you, Lady? Shall we—   (*To* Phil.

Lady L. I can hold no longer.   (*Aside.*

Pray, Sir, are not you the Viscount *Sans-Terre*?

Merr. Pretty Creature, I am.

Lady L. And come with an Intention—

Merr. To make this Lady, your Aunt, happy in a Husband, if she pleases.

Lady L. I tell you, Sir, I am that Lady you speak of; and that is my Niece *Philadelphia*.

Merr. Ha, ha, ha! Your Niece, quotha! Why sure you think to put some Trick upon me. This motherly grave Lady your Niece! No, no; I thank you, Madam, I am not to be persuaded out of my Reason.

Lady L. He makes me almost mad.   (*Aside.*
I say again, that I am call'd the Lady *Laycock;* and that pert Minx, my Niece, who was left in Charge with me till she be of Age.

Merr. 'Sdheart, 'tis impossible! You look twenty Years younger than that Lady you call your Niece.

The Amorous Widow: Or, The Wanton Wife

Lady L. Oh, dear Sir! That indeed may well be. A great many do allow, I appear to be something younger than I altogether am.

Merr. How could I be so much mistaken! Sure, Madam, you but jest with me.

Lady L. Indeed, Sir, these Gentlemen know I speak Truth.

Cun. 'Tis very true indeed, my Lord.

Merr. Well, since it happens so, I like it the better; for to say Truth, I had fix'd my Eye on you at my first Entrance. Ah! Wou'd 'twere over once. Methinks I long to have thee in my Arms. Oh! How I would employ my Faculties, and surfeit with delight. What say you, Lady? Never stand to consider on't, but send for a Parson to say Grace, that I may fall to. Odds so, I'm very hungry—Very sharp set; I long to be doing.

Lady L. Pray, my Lord, walk in, and refresh your self after your Journey. I was unmannerly not to ask you before. *Prudence*, Come hither. See that all things are in readiness. Oh, *Prudence*! I am impatient to be alone with him.

Exit Pru.

My Lord, you will excuse the Disorder you have found me in.

Merr. Never trouble your self about it. Join but your Forces with mine, and we'll beget a Race of People, that shall be immortal. A Race, that shall create a second War with *Jove*, and raise *Olympus* top equal with the Seat of him that hurls the Thunder.[17]

Lady L. No more, my Lord. Pray walk in.

Merr. All your Commands are absolute.

(Exit [Merryman as] Viscount leading Lady L., who pushes out Phil.[18]

Love. Was there ever such a Piece of Fly-Flesh?[19]

Cun. The Rogue acted it to the Life, and came very seasonably to my Rescue. Had he staid a Moment longer, I had been forc'd to have given up the Ghost.

Love. That ever Nature should suffer such a Lump of Rubbish in the World for Men to stumble over.

---

[17] *A Race*: Merryman recalls the Greek myth of the Titans, mythical children of Uranus and Gaia, and overthrown by the Gods of Olympus, led by Zeus. He omits to mention that the Titans were then imprisoned in perpetuity.

[18] *Lady L* is described here as 'the Widow' in Q1 and Q2.

[19] *Fly-flesh*: maggoty – a disparaging reference to Lady Laycock's decayed state. Not in OED.

The Amorous Widow: Or, The Wanton Wife

Cun. Pox on her old mouldy Chops. She's for engrossing all to her self. How she thrust her Niece in before her! I'll in, and try to beckon her into the Garden, if you'll interpose, shou'd the Aunt miss her, and follow us.

Love. 'Sdeath! Would'st have me run into the Lion's Den, just when I have scap'd his Paw! No, I have hazarded too much already to venture more, I thank you. I now have better Game in Chace. You know pretty Mrs. *Brittle*, Sir *Peter Pride*'s Daughter?

Cun. What of her?

Love. Oh, 'tis the sweetest little Creature! So Fair, so Witty, so Kind, and so Promising! I'm just now sending this Letter, in order to appoint a Meeting with her. But her Husband is so jealous (as indeed I hope to give him Cause for't) his Eye is hardly ever off her. I am thinking what way it can be deliver'd without Suspicion. Let me see—   (*Studies.*

Cun. I'll take my Leave; for I find I interrupt your Meditations.

Love. Farewell, my Friend; and may both our Wishes prosper.   (*Exit* Cun. *Jeffrey*!

Enter Jeffrey.

Jeff. Sir.

Love. Can'st thou contrive to carry this Letter to a young Gentlewoman, and bring an Answer, without being suspected? If thou dost, *Jeffrey*, thou shalt be well rewarded for thy Pains.

Jeff. Is she Widow, Wife, or Maid, pray Sir?

Love. Why dost thou ask?

Jeff. For a private Reason I have.

Love. Well then, to satisfy thy Curiosity, *Jeffrey*, know she's a Wife; a Young, a Handsome, and a Melting one! I am all Ecstasy, and impatient till I possess her. Good *Jeffrey*, look on the Superscription, and about it with all Speed.

Jeff. I dare not touch it. Don't trust me with it.

Love. Why so, good *Jeffrey*?

Jeff. I say again, do not trust me.

Love. Your Reason, *Jeffrey*?

Jeff. I don't care to meddle in a Cause, where there's a Process of Cuckoldom going forward.

The Amorous Widow: Or, The Wanton Wife

Love. Prithee, why so?

Jeff. Why, Sir, I'll tell you. You must know, Sir, I love *Prudence*, my Lady *Laycock*'s Woman, and I believe there's no Love lost between us; nor do I know how soon we may exchange our Persons for better and for worse. Now, Sir, if I should be the Instrument (by carrying this Letter) of your making this honest Man a Cuckold, who knows but, in return of such a monstrous Deed, it may be my own Case next; therefore, Sir, I don't care to meddle in't.

Love. Give me the Letter again; I did but try thee. Thy Master, indeed, has often told me, how scrupulous thou wert about these Matters, but I ne'er believ'd it till now. Stick to thy Principles, and be what thou deserv'st; thou mayst come to Good at last. I have no farther Service at present. Prithee leave me, I have Business of Moment.   (*Exit* Jeff.

I had been finely serv'd if I had sent this conscientious Rogue. What shall I do? The Viscount brought an ignorant Country Fellow up with him, that won't be suspected in the least. 'Tis well thought of; I'll entrust him, and send it immediately. Soft—Who comes here?—Oh! 'tis the Husband.

Enter Barnaby Brittle.

Your Servant, Mr. *Brittle;* is the Lady *Laycock* at home, can you tell?

Brit. Yes, yes, I believe she is.

Love. I have a little Business, and must needs speak with her. Sir, your Servant.   (*Exit* Love.

Britt. A little Business, quotha! A fine Trade this doating old Widow drives; my House is become as common for all Comers and Goers, as the *Mall* or *Spring-Garden*:[20] But I shall put a stop to it in a little time, I believe.

Enter Mrs. Brittle *in haste, dress'd very airy; he stops her.*

Britt. How now—Whither away in such haste?

Mrs. Britt. I'm going abroad, Husband. Good bye.

Britt. Hold, hold, by your Leave, I'll know for what, and whither your sweet Ladyship is going?

---

[20] *Mall or Spring-Garden*: the Mall, adjoining St James's Park and a fashionable locale, was created in 1660–1 using designs by André Le Notre. The Spring Gardens at Charing Cross, open to the public at least from the 1630s, soon acquired a reputation for drunken behaviour.

Mrs. Britt. Why, to the Play, sweet Husband.

Britt. Hum! to the Play.

Mrs. Britt. Well, Good bye, Husband—I shall be too late, and then there'll be such crowding, I shan't get the first Row in the Box, for 'tis a new Play; and I had as lief not go, as sit behind. (*Is going.*

Britt. Hold, hold, pray stay, if you please.

Mrs. Britt. Indeed but I can't.

Britt. Indeed but you must not go, Wife.

Mrs. Britt. Indeed, Husband, but I shall.

Britt. I say again, you must not.

Mrs. Britt. Must not! Who shall hinder me?

Britt. Why, that will I.

Mrs. Britt. I say, no.

Britt. But I say, yes.

Mrs. Britt. Don't you pretend to't.

Britt. Don't you provoke me, I say. Is this the Trade you always intend to drive?

Mrs. Britt. Yes indeed is it.

Britt. I say, no.

Mrs. Britt. But I say, yes. Do you think you shall keep me always stifling within Doors, where there's no body to be seen but your old fusty self? No, I'll to the Play, where there's all sorts of Company and Diversion; where the Actors represent all the Briskness and Gaiety of Life and Pleasure; where one is entertain'd with airy Beaux, and fine Gallants, which ogle, sigh, and talk the prettiest things in the World. Methinks 'tis rare to hear a young brisk Fellow court a handsome young Lass, and she all the while making such pretty dumb Signs: first turns aside to see who observes, then spreads her Fan before her Face, heaves up her Breasts, and sighs—at which he still swears he loves her above all the World—and presses hard his Suit; tells her, what Force her Beauty, her Wit, her Shape, her Mien, all join'd in one, are of. At which she blushing curtesies low, and to her self replies, What charming Words he speaks! His Person's heavenly, and his Voice divine. By your Leave, Husband, you make me stay long. (*Is going.*

Britt. Not in the least—there will be no great miss of you, if you don't go. And now you talk of Gallants, bless us!—What a Dress is there! Do you think that fit for a Tradesman's Wife?

Mrs. Britt. No;—but I think it fit for Sir *Peter Pride*'s Daughter, such as I am. I warrant you'd have me go abroad like one that sells Butter and Eggs—Or like one that cries, Come buy my dainty fine pickled Cucumbers.[21] No, no, I'm resolv'd to dress—put on all the Airs I can—go abroad—see and be seen—take my Fill of Pleasure, and not be shut up in a Nunnery, to pine and sigh, and waste my youthful Days in fruitless Wishes. No, I'm not so weary of my Life yet, tho' you do all you can to make me so. And I would have you to know, tho' you have forc'd me to wed my self with old Age and ill Humours, I am not wedded to my Grave!—'tis time enough forty Years hence to think of that, and I have a great deal to do before that time comes; therefore I must, and I will go abroad.

Britt. Stir one Step if you dare.   (*Spits in his Fist.*
If you go to that, I'll try who wears the Breeches, you or I. You shall stay at home, and keep me Company; I'll spoil your going to Plays, your Appointments, and your Intrigues—I'll make you know, that I am your Husband, and that you shall do what I please. 'Slife, What's here to do! What, have you forgot your Marriage Vows already? Pray, who am I? Am I not your Husband? Are you not married to me?

Mrs. Britt. No—You forc'd me; I never gave you my Consent in Word or in Deed. Could you think I was in Love with Avarice, with Age and Impotence?

Britt. Give me Patience! How! How!

Mrs. Britt. No, you basely bought me of my Father and Mother.

Britt. Would I could sell thee again.

Mrs. Britt. Like a Slave you bought me, and so you intend to use me, were I Fool enough, but I'll see you hang'd first.

Britt. Why, what will your sweet Ladyship do? I bought you, you say?

Mrs. Britt. Yes. Had you my Consent? Or did you once ask it? Or if you had, my Affections were plac'd elsewhere, and so they shall remain, in spight of all your Threats and boasted Power! I'll not be us'd at this Rate!

Britt. Good lack!

---

[21] Cp. Etherege, *The Man of Mode*: 'There's music in the worst cry in London! "My dill and cucumbers to pickle"'; in the New Mermaids edition by Michael Neill, V.ii.380–1 (p.149).

The Amorous Widow: Or, The Wanton Wife

Mrs. Britt. I that am a Gentlewoman, descended from the worshipful Family of the *Pride*'s by the Father's side—

Britt. Ay, so 'tis a sign by your Dress. *Pride*'s, quotha!

Mrs. Britt. And a Gentlewoman descended from the Honourable Family of the *Laycock*'s by the Mother's side. 　　　　　　　　　　　(*She cries.*
And to be us'd at this Rate by an old nasty Shop-keeper! I might have married a Merchant, and have kept my Glass Coach, my tall Footmen in fine Liveries, have gone abroad when I pleas'd without Controul, visited Quality, nay, took Place of 'em at the Play-house, and met with Respect from the best; and is it come to this? But I'll to my honourable Father and Mother, and tell 'em all, who, I'm sure, won't suffer their Daughter to be thus abus'd. 　　　　　　　　　　　　　　　　　(*Cries still.*

I cannot, nor will not endure it any longer. 　　　　　　　　　(*Exit.*

Britt. This 'tis for a Tradesman to marry a Gentlewoman. A Curse on such Gentility! What shall I do? I shall be damnably plagu'd with her Father and Mother. Well, next Month I must take up in *Bedlam*; a Judgment which every Citizen deserves, that marries above his Quality. 　　　　　(*Exit.*

ACT III.

SCENE, A Street before a Glass-Shop.

Enter Brittle *Solus.*

Britt. Well! What a Plague 'tis to be married! I must incorporate with one above my Quality too, and not be content with something in my own Sphere, like one that had a Mind to live in Peace and Quietness, but nothing would serve me but a Gentlewoman, altho' I took her with never a Tatter[22] to her Back, forsooth; and now, I think, I'm fitted with a Vengeance. Would I were but fairly rid of her and her Gentility once, the Devil should take all such Gentility before I'd ever concern my self with it again. But who have we here?

Enter Clodpole *as out of* Brittle's *House, looking about him as afraid to be seen.*

Clod. Hush!—Softly!—Mum—No body sees—Ha, ha, ha—No body sees! Softly!—Ods my Life, who's that?—Mum!—Not a Word— 　(*Is stealing off.*

---

[22]　*Tatter*: 'An irregularly torn piece, strip, shred, or scrap of cloth or similar substance, hanging loose from the main body, esp. of a garment' (OED 1).

Britt. Friend, hist—Friend—Pray stay a little. What Business might you have in that House?

Clod. Wou'd you know now? Softly!—Not a Word. Ha, ha, ha, you understand me.

Britt. But you must know—

Clod. Yes, yes, I do know already, but am not such a Fool to tell you. You shan't get a Word out of me. You understand me.

Britt. Yes, very well, but—

Clod. Softly!—Not a Word.

Britt. I know that; but who was you to speak with in that House?

Clod. Softly!—Can no body hear? For you must know, the old Cuckold of that House, they say, is damnably given to be jealous; I would not for ne'er so much he should see me.

Britt. No, no, I'll warrant you.

Clod. You must not say any thing—

Britt. No, no, not a Word.

Clod. His Wife's a main pretty smirking Rogue, as a Man would wish to lay his Leg o'er. Softly!—Is no body coming?

Britt. I'll warrant thee—Prithee go on.

Clod. What? You want to know all, do you? But I'll not trust you. Mum! Not a Word. You understand me.

Britt. Yes, yes, I understand you well enough—But you may trust me, I shan't say a Word.

Clod. Why luck now!—Ha, ha, ha, wou'd you, wou'd you? But you shall get nothing out of me. I'll warrant you'd have me tell you now, that I brought a Letter to the Gentlewoman of that House—

Britt. Hum!

Clod. And that I deliver'd it to none but her self—as I was order'd—

Britt. So.

Clod. You understand me?

Britt. Yes, yes, perfectly well.

Clod. And that I stay'd for an Answer—

The Amorous Widow: Or, The Wanton Wife

Britt. Well, and I hope you got one?

Clod. Mum! Not a Syllable! No body must know!—If it should come to the Knowledge of the Cuckold her Husband, 'twill spoil all.

Britt. Oh never fear.

Clod. You'll say nothing of what I have told you?

Britt. No, no, not a Word.

Clod. For you must know, Mr. *Lovemore* charg'd me, when he sent me, to say never a Word.

Britt. Is the Gentleman's Name *Lovemore*, say you?

Clod. Why, do you know him?

Britt. Oh, very well; a tall, proper, handsome Man, and always very generous.

Clod. The same, the same.

Britt. And lives just—

Clod. At the lower end of this Street on t'other side of the way, over against the *Golden Ball.*[23] I find you do know him.

Britt. Know him! Why he's my very good Friend.
A Pox of all such Friendship. (*Aside.*

Clod. Odd, he's a fine Gentleman as ever I met with in all my Life.

Brit. Yes, yes, he's a very fine Gentleman indeed.
I wou'd the Devil had him. (*Aside.*

Clod. He gave me this Piece of Gold to carry a Letter for him, which I deliver'd to the Gentlewoman of that House but now.

Britt. Oh, he's a very civil Gentleman; I have been long acquainted with him. Well, and what Answer did you get? A very pleasing one, I'll warrant you.

Clod. Softly, you must not tell a Syllable of this to the Husband, nor that she'll send my Master an Answer, as soon as ever she can get the Cuckold out of the way. But no body must know. You understand me.

Britt. Oh, I'll keep your Counsel, never fear.

---

[23] *Golden Ball*: traditionally the sign of a pawnbroker, in this case suggesting that Lovemore is hardly well-to-do. Pawnshops were so prolific and rapacious in Restoration London that proposals were advanced to regulate them. Given the earlier reference to Eaton's – a lace shop in the city – a plausible candidate in this case is the Golden Ball in Hosier Lane, west of Smithfield.

Clod. She bade me tell him, she'd meet him this Evening, if she can.

Britt. Ay.

Clod. And that she's very sensibly ob—ob—obliged to him, for his Kindness to her.

Britt. Ay, no doubt on't.

Clod. And takes it mighty kind of him.

Britt. She does.

Clod. Odd, she's a pretty Bit; and then there's a handsome Maid that waits upon her, and is Assistant to her in these Matters, one *Dam—Damaris*, I think they call her.

Britt. Ay, like enough.

Clod. And you must know I like her hugely. She gave me two or three such loving Looks, that I am half persuaded she likes me. So that if my Master gets acquainted with the Mistress, I intend to strike in with her Maid.

Britt. Oh, all but Reason.

Clod. But no body must know of it. You understand me. Well, good bye to you. My Master will wonder I stay so long. Be sure you say nothing now. You understand me. (*Exit.*

Britt. Yes, yes, I do so; farewell. Well, *Barnaby Brittle*, now thou see'st what comes of marrying of a Gentlewoman. I believe thou wilt be married to something else in a little time, if thou art not so already. (*Points to his Head.*[24]

Enter Sir Peter Pride and Lady Pride.

Sir Pet. You seem disorder'd, Son-in-law.

Britt. And I have Reason to be so, if ever any Man had.   (*Walks to and fro in a hurry.*

Lady P. Good lack! And why so short, Son-in-law?

Britt. I shall grow taller in a little time, good Mother-in-law, if this Trade holds.   (*Points to his Head.*

Sir Peter. Explain your Meaning, Son-in-law.

Britt. 'Twill explain it self shortly.   (*Walks up and down.*

---

[24]   *Points to his Head*: i.e. to cuckold's horns.

Lady P. What, is that Hat of yours nail'd on? Do you know who we are? And the Respect due to Persons of our Quality, good Son-in-law?

Britt. Ah! wou'd I did not; but now I know to my Sorrow, since you will have me speak, good Mother-in-law.

Lady P. Will you never leave that saucy Word, of calling me Mother-in-law?

Britt. Good Lord! Why what must I call you then?

Lady P. You ought to say, Madam and Sir, when you speak to us; or when you speak of us, you should say, Sir *Peter*, and her Ladyship. For tho' you have married our Daughter, yet there is a great deal of distinction betwixt you and Persons of our Rank and Quality.

Sir Peter. Go to, it is enough for me to let him know his Duty, without your Instructions. Sure, I best know my self what to do. Son-in-law, you are an impudent Fellow to use us at this rate. How often must we put you in mind of your Duty and Respect, e'er you'll know it? Hence-forward learn to behave your self as you ought, or you shall hear on't in other sort of Terms. You must not think because you've married our Daughter, that we will be satisfied with such indifferent Ceremonies and Duty you might have paid, had you married one equal with your self; nor ought you indeed to say, your Wife, when you speak of our Daughter.

Britt. Good lack! — Is not your Daughter my Wife?

Sir Peter. She is — But you ought not to call her so.

Britt. I know that too well, now 'tis too late. I'd give a thousand Pounds she were not my Wife.

Sir Peter. At it again? I tell you, tho' you have married her, yet as she is our Daughter, you must not treat her after that familiar way.

Britt. You make me mad—Is not my Wife my Wife?

Sir Peter. I tell you, tho' she be your Wife, you must not call her so. When you speak of her as being our Daughter, you must say Madam.

Britt. Well, Madam then; since it must be Madam, I did not care if she were a Dutchess, so I were but fairly rid of her. Here's such a stir about your Gentility, and your Honour: but I believe if I had not married your Daughter, and with my good Money redeem'd your Estate, your Gentility had been left in the Mud—for all your great Families, and your nice Honour.

Sir Peter. Then do you think it no Honour to be ally'd to the Worshipful Family of the *Pride*'s?

Lady P. And to the Honourable Family of the *Laycock*'s? Go, Clown. 'Tis a Shame our Daughter should be wedded to such a Brute. We have been told at what a rate you treat her. What is the Reason of it, Son-in-law?

Britt. Why, you shall know, good Mother-in-law.

Lady P. Again at that affronting way! How often have you been told to say Madam?

Britt. Well, Madam then; I always forget these fine Words. But, Madam, if you wou'd please, Madam, to hear me speak, you shall know, Madam, whether I have not Cause to wish, I never had seen my Wi—your Daughter, Madam, if I must call her nothing else.

Sir Peter. Well, Sir, proceed.

Britt. Why, in the first Place, I am in a fair way to be made a Cuckold, if I am not one already.

Sir Peter. How, Son-in-law? Have a Care what you say.

Britt. Believe me, what I say, I can make appear.

Sir Peter. Do it then presently.

Britt. Why, she has just now receiv'd a Letter from her Gallant, and made an Appointment to meet him this Evening; and judge how small a time a Pair of Horns are a-grafting.

Sir Peter. How came you to know this, Son-in-law?

Britt. Why, just now—I caught the Fellow that brought her the Letter, coming out of my House, and not knowing who I was, I got out of him all the Business; and that his Master, Mr. *Lovemore*—

Sir Peter. Is that the Gentleman's Name?

Britt. Yes, so his Man told me. I have often seen him taking a View about my House, and looking up to the Windows; and 'tis plain what his Designs were.

Lady P. If this be true, I'll tear her Eyes out.

Sir Peter. Nay, if it be, this good Sword (never yet drawn in vain) shall do you Right. Where is she, Son-in-law?

Britt. Within, I'll warrant, studying what Excuse to make, to get abroad, and meet her Gallant.

Lady P. I'll call her to answer for her self. Be sure you wrong her not, Son-in-law. (*Exit* Lady P.

Britt. Nay, nay, I make no doubt but she is to be believ'd before me; and she ne'er wants Cunning to bring her self off, I'll say that for her, tho' the Case be ne'er so plain.

Sir Peter. By this good Light, if she dares be false to her Marriage Vows, she dies; and that base Rifler[25] of her Fame shall bear her Company.

Britt. Oh! Here he comes, that Spoiler of my Honour; that's he.

    Enter Lovemore. *Sir* Peter *meets him. They stare each other i'th' Face.*

Sir Peter. Do you know who I am, Sir?

Love. I don't well remember I ever had much Acquaintance with you.

Sir Peter. I am call'd Sir *Peter Pride.*

Love. It may be so. I've heard of you, Sir.

Sir Peter. My Family, Sir, has stood these many Years with unblemish'd Fame and Honour.

Love. Very likely, Sir.

Sir Peter. How far you have endeavour'd to stain that spotless Fame, be judge your self.

Love. Pray, Sir, explain this Riddle.

Sir Peter. I have a Daughter young, fair, well-bred, has Sense; she is indeed the Wonder of her Sex, and this Man, whom you see here, has the Honour to be married to her.

Britt. Ah! 'Tis an Honour, that I cou'd have spar'd.   (*Aside.*

Sir Peter. Now, Sir, I'm told, that you endeavour to corrupt her Honour, and defile her Marriage-Bed. Sir, I have had the Honour to command abroad, and with Success, both to my King and my Country—As have also the Chief Part of all our great Race; even from *William the Conqueror*, to this present Reign, have our unquestion'd Glories stood a Pattern to our yet rising Fame. And he who dares presume to rob us of that precious Jewel, Honour, must not think to 'scape unpunish'd, tho' with the Hazard o'th' last Drop of Blood that is left, to wash off the Stain. My Daughter's Honour, Sir, is as dear to me, as this vital Air, by which I breathe and live.

Love. Pray Sir, who told you this?

Sir Peter. Believe me, Sir, whate'er I say, I can quote my Author for it.

---

25   *Rifler:* 'A robber, a plunderer, a looter' (OED 1).

Love. Then who-ever told you is a Rascal; and were he here, I'd ram the Lie down his Throat, or make him eat a Piece of my Sword.

Sir Peter. Why he told me—This Man—Her Husband here justified it to my Face, and said he had Proof.

Love. How, Sir! Did you frame this abominable Falsehood? 'Tis well you have the Honour to be ally'd to this worthy Knight, Sir *Peter Pride*, here; or you should know what it is to father such a Lie upon a Man of my Reputation.

Sir Peter. Oh! Here comes my Daughter.

Enter Lady Pride, *Mrs.* Brittle, *and* Damaris.

Love. Did you, Madam, tell your Husband a strange Story, that I should make Love to you, and endeavour'd to corrupt your Honour?

Mrs. Britt. I tell him! Why, when did you make Love to me, Sir? I assure you, had you let me know of your Passion, it shou'd not have gone unrewarded. Pray, next time you send, let it be one that knows how to take more Care. However, you have no great Reason to despair; for since he complains without any manner of Reason, I am resolv'd he shall have Cause. Therefore if you do love me, Sir, pray let me know it, and I do assure you, you shall not want Encouragement. He shall not use me at this rate for nothing.

Love. Madam, believe me, 'tis all a Riddle to me; for, till this Hour, I never heard any thing mention'd like it. I am an absolute Stranger to it.

Lady P. Do you hear that, you Clown? Are you not asham'd to abuse a Gentlewoman continually, without any Cause?

Sir Peter. What is the Meaning of this, Son-in-law?

Britt. Pray, do but hear me.

Sir Peter. Troth, Son-in-law, you are a very impudent Fellow.

Britt. Hear me but speak?

Sir Peter You shall not speak. We have heard too much already.

Mrs. Britt. I am sure *Damaris* knows, I never have any body comes near me, but such as himself; nor ever receiv'd any Message, either by Letter, or otherwise— I never committed any Crime against him, that I know of, unless sitting by my self all Day, and poring over two or three good Books be an Offence. Speak, *Damaris*, did I ever give him any Cause for these Suspicions, and this Usage? Thou know'st all I say or do.

The Amorous Widow: Or, The Wanton Wife

Damaris. Madam, I know no Reason; nor can I bear to see the Hardship you endure! Like a barbarous Man as he is—To abuse so good a Lady! So virtuous, so innocent, and so pious a Lady! I am sure it makes me weep to think on't—I am afraid he'll break her Heart in a little time, if—   (*Weeps.*

Britt. Hold your Tongue, you Jade, or I'll make you feel my double Fist. You are not a Gentlewoman— I may do what I please with you.

Mrs. Britt. Oh, my dear Father!   (*Cries.*
I am not able to endure this any longer. Never was any Woman abus'd as I am. I beg you will do me Justice, for I can bear it no longer.   (*Exit crying.*

Lady P. Damaris, let's follow her, and endeavour to comfort her. Oh, thou Clown, to use a Gentlewoman with so much Cruelty!

Dam. I fear he'll be the Death of her at one time or another.   (*Exit* Lady P.
and Damaris.

Sir Peter. What do you think of all this, Sir? Are not you a very pretty Fellow? Come hither, Son-in-law, ask this Gentleman Pardon, for the Affront you have put upon him in belying of him.

Britt. How! Ask his Pardon, that would have made me a Cuckold?

Love. Sir *Peter,* pray—

Sir Peter. I say no more Words. He has wrong'd a Gentleman; and the least he can do, is begging Pardon.

Britt. 'Tis very well! He offends, and I must ask Pardon.

Sir Peter. No matter for that, you hear he denies it; and 'tis enough, if a Gentleman unsays what he has said.

Britt. So that if I catch him making me a Cuckold, and he denies it, I must not believe it, because a Gentleman said it.

Sir Peter. I say, you shall ask Pardon. Therefore no more Words, but do't.

Britt. I shall run mad. Well, what must I do?

Sir Peter. Come hither: Take your Hat off— Kneel down, and say after me.

Britt. Well, since it must be so—   (*Kneels.*
This 'tis to be marry'd to a Gentlewoman, forsooth.

Sir Peter. Sir, I ask your Pardon.

Britt. Sir, I ask your Pardon.   (*In the same Tone.*

Sir Peter. For the Affront I have put upon you.

The Amorous Widow: Or, The Wanton Wife

Britt. For the Affront I have put upon you.

Sir Peter. By falsely accusing you—

Britt. How! Falsely accusing him!

Sir Peter. I say no more Words. Say after me.

Britt. Say after me.

Sir Peter. Accusing you, of having a Design to corrupt my Wife's Honour.

Britt. Accusing you of Truth—And having a Design to corrupt my Wife's Honour.

Sir Peter. For which, knowing my self in the wrong, I do ask your Pardon.

Britt. For which, knowing my self not in the wrong, I'm forc'd to ask your Pardon.

Love. Well, Sir, upon Sir *Peter Pride's* Account I am content to pass it by this time; but let me hear no more Complaints.   (*Brittle rises, and runs off.*

Sir Peter. Sir, now all is well, I humbly take my Leave.   (*Exit Sir* Peter.

Love. Was there ever such a lucky Rogue as I? For her to encourage me to make Love to her before her Husband's Face! Nay, and before her Father and Mother too! Oh, I am all on Fire till I have her in my Arms! But soft! Who comes here?

Enter Prudence.

Well, my little Scout, what News? How fares my Friend? Is *Philadelphia* kind? Where's thy Lady?

Pru. Where-e'er her Person is, I'm sure her best Thoughts are still employ'd on you. And however she may pretend a Passion for Mr. *Cuningham*, she loves none but you. Pray, Sir, do but try her.

Love. Oh racking Thought! I'd rather make Love to a Convocation of Cats at a Witch's Up-sitting,[26] than but speak to her. Where's my Friend? Oh! Here he comes, and his fair Consort.

Enter Cuningham *and* Philadelphia.

Cun. Be not so cruel to say, you want the Power. If we neglect this Opportunity, which kindly presents it self, the next perhaps may not be ours.

---

[26] *Up-sitting*: i.e. a late night meeting.

The Amorous Widow: Or, The Wanton Wife

Phil. Would you then have me dispose of my self without my Aunt's Consent? Do not urge me to that, since I have promised not to wed without it.

Cun. I ask not her Consent, but yours. Grant me but that, and leave the rest to Time and Chance.

Pru. Madam, how can you deny him that, since I know you love him?

Cun. Ha! Oh, the charming Sound! And will you not consent to make me happy? Or do you not believe I love you? By all those Fires that burn within my Soul, I swear—

Pru. Hold! Hold, Sir! You have sworn enough already to corrupt a whole Nunnery of sighing, praying and wishing young Votaries. Why don't you give him your Hand, since he has your Heart? I believe you love to hear him swear and—Give him your Hand, or, I'll discover all.

Phil. Well, there 'tis then.   (*Gives her Hand to* Cuningham.

But I promise nothing else. I fear I have given too much already.

Cun. Oh, never! Never! I'll pay thee back so vast a store of Love and Constancy, as shall weary thee with still receiving.

Pru. Madam, Madam, your Aunt's behind you.

Enter Lady Laycock.[27]

Phil. Ha! My Aunt! What shall I do?

Cun. Fear nothing, Madam, but give me your Hand. I'll bring all off.
                    (*Pretends to tell her Fortune.*

This Line seems to Point out some unexpected Cross. And this Line thwarting the Line of Life, signifies a retir'd Life; and this joining with it, shews you'll be in Danger of ending the latter part of your Days in a Nunnery.   (*Lady l. behind them.*

Lady L. How, Mr. *Cuningham*! Can you tell Fortunes?

Cun. I understand a little Palmistry, Madam, and can give a Guess at Physiognomy.[28]

---

27   This s.d. is given as 'Enter Widow' in Q1 and Q2 and designated as such (or 'Wid.') in those texts for the remainder of the play.

28   *Physiognomy*: study of the face as an index of character. This pseudo-science had been linked with palmistry at least since Johannes Indagine's early sixteenth-century *The Book of Palmestry and Physiognomy*, which appeared in English editions in 1651, 1666, 1671, 1676, and 1683.

Lady L. 'Tis very well. When I enter'd first, I thought you had been making Love to my Niece; I am glad to find it otherwise. But where's the Viscount?

Pru. In the next Room, Madam.

Love. I'll wait upon him: I'd feign try whether his Inside be answerable to his outward Appearance. (*Is going.*

Cun. Nay, prithee stay; I can assure you, he is not to be equall'd either in Person or Discourse.

Pru. He is indeed a fine proper Man, as one would wish to see.

Lady L. Why, really his Lordship has Parts. *Philadelphia* — You and *Prudence* go find him out, and bear him Company awhile; I'll wait on him immediately, tell him.
You, Sir, may go with 'em, if you please. (*To* Love.

Love. Madam, most willingly.

Cun. 'Sdeath! You won't leave me? (*Aside to* Love.

Love. Faith, but I will; dost think I'll stay to endure a second Hell? For if there be one upon Earth, 'tis being left alone with her.
Madam, Your Ladyship shall ever command me. (*To* Lady L.
Come, Lady, if you please, the Honour of your fair Hand. (*To* Phil.
(*Exit with* Phil. *and* Pru.

Cun. What will become of me now? (*Aside.*

Lady L. Well, Mr. *Cuningham,* I have long'd for some time to be alone with you, that I might speak more freely to you.

Cun. Madam, 'tis too great an Honour.

Lady L. I wonder, Sir, you never think of Marrying?

Cun. Madam, as yet I dare not think on't.

Lady L. Oh, dear Sir! Pray, why so?

Cun. Because I have not well consider'd it; and I have been told, 'tis a dangerous Undertaking, without having well thought before-hand.

Lady L. Pray, Sir, why should you think so? I'll vow 'tis an odd Thought, Sir, for one of your Understanding. Why, Sir, I'll tell you. I have had three Husbands, and yet I have no great Reason to complain. Tho' in my last Husband's time, I had not altogether that real Satisfaction, as I had with the other two; for to deal freely with you, Sir, my Husband Sir *Oliver Laycock,* though he was a very well-bred Man, yet he had his Humours sometimes, and would be a little given to Jealousy, so that I seldom led a quiet Hour when the Fit was upon him. But in my first Husband's Days, sure never Woman liv'd so happy! I would not a-been unmarried to have had all the Riches of the Earth laid at my Feet. But when I married with Sir *Oliver,* and had once seen his Temper, nothing I had in the World but what I would a given to a-been free again; and indeed in my Passion I often vow'd never (if please Heav'n Sir *Oliver* died) to marry any more.

Cun. 'Twas rashly done. But no doubt, were there that Man fitting to merit your Favour, and equally deserving your Person and your Estate, and one whom your Ladyship could like, you might perhaps be persuaded to break your Vow, and venture once again.

Lady L. I'll swear I hardly think it, and yet one don't know how one may be tempted; tho' if I were to be persuaded (and I will not forswear any thing), I know not any one, that can so soon persuade me to it as you, Mr. *Cuningham.*

Cun. Death and the Devil! What have I brought upon my self! (*Aside.* Oh Madam! You make me blush. But Madam! How cou'd you with Honour put off the Viscount, who you know loves you, and is come on purpose to marry you?

Lady L. Why, I intend him for my Niece, you must know, who no doubt will be much better pleas'd with the Change. For, to say Truth, Mr. *Cuningham,* I have always had more than a common Esteem for you, and for your Behaviour; and have long since resolv'd, that if I do alter my Condition, you are the Man alone I have plac'd my Thoughts upon.

Cun. You make me blush, Madam.
Wou'd I were a League under-ground, or in any Hell but this. (*Aside.*
You cannot sure. (*To her.*

Lady L. I vow 'tis true, and yet—

Cun. Hear me but speak, Madam?

Lady L. 'Tis odd, that Love shou'd over-power People at so strange a rate.

Cun. But I should be unjust to my Friend, who I know loves you dearer than his Life.

Lady L. Oh dear! Who's that I beseech you, Sir?

Cun. Mr. *Lovemore,* Madam.

Lady L. Mr. *Lovemore!* I'll swear I don't believe it.

Cun. Oh Madam! 'Tis but too true, as will appear I'm afraid, when he knows you place your Affections on any other Man.

Lady L. I'll vow you much surprize me, Mr. *Cuningham*; but how came you to know it?

Cun. Oft has he begg'd me to bear him Company in some lonely Place, where he wou'd sigh, and tell such things of his distress'd Passion, as wou'd have mov'd the most obdurate Heart; and when I ask'd him, why he did not acquaint your Ladyship with his Love, he would sigh, with Arms a-cross, as if his Heart would force its way through his Breast, and cry, Oh that's my Grief, my Friend, I cannot—dare not tell her! For should I attempt it once, and meet her scorn, (for oh! thou know'st her Vow) I shou'd be for ever lost. Then ran o'er a thousand Tales of Love, so soft, so moving, and how he priz'd you, that cannot be express'd by any, except one who loves like him.

Lady L. Truly, Sir, if it be so—

Cun. If it be so! Were your Ladyship to observe his distracted Throes, you'd pity him.

Lady L. But why should he not declare it to me?

Cun. That's what I tell him, Madam; urging that your Ladyship—But mum! who have we here?

    Enter [Merryman *as*] Viscount, Philadelphia *and* Prudence.

Merr. Ha! Whispering! And so close! I like it not.

Lady L. The Viscount! This is unlucky. He looks disturb'd!
Good Sir, some other time we'll end this Discourse.   (*to* Cun.

Merr. Ha! What are you, Sir, that thus dares to encroach upon my Territories, and invade my Right?

Lady L. Nay, pray my Lord, be not displeas'd. This Gentleman, you must know, has a Law suit depending, and is come to entreat a Line of Commendation from me to my Lawyer.

Merr. Enough; I do believe all you can say. Ah, those Eyes of yours! What Looks are there! They enflame my very Soul.

Lady L. Ah, *Prudence*, how I long to be alone with him!

Merr. I am impatient of this Delay; when shall we be married?

Lady L. Pray moderate your Passion, Sir.

The Amorous Widow: Or, The Wanton Wife

Merr. What, you are afraid of that melancholy Gentleman, that stands so silently there?

Lady L. Speak softly, I am afraid he hears you, Sir.

Merr. What care I if he does?

Enter a Servant.

Serv. My Lord, the Dancers you spoke for, wait without.

Merr. Let 'em enter. Will you please to sit, Ladies?

A DANCE.[29]

Lady L. Prudence, go tell Mr. *Lovemore,* I'd speak with him this Evening.
(*Exit* Pru.

Philadelphia —you may take a Turn in the Garden.
And, Sir, if you think it no Trouble, you may bear her Company. (*To* Cun.

Cun. Madam, most willingly. (*Exit with* Phil.

Lady L. Why are you so melancholy, my Lord?

Merr. Nothing that's worth the naming. But if you'll walk into the next Room, I'll tell you.

Lady L. My Lord, you are a Man of Honour, and I dare trust my self with you.

Merr. Madam, if I deserve it not, may you always keep a Whip and a Bell, to scourge me from you like a Cur.

---

[29] A succession of different dancers performed in the play during the early eighteenth century. For the performance at Lincoln's Fields Theatre on 26 June 1704 there was 'A New Dance by Four Scaramouches to Faranoll's Ground, never perform'd but once', and 'A Scotch and Irish Dance … By Firbank and his Scholar' (LS2 69); at the Queen's Theatre Haymarket on 20 February 1705 the dancers were 'Mlle de la Val, Mrs Elford, l'Abbé's Brother and Scholar' (LS2 88); at the same theatre on 20 November 1705 the dancers were 'l'Abbé, de Barques, Mrs Elford, Mlle Noisy, and others' (LS2 107). Anthony L'Abbé (c.1667–c.1758), dancer at the Paris Opera from 1688, was the most distinguished among them. He was performing in London at least from May 1698 (according to *The Post Boy,* 14–17 May 1698, he was already performing 'at the playhouse'). He returned home late in 1705 after a series of contractual disputes. Downes blamed Betterton for bringing over French dancers at huge expense and 'vast gain to themselves' (p.97).

The Amorous Widow: Or, The Wanton Wife

ACT IV.

> ⟨ *Enter* Clodpole *and* Damaris. *He gives her a Letter.*

Dam. You are a fine Spark, are you not, to discover all the Business, and let it come to my Master's Hearing?

Clod. Why ay, that's true, as you say; but who wou'd have thought that he could have known it! But now to our own Business, *Damaris*— Dost thou not love me, *Damaris*? Thou know'st I love thee with all my Heart. Good lack! How it beats!—Odd, you may hear it thump all over the House. *Damaris*—How can'st thou be so hard-hearted?

Dam. 'Pshaw! Prithee leave fooling.

Clod. One Kiss, *Damaris*, to revive me.   (*Kisses her.*

Dam. Pray, Clodpole, be civil.

Clod. Damaris!—Canst thou not spare a little Bit afore-hand?

Dam. Of what, Fool?

Clod. Why, of—Odd, you know well enough, What, I need not name it to thee.

Dam. I know nothing of the Matter.

Clod. Ay, but you do. Why, I ask but a little tiney, tiney Bit. Do, prithee now do.

Dam. I'll see you at the Devil first.

Clod. Do, *Damaris*—Spare but a Bit now; and 'bate[30] me as much on the Wedding-Night.

Dam. No, I thank you, good *Clodpole*;
I have too often been snapt that way already.   (*Aside.*

But see—yonder comes my Lady and my Master— Step with me into the next Room, he must not see you.

Clod. Ay, any where, any where. Quickly, good *Damaris*.   (*Exit.*

> *Enter* Barnaby Brittle *and Mrs.* Brittle.

Britt. I tell you again, that Marriage is a very sacred Thing, and ought not to be profan'd at this Rate.

---

[30]   *bate*: i.e. abate – he will settle for less sex on their wedding night if he can have some now.

The Amorous Widow: Or, The Wanton Wife

Mrs. Britt. What do you tell me of Marriage? I have other things to mind.

Britt. Truly, I do believe as much; that's the truest Word you ever spoke. But I think you ought to mind what I say. Am I not your Husband? And are not you bound in Duty by that Tye, to be obedient and just in all your Ways?

> *Enter* Lovemore *on the other side bowing.*
> *She sees him, and Curtesies to him.*

What's that for? What, do you banter me?

Mrs. Britt. Keep your Instructions for those that want 'em; my Thoughts are other ways employ'd.   (*She Curtesies,* Lovemore *bows.* Brittle *sees him not, and thinks she does it in scorn to him.*

Britt. What, you are practising your Airs against you meet your Gallant, are you? And trying how to behave your self to him? But I shall spoil your Design, I shall.   (Lovemore *bows, she curtesies again.*[31] Leave off your Tricks with a Vengeance, and mind what I say to you.
   (Lovemore *keeps bowing to her.*
Again, don't provoke me, I say, don't; if you do, you may chance to repent it. I say, that Marriage—

Mrs. Britt. I know it, Dear; you need say no more.
   (*She takes* Brittle *round the Neck, and beckons* Lovemore, *who comes and kisses her Hand over her Husband's Shoulders all the while.*
You know I love you dearly, by this I do.   (*Kisses him.*
Why will you not be satisfied? Had I the World to give, it cou'd not make me more happy than this Minute.   (Lovemore *still kisses her Hand.*

Britt. Ah dissembling Crocodile? What, now you think to wheedle me.

Mrs. Britt. Be satisfied with this: Hence-forward, if you deserve it, I give you my Heart for ever, which, till this Minute, I did not think to do.
   (*She speaks to* Lovemore.
Britt. Ah, would 'twere in your Power to keep your Word.

Mrs. Britt. Indeed I will, let that content you, and learn to merit that rich Jewel, which this Moment I put within your Power.   (*Beckons* Lovemore, *who bows, and Exit.*

---

[31]   Q1 and Q2 have 'He Bows' here, wrongly suggesting that it is Brittle who bows.

The Amorous Widow: Or, The Wanton Wife

Britt. If thou would'st be thus kind always, how happy should I be! But that's impossible! Would you but think sometimes upon the Vow you made in Church, that solemn Vow of Marriage, 'twou'd put you in Mind of your Duty.

Mrs. Britt. How can I think of any thing, when you will not give me leave so much as to peep abroad for Air? Do you think a Woman can ever be in a good Humour, that is lock'd up, and kept from what she likes? But I'm resolv'd to bear it no longer.   (*She walks backward and forward.*

Britt. Good lack! What's your Mind chang'd already? I thought 'twas too good to last long.

Mrs. Britt. But hence-forward you shan't think to make a Fool of me at this rate. I'll find a way to get out, for all your Spies; and then look to't—I'll use you as you deserve.

Britt. Tempt me no farther, I beseech you; if you do, I shall use you as you deserve. Patience! And I have need enough of it at this time.

Mrs. Britt. I'm resolv'd to encourage every Man that makes Love to me. I'll kiss and be wanton, since you provoke me to't. Love, and be belov'd—and not be subject to the nasty Humours of an old Jealous—I can't find a Name bad enough for thee.

(*He spits in his Hand.*

Britt. Odd, I've a great Mind to spoil that handsome Face. The Devil tempts me strangely. I must be gone; for if I stay, I shall certainly be provok'd to do her a Mischief.   (*Runs off.*

Enter Damaris *with a Letter.*

Dam. I waited till my Master was gone, to deliver you this Letter, Madam. Mr. *Lovemore's* Man is within, and waits for an Answer.

Mrs. Britt. Give it me, *Damaris,* quickly.

Dam. I need not bid you read it, since you know from whom it comes.

Mrs. Britt. Oh! 'tis extremely pretty, *Damaris.* I'll in, and write an Answer presently.   (*Exit.*

Dam. So she has snapt the Bait at the first Angling; how she'll get clear of the Hook, I know not. Ha! He's here himself!

Enter Lovemore *and* Clodpole.

Love. Pretty Mrs. *Damaris,* I'm glad to see you. Is your Lady within?

The Amorous Widow: Or, The Wanton Wife

Dam. Yes, Sir, writing an Answer to your Letter, I suppose. You see, I deliver'd it with Care.

Love. Oh, I understand you; there's for thy Pains. (*Gives her Money, she puts her Hand behind her, and takes it.*

Dam. Oh, dear Sir, by no means. But since you will have it so, pray command me.

Love. Can'st thou contrive to let me speak with thy Mistress?

Dam. If you please, Sir, I'll shew you to her.

Love. Thou wilt oblige me for ever.   (*Exit* Love. *and* Dam.

Clod. Hist! *Damaris!*—Odd, I shall have a rare Wife of her, if she gets Money so fast. Here's a piece of Gold got without the least Trouble, as they say. But softly!—Who have we here?

Enter Brittle.

Oh! are you there, Mr. *Babbler*? You are a pretty Fellow indeed; you have made fine Work! You cannot be told a Secret, but you must tell the Husband presently. You understand me.

Britt. Who, I tell the Husband, Friend?

Clod. Yes, you; but I'll see you hang'd before you shall get any thing more out of me. You have made fine Work! All's discover'd!—The Cuckold, her Husband, knows all the Business.

Britt. Well, but—

Clod. You may as well hold your Tongue, for you shan't get a Word out of me. No, no, I have found you out, i'faith.

Britt. This Fellow may be useful to affirm it to her Father and Mother. I'll try to bribe him.   (*Aside.*
                          (*Puts his Hand in his Pocket to give him Money.*

Why look you, Friend, I'm sorry this Matter is—

Clod. Mum! You understand me. I know what you'd say now, but 'twill not do. You'd have me to tell you what I know, but Mum!—Softly!—Not a Word. I'll warrant, you'd have me tell you what Answer she gave to the Letter.

Britt. No, no, Friend; but—

Clod. Softly!—You shall get nothing out of me. You think I'll tell you now, that the Wife promis'd to meet him, and that they are together now in that

The Amorous Widow: Or, The Wanton Wife

Room; but I'm not such a Fool. No, no, you'll tell the Husband again; you cannot be secret, and so good bye to you. You shall get nothing out of me. You understand me. (*Exit.*

Britt. I'm sorry I can't make that use of him as I intended; but however, he has discover'd something to me, that may do as well. He said her Gallant is with her now; I'll listen. (*Goes to the Door.*
Oh Sadness! 'tis but too true. Here's fine Doings. But I'll send for her Parents. Now they shall see who's in the wrong, and who's in the right. She can't scape me now, unless the Devil assist her; and see where they come in a lucky Hour.

Enter Sir Peter Pride and Lady Pride.

Father-in-law, you're welcome; and you, Madam. I'm glad you are come, I was just going to send for you.

Sir Peter. Why, what's the Matter, Son-in-law?

Britt. Now you see what a fine Daughter you have.

Sir Peter. What! More Complaints! What is the Reason of all this?

Britt. Do but hear me, and you shall know. Here has been her Gallant, and—

Sir Peter. Son-in-law, I'll not believe it. Will you never leave this fooling? We'll hear no more.

Britt. No, no; I knew you wou'd never believe a Word I say, but she can be credited, because she's a Gentlewoman, forsooth. Now you shall see what a Gentlewoman I have got for a Wife. I have her fast now, fast in that Room with her Gallant, and that I hope will convince you.

Lady P. 'Tis false, thou base Villain. I know she scorns to do so base a thing.

Britt. Pray now don't believe me, but walk in. If you find it not true, never mind any thing I say, as long as I live.

Sir Peter. Lead, Son-in law. If I find 'em together, by this good Sword they both shall die.

Lady P. But if 'tis not so, which I do believe 'tis only your Jealousy again, look to your self, Son-in-law, I'll suffer these Affronts no longer.

Britt. If they are not there now, I am a very Villain. Come along—Softly—
(*They all go in.*

SCENE Changes to a Chamber, and discovers Lovemore,
Mrs. Brittle, and Damaris.

Love. You question your own Power, when you mistrust my Honour, Madam. Such Charms can never want Force to allay all Thoughts of wronging so much Goodness.

Mrs. Britt. Well, Sir, I do believe you to be a Man of Honour, and hope you will not wrong my good Opinion.

Enter Sir Peter, *Lady* Pride *and* Brittle, *behind them. They grow enrag'd to see 'em together, and make Signs of Revenge. Sir* Peter *lays his Hand upon his Sword.*

Therefore meet me this Evening at the Garden-Door about Nine, and there we'll discourse farther. If I find what you say be real, perhaps I may be prevail'd upon to venture farther.

Love. Madam, you bless me! (*Kisses her Hand.*

Britt. Have a little Patience — Let's draw nearer, and hear what they say. (*They go nearer.*

Dam. Oh Madam! Madam! My Master, Sir *Peter*, and my Lady, are just behind you.

Mrs. Britt. Ha! Undone for ever!

Love. What will become of me then?

Mrs. Britt. Let me alone to bring it off. Be not you surpriz'd at any thing I say, but seem to humour it. (*To* Love. *Aside.*[32]
I'll hear no more. What do you tell me of your being amaz'd! Did you ever see any thing in me, that cou'd encourage you to believe I was that Woman you took me for? I'll warrant you thought, because I seem'd to give you Encouragement before my Husband Yesterday, when he had enrag'd me, that I was in earnest? (*Seems to be angry with* Lovemore.[33]

(*They over-hear, seem angry, and to threaten* Brittle, *who pretends by Signs to excuse himself.*

Love. What mean you, Madam? (*Confusedly.*

Mrs. Britt. But you will find your self deceiv'd. For tho' my Husband gives me Provocations to use him at any rate, yet, Sir, I'd have you to know, I scorn

---

[32] Q1 and Q2 place this after 'bring it off', but clearly it also applies to the subsequent sentence.

[33] Q1 and Q2 place this after 'I'll hear no more', where clearly it applies to the whole of her subsequent speech.

The Amorous Widow: Or, The Wanton Wife

Revenge; and will not be brib'd to stain my Honour, tho' all the Wealth of the whole World were laid at my Feet.

Lady P. Do you hear that, Son-in-law? *(They still threaten, he looks sneakingly.*

Mrs. Britt. No, Sir, my honourable Parents brought me up with the strictest Care; taught me the nice Paths that lead to Everlasting Fame and Glory. And he who dares attempt to make me lose my Way, deserves to be us'd thus, thus, and thus, Sir.

(Gets near Sir Peter, *snatches his Cane, and runs at* Lovemore, *who gets behind* Brittle. *She beats* Brittle *unmercifully, while* Lovemore *gets off.*

Britt. Oh, hold! Hold! What, will you murder me? (Brittle *rubs his Shoulders.*

Sir Peter. Troth, Son-in-law, she serv'd you right.

Lady P. You have not half what you deserve; And I cou'd find in my Heart to—

Sir Peter. Let him alone: I'll correct him. Son-in-law, you are a very impudent Fellow to use your Wife thus. What can you say for your self?

Britt. Say for my self! Why, I say, 'tis all a Trick—And a Contrivance to blind the Matter. *(Feels his Arms and Head.*[34]

Sir Peter. Is it not plain, you have wrong'd her? Do you not see she is a virtuous and a good Wife?

Lady P. Too good for him, a Clown.

Britt. Well, well, I am over-reach'd, I see.

Sir Peter. Son-in-law, I charge you let me hear no more of this. And instantly ask your Wife's Pardon.

Britt. How, Sir!

Mrs. Britt. Oh! let him alone; 'twill be to no purpose. I'm a little out of Order. *Damaris*, lead me to my Chamber. *(Exit with* Damaris.

Sir Peter. I say follow her, and ask her Pardon.

Britt. If I do, the Curse of Cuckoldom fall upon me. *(Runs out another way.*

Lady P. Ah, graceless Clown. Come, Sir *Peter*, let's follow, and see how she does. *(Are going.*

---

[34] Q1 and Q2 misleadingly place this s.d. next to Sir Peter's speech.

The Amorous Widow: Or, The Wanton Wife

Enter Prudence

Pru. Madam, my Lady presents her Service to your Ladyship and Sir *Peter*; and would desire your good Company at a Ball the Viscount treats her with.

Lady P. Our humble Thanks to her Ladyship. We will not fail to wait upon her.   (*Exit Sir* Peter *and Lady P.*

Enter Lady Laycock, *meeting* Lovemore.

Lady L. Oh, Mr. Lovemore! I have expected you; I am glad you're come.

Love. Madam, Your Ladyship does me too much Honour. Pray, Madam, when saw you Mr. *Cuningham*?

Lady L. Oh, Sir! He has told me all. And now you talk of Mr. *Cuningham*— *Prudence*, go find out my Niece, and have an Eye over her.   (*Exit* Pru. Well, Sir, I am sorry you shou'd make your self so great a Stranger to me. In such Cases I am not ungrateful. And where Love is real, there's a double Obligation.

Love. Ha! What does she mean by Love and double Obligations?   (*Aside.*

Lady L. I see indeed you seem to be in some Disorder, that I should know it; but had you let me known it sooner, I shou'd perhaps have sav'd you a great many Sighs and Heart-Akings, which your Bashfulness has caus'd.

Love. Sure she's mad!   (*Aside.*
Madam—

Lady L. And yet 'tis never too late to serve a Friend, and one that loves so dearly. Nor am I yet so far engag'd, but I can pity, nay make Return, when Love is sincere, and so constant.

Love. Madam, you much amaze me! Nor can I guess what you drive at!

Lady L. Ah, dear Sir! I know you are unwilling to let me know it. But shall I be sincere in asking you one Question?

Love. Most freely; so it be not any thing that leads me farther into the dark.

Lady L. Do you not love me, Sir?

Love. Love you, Madam! Why truly I hate no body.

Lady L. Well, but love me so, that it much disturbs you, and that you fear I am engag'd to another.

Love. The Devil take me if I ever lov'd you, or can think what you wou'd be at.

The Amorous Widow: Or, The Wanton Wife

Lady L. Nay, I was told you would deny it. But pray, Sir, tell me truly; for indeed, Sir, I am sorry you should suffer for my Sake. And should you do otherwise than well, I vow it would be a Means of giving me Disquiet as long as I live.

Love. Pray, Madam, who told you this?

Lady L. Your Friend Mr. *Cuningham*, who is much concern'd for you, Sir. And since you find it is discover'd, you need not be asham'd to own the Truth.

Enter Prudence, *and listens.*

Love. Faith, Madam, to deal freely with you, you're abus'd, for hang me if ever I had a thought that way; nor do I love you, or ever can.

Lady L. You're pleas'd to be merry, Sir, but I must tell you, I have observ'd it in your Looks; and since it is so, own it boldly to the World, and I promise you, I'll not be asham'd, nor disown mine. Come, come, Mr. *Lovemore*, you must not deny me that; for since I dare own it, why should you think it still amiss?

Love. Well! Since all must out, prepare to hear me. Mr. *Cuningham* has begun, and I must make an End. You must know, Madam, Mr. *Cuningham* loves you to that degree himself, that he's asham'd, knowing how near a-kin he is to you, to let you know it, and so has form'd this Story upon me, the better to make for him.

Lady L. Mr. *Cuningham* a-kin to me, Sir!

Love. Ay, Madam, your Nephew, your Brother's Son, whom he had in *Paris* by Madam *D'Olone*,[35] but for some Reason he since has chang'd his Name.

Lady L. Truly, Sir, you surprize me much! My Brother in *Paris* I heard had a Son, but what became of him I know not.

Love. Madam, this *Cuningham*, my Friend, has the Misfortune (Misfortune I think it, and he thinks so too, because he loves so dearly) to be related to you.

Lady L. I'm sorry, if he does love so well, that he shou'd be so near a-kin.

Pru. Madam, Mr. *Cuningham* is just come in.

---

[35]   *D'Olone*: Betterton probably derived the name from Louis de La Trémoille, Comte d'Olonne, a friend of Louis XIV who was subsequently banished from court. He is mentioned in St Evremond's *Recueil de diverses pieces faites pour plusieurs personnes illustres*, a three-volume collection of St Evremond's work published in La Haye in 1669, and which Betterton owned (see PB 75).

The Amorous Widow: Or, The Wanton Wife

Love. I'll leave you, Madam, for I have a little Business that I must dispatch— Besides, 'twou'd not be convenient for me to interrupt what Disputes you two may have.

Lady L. Sir, your Servant.

(As he goes out, meets Cuningham ent'ring.

Love. Had you no body to put your Tricks on, but me? But I think I have been even with you. (Exit Love.

Cun. What can he mean?

Lady L. Mr. *Cuningham,* you do not deal like a Friend by me; you might have trusted me with a Secret of greater weight.

Cun. I do not understand you, Madam!
What has he been saying to her? (Aside.

Lady L. You knew one Mrs. *D'Olone,* I suppose?

Cun. What shall I say now? (Aside.

Pru. Was your Brother then Mrs. *D'Olone's* Husband, Madam, and Mr. *Cuningham's* Father?

Lady L. Who bid you speak? Yes he was. What then?

Cun. Oh, I begin to smoke it.[36] (Aside.

Pru. Nothing, Madam, but then Mr. *Cuningham* is your Nephew.

Lady L. Indeed, I wish he were not; but since it is so, we must be satisfied with our Fate, Mr. *Cuningham.* Tho' you are much to blame, Sir, you did not let me know it sooner before Matters went so far.

Cun. Madam, I confess my Fault, and do ask your Ladyship's Forgiveness.

Enter Philadelphia.

Lady L. Well, Mr. *Cuningham,* since you are my Nephew, we may venture to embrace without a Blush. (She embraces him.

Phil. Is Mr. *Cuningham* your Nephew, Madam?

Lady L. Yes, Mistress Pert, what then?

Phil. Then he's my Cousin, and I may embrace him too. (Runs and embrace each other.

---

[36] *Smoke*: suspect, find out.

The Amorous Widow: Or, The Wanton Wife

Cun. Ay, my dear, dear Cousin.

Lady L. Why how now, saucy, impertinent Slut. How dare you take this Liberty?

Phil. Why, is there any Harm in embracing one's own Cousin?

Lady L. Get you in, Hussy, and dare not to come but when I call you.

Pru. He's none of your Cousin, Madam.   (*Aside to* Phil. *as she goes out.*

Phil. I know it. I met Mr. *Lovemore* laughing by the way, who told me all. Adieu, my dear Cousin.   (*Exit.*

Cun. My charming Cousin, farewell.

Lady L. I'll swear, Mr. *Cuningham,* you'll spoil that Girl. Methinks you embrac'd her something of the hardest.   (*Seems disturb'd.*
I call her Girl, and yet she's near five and twenty—But as I was going to tell you, Sir, You must know, this Brother was not indeed my own Brother, but something a-kin afar off. He was my first Husband's first Wife's Brother, and no kin to me. But because my Husband us'd to call him Brother, I would sometimes do so too; and by this Means was thought, by those that knew no other, to be my Brother.

Pru. Then he is not so near a-kin, but he may marry your Ladyship?

Cun. Oh!—   (*Sighs.*

Lady L. Why, truly, Mr. *Cuningham*—

Enter Jeffrey *in haste.*

Jeff. Sir, your Lawyer bid me tell you, your Cause is just now coming on; and if you do not appear, you'll be non-suited.

Lady L. Dear Sir, do not neglect your Business, nor let your being a-kin trouble you, when next I see you.

Cun. Oh, Madam! Wou'd I had never seen you, then I'd been happy; but where the Tye of Blood bars our Hopes, there's nothing but Despair in view. Madam, farewell.
Find some way to excuse me, you Dog, or I'll cut your Throat.   (*To* Jeffrey
as he goes out.

Jeff. What shall I say? My Master has begun a Lie, and I must end it. (*Aside*[37]

---

[37]   Q1 and Q2 place the s.d. after the first sentence.

Lady L. Come hither, *Jeffrey*. Dost think thy Master loves me so well as he says?

Jeff. Faith, Madam, I believe he loves your Ladyship but too well! But Mr. *Lovemore* dies, unless you take pity on him.

Lady L. Dost think he loves me better than thy Master?

Jeff. Oh, Madam! They ought not to be nam'd together. Mr. *Lovemore*, poor Gentleman, is perfectly beside himself about it.

Lady L. Didst ever hear 'em talk about me?

Jeff. A thousand times. Mr. *Lovemore* can talk of nothing else.

Lady L. 'Tis strange he should deny it to me.

Jeff. You must know, Madam, my Master was in Love elsewhere.

Lady L. How, *Jeffrey*?

Jeff. If your Ladyship will have Patience to hear me out, you shall know the whole Story.

Lady L. With all my Heart, *Jeffrey*.

Jeff. Why, you must know, Madam, my Master had the Misfortune to quarrel with a Gentleman, who urg'd him to fight; my Master kill'd him. Upon which he was forc'd to change his Habit and his Name—from *Cuningham* to *Bontefeu*.[38] But thinking it not safe to stay here, fled; and in his Journey happen'd into a Viscount's Castle, but the Viscount was gone a Journey. However, this Viscount had a very beautiful Sister, that had the Command in her Brother's Absence; she entertain'd my Master very splendidly. At last he fell in love with her, and she with him.

Lady L. Methinks she was very forward, *Jeffrey*.

Jeff. She was so indeed, Madam; for before my Master left her, she prov'd with Child.

Lady L. How! With Child, and not married, Jeffrey!

Jeff. My Master had promis'd her Marriage, Madam.

---

[38]   *Bontefeu*: Q1 has 'Bootefeu', which may in turn be an attempt at the French name of 'Boutefeu'. However, 'Bontefeu' was a synonym for a religiously inspired terrorist (usually a Catholic), as in William Bedloe's 'Epistle Dedicatory to the Surviving Citizens of London Ruined by Fire', in his *A Narrative and Impartial Discovery of the Horrid Popish Plot* (London: Robert Boulter et al., 1679), n.p. As with *Sans-Terre*, the joke is that Lady Laycock cannot hear a metaphorical alarm bell ringing.

Lady L. Oh, the impudent Creature! And thy Master was to blame, not to keep his Word, *Jeffrey.*

Jeff. Not at all, Madam, when you have heard all. You must know, my Master grew jealous of one of the Servants, as indeed he had Reason; and one Day pretended to ride out, and he shou'd not return that Night, but left me to let him in, when the Servants were all a-bed, which I did. Going up to this Lady's Bed-Chamber, and not being expected that Night, found the Servant in Bed with her.

Lady L. Unheard of Impudence! At first I was going to condemn thy Master, for deceiving a young Creature; but 'tis likely he was not the first that had to do with her.

Jeff. Very likely so, Madam. Next Day my Master was for packing up his Awls,[39] and for going; she cry'd, and urg'd his stay, and his Vows to marry her.

Lady L. He had been more to blame to have done that.

Jeff. In the mean time the Viscount return'd, found his Sister in Tears, wou'd know the Reason, was told all. He swore, if ever he could get hold of him, he'd hang him at his Castle Gate, but my Master was got off safe. What it will come to, it they should ever meet, I know not, but fear the Event.

Pru. A well invented Lye the Rogue has told.   (*Aside.*
What was this Viscount's Name?

Jeff. The Viscount *Sans-Terre*, I think he was call'd.

Pru. The Viscount *Sans-Terre*!

Lady L. Why, he's in this House.

Jeff. What, in this very House?

Pru. In this very House; in the next Room.

Jeff. Ah, my poor Master! He's but a dead Man, if he's found; for he'll certainly be hang'd.

Pru. Here he comes. Hold your Peace!

Enter [Merryman as the] Viscount.

Lady L. My Lord, your Servant. I have a Question to ask of you.

---

[39]   *Awls*: OED 2c lists the phrase as a colloquialism, punning on 'all'.

The Amorous Widow: Or, The Wanton Wife

Jeff. What shall I do to make him understand?   (*Aside.*
Humour her in all she says, my Lord.

Merr. Ask what thou wilt, I'll deny thee nothing.

Lady L. You had a Sister.

Merr. I had so. Go on.

Lady L. And she was unfortunately wrong'd by a base Fellow.

Merr. What must I say next?   (*To* Pru.

Pru. 'Twas not well done to debauch her, and then to leave her; but Woe be to him, if your Lordship catch him.   (*To* Merr.

Merr. If ever I do find the Son of a Whore, I'll hang him at my Castle Gate.

Lady L. He was very much to blame indeed; but yet, all things consider'd, he was not in all the Blame neither, counting what a Trick she play'd him. He had reason to question whether the Child was his, or not.

Merr. I'm quite at a Loss. Oh! tell me what I must say next?   (*Faints into*
Jeffrey's *Arms,*
who instructs him.

Jeff. Take it in your Ear, my Lord.   (*Aside.*

Lady L. Help, *Prudence*, my Lord faints.

Pru. Pray, Madam, don't come too near, but give him Air.   (Prudence *and*
Jeffrey *tell him*
what to say.

Lady L. Oh! he recovers.

Merr. Give me a little Air. I beg your Pardon, I never hear my Sister's Wrongs mention'd, but it puts me in Disorder; but if ever I do light upon the Villain, Woe be to him.

Lady L. I'll try to get his Pardon.   (*Aside.*
My Lord, methinks her Crime being the greatest, you might pardon him.

Merr. What! Pardon him, that has deflower'd my Sister, got her with Child of a Bastard, and stain'd the Honour of our great Family! No, tho' all the World should plead for him, I'll not forgive it; he dies.

Lady L. Good, my Lord, for my Sake.

Merr. 'Tis all in vain, Lady. I'm told he's now in this House, and has chang'd his Name. But if I find him—   (*Draws.*

The Amorous Widow: Or, The Wanton Wife

Lady L. Oh hold, my Lord.
I must save him. *(Aside.*
My Lord, I have but one Request more.

Merr. 'Twill be in vain: I'll have Revenge.

Pru. Tell him you'll marry him, Madam, and try what that will do. *(Aside
to* Lady *L.*

Lady L. Give me this Gentleman's Life, and I am content to be your Wife;
otherwise—

Merr. 'Tis a hard Request; but to shew how much I love you, upon that
Condition I grant it. *(Puts up his Sword.*

Lady L. Or, if you think fit, you shall have my Niece *Philadelphia*, and with
her I'll give you ten thousand Pounds.

Merr. Do you think my Love so poor, that 'twill be brib'd? Nay, then I recall
my Promise. He dies this Hour. *(Draws and searches about.*

Pru. Oh, pray my Lord, forbear; my Lady did it but to try you! See, you
fright her.

Lady L. Well, my Lord, since it must be so, my Chaplain is within, I'm
contented he shou'd make us one; make good but your Promise.

Merr. I confirm it here. *(Kisses her.*

Pru. My Lord, the Dancers are ready to begin, and all the Company stay
for you.

Merr. Let 'em enter, and begin when they please.

Enter Sir Peter Pride, *Lady* Pride, Lovemore,
Mrs. Brittle, Cuningham *and* Philadelphia.

Love. Well, Madam, I rely upon your Promise. *(To Mrs.* Brittle.

Merr. Come, Gentlemen and Ladies, pray sit. *They Sit.*

A DANCE.[40]

After the Dance, Enter Barnaby Brittle, *who runs after
his Wife; they get between, he gets hold of her, and
carries her off after Speaking.*

---

[40]   See above, n.29.

231

Britt. Here's fine Doings! But I'll spoil your Sport. What! My House is become a Musick-house, is it?[41] But, Gentlewoman, I have something to say to you within.

Omnes. How now! What's the Meaning of this?

Britt. I say, my Wife—

Omnes. What of your Wife?

Britt. Shall keep me Company, if you please.

Omnes. You Company!

Cun. What's the matter with the Fellow? Ha!

Britt. Come along, I say. What's here to do! Is not a Man's Wife his Wife? And may he not do what he will with her? (*Carries her off.*)

Sir Peter. He's at his old Tricks again.

Lady L. Come, let's in, and endeavour to appease him, and then end our Mirth with a Banquet.

Cun. We attend your Ladyship.

Lady L. Pray, my Lord, do me the favour to lead my Sister in. Come, Gentlemen.

Merr. Hold there, I will not part with you; I have two Hands, Madam, and can lead you both.

([*Exeunt*] *Omnes.*)

ACT V.

Enter Cuningham, Philadelphia *and* Jeffrey.

Jeff. Fear nothing; by what I could learn, by this time the old Lady is gone to her Chamber, or near being a-bed.

Cun. Then we may have Time to talk more freely.

---

[41] *Musick-house*: public music concerts are often thought not to have begun until John Banister opened his music school in December 1672 (LS1 cxix); however, private music meetings were of longer duration and, at least in the imagination of Thomas Southerne, provided an opportunity for flirting; see Act 1 of *The Wives' Excuse* in Robert Jordan and Harold Love, eds., *The Works of Thomas Southerne*, 2 vols (Oxford: Clarendon Press, 1988), I.274–86. Music alone may not have been palatable to the puritanical Brittle.

The Amorous Widow: Or, The Wanton Wife

Phil. All is not so safe as you imagine. I fear another Storm before we yet can land. I know not by what means, but the Viscount is discover'd to be a Counterfeit, which I have all along suspected; but whether 'tis come to the Knowledge of my Aunt yet, I know not.

Cun. Therefore let's lose no time, but tye that Knot, which joins our Hearts and Hands for ever. That once over, we have no farther need of the Viscount.

Enter Lovemore, *and* [Merryman as] *the Viscount enrag'd, with Lights before 'em.*

Merr. Never persuade me; I'll not stay to be fool'd at this rate any longer— Go lead, Sirrah.   (*Exit with Links.*

Cun. What's the Matter now?

Love. Matter! Why there's Matter enough in hand. We are all undone; the Match is broke off again, and you are like to lose your Mistress. The Widow will not consent you shall marry her Niece; upon which, the Viscount enrag'd (as indeed he has Cause), is resolv'd to stay no longer. What 'twill come to, I know not.

Cun. This is most unlucky. What's to be thought on next?

Love. I left *Prudence* reasoning the Case with her; what will be the Conclusion, is most uncertain. Oh! here she comes.

Enter Prudence.

Pru. Oh, Madam! the saddest News!

Phil. Why? What's the Matter?

Pru. All the Business is over. Poor Mr. *Cuningham*—

Phil. Ha! What of him? Speak.

Pru. After a thousand Arguments, which I us'd to persuade her, she has at last resolv'd—I can't speak it.

Phil. On what? Prithee out with it.

Pru. Why, to marry the Viscount her self, and give you and your ten thousand Pounds to Mr. *Cuningham*.

Cun. Oh the bless'd News! What say you now, Madam?

Phil. I'll swear I was in a Fright at first. But art thou sure she'll hold in this Mind?

Love. For fear of the worst, get all things ready, and let it be done this Moment.

Pru. Here she comes. Seem concern'd to part with her, Sir, and try how she stands resolv'd.

Enter Lady Laycock.

Cun. And must I then lose her, *Prudence*! Oh, the racking Thought! Hard, hard Decree of Fate! To part with all I hold most dear! I cannot bear it.
(*Walks about.*

Lady L. Yes, Mr. *Cuningham,* our Stars will have it so. 'Tis hard indeed to part. But since there is no way left to save your Life (which more than all the World I prize), but this only, I have at last resolv'd (tho' much against my Will) to give my self to the Viscount.

Cun. Oh! do not name it, Madam; the very Thought is worse than Death.

Lady L. I'm sorry we are so near a-kin, but that's not the chief Reason. Your Vow to marry another: and yet when I consider she was false, and had to do with more than one, and that the Child might as well not be yours, I think you were in the right to part. So I am content (since my Hopes are lost) that you shou'd marry with my Niece. But believe me, you do not know how much I'm troubled, to see another take what I so much desir'd. But we must endeavour to be satisfied.

Cun. Never! Never! For since I lose you, farewell to Love and Joy. The rest of Life I'll waste in Sorrow.

Enter Clodpole, *whispers* Lovemore.

Clod. Softly! *Damaris* bade me tell you, that her Mistress stays for you at the Garden Door.

Love. Oh, very well. I'll go this Moment.

Pru. But what will you do to recall the Viscount, Madam, who left the House in Anger, nor told any one what his Designs were?

Love. I heard him bid the Link-boy lead to the Devil Tavern.[42] If you please, thither we'll go, and conclude upon the Matter. A Glass or two of Wine may fetch him about again.

---

[42] *Devil Tavern:* i.e. The Devil and St Dunstan, at the Temple Bar end of Fleet Street, established at the beginning of the seventeenth century. Its sign showed the devil pinching St Dunstan's nose.

The Amorous Widow: Or, The Wanton Wife

Lady L. Truly, Mr. *Lovemore*, I'm much oblig'd to you, and shall endeavour to return your friendly Advice. I hope we shall live as loving Neighbours ought, but now we lose time. The Viscount may perhaps be gone, should we stay longer.

Love. I'll but give some Directions to my Man, and be there almost as soon as you.

Lady L. You will oblige us, Sir.   (*Exit all but* Love. *and* Clod.

Clod. 'Tis main dark, nothing to be seen but the Sky and Stars. What can this Darkness portend! The Almanicks this Year say, that many things will be huddled in the dark.[43]

Love. Why, thou art an Astrologer, *Clodpole,* thou talk'st so learnedly.

Clod. Why, truly I am but a Piece of one; but had I been a great Schollard, I believe I shou'd have thought on things, that never had been thought on before.

Love. Very likely, truly. But hark! What Noise is that? There's *Brittle*'s House; may be she is coming out.

Enter Mrs. Brittle and Damaris.

Mrs. Britt. Softly *Damaris,* just shut the Door, we'll not be far from it.

Dam. Is your Husband fast, Madam?

Mrs. Britt. I would not stir till I saw him asleep; he's snoring like one that's drunk.

Love. That's her Voice. Madam, where are you?

Dam. There they are, Madam.

Mrs. Britt. You find, Sir, I am as good as my Word. I hope you are a Man of Honour, as you say; yet were it to do again, I should hardly venture such another bold Attempt.

---

[43]   *Almanacks*: these publications typically provided improbable weather forecasts, travel and other predictions for the forthcoming year. It was usual to predict eclipses, which means the reference is of no use in dating the play more precisely. Betterton's purpose was to illustrate Clodpole's credulity. Edward Pond's *An Almancack for the Year of our Lord God 1668* (Cambridge: John Field, 1668), foresaw lunar and solar eclipses in May and October; while Thomas Trigge's *Calendarium astrologicum, or, An Almanack for the year of our Lord 1669* (London: Stationers' Company, 1669), predicted solar eclipses in April and October, leading to 'difficulties and discommodities to Travellers, both by Sea and Land' and 'Many Abortions' (n.p.).

The Amorous Widow: Or, The Wanton Wife

Love. Fear nothing, Madam. Your Person and your Honour both are safe, whilst I am your Guard. Can none over-hear us?

Mrs. Britt. All the Family but *Damaris* and I, are gone to Bed; nor dare we be long from thence, lest my Husband should wake, and miss me.

Love. Talk not of parting e'er we well are met; that were unkind, Madam. If you please, Madam, to walk a little farther this way, here's a Place more private than the rest, and will best befit our Discourse.

Mrs. Britt. Well, Sir, I'll not question your Honour any more, but trust my self with you; as you behave your self now, expect a greater Liberty another time.

Love. I'll warrant you; this way, my Charmer.　　(*He leads her out; she takes hold of* Damaris, *who follows.*

Mrs. Britt. Damaris!

Dam. I'm here, Madam.　　　　(Clodpole *feels with his Stick for Damaris.*

Clod. Damaris!—Softly!—*Damaris!*—*Damaris!*

　　　Enter Brittle, *groping in the dark in a Cap and a Night-Gown.*

Britt. Where can she be gone at this time of Night? I heard her steal down; I'll listen.

Clod. Damaris, where art thou, *Damaris!*—Odd, 'tis main dark.

Britt. Who have we here? Here's something more than ordinary. But I'll draw nearer.　　　　　　　　(*Goes towards him.*

Clod. Damaris, Where art thou?

Britt. Here.　　　　　　　　(*In a low Voice*; Clodpole *feels him with his Stick, thinks 'tis* Damaris.

Clod. Oh! art thou there? Well, *Damaris*, must not thee and I follow the Example of thy Mistress, and my Master? I'll warrant they'll be hugeous kind to one another; for my Master, you must know, has a mighty Love for her, and so belike she has for him; or else she wou'd ne'er a left her Husband a-bed to a come to him.

Britt. Oh horrid! 'tis so.　　　　　　　　(*Aside.*

Clod. How he snores now, if a Body were to hear him! Poor Cuckold! He little dreams what his Wife and my Master are doing. Ha, ha, ha!

Britt. Oh! this is my Country Chap again.　　　　(*Aside.*

The Amorous Widow: Or, The Wanton Wife

Clod. Poor Cuckold, 'tis good enough for him. For as they say, he uses her mighty ill. But, *Damaris*, must thee and I part thus? One little Bit to stay my Stomach, *Damaris*. 'Tis fit we shou'd follow our Leaders.   (*Goes to Kiss.*

Britt. I can hold no longer. Who goes there?   (*Hits him a Box.*

Clod. Odd so! Oh! Oh! Who's that? Oh!   (*Puts his Stick a-cross, and in running out stops against the Scenes;*[44] *at last gets off.*

Britt. So— He's gone. Here's a Discovery at last! Here's a fine virtuous Wife for you! But now all will out in spite of her. I'll send instantly for her Parents; they shall see now who's in the right. Oh bless us! What, make her Husband a Cuckold! Oh monstrous!   (*Goes to the Door, and calls.*

Jeremy! The Varlet's a-sleep, I'll warrant. *Jeremy*, I say.

(*Jer. above*)[45] Do you call, Sir?

Britt. Yes, I do call. Come down quickly, I must send you to my Father-in-law's.

Jer. I come, Sir.   (*Puts a Rope out, and slides down.*

Britt. Make haste, Sirrah. How long you are coming. Ah! Villain!
     (*Jeremy treads upon his Toes, and gets from him.*
You have trod upon my Corns, and lam'd me. Come hither, and be hang'd.

Jer. I dare not, Sir; you'll beat me.

Britt. Ah! 'tis well I stand in need of thee.   (*Comes to him.*
Run to my Father and Mother-in-Law, and tell 'em, I intreat to speak with 'em this Moment; tell 'em I'll never trouble 'em again as long as I live; beg 'em by all means to come.

Jer. Yes, Sir.   (*Exit.*

Britt. Now they shall see what a Daughter they have. Now I shall sure convince 'em of their Error! But I hear some body coming! May be I shall make a farther Discovery.   (*Stands aside.*

> *Enter* Lovemore, *Mrs.* Brittle, Damaris, *and* Clodpole.

Mrs. Britt. Nay, Sir, I've stay'd long enough for one time. Should my Husband wake, and miss me, I were undone. I must be gone.

---

[44]   *against the Scenes*: i.e. between the flats flanking the stage.
[45]   *above*: presumably referring to his appearance in one of the upper side boxes.

The Amorous Widow: Or, The Wanton Wife

Love. Stay one Minute longer, I beseech you, Madam. I have not told you yet—

Mrs. Britt. No more, Sir, if you love me. Farewell.

Love. Oh, stay! How can you go, and leave me so soon? You will have time enough to lie by that dull, stupid Clod, your Husband, e'er the Morning. Methinks I grudge him the least Look of you, since he knows not how to value so rich a Jewel. Let him live, and pore o'er his Bags, his Dross, and worldly Gains, whilst we know better how to waste our youthful Hours in softest Kisses, and everlasting Joys.

Britt. Oh, blasting Sound! But I have heard enough. Now to my Post. (*Exit.*

Mrs. Britt. Good Night, Sir. Now I must be gone.

Love. When shall I be thus bless'd again?

Mrs. Britt. To Morrow I'll send for you; and, if possible, appoint another Meeting.

Love. Till then, ten thousand Angels wait on thee. One Kiss e'er we part.
(Kisses her.
Oh, I could dwell for ever on thy Lips! Sure, there's Enchantment on 'em.

Mrs. Britt. Farewell!

Love. Adieu, my lovely Charmer. (*Exit with* Clod.

Mrs. Britt. Now, *Damaris*, let's steal in. Softly! Softly!

Dam. Oh Lord, Madam! We are undone! The Door[46] is fast since we have been out. (*Pushes against it.*

Mrs. Britt. What shall we do now, *Damaris*?

Dam. I wish my Master has not been down.

Mrs. Britt. Let's call *Jeremy* softly.

Both. Jeremy! Jeremy! (*They both call up to the Window in a soft Tone.*

Brittle *at the Window above.*

Britt. Jeremy! Jeremy! (*In their Tone.*

Dam. Oh, Madam, my Master!

Mrs. Britt. Lost! Undone for ever!

---

[46]   *Door:* Restoration theatres were equipped with doors at either side of the forestage.

Britt. Ah ha! My sweet Lady! Have I caught you at last? *Jeremy! Jeremy!* Where has your sweet Ladyship been, I pray, that you are so afraid of being discover'd? Come, I know you have a Lie in readiness. Let's have it.

Mrs. Britt. No where but just with *Damaris*, to take a little of the fresh Air; that's all indeed, sweet Husband.

Britt. To take the fresh Air, quotha! Ah, I rather believe 'twas to take a Heat,[47] you Witch you.

Mrs. Britt. Pray, Husband, let the Door be open'd?

Britt. No. You shall stay there till your Parents come. I have sent for them. They shall see what Hours you keep. And know of your Gallant you just parted from, your vigorous Lover.

Dam. Madam, he over-heard all, and we are undone.   (*Aside to her.*

Britt. What, have you no Excuse ready? No Invention? You and your wicked Instrument there, that stands like the Serpent at Eve's Elbow, to tempt her to Sin. What, is your Prompter to Wickedness dumb? I'd fain hear how you intend to excuse it.

Mrs. Britt. I don't go about to excuse it, Husband—

Britt. No; that's because you don't know how.

Mrs. Britt. I do confess, I have been to meet a Gentleman, but not alone; *Damaris* was with me. And sure there was no Crime in a little harmless Chat.

Britt. No, no, not in the least; making me a Cuckold is no harm at all.

Mrs. Britt. Pray, Husband, let me in, and I'll never do the like again, as long as I live; but you shall hence-forward find me the most dutiful Wife, that you could wish for. Pray, Husband, trust me but this once.

Britt. No.

Mrs. Britt. Do not disgrace me to my Parents, by exposing me at this unseasonable Hour, in which I do confess I am much to blame—

Britt. Oh! Do you so?

Mrs. Britt. But forgive me now, I'll never do it again.

Britt. Hang them that believes you, I say.

---

[47] *Heat*: a reference to the ancient theory of humours, an imbalance of which was believed to lead to lust, especially among women.

The Amorous Widow: Or, The Wanton Wife

Mrs. Britt. I am sure I never injur'd you in all my Life; but am as innocent as the Child unborn, from doing the Ill which you suspect.

Britt. It may be so. 'Twas not your Fault then.

Mrs. Britt. Pray, dear Husband, believe me, and let me in.

Britt. No.

Mrs. Britt. On my Knees I ask your Pardon, do but open the Door.

Britt. No.

Mrs. Britt. If you let me in this time, 'twill work upon me more than all the Liberty in the World cou'd do beside.

Britt. I care not.

Mrs. Britt. Indeed, Husband, I love you dearly, and love you only. How can you then be so cruel to refuse me?

Britt. Ah, cunning Crocodile! Now you are caught, 'tis dear Husband, sweet Husband, 'tis only you I love. But at another time, 'tis good for nothing old Fool. No, no, I know you well enough, and so shall your Parents now.

Mrs. Britt. Pray, Husband, let the Door be open'd.

Britt. No.

Mrs. Britt. Try me but this once.

Britt. I tell you, no.

Mrs. Britt. Not once more?

Britt. No.

Mrs. Britt. If you provoke me, I may despair, grow desperate, and do a Deed which you may repent.

Britt. Good lack! What will your sweet Ladyship do?

Mrs. Britt. I'll kill my self with this Knife here.   (*Shews her Fan.*

Britt. Oh, very well!

Mrs. Britt. Nay, 'twill not be so well as you imagine neither. Every body knows how ill we have liv'd, and when I'm dead, People will think you murder'd me.

Britt. Ay!

Mrs. Britt. Therefore I'll kill my self, to have my Death reveng'd upon you.

The Amorous Widow: Or, The Wanton Wife

Britt. Odd, I'll trust to that. Besides, killing ones self has been a great while out of fashion. But why don't you dispatch? Methinks you are long about it.

Mrs. Britt. You may believe me, for I'll certainly do it, if you persist.

Britt. Odd, I'll venture it.

Mrs. Britt. Besides, when I am dead, my Ghost shall haunt you.

Britt. Ah, if I cou'd but once get rid of your Person here, I should not fear your Ghost hereafter.

Mrs. Britt. Have you no Pity left? I am just going to do it.

Britt. And yet you are long about it.

Mrs. Britt. Since nothing but my Death can satisfy you— There and there!
(*Pretends to stab her self with her Fan, and falls.*

Dam. Oh, she has done't! She has done't! Oh cruel, barbarous Monster, to make her kill her self!

Mrs. Britt. Now, *Damaris,* you find too late I did not jest— I know thou'lt see my Death reveng'd upon my cruel Husband, who has accus'd me falsely; for I affirm with my dying Breath, I never wrong'd him. Farewell! Death beckons me into a dark and gloomy Vale, where I must follow.

Dam. She's gone! She's gone! Oh, thou worse than Savage! To murder so sweet a Lady, so innocent and so good. Nay, I'll swear you did it.   (*Cries
over her.*

Britt. I hear no Noise!   (*Looks frighten'd.*
Is't possible the Devil shou'd be so great with her, that she cou'd kill her self to be reveng'd on me! But I'll light a Candle, and go see.   (*Goes from the
Window.*

Mrs. Britt. Now, *Damaris,* stand close in this Corner. Close, close.   (*They
stand aside.*

Enter Brittle *with a Light; they slip by him, go in,
and lock the Door. He looks about.*

Britt. Ha, ha, ha! I thought indeed how well she'd do it. Here's none of her! She made me believe she kill'd her self, and the mean while ran away. Well, e'en let her go; I shall have this Satisfaction, her Parents shall be Witness of her Hours. I'll in, and wait their coming.
(*Goes to the Door, and finds it lock'd. Knocks.*

Mrs. Brittle *and* Damaris *above at the Window, where he was.*

241

The Amorous Widow: Or, The Wanton Wife

Mrs. Britt. Away, you idle Sot; is this a time of Night for an honest Man to come home in?

Dam. Go, go, you may be asham'd!

Britt. Why, have you the Impudence—   (*Looks up, and sees 'em above.*

Mrs. Britt. How many Nights am I forc'd to sit up to wait for his coming in? And he tells the World, 'tis I am to blame. But now it shall be seen who's to blame, and who not. My Father and Mother are coming, they shall see what Hours you keep—

Britt. I confess, I stand amaz'd at this Impudence.

Mrs. Britt. They shall know all.

Britt. Why, have you the Face to deny—

Mrs. Britt. Go, go, I'll hear none of your impudent Excuses; you are drunk, you Sot, you Swine. But here comes my honourable Father and Mother.

Enter Sir Peter *and Lady* Pride.

I'm glad you are come to be Witness of what I still suffer, by this ungrateful Usage of a cruel Husband. You see what Hours he keeps; every Night at the Tavern roaring with his Companions, whilst I am forc'd to sit at home alone, waiting for his coming; and when he does come, he strait raves and abuses me at such a rate, that I am not able to endure it.

Britt. Why, was there ever such Impudence! I wish this Candle were in my Belly, if—

Mrs. Britt. I know what he'll say now, if you'll believe him; he'll tell you, that I am still in the wrong, and 'tis I that have been out at this late Hour, and as for his part, he has been within all this Evening, and knows nothing of all this Matter, not he. But I'll leave your selves to judge, if this is an Hour for an honest Husband to come home at.

Britt. Why then may I never—

Mrs. Britt. You see he's so drunk, he can hardly stand.

Lady P. Faugh!—I smell him hither. He stinks of Liquors and Tobacco like a Tarpaulin,[48] that has not been sober whilst his Twelve-Months Pay wou'd last.

Britt. I tell you, that I am not drunk, nor have I been out of my House.

---

[48] *Tarpaulin*: an ordinary merchant seaman.

The Amorous Widow: Or, The Wanton Wife

Sir Peter. Stand farther off, I cannot bear the Scent of a Drunkard.

Mrs. Britt. I told you he wou'd deny it.

Britt. I say, that 'tis she that has been out just now, and with her Gallant, and therefore I sent for you; and that I have not been out of my Doors.

Mrs. Britt. Do you hear him? But *Damaris* can justify, I have not set my Foot over the Threshold since Day-light.

Dam. If she has, never believe me more. I can assure your Honours 'tis true; for I have not been out of her Company since he went out to the Tavern.

Mrs. Britt. Therefore I do beseech you, good Father and Mother, to revenge my Cause, for I am not able to endure it any longer. If I do, you'll never see me alive another Week.

Britt. 'Tis a strange thing, that she must be believed, and I not. I tell you—

Lady P. Stand farther off. Faugh! What a Smell there's about him. (*She goes cross the Stage.*

Britt. Well then; I'll stand farther off, if you will but hear me speak. (*Goes backward.*
I shall say nothing but the Truth, and what I can prove.

Sir Peter. Again at your Proofs, and your idle Jealousies! Be dumb, Coxcomb; it were a good deed to break your Head, for sending thus for us out of our Beds, and making Fools of us still. If you ever dare to do the like again, we'll find a Means to handle you— If there be no Law (but cutting of Throats) to revenge these Affronts—I say no more—But remember you are warn'd.

Britt. If you wou'd but let me tell why I sent for you—

Sir Peter. We have heard and seen too much already. Therefore dare not to speak a Word more.

Mrs. Britt. And is this all his Punishment?

Sir Peter. No; come down, and he shall ask your Pardon. 'Tis the least he can do.

Mrs. Britt. 'Twill be to no purpose; when your Backs are turn'd, he'll be as bad again.

Sir Peter. I say no more Disputes, but do as I command. (*They come down from the Window.*

Now, Son-in-law, kneel down, and ask your Wife Forgiveness.

Mrs. Britt. Shall I forgive him? No, I desire to be divorc'd.

The Amorous Widow: Or, The Wanton Wife

Lady P. Come, Daughter, I say you must pardon him.

Mrs. Britt. Well, Madam, I'll endeavour to obey you.

Sir Peter. Why don't you kneel, and do as I command?

Britt. Well, I find there's no Remedy; she has over-reach'd me again, and I must submit. But I am resolv'd I'll get rid of this Noose, tho' I tuck my self up in another.

             (*Sir Peter makes him kneel to his Wife.*

Sir Peter. Come, say after me. Madam, I ask your Pardon.

Britt. Madam, I ask your Pardon.

Sir Peter. For the Folly I have committed—

Britt. For the Folly I have committed in marrying you.

Sir Peter. In my wild Suspicions.

Britt. In my wild Suspicions.

Sir Peter. Which I do declare were utterly false.

Britt. Which I do declare were utterly false.

Sir Peter. And that I swear never to do the like again.

Britt. And that I swear never to do the like again, if I were once unmarried.

Mrs. Britt. Here—Kiss the Book.   (*Gives her Hand.*
But if ever you do't again— You see 'tis to no purpose to turn Hagard;[49] if you do, I'll tame you.   (*Aside to him.*

Lady P. Look if the Noise has not brought all the Company hither.

 Enter [Merryman as] Viscount, *Lady* Laycock, Lovemore, Cuningham,
  Philadelphia, Prudence, Clodpole, *and* Jeffrey, *with Lights before 'em.*

Love. Your Servant, Sir *Peter.* Sir, I hope you will not take it ill; we saw a Light in your House, and so made bold. We are resolv'd to spend an Hour or two in Mirth, and hope you will all join with us.   (*To Brittle.*

Lady L. Your Ladyship I know will pardon it upon this Occasion. (*To Lady P.*

Lady P. Is your Ladyship marry'd? May we give you Joy?

Lady L. My Niece and Mr. *Cuningham* are.

---

49 *Hagard*: here, a wild male hawk caught in order to be trained (OED 1).

244

Mrs. Britt. Give you Joy then.

Cun. and *Phil.* We thank you, Madam.

Phil. Now, Sir, since our Hands are join'd, and all is reconcil'd, I have a Boon to ask.

Cun. Whate'er it be, conclude it done.

Phil. I have observ'd some Sparks of Love between *Jeffrey* and *Prudence*; and I believe they wou'd be glad to follow our Example.

Cun. What say'st thou, *Jeffrey*? If thou hast a Mind to marry, speak freely.

Jeff. Sir, I have debated much about the Matter, and am at last resolv'd to venture.

Cun. Then if you, Madam, give your Consent, and Prudence be willing, we'll put 'em together.   (*To Lady L.*

Lady L. With all my Heart; *Prudence* has been always a good Servant, I'll say that for her.

Jeff. There's my Hand then; the rest of my Body shall be forth coming.

Pru. A Match.

Love. Then let me speak. *Clodpole* loves *Damaris,* and I believe wou'd be glad to make up the Chorus; now if Mrs. *Brittle* please to part with her—

Britt. You shall have my Consent with all my Heart; and I'll give a Sum of Money to be rid of her.

Love. And I'll give *Clodpole* something to set him up in a little Farm in the Country.

Clod. Damaris!—Dost hear that?

Mrs. Britt. What say you, *Damaris*?

Dam. If I thought he'd make a good Husband, and not be jealous—

Love. That I dare answer for him.

Clod. Well, then 'tis agreed, and there's my Hand.

Dam. For better for worse.

Clod. To have and to hold; a Tenement for Life.

Cun. And now all things being thus happily concluded—

The Amorous Widow: Or, The Wanton Wife

Lady L. No, Mr. *Cuningham*, not while your Friend is unprovided. Methinks 'twere pity he shou'd be no Actor in this Comedy.

Love. Oh, Madam, my Thoughts are not yet fix'd so much upon any Object, but the next I encounter can retrieve the past.

Cun. My Friend never wants a Mistress (I'll say that for him) in any Place, if he has but an Opportunity, which he seldom wants. I have often wonder'd at his Luck.

Mrs. Britt. Say you so? I find he makes it his Business to ensnare and deceive Women at this rate. I'm glad I know it in time, whilst I have Power to make my Retreat. I had like to have been finely caught.   (*Aside*[50]
Well, Husband, seeing so many join'd in Happiness, if you'll promise never to be jealous, I'll promise from this Moment never to give you Cause, and endeavour to make you as happy as I can.

Britt. Wou'd you'd give me Cause once to believe you.

Merr. Well then, if you are all agreed, the Parson that marry'd Mr. *Cuningham* is but just by; e'en send for him, and let him end the Work he has begun. For my part, I intend to put off mine for some time longer.

Lady L. How! My Lord! Have you serv'd me thus? Did I forsake all for you, and do you pretend to—

Merr. No Words now, 'twill spoil Company; another time we'll discourse it farther. Come, let's have a Dance, and then to Bed.

Omn. With all our Hearts.

A DANCE.

Merr. 'Tis well: So now, you that are ready to taste the Sweets of Matrimony, fall to; for my part, I have no great Stomach to it yet.
And none I hope will blame me if I tarry,
Since those that wed in haste, as fast miscarry.

(*Exeunt Omnes.*

FINIS.

---

[50]   Q1 and Q2 place the s.d. after 'at this rate'.

APPENDIX: PREFACE TO THE 1706 EDITION

As it is a Formality very much in Fashion of late amongst the Writers, to Compliment their Readers, by giving them a View of their following Entertainment in a Preface; we shall make bold to follow the Example, but without making the feigned Apologies, That what is here offered to thy Candid Perusal, was published to prevent or decry any surreptitious copy; neither meerly to satisfie the Importunity of Friends: What is here presented to publick View, is a Play written some time since by one of the purest Wits this Nation e'er produc'd for Dramatick Poetry; and with the rest of his Works, has found a general Acceptance and Applause as often as it came upon the Stage, not only on the Theatre-Royal in Drury Lane, but likewise in Lincolns-Inn-Fields, Dorset Garden, and at the Queens's Theatre in the Haymarket.

Were we to reveal the Author of this incomparable Comedy, as that we durst not without a Violation of the Promise made to his exemplary Modesty, which often requested the Gentleman, to whom he bequeathed this real Treasure, never to divulge its Parent, his very Name would challenge a just Veneration from all the most sensible Part of Mankind, as well as strike Terror in the severest Critics; who, amongst all their carping Comments, cannot deny, but his Vein was as naturally good in the Tragick way as the Comick: For in the first, he was as exact in describing the several Passions, (which gives the Draught of Nature, and is the most infallible Rule for moving the Soul) as in the latter most successful in drawing the Images or Characters really Natural; for not like Plautus, who studied to please the common People, does he make a Miser more Covetous, or a morose Man more Troublesome than the Original; but, in Imitation of Terence, who endeavour'd to please the better Sort, he confines himself within the Bounds of Nature, and represents their Vices, without making them either better or worse.

If Comedy is an Image of common Life, whose End is to shew on the Stage the Faults of Particulars, in order to amend the Faults of the Publick, and to correct the People through a fear of being render'd Ridiculous; why then the following Sheets follow those general Rules, intermixt with the pleasant Turn, that Gaiety which can sustain the Delicacy of each Character, without falling into Coldness, nor into Buffoonry: And indeed the worthy

Author has made it his Business to consult principally with Reason in the Contrivance and Oeconomy of this Play; for besides a due regarding the Three Dramatick Unities of Action, Time and Place, the Decencies herein are well observ'd, the Incidents well enough prepar'd, and the Plot so finely spun, that the Catastrophe is naturally unravell'd, which is the pure and perfect Work of Judgment.

'Tis true, a Play seldom makes a Publick Entry abroad, without being usher'd by a Prologue and Epilogue, both which we were not without; but through some Negligence or Casualty the Original ones being lost, we would not impose any upon the World, that were not Genuine: However, their usual Leading and Bringing up the Front and Rear of a Play being no Part of the Play it self, 'tis hop'd their Want will be no Blemish to so excellent a Piece as this, which for a long time has been wish'd for in Print by the most competent Judges of Wit and Sense; which not only the Last Century, but the present Age affords.

BIBLIOGRAPHY

Anon. *An Account of the Life of that Celebrated Tragedian Mr. Thomas Betterton*. London: J. Robinson, 1749

Aristotle. *Poetics*. Revised Edition. Trans. T.S. Dorsch. Penguin Classics. Harmondsworth: Penguin, 1996

Backscheider, Paula R. 'Behind City Walls: Restoration Actors in the Drapers' Company'. *Theatre Survey* 45.1 (May 2004), pp. 75–87

Baggs, Zachary. *An Advertisement Concerning the Poor Actors, who, under Pretence of Hard Usage from the Patentee, are about to Desert their Service*. London: 1709

Baines, Paul and Pat Rogers. *Edmund Curll, Bookseller*. Oxford: Clarendon Press, 2007

Beaumont Francis and John Fletcher. *The Maids Tragedy*. London: R. Bentley and S. Magnes, 1686

Betterton, Thomas. *The Amorous Widow; or, the Wanton Wife: A Comedy*. London: W. Turner for J. Morphew, 1706

Borgman, Albert S. *The Life and Death of William Mountfort*. Cambridge, MA: Harvard University Press, 1935

Cibber, Colley. *An Apology for the Life of Mr Colley Cibber*, ed. Robert W. Lowe, 2 vols (London: John Nimmo, 1889)

——. *An Apology for the Life of Mr Colley Cibber, Comedian and Late Patentee of the Theatre Royal*. Ed. and intr. David Roberts. Cambridge: Cambridge University Press, 2022

——. *Xerxes: A Tragedy*. London: Richard Basset, 1699

Cicero, Marcus Tullius. *Cicero on Oratory and Orators*, trans. J.S. Watson. London: Bell & Daldy, 1871

——. *De Officiis. Libri Tres. Cato Maior, vel de senectute. Lælius, vel del amicitia. Paradoxa Stoicorum sex...* London: Richard Field, 1604

——. *De Oratore ad Q. Freterem: Ex mss. Recensuit.* Tho. Cockman. Oxford: E. Theatro Sheldoniano, 1696

——. *On Oratory and Orators*. Ed. and trans. John Selby Watson. New York: Harper and Brothers, 1860

——. *Pro Archia Poeta, cum F. Syluii Commentariis, Oratio*. Paris, 1531

Bibliography

Collier, Jeremy. *A Short View of the Immorality, and Profaneness of the English Stage Together with the Sense of Antiquity upon This Argument.* London: S Keble et al., 1698

——. *Miscellanies in Five Essays.* London: Samuel Keeble, 1694

Congreve, William. *Love for Love: A Comedy.* 4th ed. London: Jacob Tonson, 1704

——. *The Way of the World.* Ed. David Roberts. London: Methuen, 2020

Dennis, John. *The Usefulness of the Stage to the happiness of mankind, to government, and to religion.* London: Richard Parker, 1698

Downes, John. *Roscius Anglicanus, or an Historical Review of the Stage.* London: H. Playford, 1708

Dryden, John. *Troilus and Cressida, or, Truth Found too Late: A Tragedy.* London: Jacob Tonson, 1679

Faucheur, Michel Le. *An Essay upon the Action of an Orator; As to His Pronunciation and Gesture,* trans Anon. London: Nicholas Cox, 1700(?)

Greene, Thomas M., *The Light in Troy: Imitation and Discovery in Renaissance Poetry.* New Haven: Yale University Press, 1982

Harrington, James. *The Common-wealth of Oceana.* London: Livewell Chapman, 1656

Hayes, Julie C., 'Plagiarism and Legitimation in Eighteenth-Century France', *The Eighteenth Century: Theory and Interpretation* 34 (1993), pp.115–31

Hédelin, François. *The Whole Art of the Stage.* London: William Cadman, 1684

Howell, W.S. *Eighteenth-Century British Logic and Rhetoric.* Princeton: Princeton University Press, 1971

——. 'Sources of the Elocutionary Movement in England, 1700–1748', *Quarterly Journal of Speech* 45 (1959), pp.1–18

Hughes, Derek. *English Drama 1660–1700.* Oxford: Clarendon Press, 1996

Hume, Robert D. *The Development of English Drama in the Late Seventeenth Century.* Oxford: Clarendon Press, 1976

——. 'The Aims and Genre of Colley Cibber's *Apology* (1740)', *Studies in Philology* 14.3 (Summer 2017), pp.662–95.

Hutcheon, Linda, 'Literary Borrowing … and Stealing: Plagiarism, Sources, Influences, and Intertexts', *English Studies in Canada* 12 (1986), pp.229–39

Kewes, Paulina. *Authorship and Appropriation. Writing for the Stage in England, 1660–1710* (Oxford: Clarendon Press, 1997)

Kirkman, Francis. *The Wits, or Sport Upon Sport.* London: Henry Marsh, 1662

Lane, Joan. *John Hall and His Patients: The Medical Practice of Shakespeare's Son-in-Law.* Stratford-upon-Avon: The Shakespeare Birthplace Trust, 1996

Bibliography

Lennep, William van, ed. *The London Stage 1660–1800: A Calendar of Plays, Entertainments & Afterpieces Together with Casts, Box-Receipts and Contemporary Comment*. 5 vols. Carbondale: Southern Illinois University Press, 1960–8

Lucian, of Samosata. *Part of Lucian made English from the originall, in the yeare 1638 …* Trans. Jasper Mayne and Francis Hicks. Oxford: H. Hall for R. Davis, 1663

Lucretius Carus, Titus. *Titi Lucretii Cari. De Rerum Natura Libri Sex*. Cambridge: William Morden, 1675

——. *Titus Lucretius Carus his six books of Epicurean Philosophy*. Trans. Thomas Creech. Oxford: Anthony Stephens, 1683

Massinger, Philip. *The Bond-man: An Ancient Storie*. London: John Raworth for John Harrison, 1638

Milhous, Judith. *Thomas Betterton and the Management of Lincoln's Inn Fields, 1695–1708*. Carbondale: Southern Illinois University Press, 1979

Milhous, Judith and Robert D. Hume. *A Register of English Theatrical Documents, 1660–1737*. 2 vols. Carbondale: Southern Illinois University Press, 1991

Montfleury, A.I. *La Femme Juge et Partie*. Paris: Gabriel Quinet, 1669

OED Online. May 2023. Oxford University Press. www.oed.com

Orgel, Stephen, 'The Renaissance Artist as Plagiarist', *ELH* 48 (1981), pp.476–95

Palmer, Richard and David Roberts. 'Harris vs Harris: A Restoration Actor at the Court of Arches', *Huntington Library Quarterly* (forthcoming).

Pepys Samuel. *The Diary of Samuel Pepys*. Ed. Robert Latham and William Matthews. 11 vols. London: Harper Collins, 1995

Petronius Arbiter. *Satyricon*. Ed. Gareth Schmeling. Cambridge, MA: Harvard University Press, 2020

Plutarch, *Plutarch's Lives of Illustrious Men*. Trans. John Dryden. 3 vols. Vol. III. New York: American Book Exchange, 1880

——. *Plutarch's lives translated from the Greek by several hands*. London: T. Hodgkin for J. Tonson, 1683

——. *The lives of noble Grecians and Romanes*. Trans. Thomas North. London: Thomas Vautroullier, 1579

Prynne, William. *Histrio-mastix: The Players Scourge, or Actor's Tragedy*. London: Edward Allde et al., 1633.

Quintilian. *Institutes of Oratory*, trans. J.S. Watson, ed. Curtis Dozier and Lee Honeycutt. London: Amazon, 2015

Roach, Joseph R. *The Player's Passion. Studies in the Science of Acting*. Newark: University of Delaware Press, 1985

Roberts, David, ed. *Pinacotheca Bettertonaeana: The Library of a Seventeenth-Century Actor*. London: Society for Theatre Research, 2013

Bibliography

——. *Thomas Betterton: The Greatest Actor of the Restoration Stage.* Cambridge: Cambridge University Press, 2010

Rowe, Nicholas. *Tamerlane: A Tragedy.* London: Jacob Tonson, 1702

——. *The Ambitious Step-Mother: A Tragedy.* London: Peter Buck, 1701

——. *The Biter: A Comedy.* London: Jacob Tonson, 1705

——. *The Fair Penitent: A Tragedy.* London: Jacob Tonson, 1703

——. *Ulysses: A Tragedy.* London: Jacob Tonson, 1706

——. *The Works of William Shakespeare.* London: Jacob Tonson, 1709

Shakespeare, William. *Macbeth: A Tragedy.* London: H. Herringman and E. Bentley, 1689

——. *Othello, the Moor of Venice: A Tragedy.* London: R. Wellington, 1705

——. *The Tragedy of Hamlet Prince of Denmark.* London: Richard Wellington, 1703

Steele, Richard. *The Tatler,* No.1. London, 1709

Stern, Tiffany. *Rehearsal from Shakespeare to Sheridan.* Oxford: Oxford University Press, 2000

Tacitus, *The Annals of Tacitus.* Books I to VI. Trans. Aubrey V. Symonds. London: Swan Sonnenshein & Co., 1906

Tate, Nahum. *The History of King Lear.* London: E. Flesher, 1681

Tilley, Morris Palmer. *A Dictionary of the Proverbs in England in the Sixteenth and Seventeenth Centuries.* Ann Arbor: The University of Michigan Press, 1950

Tillotson, John Archbishop. *The Works of the Reverend George Whitefield.* 7 vols. London: Edward and Charles Dilly, 1771–2

Vanbrugh, John. *A Short Vindication of The Relapse and the Provok'd Wife from Immorality and Prophaneness.* London: Printed for N. Walwyn, 1698

——. *The Provok'd Wife: A Comedy.* London: J.O. for R Wellington and Sam Briscoe, 1697

Virgil, *The Aeneid of Virgil.* Trans. C. Day Lewis. Oxford: Oxford University Press, 1986

Wanko, Cheryl. *Roles of Authority. Thespian Biography and Celebrity in Eighteenth-Century Britain.* Lubbock: Texas Tech University Press, 2003

Webster, John. *Appius and Virginia, Acted at the Dukes Theater under the Name of the Roman Virgin or Unjust Judge: A Tragedy.* London: Printed, and are to be sold by most Booksellers, 1679

White, Harold Ogden. *Plagiarism and Imitation During the English Renaissance. A Study in Critical Distinctions.* Cambridge, MA: Harvard University Press, 1935

Wilson, F.P. *The Oxford Dictionary of English Proverbs.* Oxford: Oxford University Press, 1970

Bibliography

Wycherley, William. *The Country-wife: A Comedy*. London: Thomas Dring, 1675

——. *The Plain Dealer*. London: James Magnes and Richard Bentley, 1676.

——. *The Plain Dealer*. Ed. James L. Smith. London: Ernest Benn, 1979

Xenophon. *Le Festin de Xenophon*. Trans. Mr Le Fèvre. France: Saumur, 1666

INDEX

Accius, Lucius 92, 93 nn.152–3, 131
   n.260
Acting
  discipline 56–60, 70–3
  education 147
  eyes 73–5, 80, 89–95
  face and masks 86–91, 95–6
  feet 77–8
  figures of speech 138–146
  hands 76–8, 80, 82, 96–100
  mirrors 64, 73, 82, 89
  movement 63–7, 74–6, 79, 80–2,
    84–6, 96
  passions 25, 64, 72, 81, 92–4
  physique 147–8
  principles 23
  speech and pronunciation 67, 103–24
  volume 104, 114, 120
  transitions 26–7
Addison, Joseph 24, 149 n.315
Aeschylus 3, 93 n.152, 148 n.311, 151
   n.320, 155
Aesopus 26, 63, 65, 83–4, 92, 93 n.153,
   143–4
Afer, Gnaeus Domitius 105
Aristotle 149, 154–5, 157
Aston, Anthony 25, 103 n.181
Athenaeus of Naucratis 8, 155
Audran, Benöit 168–9

Bacon, Francis, Lord Verulam 65
Baggs, Zachary 43 n.9
Baines, Paul 2, 7, 22
Ballon, Claude 150–1
Barnes, Joshua 160
Barry, Elizabeth 19, 43, 54, 57, 71–3
Battersby, Nicholas 4
Behn, Aphra 13
Betterton (Saunderson), Mary 27, 31,
   49–50
Betterton, Thomas
  actor 23–7, 31, 55
  author 2, 4–5, 8, 18, 33, 53

benefit performance 43, 52
death 17, 27, 53
financial affairs 52
innovator of scenery 49
knowledge of French 57 n.52
manager 50–2
physique 25
private life 3, 6, 48, 53
roles 6, 43 n.10, 68 n.80, 101 n.177,
   121 n.236, 170 n.380, 170 n.381,
   171–175
The Amorous Widow
  play and casts 29–32, 178
  rival texts of 33–7
  text 179–246
Blackfriars Theatre 48
Boitard, François 25, 97 n.165
Booth, Barton 23, 108 n.201, 116 n.221
Bracegirdle, Anne 5, 31, 43, 61 n.63,
   81, 178
Bradshaw, Lucretia 73
Brady, Nicholas 22
Bragg, Benjamin 21 n.84
Bright, George 178
Brown, Daniel 21 n.84
Brown, William 22
Brutus, Marcus 46, 81, 97, 130
Bulwer, John 6, 98 nn.168–70
Bunyan, John 168
Burbage, Richard 1

Carneades 104
Cassius, Caius 46
Cavalli, Pier Francesco 162, 163 n.359
Cesti, Antonio 162
Charles II, King of England 170
Cibber, Colley 5, 7, 23–6, 31, 44 n.11,
   53 n.36, 54 n.40, 55 n.43, 56
   nn.45–6 & 48, 57 n.49, 58 n.54,
   60 n.61, 70 n.87, 81n.127, 83
   n.131, 103 n.181, 106 n.195, 108
   n.201, 116 n.221, 130 n.258, 159
   n.347, 168 n.375, 170 n.382

254

Index

Cicero, Marcus Tullius   5, 6 n.27, 18, 20, 26, 39 n.2, 46–7, 55, 59 n.57, 60, 63 n.70, 65, 80–1, 84, 86, 92–3, 95 nn.159–60, 96 n.161, 100 n.174, 105 n.188, 106, 108 n.200, 109, 111, 112 n.213, 115, 116 n.220, 131, 133 n.265, 134, 135 nn.273–4, 139, 140, 141 n.291, 144 n.304
 as Tully   93 n.153, 104, 107 n.198, 131 n.261, 133 n.265, 140 n.287
Clench of Barnet   167
Cleophantes of Corinth   155
Cockpit Theatre   48
Collier, Jeremy   49 n.22, 58, 59 n.56
Congreve, William   30, 31, 37, 52 n.30, 56 n.45, 81 n.127, 101 n.177, 168 n.376, 170, 171 n.383
Conrart, Valentin   20
Coppinger, Matthew   2
Cordemoy, Geraud de   6
Corelli, Arcangelo   168–9
Cowley, Abraham   167, 174
Cox, Nicholas   11, 16–17, 20
Coypel, Antoine   70, 91
Cratinus   151
Crowne, John   106 n.193, 137 n.278, 170
Curll, Edmund   1–3, 17–19, 22–3, 34, 70 n.86, 132 n.263

Dance and dancing   2, 8, 14, 29, 55 n.41, 62, 79, 85, 105, 149–58, 162
Daniel, Samuel   22
Davenant, Charles   50–1
Davenant, Sir William   3, 25, 48–9, 55, 150 n.317, 173, 175
Davis, William   21 n.84
de Grazia, Margreta   9
Demosthenes   60, 63 n.70, 64–5, 73, 82, 83 n.129, 86, 96, 112–13, 115, 134, 137–8, 142
Dennis, John   49 n.22
Doggett, Thomas   31, 43 n.9
Dorset Garden Theatre   50, 57 n.52, 247
Dowley, James   21 n.84
Downes, John   6, 29, 46 n.14, 52 n.30, 53 n.35, 57 n.51, 83 n.131, 149 n.316, 166 n.368, 173
D'Oyly, Robert   22
Drury Lane Theatre   5, 43, 48, 52, 71 n.90, 165 n.365, 167 n.370, 168 n.375, 247

Dryden, John   9–10, 26 n.101, 31, 51 n.27, 52 n.28, 56 n.48, 63 n.70, 68 n.80, 73 n.96, 75 n.106, 77 n.11, 81 n.127, 83 n.131, 100 n.175, 162 n.355, 168, 175
Dunton, John   21 n.84

Edelinck, Ludowyck   168–9
Etherege, Sir George   170, 174, 175
Eugene, Prince of Savoy   124
Euripides   14–15, 64, 65 n.74, 93 n.152, 156 n.339, 160

Fieldhouse, actor   178
Fletcher, John   10, 43 n.9, 48 nn.18–19, 169, 173–4
Foucault, Michel   4
Freeman, John   178

Gaffarel, Jacques   88
Galliard, John Ernest   164 nn.362 & 363
Gallus, Caius Cornelius   155
Garrick, David   1, 26, 130 n.257
Gilbert, Sir Geoffrey   22
Gildon, Charles
 family history   11–12
 on music   159
 on opera   55, 149, 158–71
 on tragedy   54–5, 101
 other works by   3–4, 6, 11, 13–17, 23, 35, 132 n.263
 relationship with Betterton   4–5, 27
 works with publishers   2
 writing *The Life of Mr Thomas Betterton*   1, 18–19, 33
Gildon, Richard   12
Goodman, Cardell   103
Gosling, Francis   22
Gosling, Robert   1–2, 17, 21–3, 29, 33–4
Gregory, William   15

Haines, Joseph   3
Harriman-Smith, James   26
Harrington, Sir James   60
Hart, Charles   50–2, 103 n.181
Hayes, Julie C.   9
Heidegger, John James   164
Heliodorus of Emesa   23
Hill, Aaron   23
Hills, Henry   21 n.84
Hitch, Charles   17
Homer   96 n.163, 104, 153–5, 160 n.351

255

Index

Horace (Quintus Horatius Flaccus) 34, 71, 79, 165, 166 n.367
Hortensius, Quintus 67, 80, 83–4
Howard, Edward 17
Howell, W.S. 1–2, 20
Hunt, actress 178

James II, King of England 12
Johnson, Benjamin 71
Jones, Thomas 21 n.84
Jonson, Ben 4, 10, 29, 121, 158, 170
Jordaens, Hans the Elder 69

Kewes, Paulina 8–11
Killigrew, Charles 50 n.26, 51
Kneller, Godfrey 3
Kynaston, Edward 48, 50–2

L'Abbé, Antoine 29, 157 n.343, 158
Langbaine, Gerard 9–11, 14–18, 27
Laud, William 58
Lawrence, John 21 n.84
Le Brun, Charles 70
Le Faucheur, Michel 1, 16–21, 23–6, 66 n.77, 67 n.78, 73 n.97, 74 nn.99 & 100–2, 75 nn.103 & 105, 76 nn.107 & 109, 77 n.113, 79 n.120, 80 n.123, 81 nn.124–6, 82 n.128, 83 nn.129–30, 84 n.133, 85 n.135, 86 nn.136 & 138, 88 n.143, 89 n.145, 90 nn.146–7, 91 n.148, 92 n.151, 93 nn.153–4, 95 nn.157–60, 96 nn.161–3, 97 n.166, 98 n.168, 99 nn.171–2, 100 nn.173–4, 104 nn.182–3, 105 nn.187 & 190, 106 n.194, 107 n.198, 111 n.211, 112 nn.212–13, 113 n.214, 114 nn.216–7, 115 nn.218–20, 116 n.222, 117 nn.224–5, 118 nn.226–8, 119 nn.229–31, 120 nn.232–4, 121 nn.235 & 237–8, 122 nn.239–40, 123 nn.241–3, 124 nn.244–5, 125 nn.246–7, 126 n.248, 127 n.251, 129 nn.254 & 256, 131 nn.259 & 261, 132 n.262, 133 nn.265–8, 134 nn.269–70, 135 nn.271–3, 136 n.275, 137 nn.277–9, 138 n.283, 139 nn.284–6, 140 nn.287 & 289–90, 141 nn.294 & 297, 142 nn.298 & 300, 143 nn.301–3, 144 n.304, 145 nn.305–6, 146 n.307, 147 n.308

Lee, Nathaniel 15–16, 68 n.80, 103, 175
Leigh, Anthony 26 n.101
Leigh, Elinor 30, 178
Leveridge, Rochard 159, 165 n.365
Lincoln's Inn Fields Theatre 49–50, 52, 247
Locke, John 9, 69 n.83
Long, Jane 31
Lucian of Samosata 8, 62, 63 n.68, 79 n.119, 87, 147–9, 150–2, 155–7, 160

Mayne, Jasper 8, 62, 63 n.68, 87 n.139, 148 n.311, 149 n.313, 151 n.320
Mercuriale, Girolamo 2, 153 n.330, 155
Michaelangelo Buonarotti 147
Milhous, Judith 2, 8
Milton, John 168
Molière, Jean-Baptiste Poquelin 30, 57 n.52, 170 n.383
Monck, George, 1st Duke of Albemarle 48
Mordaunt, Charles, 3rd Earl of Peterborough 19, 124, 132 nn.263–4
Mountfort, Susannah 81
Mulgrave, John Sheffield, 3rd Earl of, and 1st Duke of Buckingham & Normanby 72–3

Neoptolemus 142
Nero (Nero Claudius Caesar Augustus Germanicus) 62, 79
Nokes, James 31

Oldmixon, John 4
Oldys, William 1
Oratory for law and religion 101
Otway, Thomas 3, 19, 72 n.93, 158, 170 n.383, 175
Overton, Henry 167
Ovid (Publius Ovidius Naso) 98 n.169, 135, 141 n.292

Pantomime and dumb shows 55, 61–3, 78–9, 100, 150–2
Parker, Richard 21 n.84
Pepys, Samuel 17 n.68, 26, 48 n.18, 56 n.44
Pericles of Athens 67, 147
Perrault, Charles 22
Petronius (Gaius Petronius Arbiter) 40
Philistus of Syracuse 66–7
Philostratus, Lucius Flavius 120

256

Index

Phrynichus   151
Pindar   151
Plagiarism, definitions of   8–18, 42
Plato   7, 47, 151 n.322, 153–5
Pliny the Elder   75, 155 n.337
Pliny the Younger   80, 120
Plutarch   46 n.13, 63–5, 86, 113, 114
    n.216, 154–6, 160
Pollux, Julius   107, 110, 155
Porter, Mary   178
Prince, actress   178
Purcell, Henry   159 n.347, 165–6, 168
    n.375

Quarles, Francis   162 n.355, 168
Queen's Theatre Haymarket   43 n.9, 52,
    149 n.315, 165 n.365, 247
Quin, James   23
Quintilian   6 n.27, 18, 20–1, 23, 25,
    42, 66, 72 n.94, 76–9, 88 n.143,
    93 n.154, 95 nn.158 & 159, 96
    nn.161–3, 97 n.166, 99 n.171,
    100 n.175, 104 n.182, 105 n.189,
    109–12, 113 n.214, 115 n.220,
    116 n.221, 117 n.225, 119 nn.230
    & 231, 137 n.276, 143 n.301

Raguenet, François   164 n.362
Raphael   147, 168
Rawlinson, Christopher   16, 20
Rhodes, John   48, 49 n.20, 51 n.27
Rich, Christopher   4, 30, 43 n.9, 52
    nn.29 & 32, 57 n.50, 71 n.90, 165
    n.364
Roach, Joseph R.   1, 74 n.98
Robinson, John   1
Rogers, Pat   2, 7, 22
Roper, Abel   21 n.84
Roper, Andrew   21 n.84
Roscius, Gallus Quintus   39 n.1, 44, 46,
    60, 63, 65, 83, 84, 86, 143, 144
    n.304
Roscommon, Wentworth Dillon, Earl of
    72, 79, 164 n.361
Ross, Trevor   9
Rossi, Luigi   162, 164
Rowe, Nicholas   2, 8, 25, 43, 94 n.156, 97
    n.165, 127 n.250, 132 n.263, 175
Russen, David   22
Rymer, Thomas   73 n.96, 101 n.178, 169

St Evremond, Charles de   6, 8, 19, 39,
    158, 161–4

Satyrus   63–4
Schmidt, Melchior   20
Seneca, Lucius Annaeus   65 n.74, 106
    n.193, 107, 121, 137 n.278
Severus, Cassius   105, 107
Shadwell, Thomas   71 n.90, 170, 174–5
Shakespeare, William   2–6, 8, 10, 11, 13,
    16, 19, 24–5, 43 n.10, 44, 62, 71,
    78, 94, 97, 102–6, 116, 126–31,
    149 n.315, 158, 169–70, 173–5
Shore, John   168–69
Smith, John   91 n.150
Smith, John Harrington   31 n.6
Smith, Richard   22
Smith, William   31, 50–1
Socrates   7, 47, 151
Sophocles   64, 91 n.151, 93 n.152
Steele, Sir Richard   7, 26–7, 40, 43 n.9
Stern, Tiffany   26 n.101, 27
Strabo   155
Straw, Jack   124
Sturton, John   15, 21 n.84
Subligny, Marie-Thérèse de   157 n.343,
    158
Sura, Manlius   105
Swiney, Owen   52, 165 n.365, 166 n.368

Tacitus, Cornelius   65
Tamariscus   90
Tasso, Torquato   73
Telesis   151
Theophrastus   90, 155
Thespis   87, 151
Thomas, Tobyas   2
Thornhill, James   168
Thucydides   147
Tilenius   156
Tillotson, John   12, 59 n.57
Titian   91
Titius, Gaius   105, 160
Tofts, Catherine   159
Trachallus   66, 112
Turner, William   33
Tyler, Wat   124

Underhill, Cave   30, 178
United Company   50–2

Vanbrugh, Sir John   52, 59 n.56, 71 n.90,
    170
van Hove, Denys   168–9
Verbruggen, John   4, 30, 103 n.181, 178
Vibulenus   65–6

Index

Vinicius Publius   22, 121 n.238
Virgil   22, 51 n.28, 69, 73, 75, 77, 141, 142 n.299

Wanko, Cheryl   2–4, 23
Wilde, James   21 n.84
Wilks, Robert   55 n.43, 70
Willis, Browne   22
Willis, Elizabeth   178

Woodward, John   21 n.84
Wright, James   150 n.317
Wright, Thomas   1
Wycherley, William   40 n.6, 51 n.27, 170, 175

Xenophon   7, 47, 152–6

Zunshine, Lisa   3